NEW LIBERTY

The Libertarian Manifesto

MURRAY N. ROTHBARD

REVISED EDITION

COLLIER BOOKS

A Division of Macmillan Publishing Co., Inc.

NEW YORK

COLLIER MACMILLAN PUBLISHERS

LONDON

Macmillan Publishing Co., Inc.
866 Third Avenue, New York, N.Y. 10022
Collier Macmillan Canada, Ltd.

Library of Congress Cataloging in Publication Data

Rothbard, Murray Newton, 1926–
    For a new liberty.

    Includes bibliographical references and index.
    1. Liberty. 2. Laissez-faire. 3. United   States—
Economic policy. 4. United States—Social policy.
I. Title.
JC599.U5R66 1978   320.5'1'0973   78–12225
ISBN 0–02–074690–3

Printed in the United States of America
For a New Liberty, in its original version, is available in
a hardcover edition from Macmillan Publishing Co., Inc.

First Collier Books Edition 1978
10   9   8   7   6   5   4   3   2

TO JOEY,

still the indispensable framework

Contents

PART III: EPILOGUE

Preface

WHEN THE ORIGINAL EDITION of this book was published (1973), the new libertarian movement in America was in its infancy. In half a dozen years the movement has matured with amazing rapidity, and has expanded greatly both in quantity and quality. Hence, while the discussion of libertarianism in this book has been strengthened and updated throughout, the greatest change is in our treatment of the libertarian movement. The original chapter 1, on "The New Libertarian Movement," is now irrelevant and outdated, and it has been transformed into an appendix providing an annotated outline of the complex structure of the current movement. The new chapter 1, on "The Libertarian Heritage," provides a brief but badly needed historical background of the American and Western tradition of liberty, and of its successes and failures, setting the stage for our discussion of its rebirth in today's movement. A new chapter 9 has been added on the vital topic of inflation and the business cycle, and the roles of government and of the free market in creating or alleviating these evils. Finally, to the concluding chapter on strategy has been added a presentation and explanation of my recently gained conviction that liberty will win, that liberty will be making great strides immediately as well as in the long run, that, in short, liberty is an idea whose time has come.

I owe the origin and inspiration of this book to my first editor, Tom Mandel, who had the vision to anticipate the recent enormous growth

of interest in libertarianism. The book would neither have been conceived nor written without him. For the revised edition, Roy A. Childs,
Jr., editor of *Libertarian Review*, was extremely helpful in suggesting
needed changes. I would also like to thank Dominic T. Armentano, of
the economics department of the University of Hartford, Williamson
M. Evers, editor of *Inquiry*, and Leonard P. Liggio, editor of *The Literature
of Liberty*, for their welcome suggestions. Walter C. Mickleburgh's un-
bounded enthusiasm for this book was vitally important in preparing
the revised edition; and Edward H. Crane III, president of Cato Institute,
San Francisco, was indispensable in providing help, encouragement,
sound .advice, and suggestions for improvement.

MURRAY N. ROTHBARD
Palo Alto, California
February 1978

For a New Liberty

1

The Libertarian Heritage:
The American Revolution
and Classical Liberalism

ON ELECTION DAY, 1978, Libertarian party candidates for congressional, state, and local offices amassed 1.25 million votes throughout the country. Richard Randolph was elected to the Alaska House of Representatives on the LP ticket, and Edward Clark piled up 377,960 votes for governor of California. After the LP presidential ticket gained 174,000 votes in 32 states in 1976, the sober *Congressional Quarterly* was moved to classify the fledgling Libertarian party as the third major political party in America. The remarkable growth rate of this new party may be seen in the fact that it only began in 1971 with a handful of members gathered in a Colorado living room. The following year it fielded a presidential ticket which managed to get on the ballot in two states. And now it is America's third major party.

Even more remarkably, the Libertarian party achieved this growth while consistently adhering to a new ideological creed—"libertarianism"—thus bringing to the American political scene for the first time in a century a party interested in principle rather than in merely gaining jobs and money at the public trough. We have been told countless times by pundits and political scientists that the genius of America and of our party system is its lack of ideology and its "pragmatism" (a kind word for focusing solely on grabbing money and jobs from the hapless taxpayers). How, then, explain the amazing growth of a new party which is frankly and eagerly devoted to ideology?

One explanation is that Americans were not always pragmatic and nonideological. On the contrary, historians now realize that the American Revolution itself was not only ideological but also the result of devotion to the creed and the institutions of libertarianism. The American revolutionaries were steeped in the creed of libertarianism, an ideology which led them to resist with their lives, their fortunes, and their sacred honor the invasions of their rights and liberties committed by the imperial British government. Historians have long debated the precise causes of the American Revolution: Were they constitutional, economic, political, or ideological? We now realize that, being libertarians, the revolutionaries saw no conflict between moral and political rights on the one hand and economic freedom on the other. On the contrary, they perceived civil and moral liberty, political independence, and the freedom to trade and produce as all part of one unblemished system, what Adam Smith was to call, in the same year that the Declaration of Independence was written, the "obvious and simple system of natural liberty."

The libertarian creed emerged from the "classical liberal" movements of the seventeenth and eighteenth centuries in the Western world, specifically, from the English Revolution of the seventeenth century. This radical libertarian movement, even though only partially successful in its birthplace, Great Britain, was still able to usher in the Industrial Revolution there by freeing industry and production from the strangling restrictions of State control and urban government-supported guilds. For the classical liberal movement was, throughout the Western world, a mighty libertarian "revolution" against what we might call the Old Order—the *ancien régime* which had dominated its subjects for centuries. This regime had, in the early modern period beginning in the sixteenth century, imposed an absolute central State and a king ruling by divine right on top of an older, restrictive web of feudal land monopolies and urban guild controls and restrictions. The result was a Europe stagnating under a crippling web of controls, taxes, and monopoly privileges to produce and sell conferred by central (and local) governments upon their favorite producers. This alliance of the new bureaucratic, war-making central State with privileged merchants—an alliance to be called "mercantilism" by later historians—and with a class of ruling feudal landlords constituted the Old Order against which the new movement of classical liberals and radicals arose and rebelled in the seventeenth and eighteenth centuries.

The object of the classical liberals was to bring about individual liberty in all of its interrelated aspects. In the economy, taxes were to be drastically reduced, controls and regulations eliminated, and human energy, enterprise, and markets set free to create and produce in exchanges that would benefit everyone and the mass of consumers. Entrepreneurs were to be free at last to compete, to develop, to create. The shackles of control were to be lifted from land, labor, and capital alike. Personal freedom and civil liberty were to be guaranteed against the depredations and tyranny of the king or his minions. Religion, the source of bloody wars for centuries when sects were battling for control of the State, was to be set free from State imposition or interference, so that all religions—or nonreligions—could coexist in peace. Peace, too, was the foreign policy credo of the new classical liberals; the age-old regime of imperial and State aggrandizement for power and pelf was to be replaced by a foreign policy of peace and free trade with all nations. And since war was seen as engendered by standing armies and navies, by military power always seeking expansion, these military establishments were to be replaced by voluntary local militia, by citizen-civilians who would only wish to fight in defense of their own particular homes and neighborhoods.

Thus, the well-known theme of "separation of Church and State" was but one of many interrelated motifs that could be summed up as "separation of the economy from the State," "separation of speech and press from the State," "separation of land from the State," "separation of war and military affairs from the State," indeed, the separation of the State from virtually everything.

The State, in short, was to be kept extremely small, with a very low, nearly negligible budget. The classical liberals never developed a theory of taxation, but every increase in a tax and every new kind of tax was fought bitterly—in America twice becoming the spark that led or almost led to the Revolution (the stamp tax, the tea tax).

The earliest theoreticians of libertarian classical liberalism were the Levelers during the English Revolution and the philosopher John Locke in the late seventeenth century, followed by the "True Whig" or radical libertarian opposition to the "Whig Settlement"—the regime of eighteenth-century Britain. John Locke set forth the natural rights of each individual to his person and property; the purpose of government was strictly limited to defending such rights. In the words of the Lockean-inspired Declaration of Independence, "to secure these rights, Governments are instituted among Men, deriving their just powers from the consent of the governed. That whenever any Form of Government becomes destructive of these ends, it is the Right of the People to alter or to abolish it . . ."

While Locke was widely read in the American colonies, his abstract philosophy was scarcely calculated to rouse men to revolution. This task was accomplished by radical Lockeans in the eighteenth century, who wrote in a more popular, hard-hitting, and impassioned manner and applied the basic philosophy to the concrete problems of the government—and especially the British government—of the day. The most important writing in this vein was "Cato's Letters," a series of newspaper articles published in the early 1720s in London by True Whigs John Trenchard and Thomas Gordon. While Locke had written of the revolutionary pressure which could properly be exerted when government became destructive of liberty, Trenchard and Gordon pointed out that government *always* tended toward such destruction of individual rights. According to "Cato's Letters," human history is a record of irrepressible conflict between Power and Liberty, with Power (government) always standing ready to increase its scope by invading people's rights and encroaching upon their liberties. Therefore, Cato declared, Power must be kept small and faced with eternal vigilance and hostility on the part of the public to make sure that it always stays within its narrow bounds:

We know, by infinite Examples and Experience, that Men possessed of Power, rather than part with it, will do any thing, even the worst and the blackest, to keep it; and scarce ever any Man upon Earth went out of it as long as he could carry every thing his own Way in it. . . . This seems certain, That the Good of the World, or of their People, was not one of their Motives either for continuing in Power, or for quitting it.

It is the Nature of Power to be ever encroaching, and converting every extraordinary Power, granted at particular Times, and upon particular Occasions, into an ordinary Power, to be used at all Times, and when there is no Occasion, nor does it ever part willingly with any Advantage. . . .

Alas! Power encroaches daily upon Liberty, with a Success too evident; and the Balance between them is almost lost. Tyranny has engrossed almost the whole Earth, and striking at Mankind Root and Branch, makes the World a Slaughterhouse; and will certainly go on to destroy, till it is either destroyed itself, or, which is most likely, has left nothing else to destroy.[1]

Such warnings were eagerly imbibed by the American colonists, who reprinted "Cato's Letters" many times throughout the colonies and down to the time of the Revolution. Such a deep-seated attitude led to what the historian Bernard Bailyn has aptly called the "transforming radical libertarianism" of the American Revolution.

For the revolution was not only the first successful modern attempt

[1]See Murray N. Rothbard, *Conceived in Liberty, vol 2, "Salutary Neglect": The American Colonies in the First Half of the 18th Century* (New Rochelle, N.Y.: Arlington House, 1975), p. 194. Also see John Trenchard and Thomas Gordon, *Cato's Letters*, in D. L. Jacobson, ed., *The English Libertarian Heritage* (Indianapolis: Bobbs-Merrill Co., 1965).

to throw off the yoke of Western imperialism—at that time, of the world's mightiest power. More important, for the first time in history, Americans hedged in their new governments with numerous limits and restrictions embodied in constitutions and particularly in bills of rights. Church and State were rigorously separated throughout the new states, and religious freedom enshrined. Remnants of feudalism were eliminated throughout the states by the abolition of the feudal privileges of entail and primogeniture. (In the former, a dead ancestor is able to entail landed estates in his family forever, preventing his heirs from selling any part of the land; in the latter, the government requires sole inheritance of property by the oldest son.)

The new federal government formed by the Articles of Confederation was not permitted to levy any taxes upon the public; and any fundamental extension of its powers required unanimous consent by every state government. Above all, the military and war-making power of the national government was hedged in by restraint and suspicion; for the eighteenth-century libertarians understood that war, standing armies, and militarism had long been the main method for aggrandizing State power.[2]

Bernard Bailyn has summed up the achievement of the American revolutionaries:

The modernization of American Politics and government during and after the Revolution took the form of a sudden, radical realization of the program that had first been fully set forth by the opposition intelligentsia . . . in the reign of George the First. Where the English opposition, forcing its way against a complacent social and political order, had only striven and dreamed, Americans, driven by the same aspirations but living in a society in many ways modern, and now released politically, could suddenly act. Where the English opposition had vainly agitated for partial reforms . . . American leaders moved swiftly and with little social disruption to implement systematically the outermost possibilities of the whole range of radically liberation ideas.

In the process they . . . infused into American political culture . . . the major themes of eighteenth-century radical libertarianism brought to realization here. The first is the belief that power is evil, a necessity perhaps but an evil necessity; that it is infinitely corrupting; and that it must be controlled, limited, restricted in every way compatible with a minimum of civil order. Written constitutions;

[2]For the radical libertarian impact of the Revolution within America, see Robert A. Nisbet, *The Social Impact of the Revolution* (Washington, D.C.: American Enterprise Institute for Public Policy Research, 1974). For the impact on Europe, see the important work of Robert R. Palmer, *The Age of the Democratic Revolution*, vol. 1 (Princeton, N.J.: Princeton University Press, 1959).

the separation of powers; bills of rights; limitations on executives, on legislatures, and courts; restrictions on the right to coerce and wage war—all express the profound distrust of power that lies at the ideological heart of the American Revolution and that has remained with us as a permanent legacy ever after.[3]

Thus, while classical liberal thought began in England, it was to reach its most consistent and radical development—and its greatest living embodiment—in America. For the American colonies were free of the feudal land monopoly and aristocratic ruling caste that was entrenched in Europe; in America, the rulers were British colonial officials and a handful of privileged merchants, who were relatively easy to sweep aside when the Revolution came and the British government was overthrown. Classical liberalism, therefore, had more popular support, and met far less entrenched institutional resistance, in the American colonies than it found at home. Furthermore, being geographically isolated, the American rebels did not have to worry about the invading armies of neighboring, counterrevolutionary governments, as, for example, was the case in France.

After the Revolution

Thus, America, above all countries, was born in an explicitly libertarian revolution, a revolution against empire; against taxation, trade monopoly, and regulation; and against militarism and executive power. The revolution resulted in governments unprecedented in restrictions placed on their power. But while there was very little institutional resistance in America to the onrush of liberalism, there did appear, from the very beginning, powerful elite forces, especially among the large merchants and planters, who wished to retain the restrictive British "mercantilist" system of high taxes, controls, and monopoly privileges conferred by the government. These groups wished for a strong central and even imperial government; in short, they wanted the British system without Great Britain. These conservative and reactionary forces first appeared during the Revolution, and later formed the Federalist party and the Federalist administration in the 1790s.

During the nineteenth century, however, the libertarian impetus continued. The Jeffersonian and Jacksonian movements, the Democratic-Republican and then the Democratic parties, explicitly strived for the

---

[3]Bernard Bailyn, "The Central Themes of the American Revolution: An Interpretation," in S. Kurtz and J. Hutson, eds., *Essays on the American Revolution* (Chapel Hill, N.C.: University of North Carolina Press, 1973), pp. 26–27.

virtual elimination of government from American life. It was to be a government without a standing army or navy; a government without debt and with no direct federal or excise taxes and virtually no import tariffs—that is, with negligible levels of taxation and expenditure; a government that does not engage in public works or internal improvements; a government that does not control or regulate; a government that leaves money and banking free, hard, and uninflated; in short, in the words of H. L. Mencken's ideal, "a government that barely escapes being no government at all."

The Jeffersonian drive toward virtually no government foundered after Jefferson took office, first, with concessions to the Federalists (possibly the result of a deal for Federalist votes to break a tie in the electoral college), and then with the unconstitutional purchase of the Louisiana Territory. But most particularly it foundered with the imperialist drive toward war with Britain in Jefferson's second term, a drive which led to war and to a one-party system which established virtually the entire statist Federalist program: high military expenditures, a central bank, a protective tariff, direct federal taxes, public works. Horrified at the results, a retired Jefferson brooded at Monticello, and inspired young visiting politicians Martin Van Buren and Thomas Hart Benton to found a new party—the Democratic party—to take back America from the new Federalism, and to recapture the spirit of the old Jeffersonian program. When the two young leaders latched onto Andrew Jackson as their savior, the new Democratic party was born.

The Jacksonian libertarians had a plan: it was to be eight years of Andrew Jackson as president, to be followed by eight years of Van Buren, then eight years of Benton. After twenty-four years of a triumphant Jacksonian Democracy, the Menckenian virtually no-government ideal was to have been achieved. It was by no means an impossible dream, since it was clear that the Democratic party had quickly become the normal majority party in the country. The mass of the people were enlisted in the libertarian cause. Jackson had his eight years, which destroyed the central bank and retired the public debt, and Van Buren had four, which separated the federal government from the banking system. But the 1840 election was an anomaly, as Van Buren was defeated by an unprecedentedly demagogic campaign engineered by the first great modern campaign chairman, Thurlow Weed, who pioneered in all the campaign frills—catchy slogans, buttons, songs, parades, etc.—with which we are now familiar. Weed's tactics put in office the egregious and unknown Whig, General William Henry Harrison, but this was clearly a fluke; in 1844, the Democrats would be prepared to counter with the same campaign tactics, and they were clearly slated to recapture the presidency that year. Van Buren, of course, was supposed to resume the triumphal Jacksonian march. But then a fateful event occurred: the Democratic party was sundered on the critical issue of slavery, or rather the expansion of slavery into a new territory. Van Buren's easy renomination foundered on a split within the ranks of the Democracy over the admission to the Union of the republic of Texas as a slave state; Van Buren was opposed, Jackson in favor, and this split symbolized the wider sectional rift within the Democratic party. Slavery, the grave antilibertarian flaw in the libertarianism of the Democratic program, had arisen to wreck the party and its libertarianism completely.

The Civil War, in addition to its unprecedented bloodshed and devastation, was used by the triumphal and virtually one-party Republican regime to drive through its statist, formerly Whig, program: national governmental power, protective tariff, subsidies to big business, inflationary paper money, resumed control of the federal government over banking, large-scale internal improvements, high excise taxes, and, during the war, conscription and an income tax. Furthermore, the states came to lose their previous right of secession and other states' powers as opposed to federal governmental powers. The Democratic party resumed its libertarian ways after the war, but it now had to face a far longer and more difficult road to arrive at liberty than it had before.

We have seen how America came to have the deepest libertarian tradition, a tradition that still remains in much of our political rhetoric, and is still reflected in a feisty and individualistic attitude toward government by much of the American people. There is far more fertile soil in this country than in any other for a resurgence of libertarianism.

Resistance to Liberty

We can now see that the rapid growth of the libertarian movement and the Libertarian party in the 1970s is firmly rooted in what Bernard Bailyn called this powerful "permanent legacy" of the American Revolution. But if this legacy is so vital to the American tradition, what went wrong? Why the need now for a new libertarian movement to arise to reclaim the American dream?

To begin to answer this question, we must first remember that classical liberalism constituted a profound threat to the political and economic interests—the ruling classes—who benefited from the Old Order: the kings, the nobles and landed aristocrats, the privileged merchants, the military machines, the State bureaucracies. Despite three major violent revolutions precipitated by the liberals—the English of the seventeenth century and the American and French of the eighteenth—victories in Europe were only partial. Resistance was stiff and managed to successfully maintain landed monopolies, religious establishments, and warlike foreign and military policies, and for a time to keep the suffrage restricted to the wealthy elite. The liberals had to concentrate on widening the suffrage, because it was clear to both sides that the objective economic and political interests of the mass of the public lay in individual liberty. It is interesting to note that, by the early nineteenth century, the laissez-faire forces were known as "liberals" and "radicals" (for the purer and more consistent among them), and the opposition that wished to preserve or go back to the Old Order were broadly known as "conservatives."

Indeed, conservatism began, in the early nineteenth century, as a conscious attempt to undo and destroy the hated work of the new classical liberal spirit—of the American, French, and Industrial revolutions. Led by two reactionary French thinkers, de Bonald and de Maistre, conservatism yearned to replace equal rights and equality before the law by the structured and hierarchical rule of privileged elites; individual liberty and minimal government by absolute rule and Big Government; religious freedom by the theocratic rule of a State church; peace and free trade by militarism, mercantilist restrictions, and war for the advantage of the nation-state; and industry and manufacturing by the old feudal and agrarian order. And they wanted to replace the new world of mass consumption and rising standards of living for all by the Old Order of bare subsistence for the masses and luxury consumption for the ruling elite.

By the middle of and certainly by the end of the nineteenth century, conservatives began to realize that their cause was inevitably doomed if they persisted in clinging to the call for outright repeal of the Industrial Revolution and of its enormous rise in the living standards of the mass of the public, and also if they persisted in opposing the widening of the suffrage, thereby frankly setting themselves in opposition to the interests of that public. Hence, the "right wing" (a label based on an accident of geography by which the spokesmen for the Old Order sat on the right of the assembly hall during the French Revolution) decided to shift their gears and to update their statist creed by jettisoning outright opposition to industrialism and democratic suffrage. For the old conservatism's frank hatred and contempt for the mass of the public, the new conservatives substituted duplicity and demagogy. The new conservatives wooed the masses with the following line: "We, too, favor industrialism and a higher standard of living. But, to accomplish such ends, we must regulate industry for the public good; we must substitute organized cooperation for the dog-eat-dog of the free and competitive marketplace; and, above all, we must substitute for the nation-destroying liberal tenets of peace and free trade the nation-glorifying measures of war, protectionism, empire, and military prowess." For all of these changes, of course, Big Government rather than minimal government was required.

And so, in the late nineteenth century, statism and Big Government returned, but this time displaying a proindustrial and pro-general-welfare face. The Old Order returned, but this time the beneficiaries were shuffled a bit; they were not so much the nobility, the feudal landlords, the army, the bureaucracy, and privileged merchants as they were the army, the bureaucracy, the weakened feudal landlords, and especially the privileged manufacturers. Led by Bismarck in Prussia, the New Right fashioned a right-wing collectivism based on war, militarism, protectionism, and the compulsory cartelization of business and industry—a giant network of controls, regulations, subsidies, and privileges which forged a great partnership of Big Government with certain favored elements in big business and industry.

Something had to be done, too, about the new phenomenon of a massive number of industrial wage workers—the "proletariat." During the eighteenth and early nineteenth centuries, indeed until the late nineteenth century, the mass of workers favored laissez-faire and the free competitive market as best for their wages and working conditions as workers, and for a cheap and widening range of consumer goods as consumers. Even the early trade unions, e.g., in Great Britain, were staunch believers in laissez-faire. New conservatives, spearheaded by Bismarck in Germany and Disraeli in Britain, weakened the libertarian will of the workers by shedding crocodile tears about the condition of the industrial labor force, and cartelizing and regulating industry, not accidentally hobbling efficient competition. Finally, in the early twentieth century, the new conservative "corporate state"—then and now the dominant political system in the Western world—incorporated "responsible" and corporatist trade unions as junior partners to Big Government and favored big businesses in the new statist and corporatist decision-making system.

To establish this new system, to create a New Order which was a modernized, dressed-up version of the *ancien régime* before the American and French revolutions, the new ruling elites had to perform a gigantic con job on the deluded public, a con job that continues to this day. Whereas the existence of *every* government from absolute monarchy to military dictatorship rests on the consent of the majority of the public, a democratic government must engineer such consent on a more immediate, day-by-day basis. And to do so, the new conservative ruling elites had to gull the public in many crucial and fundamental ways. For the masses now had to be convinced that tyranny was better than liberty, that a cartelized and privileged industrial feudalism was better for the consumers than a freely competitive market, that a cartelized monopoly was to be imposed *in the name* of antimonopoly, and that war and military aggrandizement for the benefit of the ruling elites was really in the interests of the conscripted, taxed, and often slaughtered public. How was this to be done?

In all societies, public opinion is determined by the intellectual classes, the opinion moulders of society. For most people neither originate nor disseminate ideas and concepts; on the contrary, they tend to adopt those ideas promulgated by the professional intellectual classes, the professional dealers in ideas. Now, throughout history, as we shall see further below, despots and ruling elites of States have had far more need of the services of intellectuals than have peaceful citizens in a free society. For States have always needed opinion-moulding intellectuals to con the public into believing that its rule is wise, good, and inevitable; into believing that the "emperor has clothes." Until the modern world, such intellectuals were inevitably churchmen (or witch doctors), the guardians of religion. It was a cozy alliance, this age-old partnership between Church and State; the Church informed its deluded charges that the king ruled by divine command and therefore must be obeyed; in return, the king funneled numerous tax revenues into the coffers of the Church. Hence, the great importance for the libertarian classical liberals of their success at separating Church and State. The new liberal world was a world in which intellectuals could be secular—could make a living on their own, in the market, apart from State subvention.

To establish their new statist order, their neomercantilist corporate State, the new conservatives therefore had to forge a new alliance between intellectual and State. In an increasingly secular age, this meant with secular intellectuals rather than with divines: specifically, with the new breed of professors, Ph.D.'s, historians, teachers, and technocratic economists, social workers, sociologists, physicians, and engineers. This reforged alliance came in two parts. In the early nineteenth century, the conservatives, conceding reason to their liberal enemies, relied heavily on the alleged virtues of irrationality, romanticism, tradition, theocracy. By stressing the virtue of tradition and of irrational symbols, the conservatives could gull the public into continuing privileged hierar-

chical rule, and to continue to worship the nation-state and its war-
making machine. In the latter part of the nineteenth century, the new
conservatism adopted the trappings of reason and of "science." Now
it was science that allegedly required rule of the economy and of society
by technocratic "experts." In exchange for spreading this message to
the public, the new breed of intellectuals was rewarded with jobs and
prestige as apologists for the New Order and as planners and regulators
of the newly cartelized economy and society.

To insure the dominance of the new statism over public opinion, to
insure that the public's consent would be engineered, the governments
of the Western world in the late nineteenth and early twentieth centuries
moved to seize control over education, over the minds of men: over
the universities, and over general education through compulsory school
attendance laws and a network of public schools. The public schools
were consciously used to inculcate obedience to the State as well as
other civic virtues among their young charges. Furthermore, this statiz-
ing of education insured that one of the biggest vested interests in expanding statism would be the nation's teachers and professional educationists.

One of the ways that the new statist intellectuals did their work was
to change the meaning of old labels, and therefore to manipulate in
the minds of the public the emotional connotations attached to such
labels. For example, the laissez-faire libertarians had long been known
as "liberals," and the purest and most militant of them as "radicals";
they had also been known as "progressives" because they were the ones
in tune with industrial progress, the spread of liberty, and the rise in
living standards of consumers. The new breed of statist academics and
intellectuals appropriated to themselves the words "liberal" and "progressive," and successfully managed to tar their laissez-faire opponents
with the charge of being old-fashioned, "Neanderthal," and "reactionary." Even the name "conservative" was pinned on the classical liberals.
And, as we have seen, the new statists were able to appropriate the
concept of "reason" as well.

If the laissez-faire liberals were confused by the new recrudescence
of statism and mercantilism as "progressive" corporate statism, another
reason for the decay of classical liberalism by the end of the nineteenth
century was the growth of a peculiar new movement: socialism. Socialism began in the 1830s and expanded greatly after the 1880s. The peculiar
thing about socialism was that it was a confused, hybrid movement,
influenced by *both* the two great preexisting polar ideologies, liberalism
and conservatism. From the classical liberals the socialists took a frank

acceptance of industrialism and the Industrial Revolution, an early glorification of "science" and "reason," and at least a rhetorical devotion
to such classical liberal ideals as peace, individual freedom, and a rising
standard of living. Indeed, the socialists, long before the much later
corporatists, pioneered in a co-opting of science, reason, and industrialism. And the socialists not only adopted the classical liberal adherence
to democracy, but topped it by calling for an "expanded democracy,"
in which "the people" would run the economy—and each other.

On the other hand, from the conservatives the socialists took a devotion
to coercion and the statist means for trying to achieve these liberal
goals. Industrial harmony and growth were to be achieved by aggrandizing the State into an all-powerful institution, ruling the economy and
the society in the name of "science." A vanguard of technocrats was
to assume all-powerful rule over everyone's person and property in the
name of the "people" and of "democracy." Not content with the liberal
achievement of reason and freedom for scientific research, the socialist
State would install rule *by* the scientists of everyone else; not content
with liberals setting the workers free to achieve undreamt-of prosperity,
the socialist State would install rule *by* the workers of everyone else—
or rather, rule by politicians, bureaucrats, and technocrats in their name.
Not content with the liberal creed of equality of rights, of equality
before the law, the socialist State would trample on such equality on
behalf of the monstrous and impossible goal of equality or uniformity
of *results*—or rather, would erect a new privileged elite, a new class,
in the name of bringing about such an impossible equality.

Socialism was a confused and hybrid movement because it tried to
achieve the liberal goals of freedom, peace, and industrial harmony and
growth—goals which can only be achieved through liberty and the separation of government from virtually everything—by imposing the old
conservative means of statism, collectivism, and hierarchical privilege.
It was a movement which could only fail, which indeed *did* fail miserably
in those numerous countries where it attained power in the twentieth
century, by bringing to the masses only unprecedented despotism, starvation, and grinding impoverishment.

But the worst thing about the rise of the socialist movement was
that it was able to outflank the classical liberals "on the Left": that is,
as the party of hope, of radicalism, of revolution in the Western World.
For, just as the defenders of the *ancien régime* took their place on the
right side of the hall during the French Revolution, so the liberals and
radicals sat on the left; from then on until the rise of socialism, the
libertarian classical liberals *were* "the Left," even the "extreme Left,"

on the ideological spectrum. As late as 1848, such militant laissez-faire French liberals as Frederic Bastiat sat on the left in the national assembly. The classical liberals had begun as the radical, revolutionary party in the West, as the party of hope and of change on behalf of liberty, peace, and progress. To allow themselves to be outflanked, to allow the socialists to pose as the "party of the Left," was a bad strategic error, allowing the liberals to be put falsely into a confused middle-of-the-road position with socialism and conservatism as the polar opposites. Since libertarianism is nothing if not a party of change and of progress toward liberty, abandonment of that role meant the abandonment of much of their reason for existence—either in reality or in the minds of the public.

But none of this could have happened if the classical liberals had not allowed themselves to decay from within. They could have pointed out—as some of them indeed did—that socialism was a confused, self-contradictory, quasi-conservative movement, absolute monarchy and feudalism with a modern face, and that they themselves were still the only true radicals, undaunted people who insisted on nothing less than complete victory for the libertarian ideal.

Decay From Within

But after achieving impressive partial victories against statism, the classical liberals began to lose their radicalism, their dogged insistence on carrying the battle against conservative statism to the point of final victory. Instead of using partial victories as a stepping-stone for evermore pressure, the classical liberals began to lose their fervor for change and for purity of principle. They began to rest content with trying to safeguard their existing victories, and thus turned themselves from a radical into a conservative movement—"conservative" in the sense of being content to preserve the status quo. In short, the liberals left the field wide open for socialism to become the party of hope and of radicalism, and even for the later corporatists to pose as "liberals" and "progressives" as against the "extreme right wing" and "conservative" libertarian classical liberals, since the latter allowed themselves to be boxed into a position of hoping for nothing more than stasis, than absence of change. Such a strategy is foolish and untenable in a changing world.

But the degeneration of liberalism was not merely one of stance and strategy, but one of principle as well. For the liberals became content to leave the war-making power in the hands of the State, to leave the education power in its hands, to leave the power over money and banking, and over roads, in the hands of the State—in short, to concede to

State dominion over all the crucial levers of power in society. In contrast to the eighteenth-century liberals' total hostility to the executive and to bureaucracy, the nineteenth-century liberals tolerated and even welcomed the buildup of executive power and of an entrenched oligarchic civil service bureaucracy.

Moreover, principle and strategy merged in the decay of eighteenth-century and early nineteenth-century liberal devotion to "abolitionism"—to the view that, whether the institution be slavery or any other aspect of statism, it should be abolished as quickly as possible, since the immediate abolition of statism, while unlikely in practice, was to be sought after as the *only possible moral* position. For to *prefer* a gradual whittling away to immediate abolition of an evil and coercive institution is *to ratify* and sanction such evil, and therefore to violate libertarian principles. As the great abolitionist of slavery and libertarian William Lloyd Garrison explained: "Urge immediate abolition as earnestly as we may, it will, alas! be gradual abolition in the end. We have never said that slavery would be overthrown by a single blow; that it ought to be, we shall always contend."[4]

There were two critically important changes in the philosophy and ideology of classical liberalism which both exemplified and contributed to its decay as a vital, progressive, and radical force in the Western world. The first, and most important, occurring in the early to mid-nineteenth century, was the abandonment of the philosophy of natural rights, and its replacement by technocratic utilitarianism. Instead of liberty grounded on the imperative morality of each individual's right to person and property, that is, instead of liberty being sought primarily on the basis of right and justice, utilitarianism preferred liberty as generally the best way to achieve a vaguely defined general welfare or common good. There were two grave consequences of this shift from natural rights to utilitarianism. First, the purity of the goal, the consistency of the principle, was inevitably shattered. For whereas the natural-rights libertarian seeking morality and justice cleaves militantly to pure principle, the utilitarian only values liberty as an ad hoc expedient. And since expediency can and does shift with the wind, it will become easy for the utilitarian in his cool calculus of cost and benefit to plump for statism in ad hoc case after case, and thus to give principle away. Indeed, this is precisely what happened to the Benthamite utilitarians in England: beginning with ad hoc libertarianism and laissez-faire, they found it

---

[4]Quoted in William H. Pease and Jane H. Pease, eds., *The Antislavery Argument* (Indianapolis: Bobbs-Merrill Co., 1965), p. xxxv.

ever easier to slide further and further into statism. An example was
the drive for an "efficient" and therefore strong civil service and executive power, an efficiency that took precedence, indeed replaced, any
concept of justice or right.

Second, and equally important, it is rare indeed ever to find a utilitarian who is also radical, who burns for immediate abolition of evil
and coercion. Utilitarians, with their devotion to expediency, almost
inevitably oppose any sort of upsetting or radical change. There have
been no utilitarian revolutionaries. Hence, utilitarians are never immediate abolitionists. The abolitionist is such because he wishes to eliminate
wrong and injustice as rapidly as possible. In choosing this goal, there
is no room for cool, ad hoc weighing of cost and benefit. Hence, the
classical liberal utilitarians abandoned radicalism and became mere grad-
ualist reformers. But in becoming reformers, they also put themselves
inevitably into the position of advisers and efficiency experts to the
State. In other words, they inevitably came to abandon libertarian principle as well as a principled libertarian strategy. The utilitarians wound
up as apologists for the existing order, for the status quo, and hence
were all too open to the charge by socialists and progressive corporatists
that they were mere narrow-minded and conservative opponents of any
and all change. Thus, starting as radicals and revolutionaries, as the
polar opposites of conservatives, the classical liberals wound up as the
image of the thing they had fought.

This utilitarian crippling of libertarianism is still with us. Thus, in
the early days of economic thought, utilitarianism captured free-market
economics with the influence of Bentham and Ricardo, and this influence
is today fully as strong as ever. Current free-market economics is all
too rife with appeals to gradualism; with scorn for ethics, justice, and
consistent principle; and with a willingness to abandon free-market principles at the drop of a cost-benefit hat. Hence, current free-market economics is generally envisioned by intellectuals as merely apologetics
for a slightly modified status quo, and all too often such charges are
correct.

A second, reinforcing change in the ideology of classical liberals came
during the late nineteenth century, when, at least for a few decades,
they adopted the doctrines of social evolutionism, often called "social
Darwinism." Generally, statist historians have smeared such social Darwinist laissez-faire liberals as Herbert Spencer and William Graham
Sumner as cruel champions of the extermination, or at least of the disappearance, of the socially "unfit." Much of this was simply the dressing
up of sound economic and sociological free-market doctrine in the then-

fashionable trappings of evolutionism. But the really important and crippling aspect of their social Darwinism was the illegitimate carrying-over to the social sphere of the view that species (or later, genes) change very, very slowly, after millennia of time. The social Darwinist liberal came, then, to abandon the very idea of revolution or radical change in favor of sitting back and waiting for the inevitable tiny evolutionary changes over eons of time. In short, ignoring the fact that liberalism had had to break through the power of ruling elites by a series of radical changes and revolutions, the social Darwinists became conservatives preaching against any radical measures and in favor of only the most minutely gradual of changes.[5]

In fact, the great libertarian Spencer himself is a fascinating illustration of just such a change in classical liberalism (and his case is paralleled in America by William Graham Sumner). In a sense, Herbert Spencer embodies within himself much of the decline of liberalism in the nineteenth century. For Spencer began as a magnificently radical liberal, as virtually a pure libertarian. But, as the virus of sociology and social Darwinism took over in his soul, Spencer abandoned libertarianism as a dynamic, radical historical movement, although without abandoning it in pure theory. While looking forward to an eventual victory of pure liberty, of "contract" as against "status," of industry as against militarism, Spencer began to see that victory as inevitable, but only after millennia of gradual evolution. Hence, Spencer abandoned liberalism as a fighting, radical creed and confined his liberalism in practice to a weary, conservative, rearguard action against the growing collectivism and statism of his day.

But if utilitarianism, bolstered by social Darwinism, was the main agent of philosophical and ideological decay in the liberal movement, the single most important, and even cataclysmic, reason for its demise was its abandonment of formerly stringent principles against war, empire, and militarism. In country after country, it was the siren song

---

[5]Ironically enough, modern evolutionary theory is coming to abandon completely the theory of gradual evolutionary change. Instead, it is now perceived that a far more accurate picture is sharp and sudden flips from one static species equilibrium to another; this is being called the theory of "punctuational change." As one of the expounders of the new view, Professor Stephen Jay Gould, writes: "Gradualism is a philosophy of change, not an induction from nature. . . . Gradualism, too, has strong ideological components more responsible for its previous success than any objective matching with external nature. . . . The utility of gradualism as an ideology must explain much of its influence, for it became liberalism's quintessential dogma against radical change—sudden flips are against the laws of nature." Stephen Jay Gould, "Evolution: Explosion, Not Ascent," *New York Times* (January 22, 1978).

of nation-state and empire that destroyed classical liberalism. In England, the liberals, in the late nineteenth and early twentieth centuries, abandoned the antiwar, antiimperialist "Little Englandism" of Cobden, Bright, and the Manchester School. Instead, they adopted the obscenely entitled "Liberal Imperialism"—joining the conservatives in the expansion of empire, and the conservatives and the right-wing socialists in the destructive imperialism and collectivism of World War I. In Germany, Bismarck was able to split the previously almost triumphant liberals by setting up the lure of unification of Germany by blood and iron. In both countries, the result was the destruction of the liberal cause.

In the United States, the classical liberal party had long been the Democratic party, known in the latter nineteenth century as "the party of personal liberty." Basically, it had been the party not only of personal but also of economic liberty; the stalwart opponent of Prohibition, of Sunday blue laws, and of compulsory education; the devoted champion of free trade, hard money (absence of governmental inflation), separation of banking from the State, and the absolute minimum of government. It construed state power to be negligible and federal power to be virtually nonexistent. On foreign policy, the Democratic party, though less rigorously, tended to be the party of peace, antimilitarism, and antiimperialism. But personal and economic libertarianism were both abandoned with the capture of the Democratic party by the Bryan forces in 1896, and the foreign policy of nonintervention was then rudely abandoned by Woodrow Wilson two decades later. It was an intervention and a war that were to usher in a century of death and devastation, of wars and new despotisms, and also a century in all warring countries of the new corporatist statism—of a welfare-warfare State run by an alliance of Big Government, big business, unions, and intellectuals—that we have mentioned above.

The last gasp, indeed, of the old laissez-faire liberalism in America was the doughty and aging libertarians who banded together to form the Anti-Imperialist League at the turn of the century, to combat the American war against Spain and the subsequent imperialist American war to crush the Filipinos who were striving for national independence from both Spain and the United States. To current eyes, the idea of an antiimperialist who is not a Marxist may seem strange, but opposition to imperialism began with laissez-faire liberals such as Cobden and Bright in England, and Eugen Richter in Prussia. In fact, the Anti-Imperialist League, headed by Boston industrialist and economist Edwad Atkinson (and including Sumner) consisted largely of laissez-faire radicals who had fought the good fight for the abolition of slavery, and had then championed free trade, hard money, and minimal government. To them, their final battle against the new American imperialism was simply part and parcel of their lifelong battle against coercion, statism, and injustice—against Big Government in every area of life, both domestic and foreign.

We have traced the rather grisly story of the decline and fall of classical liberalism after its rise and partial triumph in previous centuries. What, then, is the reason for the resurgence, the flowering, of libertarian thought and activity in the last few years, particularly in the United States? How could these formidable forces and coalitions for statism have yielded even that much to a resurrected libertarian movement? Shouldn't the resumed march of statism in the late nineteenth and twentieth centuries be a cause for gloom rather than usher in a reawakening of a seemingly moribund libertarianism? Why didn't libertarianism remain dead and buried?

We have seen why libertarianism would naturally arise first and most fully in the United States, a land steeped in libertarian tradition. But we have not yet examined the question: Why the renaissance of libertarianism *at all* within the last few years? What contemporary conditions have led to this surprising development? We must postpone answering this question until the end of the book, until we first examine what the libertarian creed is, and how that creed can be applied to solve the leading problem areas in our society.

PART I

The Libertarian Creed

2

Property and Exchange

The Nonaggression Axiom

THE LIBERTARIAN CREED rests upon one central axiom: that no man or group of men may aggress against the person or property of anyone else. This may be called the "nonaggression axiom." "Aggression" is defined as the initiation of the use or threat of physical violence against the person or property of anyone else. Aggression is therefore synonymous with invasion.

If no man may aggress against another; if, in short, everyone has the absolute right to be "free" from aggression, then this at once implies that the libertarian stands foursquare for what are generally known as "civil liberties": the freedom to speak, publish, assemble, and to engage in such "victimless crimes" as pornography, sexual deviation, and prostitution (which the libertarian does not regard as "crimes" at all, since he defines a "crime" as violent invasion of someone else's person or property). Furthermore, he regards conscription as slavery on a massive scale. And since war, especially modern war, entails the mass slaughter of civilians, the libertarian regards such conflicts as mass murder and therefore totally illegitimate.

All of these positions are now considered "leftist" on the contemporary ideological scale. On the other hand, since the libertarian also opposes invasion of the rights of private property, this also means that he just as emphatically opposes government interference with property rights or with the free-market economy through controls, regulations, subsidies, or prohibitions. For if every individual has the right to his own property without having to suffer aggressive depredation, then he also has the right to give away his property (bequest and inheritance) and to exchange it for the property of others (free contract and the free market economy) without interference. The libertarian favors the right to unrestricted private property and free exchange; hence, a system of "laissez-faire capitalism."

In current terminology again, the libertarian position on property and economics would be called "extreme right wing." But the libertarian sees no inconsistency in being "leftist" on some issues and "rightist" on others. On the contrary, he sees his own position as virtually the *only* consistent one, consistent on behalf of the liberty of every individual. For how can the leftist be opposed to the violence of war and conscription while at the same time supporting the violence of taxation and government control? And how can the rightist trumpet his devotion to private property and free enterprise while at the same time favoring war, conscription, and the outlawing of noninvasive activities and practices that he deems immoral? And how can the rightist favor a free market while seeing nothing amiss in the vast subsidies, distortions, and unproductive inefficiencies involved in the military-industrial complex?

While opposing any and all private or group aggression against the rights of person and property, the libertarian sees that throughout history and into the present day, there has been one central, dominant, and overriding aggressor upon all of these rights: the State. In contrast to all other thinkers, left, right, or in-between, the libertarian refuses to give the State the moral sanction to commit actions that almost everyone agrees would be immoral, illegal, and criminal if committed by any person or group in society. The libertarian, in short, insists on applying the general moral law to everyone, and makes no special exemptions for any person or group. But if we look at the State naked, as it were, we see that it is universally allowed, and even encouraged, to commit all the acts which even nonlibertarians concede are reprehensible crimes. The State habitually commits mass murder, which it calls "war," or sometimes "suppression of subversion"; the State engages in enslavement into its military forces, which it calls "conscription"; and it lives and has its being in the practice of forcible theft, which it calls "taxation." The libertarian insists that whether or not such practices are supported by the majority of the population is not germane to their nature: that, regardless of popular sanction, War is Mass Murder, Conscription is

Slavery, and Taxation is Robbery. The libertarian, in short, is almost completely the child in the fable, pointing out insistently that the emperor has no clothes.

Throughout the ages, the emperor has had a series of pseudoclothes provided for him by the nation's intellectual caste. In past centuries, the intellectuals informed the public that the State or its rulers were divine, or at least clothed in divine authority, and therefore what might *look* to the naive and untutored eye as despotism, mass murder, and theft on a grand scale was only the divine working its benign and mysterious ways in the body politic. In recent decades, as the divine sanction has worn a bit threadbare, the emperor's "court intellectuals" have spun ever more sophisticated apologia: informing the public that what the government does is for the "common good" and the "public welfare," that the process of taxation-and-spending works through the mysterious process of the "multiplier" to keep the economy on an even keel, and that, in any case, a wide variety of governmental "services" could not possibly be performed by citizens acting voluntarily on the market or in society. All of this the libertarian denies: he sees the various apologia as fraudulent means of obtaining public support for the State's rule, and he insists that whatever services the government actually performs could be supplied far more efficiently and far more morally by private and cooperative enterprise.

The libertarian therefore considers one of his prime educational tasks is to spread the demystification and desanctification of the State among its hapless subjects. His task is to demonstrate repeatedly and in depth that not only the emperor but even the "democratic" State has no clothes; that all governments subsist by exploitive rule over the public; and that such rule is the reverse of objective necessity. He strives to show that the very existence of taxation and the State necessarily sets up a class division between the exploiting rulers and the exploited ruled. He seeks to show that the task of the court intellectuals who have always supported the State has ever been to weave mystification in order to induce the public to accept State rule, and that these intellectuals obtain, in return, a share in the power and pelf extracted by the rulers from their deluded subjects.

Take, for example, the institution of taxation, which statists have claimed is in some sense really "voluntary." Anyone who truly believes in the "voluntary" nature of taxation is invited to refuse to pay taxes and to see what then happens to him. If we analyze taxation, we find that, among all the persons and institutions in society, only the government acquires its revenues through coercive violence. Everyone else in society acquires income *either* through voluntary gift (lodge, charitable society, chess club) *or* through the sale of goods or services voluntarily purchased by consumers. If anyone *but* the government proceeded to "tax," this would clearly be considered coercion and thinly disguised banditry. Yet the mystical trappings of "sovereignty" have so veiled the process that only libertarians are prepared to call taxation what it is: legalized and organized theft on a grand scale.

Property Rights

If the central axiom of the libertarian creed is nonaggression against anyone's person and property, how is this axiom arrived at? What is its groundwork or support? Here, libertarians, past and present, have differed considerably. Roughly, there are three broad types of foundation for the libertarian axiom, corresponding to three kinds of ethical philosophy: the emotivist, the utilitarian, and the natural rights viewpoint. The emotivists assert that they take liberty or nonaggression as their premise purely on subjective, emotional grounds. While their own intense emotion might seem a valid basis for their own political philosophy, this can scarcely serve to convince anyone else. By ultimately taking themselves outside the realm of rational discourse, the emotivists thereby insure the lack of general success of their own cherished doctrine.

The utilitarians declare, from their study of the consequences of liberty as opposed to alternative systems, that liberty will lead more surely to widely approved goals: harmony, peace, prosperity, etc. Now no one disputes that relative consequences should be studied in assessing the merits or demerits of respective creeds. But there are many problems in confining ourselves to a utilitarian ethic. For one thing, utilitarianism assumes that we can weigh alternatives, and decide upon policies, on the basis of their good or bad *consequences*. But if it is legitimate to apply value judgments to the *consequences* of X, why is it not equally legitimate to apply such judgments to X *itself*? May there not be something about an act itself which, in its very nature, can be considered good or evil?

Another problem with the utilitarian is that he will rarely adopt a principle as an absolute and consistent yardstick to apply to the varied concrete situations of the real world. He will only use a principle, at best, as a vague guideline or aspiration, as a *tendency* which he may choose to override at any time. This was the major defect of the nineteenth-century English Radicals, who had adopted the laissez-faire view of the eighteenth-century liberals but had substituted a supposedly "scientific" utilitarianism for the supposedly "mystical" concept of natural rights as the groundwork for that philosophy. Hence the nineteenth-century laissez-faire liberals came to use laissez-faire as a vague tendency rather than as an unblemished yardstick, and therefore increasingly and fatally compromised the libertarian creed. To say that a utilitarian cannot be "trusted" to maintain libertarian principle in every specific application may sound harsh, but it puts the case fairly. A notable contemporary example is the free-market economist Professor Milton Friedman who, like his classical economist forebears, holds to freedom as against State intervention as a general tendency, but in practice allows a myriad of damaging exceptions, exceptions which serve to vitiate the principle almost completely, notably in the fields of police and military affairs, education, taxation, welfare, "neighborhood effects," antitrust laws, and money and banking.

Let us consider a stark example: Suppose a society which fervently considers all redheads to be agents of the Devil and therefore to be executed whenever found. Let us further assume that only a small number of redheads exist in any generation—so few as to be statistically insignificant. The utilitarian-libertarian might well reason: "While the murder of isolated redheads is deplorable, the executions are small in number; the vast majority of the public, as non-redheads, achieves enormous psychic satisfaction from the public execution of redheads. The social cost is negligible, the social, psychic benefit to the rest of society is great; therefore, it is right and proper for society to execute the redheads." The natural-rights libertarian, overwhelmingly concerned as he is for the *justice* of the act, will react in horror and staunchly and unequivocally oppose the executions as totally unjustified murder and aggression upon nonaggressive persons. The *consequence* of stopping the murders—depriving the bulk of society of great psychic pleasure—would not influence such a libertarian, the "absolutist" libertarian, in the slightest. Dedicated to justice and to logical consistency, the natural-rights libertarian cheerfully admits to being "doctrinaire," to being, in short, an unabashed follower of his own doctrines.

Let us turn then to the natural-rights basis for the libertarian creed, a basis which, in one form or another, has been adopted by most of the libertarians, past and present. "Natural rights" is the cornerstone of a political philosophy which, in turn, is embedded in a greater structure of "natural law." Natural law theory rests on the insight that we live in a world of more than one—in fact, a vast number—of entities, and that each entity has distinct and specific properties, a distinct "nature," which can be investigated by man's reason, by his sense perception and mental faculties. Copper has a distinct nature and behaves in a

[handwritten margin note:] what about a selfish utilitarian? *

[handwritten margin note:] essences, natural kinds

[handwritten note at bottom:] * he would fight against this as a society with such rules could easily wipe him out by s rules.
– Rand seems to be a selfish utilitarian

certain way, and so do iron, salt, etc. The species man, therefore, has a specifiable nature, as does the world around him and the ways of interaction between them. To put it with undue brevity, the activity of each inorganic and organic entity is determined by its own nature and by the nature of the other entities with which it comes in contact. Specifically, while the behavior of plants and at least the lower animals is determined by their biological nature or perhaps by their "instincts," the nature of man is such that each individual person must, in order to act, choose his own ends and employ his own means in order to attain them. Possessing no automatic instincts, each man must learn about himself and the world, use his mind to select values, learn about cause and effect, and act purposively to maintain himself and advance his life. Since men can think, feel, evaluate, and act only as individuals, it becomes vitally necessary for each man's survival and prosperity that he be free to learn, choose, develop his faculties, and act upon his knowledge and values. This is the necessary path of human nature; to interfere with and cripple this process by using violence goes profoundly against what is necessary by man's nature for his life and prosperity. Violent interference with a man's learning and choices is therefore profoundly "antihuman"; it violates the natural law of man's needs.

Individualists have always been accused by their enemies of being "atomistic"—of postulating that each individual lives in a kind of vacuum, thinking and choosing without relation to anyone else in society. This, however, is an authoritarian straw man; few, if any, individualists have ever been "atomists." On the contrary, it is evident that individuals always learn from each other, cooperate and interact with each other; and that this, too, is required for man's survival. But the point is that each individual makes the final choice of which influences to adopt and which to reject, or of which to adopt first and which afterwards. The libertarian welcomes the process of voluntary exchange and cooperation between freely acting individuals; what he abhors is the use of violence to cripple such voluntary cooperation and force someone to choose and act in ways different from what his own mind dictates.

The most viable method of elaborating the natural-rights statement of the libertarian position is to divide it into parts, and to begin with the basic axiom of the "right to self-ownership." The right to self-ownership asserts the absolute right of each man, by virtue of his (or her) being a human being, to "own" his or her own body; that is, to control that body free of coercive interference. Since each individual must think, learn, value, and choose his or her ends and means in order to survive and flourish, the right to self-ownership gives man the right to perform these vital activities without being hampered and restricted by coercive molestation.

Consider, too, the consequences of *denying* each man the right to own his own person. There are then only two alternatives: either (1) a certain class of people, *A*, have the right to own another class, *B*; or (2) everyone has the right to own his own equal quotal share of everyone else. The first alternative implies that while Class *A* deserves the rights of being human, Class *B* is in reality subhuman and therefore deserves no such rights. But since they *are* indeed human beings, the first alternative contradicts itself in denying natural human rights to one set of humans. Moreover, as we shall see, allowing Class *A* to own Class *B* means that the former is allowed to exploit, and therefore to live parasitically, *at the expense* of the latter. But this parasitism itself violates the basic economic requirement for life: production and exchange.

[margin note: this is not a partition]

The second alternative, what we might call "participatory communalism" or "communism," holds that every man should have the right to own his equal quotal share of everyone else. If there are two billion people in the world, then everyone has the right to own one two-billionth of every other person. In the first place, we can state that this ideal rests on an absurdity: proclaiming that every man is entitled to own a part of everyone else, yet is not entitled *to own himself.* Secondly, we can picture the viability of such a world: a world in which *no* man is free to take *any* action whatever without prior approval or indeed command by *everyone* else in society. It should be clear that in that sort of "communist" world, no one would be able to do anything, and the human race would quickly perish. But if a world of zero self-ownership and one hundred percent other ownership spells death for the human race, then any steps in that direction also contravene the natural law of what is best for man and his life on earth.

[margin note: interesting]

[margin note: extremists — why this monotocracy?]

Finally, however, the participatory communist world *cannot* be put into practice. For it is physically impossible for everyone to keep continual tabs on everyone else, and thereby to exercise his equal quotal share of partial ownership over every other man. In practice, then, the concept of universal and equal other-ownership is utopian and impossible, and supervision and therefore control and ownership of others necessarily devolves upon a specialized group of people, who thereby become a ruling class. Hence, in practice, any attempt at communist rule will automatically become class rule, and we would be back at our first alternative.

The libertarian therefore rejects these alternatives and concludes by adopting as his primary axiom the universal right of self-ownership, a right held by everyone by virtue of being a human being. A more difficult task is to settle on a theory of property in nonhuman objects, in the things of this earth. It is comparatively easy to recognize the practice when someone is aggressing against the property right of another's person: If A assaults B, he is violating the property right of B in his own body. But with nonhuman objects the problem is more complex. If, for example, we see X seizing a watch in the possession of Y, we cannot automatically assume that X is aggressing against Y's right of property in the watch; for may not X have been the original, "true" owner of the watch who can therefore be said to be repossessing his own legitimate property? In order to decide, we need a theory of justice in property, a theory that will tell us whether X or Y or indeed someone else is the legitimate owner.

Some libertarians attempt to resolve the problem by asserting that whoever the existing government decrees has the property title should be considered the just owner of the property. At this point, we have not yet delved deeply into the nature of government, but the anomaly here should be glaring enough: it is surely odd to find a group eternally suspicious of virtually any and all functions of government suddenly leaving it to government to define and apply the precious concept of property, the base and groundwork of the entire social order. It is particularly the utilitarian laissez-fairists who believe it most feasible to begin the new libertarian world by confirming all existing property titles; that is, property titles and rights as decreed by the very government that is condemned as a chronic aggressor.

Let us illustrate with a hypothetical example. Suppose that libertarian agitation and pressure has escalated to such a point that the government and its various branches are ready to abdicate. But they engineer a cunning ruse. Just before the government of New York state abdicates it passes a law turning over the entire territorial area of New York to become the private property of the Rockefeller family. The Massachusetts legislature does the same for the Kennedy family. And so on for each state. The government could then abdicate and decree the abolition of taxes and coercive legislation, but the victorious libertarians would now be confronted with a dilemma. Do they recognize the new property titles as legitimately private property? The utilitarians, who have no theory of justice in property rights, would, if they were consistent with their acceptance of given property titles as decreed by government, have to accept a new social order in which fifty new satraps would be collecting taxes in the form of unilaterally imposed "rent." The point is that

only natural-rights libertarians, only those libertarians who have a theory of justice in property titles that does not depend on government decree, could be in a position to scoff at the new rulers' claims to have private property in the territory of the country, and to rebuff these claims as invalid. As the great nineteenth-century liberal Lord Acton saw clearly, the natural law provides the only sure ground for a continuing critique of governmental laws and decrees.[1] What, specifically, the natural-rights position on property titles may be is the question to which we now turn.

We have established each individual's right to self-ownership, to a property right in his own body and person. But people are not floating wraiths; they are not self-subsistent entities; they can only survive and flourish by grappling with the earth around them. They must, for example, *stand* on land areas; they must also, in order to survive and maintain themselves, transform the resources given by nature into "consumer goods," into objects more suitable for their use and consumption. Food must be grown and eaten; minerals must be mined and then transformed into capital and then useful consumer goods, etc. Man, in other words, must own not only his own person, but also material objects for his control and use. How, then, should the property titles in these objects be allocated?

Let us take, as our first example, a sculptor fashioning a work of art out of clay and other materials; and let us waive, for the moment, the question of original property rights in the clay and the sculptor's tools. The question then becomes: *Who* owns the work of art as it emerges from the sculptor's fashioning? It is, in fact, the sculptor's "creation," not in the sense that he has created matter, but in the sense that he has transformed nature-given matter—the clay—into another form dictated by his own ideas and fashioned by his own hands and energy. Surely, it is a rare person who, with the case put thus, would say that the sculptor does *not* have the property right in his own product. Surely, if every man has the right to own his own body, and if he must grapple with the material objects of the world in order to survive, then the sculptor has the right to own the product he has made, by his energy and effort, a veritable *extension* of his own personality. He has placed the stamp of his person upon the raw material, by "mixing his labor" with the clay, in the phrase of the great property theorist John Locke. And the product transformed by his own energy has become the material

---

[1]See Gertrude Himmelfarb, *Lord Acton; A Study in Conscience and Politics* (Chicago: Phoenix Books, 1962), pp. 294–05. Compare also John Wild, *Plato's Modern Enemies and the Theory of Natural Law* (Chicago: University of Chicago Press, 1953), p. 176.

embodiment of the sculptor's ideas and vision. John Locke put the case this way:

. . . every man has a *property* in his own *person*. This nobody has any right to but himself. The *labour* of his body and the *work* of his hands, we may say, are properly his. Whatsoever, then, he removes out of the state that nature hath provided and left it in, he hath mixed his labour with it, and joined it to something that is his own, and thereby makes it his property. It being by him removed from the common state nature placed it in, it hath by this labour something annexed to it that excludes the common right of other men. For this labour being the unquestionable property of the labourer, no man but he can have a right to what that is once joined to . . .[2]

As in the case of the ownership of people's bodies, we again have three logical alternatives: (1) either the transformer, or "creator," has the property right in his creation; or (2) another man or set of men have the right in that creation, i.e., have the right to appropriate it by force without the sculptor's consent; or (3) every individual in the world has an equal, quotal share in the ownership of the sculpture—the "communal" solution. Again, put baldly, there are very few who would not concede the monstrous injustice of confiscating the sculptor's property, either by one or more others, or on behalf of the world as a whole. By what right do they do so? By what right do they appropriate to themselves the product of the creator's mind and energy? In this clear-cut case, the right of the creator to own what he has mixed his person and labor with would be generally conceded. (Once again, as in the case of communal ownership of persons, the world communal solution would, in practice, be reduced to an oligarchy of a *few* others expropriating the creator's work *in the name* of "world public" ownership.)

The main point, however, is that the case of the sculptor is not qualitatively different from *all* cases of "production." The man or men who had extracted the clay from the ground and had sold it to the sculptor may not be as "creative" as the sculptor, but they too are "producers," they too have mixed their ideas and their technological know-how with the nature-given soil to emerge with a useful product. They, too, are "producers," and they too have mixed their labor with natural materials to transform those materials into more useful goods and services. These persons, too, are entitled to the ownership of their products. Where then does the process begin? Again, let us turn to Locke:

[2]John Locke, *An Essay Concerning the True Original, Extent and End of Civil Government*, in E. Barker, ed., *Social Contract* (New York: Oxford University Press, 1948), pp. 17–18.

He that is nourished by the acorns he picked up under an oak, or the apples he gathered from the trees in the wood, has certainly appropriated them to himself. Nobody can deny but the nourishment is his. I ask then, when did they begin to be his? When he digested? or when he ate? or when he boiled? or when he brought them home? or when he picked them up? And 'tis plain, if the first gathering made them not his, nothing else could. That labour put a distinction between them and common. That added something to them more than Nature, the common mother of all, had done, and so they became his private right. And will any one say he had no right to those acorns or apples he thus appropriated because he had not the consent of all mankind to make them his? Was it a robbery thus to assume to himself what belonged to all in common? If such a consent as that was necessary, man had starved, notwithstanding the plenty God had given him. . . . Thus, the grass my horse has bit, the turfs my servant has cut, and the ore I have digged in my place, where I have a right to them in common with others, become my property without the assignation or consent of any body. The labour that was mine, removing them out of that common state they were in, hath fixed my property in them.

By making an explicit consent of every commoner necessary to any one's appropriating to himself any part of what is given in common, children or servants could not cut the meat which their father or master had provided for them in common without assigning to every one his peculiar part. Though the water running in the fountain be every one's, yet who can doubt but that in the pitcher is his only who drew it out? His labour hath taken it out of the hands of Nature where it was common . . . and hath thereby appropriated it to himself.

Thus the law of reason makes the deer that Indian's who killed it; 'tis allowed to be his goods who hath bestowed his labour upon it, though, before, it was the common right of every one. And amongst those who are counted the civilized part of mankind . . . this original law of nature for the beginning of property, in what was before common, still takes place, and by virtue thereof, what fish any one catches in the ocean, that great and still remaining common of mankind; or what ambergris any one takes up here is by the labour that removes it out of that common state nature left it in, made his property who takes that pains about it.[3]

If every man owns his own person and therefore his own labor, and if by extension he owns whatever property he has "created" or gathered out of the previously unused, unowned, "state of nature," then what of the last great question: the right to own or control the earth *itself?* In short, if the gatherer has the right to own the acorns or berries he picks, or the farmer the right to own his crop of wheat or peaches,

---

[3]Locke, *Civil Government*, pp. 18–19. While Locke was a brilliant property theorist, we are not claiming that he developed and applied his theory with anything like complete consistency.

who has the right to own the land on which these things have grown? It is at this point that Henry George and his followers, who have gone all the way so far with the libertarians, leave the track and deny the individual's right to own the piece of land itself, the *ground* on which these activities have taken place. The Georgists argue that, while every man should own the goods which he produces or creates, since Nature or God created the land itself, no individual has the right to assume ownership of that land. Yet, if the land is to be used at all as a resource in any sort of efficient manner, it must be owned or controlled by *someone* or some group, and we are again faced with our three alternatives: either the land belongs to the first user, the man who first brings it into production; *or* it belongs to a group of others; *or* it belongs to the world as a whole, with every individual owning a quotal part of every acre of land. George's option for the last solution hardly solves his moral problem: If the land itself should belong to God or Nature, then why is it more moral for every acre in the world to be owned by the world as a whole, than to concede individual ownership? In practice, again, it is obviously impossible for every person in the world to exercise effective ownership of his four-billionth portion (if the world population is, say, four billion) of every piece of the world's land surface. In practice, of course, a small oligarchy would do the controlling and owning, and not the world as a whole.

But apart from these difficulties in the Georgist position, the natural-rights justification for the ownership of ground land is the same as the justification for the original ownership of all other property. For, as we have seen, no producer *really* "creates" matter; he takes nature-given matter and transforms it by his labor energy in accordance with his ideas and vision. But *this* is precisely what the pioneer—the "homesteader"—does when he brings previously unused land into his own private ownership. Just as the man who makes steel out of iron ore transforms that ore out of his know-how and with his energy, and just as the man who takes the iron out of the ground does the same, so does the homesteader who clears, fences, cultivates, or builds upon the land. The homesteader, too, has transformed the character of the nature-given soil by his labor and his personality. The homesteader is just as legitimately the owner of the property as the sculptor or the manufacturer; he is just as much a "producer" as the others.

Furthermore, if the original land is nature- or God-given then so are the people's talents, health, and beauty. And just as all these attributes are given to specific individuals and not to "society," so then are land and natural resources. All of these resources are given to individuals and not to "society," which is an abstraction that does not actually exist. There is no existing entity called "society"; there are only interacting individuals. To say that "society" should own land or any other property in common, then, must mean that a group of oligarchs—in practice, government bureaucrats—should own the property, and at the expense of expropriating the creator or the homesteader who had originally brought this product into existence.

Moreover, no one can produce *anything* without the cooperation of original land, if only as standing room. No man can produce or create anything by his labor alone; he must have the cooperation of land and other natural raw materials.

Man comes into the world with just himself and the world around him—the land and natural resources given him by nature. He takes these resources and transforms them by his labor and mind and energy into goods more useful to man. Therefore, if an individual cannot own original land, neither can he in the full sense own any of the fruits of his labor. The farmer cannot own his wheat crop if he cannot own the land on which the wheat grows. Now that his labor has been inextricably mixed with the land, he cannot be deprived of one without being deprived of the other.

Moreover, if a producer is *not* entitled to the fruits of his labor, who is? It is difficult to see why a newborn Pakistani baby should have a moral claim to a quotal share of ownership of a piece of Iowa land that someone has just transformed into a wheatfield—and vice versa of course for an Iowan baby and a Pakistani farm. Land in its original state is unused and unowned. Georgists and other land communalists may claim that the whole world population *really* "owns" it, but if no one has yet used it, it is in the real sense owned and controlled by no one. The pioneer, the homesteader, the first user and transformer of this land, is the man who first brings this simple valueless thing into production and social use. It is difficult to see the morality of depriving him of ownership in favor of people who have never gotten within a thousand miles of the land, and who may not even know of the existence of the property over which they are supposed to have a claim.

The moral, natural-rights issue involved here is even clearer if we consider the case of animals. Animals are "economic land," since they are original nature-given resources. Yet will anyone deny full title to a horse to the man who finds and domesticates it—is this any different from the acorns and berries that are generally conceded to the gatherer? Yet in land, too, some homesteader takes the previously "wild," undomesticated land, and "tames" it by putting it to productive use. Mixing his labor with land sites should give him just as clear a title as in the case of animals. As Locke declared: "As much land as a man tills, plants, improves, cultivates, and can use the product of, so much is his property. He by his labour does, as it were, enclose it from the common."[4]

The libertarian theory of property was eloquently summed up by two nineteenth-century laissez-faire French economists:

If man acquires rights over things, it is because he is at once active, intelligent and free; by his activity he spreads over external nature; by his intelligence he governs it, and bends it to his use; by his liberty, he establishes between himself and it the relation of cause and effect and makes it his own. . . .

Where is there, in a civilized country, a clod of earth, a leaf, which does not bear this impress of the personality of man? In the town, we are surrounded by the works of man; we walk upon a level pavement or a beaten road; it is man who made healthy the formerly muddy soil, who took from the side of a far-away hill the flint or stone which covers it. We live in houses; it is man who has dug the stone from the quarry, who has hewn it, who has planed the woods; it is the thought of man which has arranged the materials properly and made a building of what was before rock and wood. And in the country, the action of man is still everywhere present; men have cultivated the soil and generations of laborers have mellowed and enriched it; the works of man have dammed the rivers and created fertility where the waters had brought only desolation. . . . Everywhere a powerful hand is divined which has moulded matter, and an intelligent will which has adapted it . . . to the satisfaction of the wants of one same being. Nature has recognized her master, and man feels that he is at home in nature. Nature has been *appropriated* by him for his use; she has become his *own;* she is his *property.* This property is legitimate; it constitutes a right as sacred for man as is the free exercise of his faculties. It is his because it has come entirely from himself, and is in no way anything but an emanation from his being. Before him, there was scarcely anything but matter; since him, and by him, there is interchangeable wealth, that is to say, articles having acquired a value by some industry, by manufacture, by handling, by extraction, or simply by transportation. From the picture of a great master, which is perhaps of all material production that in which matter plays the smallest part, to the pail of water which the carrier draws from the river and takes to the consumer, wealth, whatever it may be, acquires its value only by communicated qualities, and these qualities are part of human activity, intelligence, strength. The producer has left a fragment of his own person in the thing which has thus become valuable, and may hence be regarded as a prolongation of the faculties of man acting upon external nature. As a free being he belongs to himself; now the cause, that is to say, the productive force, is himself; the effect, that is to say, the wealth produced, is still himself. Who shall dare

---

[4]Locke, *Civil Government,* p. 20.

contest his title of ownership so clearly marked by the seal of his personality? . . .

It is then, to the human being, the creator of all wealth, that we must come back . . . it is by labor that man impresses his personality on matter. It is labor which cultivates the earth and makes of an unoccupied waste an appropriated field; it is labor which makes of an untrodden forest a regularly ordered wood; it is labor, or rather, a series of labors often executed by a very numerous succession of workmen, which brings hemp from seed, thread from hemp, cloth from thread, clothing from cloth; which transforms the shapeless pyrite, picked up in the mine, into an elegant bronze which adorns some public place, and repeats to an entire people the thought of an artist. . . .

Property, made manifest by labor, participates in the rights of the person whose emanation it is; like him, it is inviolable so long as it does not extend so far as to come into collision with another right; like him, it is individual, because it has origin in the independence of the individual, and because, when several persons have cooperated in its formation, the latest possessor has purchased with a value, the fruit of his personal labor, the work of all the fellow-laborers who have preceded him: this is what is usually the case with manufactured articles. When property has passed, by sale or by inheritance, from one hand to another, its conditions have not changed; it is still the fruit of human liberty manifested by labor, and the holder has the rights as the producer who took possession of it by right.[5]

Society and the Individual

We have talked at length of individual rights; but what, it may be asked, of the "rights of society"? Don't they supersede the rights of the mere individual? The libertarian, however, is an individualist; he believes that one of the prime errors in social theory is to treat "society" as if it were an actually existing entity. "Society" is sometimes treated as a superior or quasi-divine figure with overriding "rights" of its own; at other times as an existing evil which can be blamed for all the ills of the world. The individualist holds that only individuals exist, think, feel, choose, and act; and that "society" is not a living entity but simply a label for a set of interacting individuals. Treating society as a thing that chooses and acts, then, serves to obscure the real forces at work. If, in a small community, ten people band together to rob and expropriate three others, then this is clearly and evidently a case of a group of individuals acting in concert against another group. In this situation, if the ten people presumed to refer to themselves as "society" acting in "its" interest, the rationale would be laughed out of court; even the

[5]Leon Wolowski and Émile Levasseur, "Property," in *Lalor's Cyclopedia of Political Science* . . . (Chicago: M. B. Cary & Co., 1884), III, pp. 392–93.

ten robbers would probably be too shamefaced to use this sort of argument. But let their size increase, and this kind of obfuscation becomes rife and succeeds in duping the public.

The fallacious use of a collective noun like "nation," similar in this respect to "society," has been trenchantly pointed out by the historian Parker T. Moon:

When one uses the simple monosyllable "France" one thinks of France as a unit, an entity. When . . . we say "France sent *her* troops to conquer Tunis"— we impute not only unit but personality to the country. The very words conceal the facts and make international relations a glamorous drama in which personalized nations are the actors, and all too easily we forget the flesh-and-blood men and women who are the true actors . . . if we had no such word as "France". . . then we should more accurately describe the Tunis expedition in some such way as this: "A few of these thirty-eight million persons sent thirty thousand others to conquer Tunis." This way of putting the fact immediately suggests a question, or rather a series of questions. Who were the "few"? Why did they send the thirty thousand to Tunis? And why did these obey? Empire-building is done not by "nations," but by men. The problem before us is to discover the men, the active, interested minorities in each nation, who are directly interested in imperialism and then to analyze the reasons why the majorities pay the expense and fight the war necessitated by imperialist expansion.[6]

The individualist view of "society" has been summed up in the phrase: *"Society" is everyone but yourself.* Put thus bluntly, this analysis can be used to consider those cases where "society" is treated, not only as a superhero with superrights, but as a supervillain on whose shoulders massive blame is placed. Consider the typical view that not the individual criminal, but "society," is responsible for his crime. Take, for example, the case where Smith robs or murders Jones. The "old-fashioned" view is that Smith is responsible for his act. The modern liberal counters that "society" is responsible. This sounds both sophisticated and humanitarian, until we apply the individualist perspective. Then we see that what liberals are *really* saying is that *everyone but* Smith, including of course the victim Jones, is responsible for the crime. Put this baldly, almost everyone would recognize the absurdity of this position. But conjuring up the fictive entity "society" obfuscates this process. As the sociologist Arnold W. Green puts it: "It would follow, then, that if society is responsible for crime, and criminals are not responsible for crime, only those members of society who do not commit crime can

[6]Parker Thomas Moon, *Imperialism and World Politics* (New York: Macmillan, 1930), p. 58.

be held responsible for crime. Nonsense this obvious can be circumvented only by conjuring up society as devil, as evil being apart from people and what they do."[7]

The great American libertarian writer Frank Chodorov stressed this view of society when he wrote that "Society Are People."

Society is a collective concept and nothing else; it is a convenience for designating a number of people. So, too, is family or crowd or gang, or any other name we give to an agglomeration of persons. Society . . . is not an extra "person"; if the census totals a hundred million, that's all there are, not one more, for there cannot be any accretion to Society except by procreation. The concept of Society as a metaphysical person falls flat when we observe that Society disappears when the component parts disperse; as in the case of a "ghost town" or of a civilization we learn about by the artifacts they left behind. When the individuals disappear so does the whole. The whole has no separate existence. Using the collective noun with a singular verb leads us into a trap of the imagination; we are prone to personalize the collectivity and to think of it as having a body and a psyche of its own.[8]

Free Exchange and Free Contract

The central core of the libertarian creed, then, is to establish the absolute right to private property of every man: first, in his own body, and second, in the previously unused natural resources which he first transforms by his labor. These two axioms, the right of self-ownership and the right to "homestead," establish the complete set of principles of the libertarian system. The entire libertarian doctrine then becomes the spinning out and the application of all the implications of this central doctrine. For example, a man, X, owns his own person and labor and the farm he clears on which he grows wheat. Another man, Y, owns the fish he catches; a third man, Z, owns the cabbages he has grown and the land under it. But if a man owns anything, he then has the right to *give away* or *exchange* these property titles to someone else, after which point the other person also has absolute property title. From this corollary right to private property stems the basic justification for free contract and for the free-market economy. Thus, if X grows wheat, he may and probably will agree to exchange some of that wheat for some of the fish caught by Y or for some of the cabbages grown by Z.

[7]Arnold W. Green, "The Reified Villain," *Social Research* (Winter, 1968), p. 656.

[8]Frank Chodorov, *The Rise and Fall of Society* (New York: Devin Adair, 1959), pp. 29–30.

With both X and Y making voluntary agreements to exchange property titles (or Y and Z, or X and Z) the property then becomes with equal legitimacy the property of the other person. If X exchanges wheat for Y's fish, then that fish becomes X's property to do with as he wishes, and the wheat becomes Y's property in precisely the same way.

Further, a man may exchange not only the tangible objects he owns but also his own labor, which of course he owns as well. Thus, Z may sell his labor services of teaching farmer X's children in return for some of the farmer's produce.

It so happens that the free-market economy, and the specialization and division of labor it implies, is by far the most productive form of economy known to man, and has been responsible for industrialization and for the modern economy on which civilization has been built. This is a fortunate utilitarian result of the free market, but it is not, to the libertarian, the *prime* reason for his support of this system. That prime reason is moral and is rooted in the natural-rights defense of private property we have developed above. Even if a society of despotism and systematic invasion of rights could be shown to be more productive than what Adam Smith called "the system of natural liberty," the libertarian would support this system. Fortunately, as in so many other areas, the utilitarian and the moral, natural rights and general prosperity, go hand in hand.

The developed-market economy, as complex as the system appears to be on the surface, is nothing more than a vast network of voluntary and mutually agreed-upon two-person exchanges such as we have shown to occur between wheat and cabbage farmers, or between the farmer and the teacher. Thus, when I buy a newspaper for a dime, a mutually beneficial two-person exchange takes place: I transfer my ownership of the dime to the newsdealer and he transfers ownership of the paper to me. We do this because, under the division of labor, I calculate that the paper is worth more to me than the dime, while the newsdealer prefers the dime to keeping the paper. Or, when I teach at a university, I estimate that I prefer my salary to not expending my labor of teaching, while the university authorities calculate that they prefer gaining my teaching services to not paying me the money. If the newsdealer insisted on charging 50¢ for the paper, I might well decide that it isn't worth the price; similarly, if I should insist on triple my present salary, the university might well decide to dispense with my services.

Many people are willing to concede the justice and propriety of property rights and the free-market economy, to concede that the farmer should be able to charge whatever his wheat will bring from consumers or the worker to reap whatever others are willing to pay for his services. But they balk at one point: inheritance. If Willie Stargell is ten times as good and "productive" a ball player as Joe Jack, they are willing to concede the justice of Stargell's earning ten times the amount; but what, they ask, is the justification for someone whose only merit is being born a Rockefeller inheriting far more wealth than someone born a Rothbard? The libertarian answer is to concentrate *not* on the recipient, the child Rockefeller or the child Rothbard, but to concentrate on the *giver*, the man who bestows the inheritance. For if Smith and Jones and Stargell have the right to their labor and property and to exchange the titles to this property for the similar property of others, they also have the right to *give* their property to whomever they wish. And of course most such gifts consist of the gifts of the property owners to their children—in short, inheritance. If Willie Stargell owns his labor and the money he earns from it, then he has the right to give that money to the baby Stargell.

In the developed free-market economy, then, the farmer exchanges the wheat for money; the wheat is bought by the miller who processes and transforms the wheat into flour; the miller sells the flour to the baker who produces bread; the baker sells the bread to the wholesaler, who in turn sells it to the retailer, who finally sells it to the consumer. And at each step of the way, the producer may hire the labor services of the workers in exchange for money. How "money" enters the equation is a complex process; but it should be clear that *conceptually* the use of money is equivalent to any single or group of useful commodities that are exchanged for the wheat, flour, etc. Instead of money, the commodity exchanged could be cloth, iron, or whatever. At each step of the way, mutually beneficial exchanges of property titles are agreed upon and transacted.

We are now in a position to see how the libertarian defines the concept of "freedom" or "liberty." Freedom is a condition in which a person's ownership rights in his own body and his legitimate material property are *not* invaded, are not aggressed against. A man who steals another man's property is invading and restricting the victim's freedom, as does the man who beats another over the head. Freedom and unrestricted property right go hand in hand. On the other hand, to the libertarian, "crime" is an act of aggression against a man's property right, either in his own person or his materially owned objects. Crime is an invasion, by the use of violence, against a man's property and therefore against his liberty. "Slavery"—the opposite of freedom—is a condition in which the slave has little or no right of self-ownership; his person and his produce are systematically expropriated by his master by the use of violence.

The libertarian, then, is clearly an individualist but *not* an egalitarian. The only "equality" he would advocate is the equal right of every man to the property in his own person, to the property in the unused resources he "homesteads," and to the property of others he has acquired either through voluntary exchange or gift.

Property Rights and "Human Rights"

Liberals will generally concede the right of every individual to his "personal liberty," to his freedom to think, speak, write, and engage in such personal "exchanges" as sexual activity between "consenting adults." In short, the liberal attempts to uphold the individual's right to the ownership of his own body, but then denies his right to "property," i.e., to the ownership of material objects. Hence, the typical liberal dichotomy between "human rights," which he upholds, and "property rights," which he rejects. Yet the two, according to the libertarian, are inextricably intertwined; they stand or fall together.

Take, for example, the liberal socialist who advocates government ownership of all the "means of production" while upholding the "human" right of freedom of speech or press. How is this "human" right to be exercised if the individuals constituting the public are denied their right to ownership of property? If, for example, the government owns all the newsprint and all the printing shops, how is the right to a free press to be exercised? If the government owns all the newsprint, it then necessarily has the right and the power to allocate that newsprint, and someone's "right to a free press" becomes a mockery if the government decides not to allocate newsprint in his direction. And since the government must allocate scarce newsprint in *some* way, the right to a free press of, say, minorities or "subversive" antisocialists will get short shrift indeed. The same is true for the "right to free speech" if the government owns all the assembly halls, and therefore allocates those halls as it sees fit. Or, for example, if the government of Soviet Russia, being atheistic, decides not to allocate many scarce resources to the production of matzohs, for Orthodox Jews the "freedom of religion" becomes a mockery; but again, the Soviet government can always rebut that Orthodox Jews are a small minority and that capital equipment should not be diverted to matzoh production.

The basic flaw in the liberal separation of "human rights" and "property rights" is that people are treated as ethereal abstractions. If a man has the right to self-ownership, to the control of his life, then in the real world he must also have the right to sustain his life by grappling with and transforming resources; he must be able to own the ground and the resources on which he stands and which he must use. In short, to sustain his "human right"—or his property rights in his own person— he must also have the property right in the material world, in the objects which he produces. Property rights *are* human rights, and are essential to the human rights which liberals attempt to maintain. The human right of a free press depends upon the human right of private property in newsprint.

In fact, there *are no* human rights that are separable from property rights. The human right of free speech is simply the property right to hire an assembly hall from the owners, or to own one oneself; the human right of a free press is the property right to buy materials and then print leaflets or books and to sell them to those who are willing to buy. There is no extra "right of free speech" or free press beyond the property rights we can enumerate in any given case. And furthermore, discovering and identifying the property rights involved will resolve any apparent conflicts of rights that may crop up.

Consider, for example, the classic example where liberals generally concede that a person's "right of freedom of speech" must be curbed in the name of the "public interest": Justice Holmes' famous dictum that no one has the right to cry "fire" falsely in a crowded theater. Holmes and his followers have used this illustration again and again to prove the supposed necessity for all rights to be relative and tentative rather than precise and absolute.

But the problem here is *not* that rights cannot be pushed too far, but that the whole case is discussed in terms of a vague and wooly "freedom of speech" rather than in terms of the rights of private property. Suppose we analyze the problem under the aspect of property rights. The fellow who brings on a riot by falsely shouting "fire" in a crowded theater is, necessarily, either the owner of the theater (or the owner's agent) or a paying patron. If he is the owner, then he has committed fraud on his customers. He has taken their money in exchange for a promise to put on a movie or play, and now, instead, he disrupts the show by falsely shouting "fire" and breaking up the performance. He has thus welshed on his contractual obligation, and has thereby stolen the property—the money—of his patrons and has violated their property rights.

Suppose, on the other hand, that the shouter is a patron and not the owner. In that case, he is violating the property right of the owner—

as well as of the other guests to their paid-for performance. As a guest, he has gained access to the property on certain terms, including an obligation not to violate the owner's property or to disrupt the performance the owner is putting on. His malicious act, therefore, violates the property rights of the theater owner and of all the other patrons.

There is no need, therefore, for individual rights to be restricted in the case of the false shouter of "fire." The rights of the individual are *still* absolute; but they are *property* rights. The fellow who maliciously cried "fire" in a crowded theater is indeed a criminal, but *not* because his so-called "right of free speech" must be pragmatically restricted on behalf of the "public good"; he is a criminal because he has clearly and obviously violated the property rights of another person.

3
The State

The State as Aggressor

THE CENTRAL THRUST of libertarian thought, then, is to oppose any and all aggression against the property rights of individuals in their own persons and in the material objects they have voluntarily acquired. While individual and gangs of criminals are of course opposed, there is nothing unique here to the libertarian creed, since almost all persons and schools of thought oppose the exercise of random violence against persons and property.

There is, however, a difference of emphasis on the part of libertarians even in this universally accepted area of defending people against crime. In the libertarian society there would be no "district attorney" who prosecutes criminals in the name of a nonexistent "society," even against the wishes of the victim of crime. The victim would himself decide whether to press charges. Furthermore, as another side to the same coin, in a libertarian world the victim would be able to press suit against a wrongdoer without having to convince the same district attorney that he should proceed. Moreover, in the system of criminal punishment in the libertarian world, the emphasis would never be, as it is now, on "society's" jailing the criminal; the emphasis would necessarily be on compelling the criminal to make restitution to the victim of his crime. The present system, in which the victim is not recompensed but instead

45

has to pay taxes to support the incarceration of his own attacker—would be evident nonsense in a world that focuses on the defense of property rights and therefore on the victim of crime.

Furthermore, while most libertarians are not pacifists, they would not join the present system in interfering with people's *right* to be pacifists. Thus, suppose that Jones, a pacifist, is aggressed against by Smith, a criminal. If Jones, as the result of his beliefs, is against defending himself by the use of violence and is therefore opposed to any prosecution of crime, then Jones will simply fail to prosecute, and that will be the end of it. There will be no governmental machinery that pursues and tries criminals even against the wishes of the victim.

But the critical difference between libertarians and other people is not in the area of private crime; the critical difference is their view of the role of the State—the government. For libertarians regard the State as the supreme, the eternal, the best organized aggressor against the persons and property of the mass of the public. *All* States everywhere, whether democratic, dictatorial, or monarchical, whether red, white, blue, or brown.

The State! Always and ever the government and its rulers and operators have been considered above the general moral law. The "Pentagon Papers" are only one recent instance among innumerable instances in history of men, most of whom are perfectly honorable in their private lives, who lie in their teeth before the public. Why? For "reasons of State." Service to the State is supposed to excuse all actions that would be considered immoral or criminal if committed by "private" citizens. The distinctive feature of libertarians is that they coolly and uncompromisingly apply the general moral law to people acting in their roles as members of the State apparatus. Libertarians make no exceptions. For centuries, the State (or more strictly, individuals acting in their roles as "members of the government") has cloaked its criminal activity in high-sounding rhetoric. For centuries the State has committed mass murder and called it "war"; then ennobled the mass slaughter that "war" involves. For centuries the State has enslaved people into its armed battalions and called it "conscription" in the "national service." For centuries the State has robbed people at bayonet point and called it "taxation." In fact, if you wish to know how libertarians regard the State and any of its acts, simply think of the State as a criminal band, and all of the libertarian attitudes will logically fall into place.

Let us consider, for example, what it is that sharply distinguishes government from all other organizations in society. Many political scientists and sociologists have blurred this vital distinction, and refer to all organizations and groups as hierarchical, structured, "governmental," etc. Left-wing anarchists, for example, will oppose equally government *and* private organizations such as corporations on the ground that each is equally "elitist" and "coercive." But the "rightist" libertarian is not opposed to inequality, and his concept of "coercion" applies only to the use of violence. The libertarian sees a crucial distinction between government, whether central, state, or local, and all other institutions in society. Or rather, two crucial distinctions. First, every other person or group receives its income by voluntary payment: either by voluntary contribution or gift (such as the local community chest or bridge club), *or* by voluntary purchase of its goods or services on the market (i.e., grocery store owner, baseball player, steel manufacturer, etc.). *Only* the government obtains its income by coercion and violence—i.e., by the direct threat of confiscation or imprisonment if payment is not forthcoming. This coerced levy is "taxation." A second distinction is that, apart from criminal outlaws, *only* the government can use its funds to commit violence against its own or any other subjects; only the government can prohibit pornography, compel a religious observance, or put people in jail for selling goods at a higher price than the government deems fit. Both distinctions, of course, can be summed up as: *only* the government, in society, is empowered to aggress against the property rights of its subjects, whether to extract revenue, to impose its moral code, or to kill those with whom it disagrees. Furthermore, any and all governments, even the least despotic, have always obtained the bulk of their income from the coercive taxing power. And historically, by far the overwhelming portion of all enslavement and murder in the history of the world have come from the hands of government. And since we have seen that the central thrust of the libertarian is to oppose all aggression against the rights of person and property, the libertarian necessarily opposes the institution of the State as the inherent and overwhelmingly the most important enemy of those precious rights.

There is another reason why State aggression has been far more important than private, a reason apart from the greater organization and central mobilizing of resources that the rulers of the State can impose. The reason is the absence of any check upon State depredation, a check that does exist when we have to worry about muggers or the Mafia. To guard against private criminals we have been able to turn to the State and its police; but who can guard us against the State itself? No one. For another critical distinction of the State is that it compels the monopolization of the service of protection; the State arrogates to itself a virtual monopoly of violence and of ultimate decision-making in soci-

ety. If we don't like the decisions of the State courts, for example, there
are no other agencies of protection to which we may turn.

It is true that, in the United States, at least, we have a constitution
that imposes strict limits on some powers of government. But, as we
have discovered in the past century, no constitution can interpret or
enforce itself; it must be interpreted by *men*. And if the ultimate power
to interpret a constitution is given to the government's own Supreme
Court, then the inevitable tendency is for the Court to continue to place
its imprimatur on ever-broader powers for its own government. Furthermore, the highly touted "checks and balances" and "separation of powers" in the American government are flimsy indeed, since in the final
analysis all of these divisions are part of the same government and are
governed by the same set of rulers.

One of America's most brilliant political theorists, John C. Calhoun,
wrote prophetically of the inherent tendency of a State to break through
the limits of its written constitution:

A written constitution certainly has many and considerable advantages, but it
is a great mistake to suppose that the mere insertion of provisions to restrict
and limit the powers of the government, without investing those for whose
protection they are inserted with the means of enforcing their observance, will
be sufficient to prevent the major and dominant party from abusing its powers.
Being the party in possession of the government, they will . . . be in favor of
the powers granted by the constitution and opposed to the restrictions intended
to limit them. As the major and dominant parties, they will have no need of
these restrictions for their protection. . . .

The minor or weaker party, on the contrary, would take the opposite direction
and regard them as essential to their protection against the dominant party.
. . . But where there are no means by which they could compel the major
party to observe the restrictions, the only resort left them would be a strict
construction of the constitution. . . . To this the major party would oppose a
liberal construction—one which would give to the words of the grant the broadest meaning of which they were susceptible. It would then be construction
against construction—the one to contract and the other to enlarge the powers
of the government to the utmost. But of what possible avail could the strict
construction of the minor party be, against the liberal interpretation of the
major, when the one would have all the powers of the government to carry
its construction into effect and the other be deprived of all means of enforcing
its construction? In a contest so unequal, the result would not be doubtful.
The party in favor of the restrictions would be overpowered. . . . The end of
the contest would be the subversion of the constitution . . . the restrictions
. would ultimately be annulled and the government be converted into one of
unlimited powers.

Nor would the division of government into separate and, as it regards each other, independent departments prevent this result . . . as each and all the departments—and, of course, the entire government—would be under the control of the numerical majority, it is too clear to require explanation that a mere distribution of its powers among its agents or representatives could do little or nothing to counteract its tendency to oppression and abuse of power.[1]

But why worry about the weakness of limits on governmental power? Especially in a "democracy," in the phrase so often used by American liberals in their heyday before the mid-1960s when doubts began to creep into the liberal utopia: "Are *we* not the government?" In the phrase "we are the government," the useful collective term "we" has enabled an ideological camouflage to be thrown over the naked exploitative reality of political life. For if *we* truly *are* the government, then *anything* a government does to an individual is not only just and not tyrannical; it is also "voluntary" on the part of the individual concerned. If the government has incurred a huge public debt which must be paid by taxing one group on behalf of another, this reality of burden is conveniently obscured by blithely saying that "we owe it to ourselves" (but *who* are the "we" and *who* the "ourselves"?). If the government drafts a man, or even throws him into jail for dissident opinions, then he is only "doing it to himself" and therefore nothing improper has occurred. Under this reasoning, then, Jews murdered by the Nazi government were *not* murdered; they must have "committed suicide," since they *were* the government (which was democratically chosen), and therefore anything the government did to them was only voluntary on their part. But there is no way out of such grotesqueries for those supporters of government who see the State merely as a benevolent and voluntary agent of the public.

And so we must conclude that "we" are *not* the government; the government is *not* "us." The government does not in any accurate sense "represent" the majority of the people, but even if it did, even if 90% of the people decided to murder or enslave the other 10%, this would *still* be murder and slavery, and would not be voluntary suicide or enslavement on the part of the oppressed minority. Crime is crime, aggression against rights is aggression, no matter how many citizens agree to the oppression. There is nothing sacrosanct about the majority; the lynch mob, too, is the majority in its own domain.

But while, as in the lynch mob, the majority can become actively

[1]John C. Calhoun, *A Disquisition on Government* (New York: Liberal Arts Press, 1953), pp. 25–27.

tyrannical and aggressive, the normal and continuing condition of the State is *oligarchic* rule: rule by a coercive elite which has managed to gain control of the State machinery. There are two basic reasons for this: one is the inequality and division of labor inherent in the nature of man, which gives rise to an "Iron Law of Oligarchy" in all of man's activities; and second is the parasitic nature of the State enterprise itself.

We have said that the individualist is not an egalitarian. Part of the reason for this is the individualist's insight into the vast diversity and individuality within mankind, a diversity that has the chance to flower and expand as civilization and living standards progress. Individuals differ in ability and in interest both within and between occupations; and hence, in all occupations and walks of life, whether it be steel production or the organization of a bridge club, leadership in the activity will inevitably be assumed by a relative handful of the most able and energetic, while the remaining majority will form themselves into rank-and-file followers. This truth applies to all activities, whether they are beneficial or malevolent (as in criminal organizations). Indeed, the discovery of the Iron Law of Oligarchy was made by the Italian sociologist Robert Michels, who found that the Social Democratic Party of Germany, despite its rhetorical commitment to egalitarianism, was rigidly oligarchical and hierarchical in its actual functioning.

A second basic reason for the oligarchic rule of the State is its parasitic nature—the fact that it lives coercively off the production of the citizenry. To be successful to its practitioners, the fruits of parasitic exploitation must be confined to a relative minority, otherwise a meaningless plunder of all by all would result in no gains for anyone. Nowhere has the coercive and parasitic nature of the State been more clearly limned than by the great late nineteenth-century German sociologist, Franz Oppenheimer. Oppenheimer pointed out that there are two and only two mutually exclusive means for man to obtain wealth. One, the method of production and voluntary exchange, the method of the free market, Oppenheimer termed the "economic means"; the other, the method of robbery by the use of violence, he called the "political means." The political means is clearly parasitic, for it requires previous production for the exploiters to confiscate, and it subtracts from instead of adding to the total production in society. Oppenheimer then proceeded to define the State as the "organization of the political means"— the systematization of the predatory process over a given territorial area.[2]

[2]Franz Oppenheimer, *The State* (New York: Vanguard Press, 1926), pp. 24–27 and passim.

In short, private crime is, at best, sporadic and uncertain; the parasitism is ephemeral, and the coercive, parasitic lifeline can be cut at any time by the resistance of the victims. The State provides a legal, orderly, systematic channel for predation on the property of the producers; it makes certain, secure, and relatively "peaceful" the lifeline of the parasitic caste in society. The great libertarian writer Albert Jay Nock wrote vividly that "the State claims and exercises the monopoly of crime. . . . It forbids private murder, but itself organizes murder on a colossal scale. It punishes private theft, but itself lays unscrupulous hands on anything it wants, whether the property of citizen or of alien."[3]

At first, of course, it is startling for someone to consider taxation as robbery, and therefore government as a band of robbers. But anyone who persists in thinking of taxation as in some sense a "voluntary" payment can see what happens if he chooses not to pay. The great economist Joseph Schumpeter, himself by no means a libertarian, wrote that "the state has been living on a revenue which was being produced in the private sphere for private purposes and had to be deflected from these purposes by political force. The theory which construes taxes on the analogy of club dues or of the purchase of the services of, say, a doctor only proves how far removed this part of the social sciences is from scientific habits of mind."[4] The eminent Viennese "legal positivist" Hans Kelsen attempted, in his treatise, *The General Theory of Law and the State*, to establish a political theory and justification of the State, on a strictly "scientific" and value-free basis. What happened is that early in the book, he came to the crucial sticking-point, the *pons asinorum* of political philosophy: *What* distinguishes the edicts of the State from the commands of a bandit gang? Kelsen's answer was simply to say that the decrees of the State are "valid," and to proceed happily from there, without bothering to define or explain this concept of "validity." Indeed, it would be a useful exercise for nonlibertarians to ponder this question: *How* can you define taxation in a way which makes it different from robbery?

To the great nineteenth-century individualist anarchist—and constitutional lawyer—Lysander Spooner, there was no problem in finding the answer. Spooner's analysis of the State as robber group is perhaps the most devastating ever written:

---

[3]Albert Jay Nock, *On Doing the Right Thing, and Other Essays* (New York: Harper & Bros., 1928), p. 145.

[4]Joseph A. Schumpeter, *Capitalism, Socialism, and Democracy* (New York: Harper & Bros., 1942), pp. 198 and 198n.

It is true that the *theory* of our Constitution is, that all taxes are paid voluntarily; that our government is a mutual insurance company, voluntarily entered into by the people with each other. . . .

But this theory of our government is wholly different from the practical fact. The fact is that the government, like a highwayman, say to a man: "Your money, or your life." And many, if not most, taxes are paid under the compulsion of that threat.

The government does not, indeed, waylay a man in a lonely place, spring upon him from the roadside, and holding a pistol to his head, proceed to rifle his pockets. But the robbery is none the less a robbery on that account; and it is far more dastardly and shameful.

The highwayman takes solely upon himself the responsibility, danger, and crime of his own act. He does not pretend that he has any rightful claim to your money, or that he intends to use it for your own benefit. He does not pretend to be anything but a robber. He has not acquired impudence enough to profess to be merely a "protector," and that he takes men's money against their will, merely to enable him to "protect" those infatuated travellers, who feel perfectly able to protect themselves, or do not appreciate his peculiar system of protection. He is too sensible a man to make such professions as these. Furthermore, having taken your money, he leaves you, as you wish him to do. He does not persist in following you on the road, against your will; assuming to be your rightful "sovereign," on account of the "protection" he affords you. He does not keep "protecting" you, by commanding you to bow down and serve him; by requiring you to do this, and forbidding you to do that; by robbing you of more money as often as he finds it for his interest or pleasure to do so; and by branding you as a rebel, a traitor, and an enemy to your country, and shooting you down without mercy, if you dispute his authority, or resist his demands. He is too much of a gentleman to be guilty of such impostures, and insults, and villainies as these. In short, he does not, in addition to robbing you, attempt to make you either his dupe or his slave.[5]

If the State is a group of plunderers, *who* then constitutes the State? Clearly, the ruling elite consists at any time of (a) the full-time *apparatus*—the kings, politicians, and bureaucrats who man and operate the State; and (b) the groups who have maneuvered to gain privileges, subsidies, and benefices from the State. The remainder of society constitutes the ruled. It was, again, John C. Calhoun who saw with crystal clarity that, no matter how small the power of government, no matter how low the tax burden or how equal its distribution, the very nature of government creates two unequal and inherently conflicting classes in society: those who, on net, *pay* the taxes (the "tax-payers"), and those who, on

---

[5]Lysander Spooner, *No Treason, No. VI: The Constitution of No Authority* (1870, reprinted in Larkspur, Colo.: Pine Tree Press, 1966), p. 17.

net, *live off* taxes (the "tax-consumers"). Suppose that the government imposes a low and seemingly equally distributed tax to pay for building a dam. This very act takes money from most of the public to pay it out to net "tax-consumers": the bureaucrats who run the operation, the contractors and workers who build the dam, etc. And the greater the scope of government decision-making, the greater its fiscal burdens, Calhoun went on, the greater the burden and the artificial inequality it imposes between these two classes:

Few, comparatively, as they are, the agents and employees of the government constitute that portion of the community who are the exclusive recipients of the proceeds of the taxes. Whatever amount is taken from the community in the form of taxes, if not lost, goes to them in the shape of expenditures or disbursements. The two—disbursement and taxation—constitute the fiscal action of the government. They are correlatives. What the one takes from the community under the name of taxes is transferred to the portion of the community who are the recipients under that of disbursements. But as the recipients constitute only a portion of the community, it follows, taking the two parts of the fiscal process together, that its action must be unequal between the payers of the taxes and the recipients of their proceeds. Nor can it be otherwise; unless what is collected from each individual in the shape of taxes shall be returned to him in that of disbursements, which would make the process nugatory and absurd. . . .

The necessary result, then, of the unequal fiscal action of the government is to divide the community into two great classes: one consisting of those who, in reality, pay the taxes and, of course, bear exclusively the burden of supporting the government; and the other, of those who are the recipients of their proceeds through disbursements, and who are, in fact, supported by the government; or, in fewer words, to divide it into tax-payers and tax-consumers.

But the effect of this is to place them in antagonistic relations in reference to the fiscal action of the government—and the entire course of policy therewith connected. For the greater the taxes and disbursements, the greater the gain of the one and the loss of the other, and vice versa. . . . The effect, then, of every increase is to enrich and strengthen the one, and impoverish and weaken the other.[6]

If states have everywhere been run by an oligarchic group of predators, how have they been able to maintain their rule over the mass of the population? The answer, as the philosopher David Hume pointed out over two centuries ago, is that in the long run *every* government, no matter how dictatorial, rests on the support of the majority of its subjects. Now this does not of course render these governments "voluntary,"

---

[6]Calhoun, *Disquisition on Government*, pp. 16–18.

since the very existence of the tax and other coercive powers shows how much compulsion the State must exercise. Nor does the majority support have to be eager and enthusiastic approval; it could well be mere passive acquiescence and resignation. The conjunction in the famous phrase "death and taxes" implies a passive and resigned acceptance to the assumed inevitability of the State and its taxation.

The tax-consumers, the groups that benefit from the operations of the State, will of course be eager rather than passive followers of the State mechanism. But these are only a minority. How is the compliance and acquiescence of the mass of the population to be secured? Here we come to the central problem of political philosophy—that branch of philosophy that deals with politics, the exercise of regularized violence: the mystery of civil obedience. Why do people obey the edicts and depredations of the ruling elite? Conservative writer James Burnham, who is the reverse of libertarian, put the problem very clearly, admitting that there is no rational justification for civil obedience: "Neither the source nor the justification of government can be put in wholly rational terms . . . why should I accept the hereditary or democratic or any other principle of legitimacy? Why should a principle justify the rule of that man over me?" His own answer is hardly calculated to convince many others: "I accept the principle, well . . . because I do, because that is the way it is and has been."[7] But suppose that one does *not* accept the principle; what will the "way" be then? And why have the bulk of subjects agreed to accept it?

The State and the Intellectuals

The answer is that, since the early origins of the State, its rulers have always turned, as a necessary bolster to their rule, to an alliance with society's class of intellectuals. The masses do not create their own abstract ideas, or indeed think through these ideas independently; they follow passively the ideas adopted and promulgated by the body of intellectuals, who become the effective "opinion moulders" in society. And since it is precisely a moulding of opinion on behalf of the rulers that the State almost desperately needs, this forms a firm basis for the age-old alliance of the intellectuals and the ruling classes of the State. The alliance is based on a *quid pro quo:* on the one hand, the intellectuals spread among the masses the idea that the State and its rulers are wise,

7James Burnham, *Congress and the American Tradition* (Chicago: Henry Regnery, 1959), pp. 6–8.

good, sometimes divine, and at the very least inevitable and better than any conceivable alternatives. In return for this panoply of ideology, the State incorporates the intellectuals as part of the ruling elite, granting them power, status, prestige, and material security. Furthermore, intellectuals are needed to staff the bureaucracy and to "plan" the economy and society.

Before the modern era, particularly potent among the intellectual handmaidens of the State was the priestly caste, cementing the powerful and terrible alliance of warrior chief and medicine man, of Throne and Altar. The State "established" the Church and conferred upon it power, prestige, and wealth extracted from its subjects. In return, the Church anointed the State with divine sanction and inculcated this sanction into the populace. In the modern era, when theocratic arguments have lost much of their lustre among the public, the intellectuals have posed as the scientific cadre of "experts" and have been busy informing the hapless public that political affairs, foreign and domestic, are much too complex for the average person to bother his head about. Only the State and its corps of intellectual experts, planners, scientists, economists, and "national security managers" can possibly hope to deal with these problems. The role of the masses, even in "democracies," is to ratify and assent to the decisions of their knowledgeable rulers.

Historically, the union of Church and State, of Throne and Altar, has been the most effective device for inducing obedience and support among the subjects. Burnham attests to the power of myth and mystery in inducing support when he writes that "In ancient times, before the illusions of science had corrupted traditional wisdom, the founders of Cities were known to be gods or demi-gods."[8] To the established priestcraft, the ruler was either anointed by God or, in the case of the absolute rule of many Oriental despotisms, was even himself God; hence, any questioning or resistance to his rule would be blasphemy.

Many and subtle are the ideological weapons the State and its intellectuals have used over the centuries to induce their subjects to accept their rule. One excellent weapon has been the power of *tradition*. The longer lasting the rule of any given State, the more powerful this weapon; for then the X-Dynasty or the Y-State has the seeming weight of centuries of tradition behind it. Worship of one's ancestors then becomes a none-too-subtle means of cultivating worship of one's ancestral rulers. The force of tradition is, of course, bolstered by ancient *habit*, which confirms the subjects in the seeming propriety and legitimacy of the

[8]Burnham, *op. cit.*, p. 3.

rule under which they live. Thus, the political theorist Bertrand De Jouvenel has written:

The essential reason for obedience is that it has become a habit of the species. . . . Power is for us a fact of nature. From the earliest days of recorded history it has always presided over human destinies . . . the authorities which ruled . . . in former times did not disappear without bequeathing to their successors their privilege nor without leaving in men's minds imprints which are cumulative in their effect. The succession of governments which, in the course of centuries, rule the same society may be looked on as one underlying government which takes on continuous accretions.[9]

Another potent ideological force is for the State to deprecate the *individual* and exalt either the past or the present collectivity of society. Any isolated voice, any raiser of new doubts, can then be attacked as a profane violator of the wisdom of his ancestors. Moreover, any new idea, much less any new *critical* idea, must necessarily *begin* as a small minority opinion. Therefore, in order to ward off any potentially dangerous idea from threatening majority acceptance of its rule, the State will try to nip the new idea in the bud by ridiculing any view that sets itself against mass opinion. The ways in which the State rulers in ancient Chinese despotisms used religion as a method of binding the individual to the State-run society were summarized by Norman Jacobs:

Chinese religion is a social religion, seeking to solve the problems of social interests, not individual interests. . . . Religion is essentially a force of impersonal social adjustment and control—rather than a medium for the personal solutions of the individual—and social adjustment and control are effected through education and reverence for superiors. . . . Reverence for superiors—superior in age and hence in education and experience—is the ethical foundation of social adjustment and control. . . . In China, the inter-relationship of political authority with orthodox religion equated heterodoxy with political error. The orthodox religion was particularly active in persecuting and destroying heterodox sects; in this it was backed by the secular power.[10]

The general tendency of government to seek out and thwart any heterodox views was outlined, in typically witty and delightful style, by the libertarian writer H. L. Mencken:

All [that government] can see in an original idea is potential change, and hence an invasion of its prerogatives. The most dangerous man, to any government,

[9]Bertrand De Jouvenel, *On Power* (New York: Viking Press, 1949), p. 22.

[10]Norman Jacobs, *The Origin of Modern Capitalism and Eastern Asia* (Hong Kong: Hong Kong University Press, 1958), pp. 161–63, 185. The great work on all aspects of Oriental despotism is Karl A. Wittfogel, *Oriental Despotism: A Comparative Study of Total Power* (New Haven: Yale University Press, 1957).

is the man who is able to think things out for himself, without regard to the prevailing superstitions and taboos. Almost inevitably he comes to the conclusion that the government he lives under is dishonest, insane and intolerable, and so, if he is romantic, he tries to change it. And even if he is not romantic personally he is very apt to spread discontent among those who are.[11]

It is also particularly important for the State to make its rule seem *inevitable:* even if its reign is disliked, as it often is, it will then be met with the passive resignation expressed in the familiar coupling of "death and taxes." One method is to bring to its side historical determinism: if X-State rules us, then this has been inevitably decreed for us by the Inexorable Laws of History (or the Divine Will, or the Absolute, or the Material Productive Forces), and nothing that any puny individuals may do can change the inevitable. It is also important for the State to inculcate in its subjects an aversion to any outcropping of what is now called "a conspiracy theory of history." For a search for "conspiracies," as misguided as the results often are, means a search for motives, and an attribution of individual responsibility for the historical misdeeds of ruling elites. If, however, any tyranny or venality or aggressive war imposed by the State was brought about *not* by particular State rulers but by mysterious and arcane "social forces," or by the imperfect state of the world—or if, in some way, *everyone* was guilty ("We are *all* murderers," proclaims a common slogan), then there is no point in anyone's becoming indignant or rising up against such misdeeds. Furthermore, a discrediting of "conspiracy theories"—or indeed, of anything smacking of "economic determinism"—will make the subjects more likely to believe the "general welfare" reasons that are invariably put forth by the modern State for engaging in any aggressive actions.

The rule of the State is thus made to seem inevitable. Furthermore, any alternative to the existing State is encased in an aura of fear. Neglecting its own monopoly of theft and predation, the State raises the spectre among its subjects of the chaos that would supposedly ensue if the State should disappear. The people on their own, it is maintained, could not possibly supply their own protection against sporadic criminals and marauders. Furthermore, each State has been particularly successful over the centuries in instilling fear among its subjects of *other* State rulers. With the land area of the globe now parcelled out among particular States, one of the basic doctrines and tactics of the rulers of each State has been to identify *itself* with the territory it governs. Since most men tend to love their homeland, the identification of that land and its popula-

[11]H. L. Mencken, *A Mencken Crestomathy* (New York: Alfred A. Knopf, 1949), p. 145.

tion with the State is a means of making natural patriotism work to the State's advantage. If, then, "Ruritania" is attacked by "Walldavia," the first task of the Ruritanian State and its intellectuals is to convince the people of Ruritania that the attack is really upon *them*, and not simply upon their ruling class. In this way, a war between *rulers* is converted into a war between *peoples*, with each people rushing to the defense of their rulers in the mistaken belief that the rulers are busily defending *them*. This device of nationalism has been particularly successful in recent centuries; it was not very long ago, at least in Western Europe, when the mass of subjects regarded wars as irrelevant battles between various sets of nobles and their retinues.

Another tried and true method for bending subjects to one's will is the infusion of guilt. Any increase in private well-being can be attacked as "unconscionable greed," "materialism," or "excessive affluence"; and mutually beneficial exchanges in the market can be denounced as "selfish." Somehow the conclusion always drawn is that more resources should be expropriated from the private sector and siphoned into the parasitic "public," or State, sector. Often the call upon the public to yield more resources is couched in a stern call by the ruling elite for more "sacrifices" for the national or the common weal. Somehow, however, while the public is supposed to sacrifice and curtail its "materialistic greed," the sacrifices are always one way. The *State* does not sacrifice; the State eagerly grabs more and more of the public's material resources. Indeed, it is a useful rule of thumb: when your ruler calls aloud for "sacrifices," look to your own life and pocketbook!

This sort of argumentation reflects a general double standard of morality that is always applied to State rulers but not to anyone else. No one, for example, is surprised or horrified to learn that businessmen are seeking higher profits. No one is horrified if workers leave lower-paying for higher-paying jobs. All this is considered proper and normal behavior. But if anyone should dare assert that politicians and bureaucrats are motivated by the desire to maximize *their* incomes, the hue and cry of "conspiracy theorist" or "economic determinist" spreads throughout the land. The general opinion—carefully cultivated, of course, by the State itself—is that men enter politics or government purely out of devoted concern for the common good and the public weal. What gives the gentlemen of the State apparatus their superior moral patina? Perhaps it is the dim and instinctive knowledge of the populace that the State *is* engaged in systematic theft and predation, and they may feel that only a dedication to altruism on the part of the State makes these actions tolerable. To consider politicians and bureaucrats subject to the same monetary aims as everyone else would strip the Robin Hood veil from State predation. For it would then be clear that, in the Oppenheimer phrasing, ordinary citizens were pursuing the peaceful, productive "economic means" to wealth, while the State apparatus was devoting itself to the coercive and exploitative organized "political means." The emperor's clothes of supposed altruistic concern for the common weal would then be stripped from him.

The intellectual arguments used by the State throughout history to "engineer consent" by the public can be classified into two parts: (1) that rule by the existing government is inevitable, absolutely necessary, and far better than the indescribable evils that would ensue upon its downfall; and (2) that the State rulers are especially great, wise, and altruistic men—far greater, wiser, and better than their simple subjects. In former times, the latter argument took the form of rule by "divine right" or by the "divine ruler" himself, or by an "aristocracy" of men. In modern times, as we indicated earlier, this argument stresses not so much divine approval as rule by a wise guild of "scientific experts" especially endowed in knowledge of statesmanship and the arcane facts of the world. The increasing use of scientific jargon, especially in the social sciences, has permitted intellectuals to weave apologia for State rule which rival the ancient priestcraft in obscurantism. For example, a thief who presumed to justify his theft by saying that he was really helping his victims by his spending, thus giving retail trade a needed boost, would be hooted down without delay. But when this same theory is clothed in Keynesian mathematical equations and impressive references to the "multiplier effect," it carries far more conviction with a bamboozled public.

In recent years, we have seen the development in the United States of a profession of "national security managers," of bureaucrats who never face electoral procedures, but who continue, through administration after administration, secretly using their supposed special expertise to plan wars, interventions, and military adventures. Only their egregious blunders in the Vietnam war have called their activities into any sort of public question; before that, they were able to ride high, wide, and handsome over the public they saw mostly as cannon fodder for their own purposes.

A public debate between "isolationist" Senator Robert A. Taft and one of the leading national security intellectuals, McGeorge Bundy, was instructive in demarking both the issues at stake and the attitude of the intellectual ruling elite. Bundy attacked Taft in early 1951 for opening a public debate on the waging of the Korean war. Bundy insisted that

only the executive policy leaders were equipped to manipulate diplo-
matic and military force in a lengthy decades-long period of limited
war against the communist nations. It was important, Bundy maintained,
that public opinion and public debate be excluded from promulgating
any policy role in this area. For, he warned, the public was unfortunately
not committed to the rigid national purposes discerned by the policy
managers; it merely responded to the *ad hoc* realities of given situations.
Bundy also maintained that there should be no recriminations or even
examinations of the decisions of the policy managers, because it was
important that the public accept their decisions without question. Taft,
in contrast, denounced the secret decision-making by military advisers
and specialists in the executive branch, decisions effectively sealed off
from public scrutiny. Furthermore, he complained, "If anyone dared
to suggest criticism or even a thorough debate, he was at once branded
as an isolationist and a saboteur of unity and the bipartisan foreign
policy."[12]

Similarly, at a time when President Eisenhower and Secretary of State
Dulles were privately contemplating going to war in Indochina, another
prominent national security manager, George F. Kennan, was advising
the public that "There are times when, having elected a government,
we will be best advised to let it govern and let it speak for us as it
will in the councils of the nations."[13]

We see clearly why the State needs the intellectuals; but why do
the intellectuals need the State? Put simply, the intellectual's livelihood
in the free market is generally none too secure; for the intellectual,
like everyone else on the market, must depend on the values and choices
of the masses of his fellow men, and it is characteristic of these masses
that they are generally uninterested in intellectual concerns. The State,
on the other hand, is willing to offer the intellectuals a warm, secure,
and permanent berth in its apparatus, a secure income, and the panoply
of prestige.

The eager alliance between the State and the intellectuals was symbolized by the avid desire of the professors at the University of Berlin,
in the nineteenth century, to form themselves into what they themselves
proclaimed as the "intellectual bodyguard of the House of Hohenzollern." From a superficially different ideological perspective, it can be
seen in the revealingly outraged reaction of the eminent Marxist scholar

---

[12]See Leonard P. Liggio, *Why the Futile Crusade?* (New York: Center for Libertarian
Studies, April 1978), pp. 41–43.

[13]George F. Kennan, *Realities of American Foreign Policy* (Princeton: Princeton University
Press, 1954), pp. 95–96.

of ancient China, Joseph Needham, to Karl Wittfogel's acidulous critique of ancient Chinese despotism. Wittfogel had shown the importance for bolstering the system of the Confucian glorification of the gentleman-scholar officials who manned the ruling bureaucracy of despotic China. Needham charged indignantly that the "civilization which Professor Wittfogel is so bitterly attacking was one which could make poets and scholars into officials."[14] What matter the totalitarianism so long as the ruling class is abundantly staffed by certified intellectuals!

The worshipful and fawning attitude of intellectuals toward their rulers has been illustrated many times throughout history. A contemporary American counterpart to the "intellectual bodyguard of the House of Hohenzollern" is the attitude of so many liberal intellectuals toward the office and person of the President. Thus, to political scientist Professor Richard Neustadt, the President is the "sole crown-like symbol of the Union." And policy manager Townsend Hoopes, in the winter of 1960, wrote that "under our system the people can look only to the President to define the nature of our foreign policy problem and the national programs and sacrifices required to meet it with effectiveness."[15] After generations of such rhetoric, it is no wonder that Richard Nixon, on the eve of his election as President, should thus describe his role: "He [the President] must articulate the nation's values, define its goals and marshall its will." Nixon's conception of his role is hauntingly similar to Ernst Huber's articulation, in the Germany of the 1930s, of the *Constitutional Law of the Greater German Reich.* Huber wrote that the head of State "sets up the great ends which are to be attained and draws up the plans for the utilization of all national powers in the achievement of the common goals . . . he gives the national life its true purpose and value."[16]

The attitude and motivation of the contemporary national security intellectual bodyguard of the State has been caustically described by Marcus Raskin, who was a staff member of the National Security Council during the Kennedy administration. Calling them "megadeath intellectuals," Raskin writes that:

[14]Joseph Needham, "Review of Karl A. Wittfogel, *Oriental Despotism,*" *Science and Society* (1958), p. 65. For an attitude in contrast to Needham's, see John Lukacs, "Intellectual Class or Intellectual Profession?," in George B. deHuszar, ed., *The Intellectuals* (Glencoe, Ill.: The Free Press, 1960), p. 522.

[15]Richard Neustadt, "Presidency at Mid-Century," *Law and Contemporary Problems* (Autumn, 1956), pp. 609–45; Townsend Hoopes, "The Persistence of Illusion: The Soviet Economic Drive and American National Interest," *Yale Review* (March 1960), p. 336.

[16]Quoted in Thomas Reeves and Karl Hess, *The End of the Draft* (New York: Vintage Books, 1970), pp. 64–65.

. . . their most important function is to justify and extend the existence of
their employers. . . . In order to justify the continued large-scale production
of these [thermonuclear] bombs and missiles, military and industrial leaders
needed some kind of theory to rationalize their use. . . . This became particularly urgent during the late 1950's, when economy-minded members of the Eisenhower Administration began to wonder why so much money, thought, and
resources were being spent on weapons if their use could not be justified. And
so began a series of rationalizations by the "defense intellectuals" in and out
of the universities. . . . Military procurement will continue to flourish, and
they will continue to demonstrate why it must. In this respect they are no
different from the great majority of modern specialists who accept the assumptions of the organizations which employ them because of the rewards in money
and power and prestige. . . . They know enough not to question their employers' right to exist.[17]

This is not to say that all intellectuals everywhere have been "court
intellectuals," servitors and junior partners of power. But this has been
the ruling condition in the history of civilizations—generally in the
form of a priestcraft—just as the ruling condition in those civilizations
has been one or another form of despotism. There have been glorious
exceptions, however, particularly in the history of Western civilization,
where intellectuals have often been trenchant critics and opponents of
State power, and have used their intellectual gifts to fashion theoretical
systems which could be used in the struggle for liberation from that
power. But invariably, these intellectuals have only been able to arise
as a significant force when they have been able to operate from an
independent power base—an independent property base—separate from
the apparatus of the State. For wherever the State controls all property,
wealth, and employment, everyone is economically dependent on it,
and it becomes difficult, if not impossible, for such independent criticism
to arise. It has been in the West, with its decentralized foci of power,
its independent sources of property and employment, and therefore of
bases from which to criticize the State, where a body of intellectual
critics has been able to flourish. In the Middle Ages, the Roman Catholic
Church, which was at least separate if not independent from the State,
and the new free towns were able to serve as centers of intellectual
and also of substantive opposition. In later centuries, teachers, ministers,
and pamphleteers in a relatively free society were able to use their independence from the State to agitate for further expansion of freedom.
In contrast, one of the first libertarian philosophers, Lao-tse, living in

---

[17]Marcus Raskin, "The Megadeath Intellectuals," *The New York Review of Books* (November 14, 1963), pp. 6–7. Also see Martin Nicolaus, "The Professor, the Policeman, and the
Peasant," *Viet-Report* (June–July 1966), pp. 15–19.

the midst of ancient Chinese despotism, saw no hope for achieving liberty in that totalitarian society except by counseling quietism, to the point of the individual's dropping out of social life altogther.

With decentralized power, with a Church separate from the State, with flourishing towns and cities able to develop outside the feudal power structure, and with freedom in society, the economy was able to develop in Western Europe in a way that transcended all previous civilizations. Furthermore, the Germanic—and particularly the Celtic— tribal structure which succeeded the disintegrating Roman Empire had strong libertarian elements. Instead of a mighty State apparatus exerting a monopoly of violence, disputes were solved by contending tribesmen consulting the elders of the tribe on the nature and application of the tribe's customary and common law. The "chief" was generally merely a war leader who was only called into his warrior role whenever war with other tribes was under way. There was no permanent war or military bureaucracy in the tribes. In Western Europe, as in many other civilizations, the typical model of the origin of the State was not via a voluntary "social contract" but by the conquest of one tribe by another. The original liberty of the tribe or the peasantry thus falls victim to the conquerors. At first, the conquering tribe killed and looted the victims and rode on. But at some time the conquerors decided that it would be more profitable to settle down among the conquered peasantry and rule and loot them on a permanent and systematic basis. The periodic tribute exacted from the conquered subjects eventually came to be called "taxation." And, with equal generality, the conquering chieftains parcelled out the land of the peasantry to the various warlords, who were then able to settle down and collect feudal "rent" from the peasantry. The peasants were often enslaved, or rather enserfed, to the land itself to provide a continuing source of exploited labor for the feudal lords.[18]

We may note a few prominent instances of the birth of a modern State through conquest. One was the military conquest of the Indian peasantry in Latin America by the Spaniards. The conquering Spanish not only established a new State over the Indians, but the land of the peasantry was parcelled out among the conquering warlords, who were

[18]On the typical genesis of the State, see Oppenheimer, *op. cit.*, Chapter II. While scholars such as Lowie and Wittfogel (*op. cit.*, pp. 324–25) dispute the Gumplowicz-Oppenheimer-Rüstow thesis that the State *always* originated in conquest, they concede that conquest often entered into the alleged internal development of States. Furthermore, there is evidence that in the first great civilization, Sumer, a prosperous, free and Stateless society existed until military *defense* against conquest induced the development of a permanent military and State bureaucracy. Cf. Samual Noah Kramer, *The Sumerians* (Chicago: University of Chicago Press, 1963), pp. 73ff.

ever after to collect rent from the tillers of the land. Another instance was the new political form imposed upon the Saxons of England after their conquest by the Normans in 1066. The land of England was parcelled out among the Norman warrior lords, who thereby formed a State and feudal-land apparatus of rule over the subject population. For the libertarian, the most interesting and certainly the most poignant example of the creation of a State through conquest was the destruction of the libertarian society of ancient Ireland by England in the seventeenth century, a conquest which established an imperial State and ejected numerous Irish from their cherished land. The libertarian society of Ireland, which lasted for a thousand years—and which will be described further below—was able to resist English conquest for hundreds of years because of the absence of a State which could be conquered easily and then used by the conquerors to rule over the native population.

But while throughout Western history, intellectuals have formulated theories designed to check and limit State power, each State has been able to use its own intellectuals to turn those ideas around into further legitimations of its own advance of power. Thus, originally, in Western Europe the concept of the "divine right of kings" was a doctrine promoted by the Church to *limit* State power. The idea was that the king could not just impose his arbitrary will. His edicts were limited to conforming with the divine law. As absolute monarchy advanced, however, the kings were able to turn the concept around to the idea that God put his stamp of approval on any of the king's actions; that he ruled by "divine right."

Similarly, the concept of parliamentary democracy began as a popular check on the absolute rule of the monarch. The king was limited by the power of parliament to grant him tax revenues. Gradually, however, as parliament displaced the king as head of State, the parliament itself became the unchecked State sovereign. In the early nineteenth century, English utilitarians, who advocated additional individual liberty in the name of social utility and the general welfare, were to see these concepts turned into sanctions for expanding the power of the State.

As De Jouvenel writes:

Many writers on theories of sovereignty have worked out one or the other of these restrictive devices. But in the end every single such theory has, sooner or later, lost its original purpose, and come to act merely as a springboard to Power, by providing it with the powerful aid of an invisible sovereign with whom it could in time successfully identify itself.[19]

[19]De Jouvenel, *op. cit.*, p. 27.

Certainly, the most ambitious attempt in history to impose limits on the State was the Bill of Rights and other restrictive parts of the United States Constitution. Here, written limits on government became the fundamental law, to be interpreted by a judiciary supposedly independent of the other branches of government. All Americans are familiar with the process by which John C. Calhoun's prophetic analysis has been vindicated; the State's own monopoly judiciary has inexorably broadened the construction of State power over the last century and a half. But few have been as keen as liberal Professor Charles Black—who hails the process—in seeing that the State has been able to transform judicial review itself from a limiting device into a powerful instrument for gaining legitimacy for its actions in the minds of the public. If a judicial decree of "unconstitutional" is a mighty check on governmental power, so too a verdict of "constitutional" is an equally mighty weapon for fostering public acceptance of ever greater governmental power.

Professor Black begins his analysis by pointing out the crucial necessity for "legitimacy" of any government in order to endure; that is, basic majority acceptance of the government and its actions. Acceptance of legitimacy, however, becomes a real problem in a country like the United States, where "substantive limitations are built into the theory on which the government rests." What is needed, adds Black, is a method by which the government can assure the public that its expanding powers are indeed "constitutional." And this, he concludes, has been the major historic function of judicial review. Let Black illustrate the problem:

The supreme risk [to the government] is that of disaffection and a feeling of outrage widely disseminated throughout the population, and loss of moral authority by the government as such, however long it may be propped up by force or inertia or the lack of an appealing and immediately available alternative. Almost everybody living under a government of limited powers, must sooner or later be subjected to some governmental action which as a matter of private opinion he regards as outside the power of government or positively forbidden to government. A man is drafted, though he finds nothing in the Constitution about being drafted. . . . A farmer is told how much wheat he can raise; he believes, and he discovers that some respectable lawyers believe with him, that the government has no more right to tell him how much wheat he can grow than it has to tell his daughter whom she can marry. A man goes to the federal penitentiary for saying what he wants to, and he paces his cell reciting . . . "Congress shall make no laws abridging the freedom of speech.". . . A businessman is told what he can ask, and must ask, for buttermilk.

The danger is real enough that each of these people (and who is not of their number?) will confront the concept of governmental limitation with the reality (as he sees it) of the flagrant overstepping of actual limits, and draw the obvious conclusion as to the status of his government with respect to legitimacy.[20]

This danger is averted, Black adds, by the State's propounding the doctrine that *some one* agency must have the ultimate decision on constitutionality, and that this agency must be part of the federal government itself. For while the seeming independence of the federal judiciary has played a vital role in making its actions virtual Holy Writ for the bulk of the population, it is also true that the judiciary is part and parcel of the government apparatus and is appointed by the executive and legislative branches. Professor Black concedes that the government has thereby set itself up as a judge in its own case, and has thus violated a basic juridical principle for arriving at any kind of just decision. But Black is remarkably lighthearted about this fundamental breach: "The final power of the State . . . must stop where the law stops it. And who shall set the limit, and who shall enforce the stopping, against the mightiest power? Why, the State itself, of course, through its judges and its laws. Who controls the temperate? Who teaches the wise? . . ."[21] And so Black admits that when we have a State, we hand over all our weapons and means of coercion to the State apparatus, we turn over all of our powers of ultimate decision-making to this deified group, and *then* we must jolly well sit back quietly and await the unending stream of justice that will pour forth from these institutions—even though they are basically judging their own case. Black sees no conceivable alternative to this coercive monopoly of judicial decisions enforced by the State, but here is precisely where our new movement challenges this conventional view and asserts that there *is* a viable alternative: libertarianism.

Seeing no such alternative, Professor Black falls back on mysticism in his defense of the State, for in the final analysis he finds the achievement of justice and legitimacy from the State's perpetual judging of its own cause to be "something of a miracle." In this way, the liberal Black joins the conservative Burnham in falling back on the miraculous and thereby admitting that there is no satisfactory rational argument in support of the State.[22]

[20]Charles L. Black, Jr., *The People and the Court* (New York: Macmillan, 1960), pp. 42–43.

[21]*Ibid.*, pp. 32–33.

[22]In contrast to the complacency of Black was the trenchant critique of the Constitution and the powers of the Supreme Court by the political scientist J. Allen Smith. Smith wrote that "Clearly, common sense required that no organ of the government should be able to determine its own powers." J. Allen Smith, *The Growth and Decadence of Constitutional Government* (New York: Henry Holt and Co., 1930), p. 87. Clearly, common sense and "miracles" dictate very different views of government.

Applying his realistic view of the Supreme Court to the famous conflict between the Court and the New Deal in the 1930s, Professor Black chides his liberal colleagues for their shortsightedness in denouncing judicial obstructionism:

. . . the standard version of the story of the New Deal and the Court, though accurate in its way, displaces the emphasis. . . . It concentrates on the difficulties; it almost forgets how the whole thing turned out. The upshot of the matter was (and this is what I like to emphasize) that after some twenty-four months of balking . . . the Supreme Court, without a single change in the law of its composition, or, indeed, in its actual manning, *placed the affirmative stamp of legitimacy on the New Deal, and on the whole new conception of government in America.* [*Italics the author's.*][23]

In this way, the Supreme Court was able to put the quietus to the large body of Americans who had strong constitutional objections to the expanded powers of the New Deal:

Of course, not everyone was satisfied. The Bonnie Prince Charlie of constitutionally commanded laissez-faire still stirs the hearts of a few zealots in the Highlands of choleric unreality. But there is no longer any significant or dangerous public doubt as to the constitutional power of Congress to deal as it does with the national economy. . . . We had no means, other than the Supreme Court, for imparting legitimacy to the New Deal.[24]

Thus, even in the United States, unique among governments in having a constitution, parts of which at least were meant to impose strict and solemn limits upon its actions, even here the Constitution has proved to be an instrument for ratifying the expansion of State power rather than the opposite. As Calhoun saw, any written limits that leave it to government to interpret its own powers are bound to be interpreted as sanctions for expanding and not binding those powers. In a profound sense, the idea of binding down power with the chains of a written constitution has proved to be a noble experiment that failed. The idea of a strictly limited government has proved to be utopian; some other, more radical means must be found to prevent the growth of the aggressive State. The libertarian system would meet this problem by scrapping the entire notion of creating a government—an institution with a coercive monopoly of force over a given territory—and *then* hoping to find ways to keep that government from expanding. The libertarian alternative is to abstain from such a monopoly government to begin with.

---

[23] *Ibid.*, p. 64.
[24] *Ibid.*, p. 65.

We will explore the entire notion of a State-less society, a society without formal government, in later chapters. But one instructive exercise is to try to abandon the habitual ways of seeing things, and to consider the argument for the State *de novo*. Let us try to transcend the fact that for as long as we can remember, the State has monopolized police and judicial services in society. Suppose that we were all starting completely from scratch, and that millions of us had been dropped down upon the earth, fully grown and developed, from some other planet. Debate begins as to how protection (police and judicial services) will be provided. Someone says: "Let's all give all of our weapons to Joe Jones over there, and to his relatives. And let Jones and his family decide all disputes among us. In that way, the Joneses will be able to protect all of us from any aggression or fraud that anyone else may commit. With all the power and all the ability to make ultimate decisions on disputes in the hands of Jones, we will all be protected from one another. And then let us allow the Joneses to obtain their income from this great service by using their weapons, and by exacting as much revenue by coercion as they shall desire." Surely in that sort of situation, no one would treat this proposal with anything but ridicule. For it would be starkly evident that there would be no way, in that case, for any of us to protect ourselves from the aggressions, or the depredations, of the Joneses themselves. No one would then have the total folly to respond to that long-standing and most perceptive query: "Who shall guard the guardians?" by answering with Professor Black's blithe: "Who controls the temperate?" It is only because we have become accustomed over thousands of years to the existence of the State that we now give precisely this kind of absurd answer to the problem of social protection and defense.

And, of course, the State never really did begin with this sort of "social contract." As Oppenheimer pointed out, the State generally began in violence and conquest; even if at times internal processes gave rise to the State, it was certainly never by general consensus or contract.

The libertarian creed can now be summed up as (1) the absolute right of every man to the ownership of his own body; (2) the equally absolute right to own and therefore to control the material resources he has found and transformed; and (3) therefore, the absolute right to exchange or give away the ownership to such titles to whoever is willing to exchange or receive them. As we have seen, each of these steps involves *property* rights, but even if we call step (1) "personal" rights, we shall see that problems about "personal liberty" inextricably involve the rights of material property or free exchange. Or, briefly, the rights of personal liberty and "freedom of enterprise" almost invariably intertwine and cannot really be separated.

We have seen that the exercise of personal "freedom of speech," for example, almost invariably involves the exercise of "economic freedom"—i.e., freedom to own and exchange material property. The holding of a meeting to exercise freedom of speech involves the hiring of a hall, traveling to the hall over roads, and using some form of transportation, etc. The closely related "freedom of the press" even more evidently involves the cost of printing and of using a press, the sale of leaflets to willing buyers—in short, all the ingredients of "economic freedom." Furthermore, our example of "shouting 'fire' in a crowded theater" provides us with the clear guideline for deciding *whose* rights must be defended in any given situation—the guidelines being provided by our criterion: the rights of property.

PART II

Libertarian Applications
to Current Problems

4

The Problems

LET US TAKE A BRIEF LOOK at the major problem areas of our society and see if we can detect any "red thread" that runs through all of them.

High taxes. High and rising taxes have crippled almost everyone and are hampering productivity, incentives, and thrift, as well as the free energies of the people. On the federal level, there is a rising rebellion against the burden of income taxes, and there is a flourishing tax rebel movement, with its own organizations and magazines, which refuses to pay a tax which it regards as predatory and unconstitutional. On the state and local levels, there is a rising tide of sentiment against oppressive property taxes. Thus, a record 1.2 million California voters signed the petition for the Jarvis-Gann initiative on the 1978 ballot, a proposal which would drastically and permanently lower property taxes by two-thirds to one percent and place ceilings upon the assessed value of the property. Furthermore, the Jarvis-Gann initiative enforces the freeze by requiring the approval of two-thirds of *all* registered voters in the state of California to raise property taxes beyond the one-percent ceiling. And, to make sure that the state doesn't simply substitute some other tax, the initiative also requires a two-thirds vote by the state legislature to increase *any other* tax in the state.

Furthermore, in the fall of 1977, scores of thousands of homeowners in Cook County, Illinois, engaged in a tax strike against the property tax, which had increased dramatically due to higher assessments.

It need hardly be emphasized that taxation, of income, property, or whatever, is the exclusive monopoly of government. No other individual or organization enjoys the privilege of taxation, of acquiring its income by coercion.

Urban fiscal crisis. Throughout the nation, states and localities are having difficulty paying interest and principal due on their swollen public debt. New York City has already pioneered in a partial default on its contractual obligations. The urban fiscal crisis is simply a matter of urban governments spending too much, more even than the high taxes they extract from us. Again, how much urban or state governments spend is up to them; once again, government is to blame.

Vietnam and other foreign interventions. The war in Vietnam was a total disaster for American foreign policy; after countless people were murdered and the land devastated, and at an enormous cost in resources, the American-supported government finally collapsed in early 1975. The disaster of the Vietnam war has properly called the rest of America's interventionist foreign policy into severe question, and was partly responsible for Congress's putting a brake on U.S. military intervention in the Angolan fiasco. Foreign policy, of course, is also an exclusive monopoly of the federal government. The war was waged by our armed forces which, again, are a compulsory monopoly of the same federal government. So the government is wholly responsible for the entire war and foreign policy problem, as a whole and in all of its aspects.

Crime in the streets. Consider: the crime in question is being committed, by definition, on the streets. The streets are owned, almost universally, by government, which thereby has a virtual monopoly of street-ownership. The police, who are supposed to guard us against this crime, are a compulsory monopoly of the government. And the courts, which are in the business of convicting and punishing criminals, are also a coercive monopoly of the government. So government has been in charge of every single aspect of the crime-in-the-streets problem. The failure here, just as the failure in Vietnam, must be chalked up solely to government.

Traffic congestion. Once again, this occurs solely on government-owned streets and roads.

The military-industrial complex. This complex is entirely a creature of the federal government. It is the government that decides to spend countless billions on overkill weaponry, it is the government that hands out contracts, the government that subsidizes inefficiency through cost-plus guarantees, the government that builds plants and leases or gives them outright to contractors. Of course, the businesses involved lobby for these privileges, but it is only through *government* that the mechanism for this privilege, and this wasteful misallocation of resources, can possibly exist.

Transportation. The crisis of transportation involves not only congested streets, but also decaying railroads, overpriced airlines, airport congestion at peak hours, and subways (e.g., New York City) that are suffering deficits and visibly heading toward collapse. Yet: the railroads were overbuilt from extensive government subsidies (federal, state, and local) during the nineteenth century, and have been the most heavily regulated industry for the longest period of time in American history. Airlines are cartelized through regulation by the Civil Aeronautics Board and subsidized through such regulation, mail contracts, and virtually free airports. Airports for commercial lines are all owned by branches of the government, largely local. The New York City subways have been government-owned for decades.

River pollution. The rivers are, in effect, unowned, i.e., they have been kept as "public domain" owned by government. Furthermore, by far the biggest culprits in water pollution are the municipally owned sewage disposal systems. Again: government is at the same time the largest polluter, as well as the careless "owner" of the resource.

Water shortages. Water shortages are chronic in some areas of the country, and intermittent in others, such as New York City. Yet the government, (1) via its ownership of the public domain, owns the rivers from which much of the water comes, and (2) as virtually the only commercial *supplier* of water, the government owns the reservoirs and water conduits.

Air pollution. Again, the government, as owner of the public domain, "owns" the air. Furthermore, it has been the courts, owned solely by the government, which, as an act of deliberate policy, have for generations failed to protect our property rights in our bodies and orchards from the pollution generated by industry. Moreover, much of the direct pollution comes from government-owned plants.

Power shortages and blackouts. Throughout the land, state and local governments have created compulsory monopolies of gas and electric power and have granted these monopoly privileges to private utility companies, which are then regulated and have their rates set by government agencies to insure a permanent and fixed profit. Again, government has been the source of the monopoly and the regulation.

Telephone service. Increasingly failing telephone service comes, again, from a utility which receives a compulsory monopoly privilege from government, and which finds its rates set by government to guarantee a profit. As in the case of gas and electricity, no one is allowed to compete with the monopoly phone company.

Postal service. Suffering from heavy deficits throughout its existence, the postal service, in stark contrast to the goods and services produced by private industry on the free market, has become steadily higher in price and lower in quality. The mass of the public, using first-class mail, has been forced to subsidize businesses using second- and third-class services. Again, the Post Office has been, since the late nineteenth century, a compulsory monopoly of government. Whenever private firms have been allowed to compete, even illegally, in delivery of mail, they have invariably provided better service at a lower price.

Television. Television consists of bland programs and distorted news. Radio and television channels have been nationalized for half a century by the federal government, which grants channels as a gift to privileged licensees, and can and does withdraw these gifts when a station displeases the government's Federal Communications Commission. How can any genuine freedom of speech or of the press exist under such conditions?

Welfare system. Welfare, of course, is exclusively the province of government, largely state and local.

Urban housing. Along with traffic, one of our most conspicuous urban failures. Yet there are few other industries that have been so closely intertwined with government. Urban planning has controlled and regulated the cities. Zoning laws have ringed housing and land use with innumerable restrictions. Property taxes have crippled urban development and forced abandonment of houses. Building codes have restricted housing construction and made it more costly. Urban renewal has provided massive subsidies to real estate developers, forced the bulldozing of apartments and rental stores, lowered the supply of housing, and intensified racial discrimination. Extensive government loans have generated overbuilding in the suburbs. Rent controls have created apartment shortages and reduced the supply of residential housing.

Union strikes and restrictions. Unions have become a nuisance with power to cripple the economy, but only as a result of numerous special privileges afforded by the government; especially various immunities accorded unions, particularly the Wagner Act of 1935, still in effect, which compels employers to bargain with unions which gain a majority vote of a "bargaining unit" arbitrarily defined by the government itself.

Education. Once as revered and sacrosanct in American opinion as motherhood or the flag, the public school, in recent years, has come under widespread attack, from all parts of the political spectrum. Even its supporters would not presume to maintain that the public schools actually *teach* much of anything. And we have recently seen extreme cases in which the actions of the public schools have motivated a violent reaction in such widely different areas as South Boston and Kanawha County, West Virginia. The public schools, of course, are totally owned and operated by state and local government—with considerable assist and coordination from the federal level. The public schools are backed up by compulsory attendance laws which force all children through high school age to attend school—either public or private schools certified by governmental authorities. Higher education, too, has become closely intertwined with government in recent decades: many universities are government-owned, and the others are systematic receivers of grants, subsidies, and contracts.

Inflation and stagflation. The United States, as well as the rest of the world, has been suffering for many years from chronic and accelerating inflation, an inflation accompanied by high unemployment and persisting through severe as well as mild recessions ("stagflation"). An explanation of these unwelcome phenomena will be presented below; here let it be said that the root cause is in a continuing expansion of the money supply, a compulsory monopoly of the federal government (anyone who presumes to compete with the government's issuing of money goes to jail for counterfeiting). A vital part of the nation's money supply is issued as "checkbook money" by the banking system, which in turn is under total control by the federal government and its Federal Reserve System.

Watergate. Finally, and not least, is the entire traumatic syndrome suffered by Americans known as "Watergate." What Watergate has meant is a total desanctifying of the President and of such previously sacrosanct federal institutions as the CIA and the FBI. The invasions of property, the police state methods, the deception of the public, the corruption, the manifold and systemic commissions of crime by a once virtually all-powerful President led to a once unthinkable impeachment of a President and of a widespread and well-justified lack of trust in all politicians and all government officials. The Establishment has often bemoaned this new, pervasive lack of trust, but has not been able to restore the naive public faith of pre-Watergate days. The liberal historian Cecilia Kenyon once chastised the Anti-Federalists—the defenders of the Articles of Confederation and opponents of the Constitution—as being "Men of Little Faith" in the institutions of government. One suspects that she would not be quite so naive if she were writing that article in the post-Watergate era.[1]

---

[1]Cecilia M. Kenyon, "Men of Little Faith: The Anti-Federalists on the Nature of Representative Government," *William and Mary Quarterly* (January 1955), pp. 3–43.

Watergate, of course, is purely and totally a governmental phenomenon. The President is the chief executive of the federal government, the "plumbers" were his instrument, and the FBI and the CIA are governmental agencies as well. And it is, quite understandably, faith and trust *in government* that was shattered by Watergate.

If we look around, then, at the crucial problem areas of our society—the areas of crisis and failure—we find in each and every case a "red thread" marking and uniting them all: the thread of government. In every one of these cases, government either has totally run or heavily influenced the activity. John Kenneth Galbraith, in his best-selling *The Affluent Society*, recognized that the government sector was the focus of our social failure—but drew instead the odd lesson that therefore still more funds and resources must be diverted from the private to the public sector. He thereby ignored the fact that the role of government in America—federal, state, and local—has expanded enormously, both absolutely and proportionately, in this century and especially in recent decades. Unfortunately, Galbraith never once raised the question: Is there something inherent in government operation and activity, something which *creates* the very failures which we see abounding? We shall investigate some of the major problems of government and of liberty in this country, see where the failures came from, and propound the solutions of the new libertarianism.

5
Involuntary Servitude

IF THERE IS ANYTHING a libertarian must be squarely and totally against, it is *involuntary servitude*—forced labor—an act which denies the most elemental right of self-ownership. "Liberty" and "slavery" have ever been recognized to be polar opposites. The libertarian, therefore, is totally opposed to slavery.[1] An academic question nowadays, one might object? But is it really? For what *is* slavery but (a) forcing people to work at tasks the slavemaster wishes, and (b) paying them either pure subsistence or, at any rate, less than the slave would have accepted voluntarily. In sort, forced labor at below free-market wages.

Thus, are we really free of "slavery," of involuntary servitude in present-day America? Is the prohibition against involuntary servitude of the Thirteenth Amendment really being obeyed?[2]

Conscription

Surely, for one example, there can be no more blatant case of involuntary servitude than our entire system of *conscription*. Every youth is

---

[1]There is one exception: the punishment of criminals who had themselves aggressed against or enslaved their victims. Such punishment in a libertarian system would at least involve forcing the criminal to work in order to pay restitution to his victim.

[2]Significantly, the Thirteenth Amendment's only exception is the punishment of convicted criminals mentioned in the previous note: "Neither slavery nor involuntary servitude except as a punishment for crime whereof the party shall have been duly convicted, shall exist within the United States, or any place subject to their jurisdiction."

forced to register with the selective service system when he turns eighteen. He is compelled to carry his draft card at all times, and, at whatever time the federal government deems fit, he is seized by the authorities and inducted into the armed forces. There his body and will are no longer his own; he is subject to the dictates of the government; and he can be forced to kill and to place his own life in jeopardy if the authorities so decree. What else is involuntary servitude if not the draft?

The utilitarian aspect permeates the argument for the conscription system. Thus the government uses the argument: *Who* will defend us against foreign attack if we do not employ coercion and conscript our defenders? There are several rebuttals for a libertarian to make to this line of reasoning. In the first place, if you and I and our next-door neighbor think that we need defending, we have no moral right to use coercion—the bayonet or the revolver—to force someone else to defend us. This act of conscripting is just as much a deed of unjustifiable aggression—of kidnapping and possibly murder—as the alleged aggression we are trying to guard ourselves against in the first place. If we add that the draftees owe their bodies and their lives, if necessary, to "society" or to "their country," then we must retort: *Who is* this "society" or this "country" that is being used as a talisman to justify enslavement? It is simply all individuals in the territorial area *except* the youths being conscripted. "Society" and "country" are in this case mythical abstractions that are being used to cloak the naked use of coercion to promote the interests of specific individuals.

Secondly, to move to the utilitarian plane, *why* is it considered necessary to conscript defenders? No one is conscripted on the free market, yet on that market people obtain, through voluntary purchase and sale, every conceivable manner of goods and services, even the most necessary ones. On the market, people can and do obtain food, shelter, clothing, medical care, etc. Why can't they hire defenders as well? Indeed, there are plenty of people being hired every day to perform dangerous services: forest firefighters, rangers, test pilots, and . . . police and private guards and watchmen. Why can't soldiers be hired in the same way?

Or, to put it another way, the government employs countless thousands of people for all sorts of services, from truck drivers to scientists to typists; how is it that none of these people have to be conscripted? Why is there no "shortage" of these occupations to supposedly force the government to resort to compulsion to obtain them? To go a step further, even within the army there is no "shortage" of officers and no need to draft them; no one conscripts generals or admirals. The answer to these questions is simple: there is no shortage of government typists because the government goes out on the market and hires them at the market wage; there is no shortage of generals because they are paid handsomely, in salaries, perquisites, and pensions. There *is* a shortage of buck privates because their pay is—or was, until very recently—abysmally below the market wage. For years, even including the monetary value of the free food, shelter, and other services supplied the GIs, the earnings of the buck private were something like one-half the salary he could have earned in civilian life. Is it any wonder that there has been a chronic shortage of enlistees? For years it has been known that the way to induce people to volunteer for hazardous jobs is to pay them extra as a compensation. But the government has been paying the men half of what they could earn in private life.[3]

There is also the special disgrace of the doctors' draft, in which physicians are subject to the draft at ages far beyond anyone else. Are doctors, then, to be penalized for their entry into the profession of medicine? What is the moral justification for onerous burdens placed on this particular, and vitally important, profession? Is this the way to cure the shortage of doctors—to put every man on notice that if he becomes a physician he will be sure to be drafted, and at a specially late age? Once again, the armed forces' need for doctors could easily be satisfied if the government were willing to pay physicians the market salary, plus enough to compensate them for the hazardous labor. If the government wishes to hire nuclear physicists or "think-tank" strategists, it finds ways of doing so at extremely handsome salaries. Are doctors lower forms of humanity?

The Army

While conscription into the armed forces is a blatant and aggravated form of involuntary servitude, there is another, far more subtle and therefore less detectable form: the structure of the army itself. Consider this: in what other occupation in the country are there severe penalties, including prison and in some cases execution, for "desertion," i.e., for quitting the particular employment? If someone quits General Motors, is he shot at sunrise?

It might be objected that, in the case of enlistees, the soldier or officer has voluntarily agreed to serve for a certain term, and he is therefore obligated to continue in service for that term of years. But the whole concept of "term of service" is part of the problem. Suppose, for example,

[3]Cf. James C. Miller III, ed., *Why the Draft?* (Baltimore: Penguin Books, 1968).

that an engineer signs a contract with ARAMCO to serve for three years in Saudi Arabia. After a few months he decides that the life is not for him and he quits. This may well be a *moral* default on his part— a breach of moral obligation. But is it a legally enforceable obligation? In short, can he or should he be forced by the monopoly of weaponry of government to keep working for the remainder of his term? If so, that would be forced labor and enslavement. For while it is true that he made a promise of future work, his body continues, in a free society, to be owned by himself alone. In practice and in libertarian theory as well, then, the engineer might be morally criticized for the breach, he may be blacklisted by other oil firms, he may be forced to return any advance pay tendered to him by the company, but he will *not* be enslaved to ARAMCO for the three-year period.

But if this is true of ARAMCO, or of any other occupation or job in private life, why should it be different in the army? If a man signs up for seven years and then quits, he should be allowed to leave. He will lose pension rights, he will be morally criticized, he may be blacklisted from similar occupations, but he cannot, as a self-owner, be enslaved against his will.

It may be protested that the armed forces is a peculiarly important occupation that needs this sort of coercive sanction that other jobs do not have. Setting aside the importance of such occupations as medicine, agriculture and transportation that need not resort to such methods, let us consider a comparable defense occupation in civilian life—the police. Surely the police perform an equally, and perhaps more vital, service—and yet every year people join the police and quit the force, and there is no coercive attempt to bind their labor through years of enlistment. In addition to demanding the end of conscription, then, the libertarian also proposes to do away with the entire concept of a *term* of enlistment and the practice of slavery this implies. Let the armed forces operate in ways similar to police, firemen, rangers, private guards, etc.—free of the blight and the moral crime of involuntary servitude.

But there is more to be said about the army as an institution, even if it were made completely voluntary. Americans have almost totally forgotten one of the noblest and strongest elements in the original American heritage: determined opposition to the entire institution of a "standing army." A government that has a permanent standing army at its disposal will always be tempted to use it, and to use it in an aggressive, interventionist, and warlike manner. While foreign policy will be dealt with below, it is clear that a permanent army is a standing temptation to the State to enlarge its power, to push around other people as well as other countries, and to dominate the internal life of the nation. The original aim of the Jeffersonian movement—a largely libertarian factor in American political life—was to abolish the standing army and navy altogether. The original American principle was that if the nation was attacked, then the citizens would hasten to join to repel the invader. A standing armed force, then, could only lead to trouble and to the aggrandizement of State power. In the course of his trenchant and prophetic attack on the proposed Constitution in the Virginia ratifying convention, Patrick Henry warned of a standing army: "Congress, by the power of taxation, by that of raising an army, and by their control over the militia, have the sword in one hand, and the purse in the other. Shall we be safe without either?"[4]

Any standing army, then, poses a standing threat to liberty. Its monopoly of coercive weapons, its modern tendency toward creating and supporting a "military-industrial complex" to supply that army, and, last, but not least, as Patrick Henry notes, the taxing power to finance that army, pose a continuing threat of the army's perpetual expansion in size and power. *Any* tax-supported institution, of course, is opposed by the libertarian as coercive, but an army is uniquely menacing for its amassing and collecting into one set of hands the massive power of modern weaponry.

Anti-Strike Laws

On October 4, 1971, President Nixon invoked the Taft-Hartley Act to obtain a court injunction forcing the suspension of a dock strike for eighty days; this was the ninth time the federal government had used the Act in a dock strike. Months earlier, the head of the New York City teachers' union went to jail for several days for defying a law prohibiting public employees from striking. It is no doubt convenient for a long-suffering public to be spared the disruptions of a strike. Yet the "solution" imposed was forced labor, pure and simple; the workers were coerced, against their will, into going back to work. There is

[4]Arthur A. Ekirch, Jr., *The Civilian and the Military* (New York: Oxford University Press, 1956), p. 28. For a trenchant attack by a Jeffersonian theorist on the American executive as commander-in-chief of the armed forces, see John Taylor of Caroline, *An Inquiry into the Principles and Policy of the Government of the United States* (1814, rep. New Haven: Yale University Press, 1950), pp. 175ff. On the important influence of seventeenth-century English libertarian theorists and their hostility to a standing army upon the American Revolution, see Bernard Bailyn, *The Ideological Origins of the American Revolution* (Cambridge: Harvard University Press, 1967), pp. 61–64. Also see Don Higgenbotham, *The War of American Independence* (New York: Macmillan, 1971), pp. 14–16.

no moral excuse, in a society claiming to be opposed to slavery and in a country which has outlawed involuntary servitude, for any legal or judicial action prohibiting strikes—or jailing union leaders who fail to comply. Slavery is all too often more convenient for the slavemasters.

It is true that the strike is a peculiar form of work stoppage. The strikers do not merely quit their jobs; they also assert that somehow, in some metaphysical sense, they still "own" their jobs and are entitled to them, and intend to return to them when the issues are resolved. But the remedy for this self-contradictory policy, as well as for the disruptive power of labor unions, is not to pass laws outlawing strikes; the remedy is to remove the substantial body of law, federal, state, and local, that confers special governmental privileges on labor unions. All that is needed, both for libertarian principle and for a healthy economy, is to remove and abolish these special privileges.

These privileges have been enshrined in federal law—especially in the Wagner-Taft-Hartley Act, passed originally in 1935, and the Norris-LaGuardia Act of 1931. The latter prohibits the courts from issuing injunctions in cases of imminent union violence; the former compels employers to bargain "in good faith" with any union that wins the votes of the majority of a work unit arbitrarily defined by the federal government—and also prohibits employers from discriminating against union organizers. It was only after the Wagner Act—and its predecessor, the NIRA in 1933—that labor unions were able to become a powerful force in American life. It was then that unions skyrocketed from something like five percent to over twenty percent of the labor force. Furthermore, local and state laws often protect unions from being sued, and they place restrictions on the employers' hiring of strikebreaking labor; and police are often instructed not to interfere in the use of violence against strikebreakers by union pickets. Take away these special privileges and immunities, and labor unions would sink back to their previous negligible role in the American economy.

It is characteristic of our statist trend that, when general indignation against unions led to the Taft-Hartley Act of 1947, the government did not repeal any of these special privileges. Instead, it added special restrictions upon unions to limit the power which the government itself had created. Given a choice, the natural tendency of the State is to add to its power, not to cut it down; and so we have the peculiar situation of the government first building up unions and then howling for restrictions against their power. This is reminiscent of the American farm programs, in which one branch of the Department of Agriculture pays farmers to *restrict* their production, while another branch of the same agency pays them to increase their productivity. Irrational, surely, from the point of view of the consumers and the taxpayers, but perfectly rational from the point of view of the subsidized farmers *and* of the growing power of the bureaucracy. Similarly, the government's seemingly contradictory policy on unions serves, first, to aggrandize the power of government over labor relations, and second, to foster a suitably integrated and Establishment-minded unionism as junior partner in government's role over the economy.

The Tax System

In a sense, the entire system of taxation is a form of involuntary servitude. Take, in particular, the *income tax*. The high levels of income tax mean that all of us work a large part of the year—several months— for *nothing* for Uncle Sam before being allowed to enjoy our incomes on the market. Part of the essence of slavery, after all, is forced work for someone at little or no pay. But the income tax means that we sweat and earn income, only to see the government extract a large chunk of it by coercion for its own purposes. What is this but forced labor at no pay?

The *withholding* feature of the income tax is a still more clear-cut instance of involuntary servitude. For as the intrepid Connecticut industrialist Vivien Kellems argued years ago, the employer is forced to expend time, labor, and money in the business of deducting and transmitting his employees' taxes to the federal and state governments—yet the employer is not recompensed for this expenditure. What moral principle justifies the government's forcing employers to act as its unpaid tax collectors?

The withholding principle, of course, is the linchpin of the whole federal income tax system. Without the steady and relatively painless process of deducting the tax from the worker's paycheck, the government could never hope to raise the high levels of tax from the workers in one lump sum. Few people remember that the withholding system was only instituted during World War II and was supposed to be a wartime expedient. Like so many other features of State despotism, however, the wartime emergency measure soon became a hallowed part of the American system.

It is perhaps significant that the federal government, challenged by Vivien Kellems to test the constitutionality of the withholding system, failed to take up the challenge. In February 1948 Miss Kellems, a small manufacturer in Westport, Connecticut, announced that she was defying the withholding law and was refusing to deduct the tax from her employees. She demanded that the federal government indict her, so that the courts would be able to rule on the constitutionality of the withholding system. The government refused to do so, but instead seized the amount due from her bank account. Miss Kellems then sued in federal court for the government to return her funds. When the suit finally came to trial in February 1951, the jury ordered the government to refund her money. But the test of constitutionality never came.[5]

To add insult to injury, the individual taxpayer, in filling out his tax form, is also forced by the government to work at no pay on the laborious and thankless task of reckoning how much he owes the government. Here again, he cannot charge the government for the cost and labor expended in making out his return. Furthermore, the law requiring everyone to fill out his tax form is a clear violation of the Fifth Amendment of the Constitution, prohibiting the government from forcing anyone to incriminate himself. Yet the courts, often zealous in protecting Fifth Amendment rights in less sensitive areas, have done nothing here, in a case where the entire existence of the swollen federal government structure is at stake. The repeal of either the income tax or the withholding or self-incriminating provisions would force the government back to the relatively minor levels of power that the country enjoyed before the twentieth century.

Retail sales, excise, and admission taxes also compel unpaid labor—in these cases, the unpaid labor of the retailer in collecting and forwarding the taxes to the government.

The high costs of tax collecting for the government have another unfortunate effect—perhaps not unintended by the powers-that-be. These costs, readily undertaken by large businesses, impose a disproportionately heavy and often crippling cost upon the small employer. The large employer can then cheerfully shoulder the cost knowing that his small competitor bears far more of the burden.

The Courts

Compulsory labor permeates our legal and judicial structure. Thus, much venerated judicial procedure rests upon *coerced testimony*. Since it is axiomatic to libertarianism that all coercion—in this case, all coerced labor—against everyone except convicted criminals be eliminated, this

[5]On the Kellems case, see Vivien Kellems, *Toil, Taxes and Trouble* (New York: E. P. Dutton, 1952).

means that compulsory testimony must be abolished as well. In recent years, it is true, the courts have been alive to the Fifth Amendment protection that no alleged criminal be forced to testify against himself—to provide the material for his own conviction. The legislatures have been significantly weakening this protection by passing immunity laws, offering immunity from prosecution if someone will testify against his fellows—and, furthermore, compelling the witness to accept the offer and testify against his associates. But compelling testimony from anyone for any reason is forced labor—and, furthermore, is akin to kidnapping, since the person is forced to appear at the hearing or trial and is then forced to perform the labor of giving testimony. The problem is not only the recent immunity laws; the problem is to eliminate *all* coerced testimony, including the universal subpoenaing of witnesses to a crime, and then forcing them to testify. In the case of witnesses, there is no question whatever of their being guilty of a crime, so the use of compulsion against them—a use that no one has questioned until now—has even less justification than compelling testimony from accused criminals.

In fact, the entire power to *subpoena* should be abolished, because the *subpoena* power compels attendance at a trial. Even the accused criminal or tortfeasor should not be forced to attend his own trial, since he has not yet been convicted. If he is indeed—according to the excellent and libertarian principle of Anglo-Saxon law—innocent until proved guilty, then the courts have no right to compel the defendant to attend his trial. For remember, the *only* exemption to the Thirteenth Amendment's prohibition of involuntary servitude is "except as a punishment for crime whereof the party shall have been duly convicted"; an accused party has not yet been convicted. The most the court should be able to do, then, is to notify the defendant that he is going to be tried, and *invite* him or his lawyer to attend; otherwise, if they choose not to, the trial will proceed *in absentia*. Then, of course, the defendant will not enjoy the best presentation of his case.

Both the Thirteenth Amendment and the libertarian creed make the exception for the convicted criminal. The libertarian believes that a criminal loses his rights to the extent that he has aggressed upon the rights of another, and therefore that it is permissible to incarcerate the convicted criminal and subject him to involuntary servitude to that degree. In the libertarian world, however, the *purpose* of imprisonment and punishment will undoubtedly be different; there will be no "district attorney" who presumes to try a case on behalf of a nonexistent "society," and then punishes the criminal on "society's" behalf. In that world the prosecutor will always represent the *individual victim*, and punishment will be exacted to redound to the benefit of that victim. Thus, a crucial focus of punishment will be to force the criminal to repay, make restitution to, the victim. One such model was a practice in colonial America. Instead of incarcerating, say, a man who had robbed a farmer in the district, the criminal was coercively indentured out to the farmer—in effect, "enslaved" for a term—there to work for the farmer until his debt was repaid. Indeed, during the Middle Ages, restitution to the victim was the dominant concept of punishment; only as the State grew more powerful did the governmental authorities—the kings and the barons—encroach more and more into the compensation process, increasingly confiscating more of the criminal's property for themselves and neglecting the hapless victim. And as the emphasis shifted from restitution to punishment for abstract crimes "committed against the State," the punishments exacted by the State upon the wrongdoer became more severe.

As Professor Schafer writes, "As the state monopolized the institution of punishment, so the rights of the injured were slowly separated from penal law." Or, in the words of the turn-of-the-century criminologist William Tallack, "It was chiefly owing to the violent greed of feudal barons and medieval ecclesiastical powers that the rights of the injured party were gradually infringed upon, and finally, to a large extent, appropriated by these authorities, who exacted a double vengeance, indeed, upon the offender, by forfeiting his property to themselves instead of to his victim, and then punishing him by the dungeon, the torture, the stake or the gibbet. But the original victim of wrong was practically ignored."[6]

At any rate, while the libertarian does not object to prisons per se, he does balk at several practices common to the present judicial and penal system. One is the lengthy jail term imposed upon the defendant while awaiting trial. The constitutional right to a "speedy trial" is not arbitrary but a way of minimizing the length of involuntary servitude *before* conviction for a crime. In fact, except in those cases where the criminal has been caught red-handed and where a certain presumption of guilt therefore exists, it is impossible to justify *any* imprisonment before conviction, let alone before trial. And even when someone is caught red-handed, there is an important reform that needs to be instituted to keep the system honest: subjecting the police and the other

---

[6]Stephen Schafer, *Restitution to Victims of Crime* (Chicago: Quadrangle Books, 1960), pp. 7–8; William Tallack, *Reparation to the Injured and the Rights of the Victims of Crime to Compensation* (London, 1900), pp. 11–12.

authorities to the same law as everyone else. As will be discussed further below, if everyone is supposed to be subject to the same criminal law, then exempting the authorities from that law gives them a legal license to commit continual aggression. The policeman who apprehends a criminal and arrests him, and the judicial and penal authorities who incarcerate him before trial and conviction—all should be subject to the universal law. In short, if they have committed an error and the defendant turns out to be innocent, then these authorities should be subjected to the same penalties as anyone else who kidnaps and incarcerates an innocent man. Immunity in pursuit of their trade should no more serve as an excuse than Lieutenant Calley was excused for committing atrocities at My Lai in the course of the Vietnam war.[7]

The granting of *bail* is a halfhearted attempt to ease the problem of incarceration before trial, but it is clear that the practice of bail discriminates against the poor. The discrimination persists even though the rise of the business of bail-bonding has permitted many more people to raise bail. The rebuttal that the courts are clogged with cases and therefore cannot grant a speedy trial is, of course, no defense of the system; on the contrary, this built-in inefficiency is an excellent argument for the abolition of government courts.

Furthermore, the setting of bail is arbitrarily in the hands of the judge, who has excessive and little-checked power to incarcerate people before they are convicted. This is particularly menacing in the case of citations for *contempt of court*, because judges have almost unlimited power to slap someone into prison, after the judge himself has acted as a one-man prosecutor, judge, and jury in accusing, "convicting," and sentencing the culprit completely free from the ordinary rules of evidence and trial, and in violation of the fundamental legal principle of not being a judge in one's own case.

Finally, there is another cornerstone of the judicial system which has unaccountably gone unchallenged, even by libertarians, for far too long. This is *compulsory jury service*. There is little difference in kind, though obviously a great difference in degree, between compulsory jury duty and conscription; both are enslavement, both compel the individual to perform tasks on the State's behalf and at the State's bidding. And both are a function of pay at slave wages. Just as the shortage of voluntary enlistees in the army is a function of a pay scale far below the market

---

[7]For a hilarious critique of the immunities of the arresting and penal authorities, see H. L. Mencken, "The Nature of Liberty," *Prejudices: A Selection* (New York: Vintage Books, 1958), pp. 138–43.

wage, so the abysmally low pay for jury service insures that, even if jury "enlistments" were possible, not many would be forthcoming. Furthermore, not only are jurors coerced into attending and serving on juries, but sometimes they are locked behind closed doors for many weeks, and prohibited from reading newspapers. What is this but prison and involuntary servitude for noncriminals?

It will be objected that jury service is a highly important civic function, and insures a fair trial which a defendant may not obtain from the judge, especially since the judge is part of the State system and therefore liable to be partial to the prosecutor's case. Very true, but precisely because the service is so vital, it is particularly important that it be performed by people who do it gladly, and voluntarily. Have we forgotten that free labor is happier and more efficient than slave labor? The abolition of jury-slavery should be a vital plank in any libertarian platform. The judges are not conscripted; neither are the opposing lawyers; and neither should the jurors.

It is perhaps not a coincidence that, throughout the United States, lawyers are everywhere exempt from jury service. Since it is almost always lawyers who write the laws, can we detect class legislation and class privilege at work?

Compulsory Commitment

One of the most shameful areas of involuntary servitude in our society is the widespread practice of compulsory commitment, or involuntary hospitalization, of mental patients. In former generations this incarceration of noncriminals was frankly carried out as a measure against mental patients, to remove them from society. The practice of twentieth-century liberalism has been superficially more humane, but actually far more insidious: now physicians and psychiatrists help incarcerate these unfortunates "for their own good." The humanitarian rhetoric has permitted a far more widespread use of the practice and, for one thing, has allowed disgruntled relatives to put away their loved ones without suffering a guilty conscience.

In the last decade, the libertarian psychiatrist and psychoanalyst Dr. Thomas S. Szasz has carried on a one-man crusade, at first seemingly hopeless but now increasingly influential in the psychiatric field, against compulsory commitment. In numerous books and articles, Dr. Szasz has delivered a comprehensive and systematic attack on this practice. He has insisted, for example, that involuntary commitment is a profound violation of medical ethics. Instead of serving the patient, the physician here serves others—the family, the State—to act against, and tyrannize over completely, the person he is supposed to be helping. Compulsory commitment and compulsory "therapy," moreover, are far more likely to aggravate and perpetuate "mental illness" than to cure it. All too often, Szasz points out, commitment is a device for incarcerating and thereby disposing of disagreeable relatives rather than a genuine aid to the patient.

The guiding rationale for compulsory commitment is that the patient might well be "dangerous to himself or to others." The first grave flaw in this approach is that the police, or the law, is stepping in, *not* when an overt aggressive act is in the process of occurring, but on someone's judgment that such an act *might* someday take place. But this provides an open sesame for unlimited tyranny. Anyone might be adjudged to be capable of or likely to commit a crime someday, and therefore on such grounds anyone may legitimately be locked up—not for a crime, but because someone *thinks* he *might* commit one. This sort of thinking justifies not only incarceration, but *permanent* incarceration, of *anyone* under suspicion. But the fundamental libertarian creed holds that every individual is capable of free will and free choice; that no one, however likely to commit a crime in the future based on a statistical or any other judgment, is inevitably determined to do so; and that, in any case, it is immoral, and itself invasive and criminal, to coerce anyone who is not an *overt* and present, rather than a suspected, criminal.

Recently Dr. Szasz was asked, "But don't you think that society has the right and the duty to care for those individuals adjudged to be 'dangerous to themselves and others'?" Szasz cogently replied:

I think the idea of "helping" people by imprisoning them and doing terrible things to them is a religious concept, as the idea of "saving" witches by torture and burning once was. As far as "dangerousness to self" is concerned, I believe, as did John Stuart Mill, that a man's body and soul are his own, not the state's. And furthermore, that each individual has the "right," if you will, to do with his body as he pleases—so long as he doesn't harm anyone else, or infringe on someone else's right.

As far as "dangerousness to others" goes, most psychiatrists working with hospitalized patients would admit this is pure fantasy. . . . There have in fact been statistical studies made which show that mental patients are much more law-abiding than the normal population.

And civil liberties lawyer Bruce Ennis adds that:

We know that 85 percent of all ex-convicts will commit more crimes in the future and that ghetto residents and teen-age males are far more likely to commit crime than the average member of the population. We also know, from recent studies, that mental patients are statistically *less* dangerous than the average guy. So if what we're really worried about is danger, why don't we, first, lock up all former convicts, and then lock up all ghetto residents, and then why don't we lock up all teen-age males? . . . The question Szasz has been asking is: If a person hasn't broken a law, what right has society to lock him up?[8]

The involuntarily committed may be divided into two classes: those who have committed no crime, and those who have. For the former, the libertarian calls unconditionally for their release. But what of the latter, what of criminals who, through insanity or other pleas, supposedly escape the "brutality" of prison punishment and instead receive medical care at the hands of the State? Here again, Dr. Szasz has pioneered in a vigorous and devastating critique of the despotism of liberal "humanitarianism." First, it is grotesque to claim that incarceration in a state mental hospital is somehow "more humane" than equivalent incarceration in prison. On the contrary, the despotism of the authorities is likely to be more severe, and the prisoner is likely to have far less recourse in defense of his rights, for as someone certified as "mentally ill" he is placed into the category of a "nonperson" whom no one feels obliged to take seriously any longer. As Dr. Szasz has jocularly said: "Being in a state mental hospital would drive anyone crazy!"

But furthermore, we must question the entire notion of taking *anyone* out from under the rule of objective law. To do so is far more likely to be damaging than helpful to the people thus singled out. Suppose, for example, that two men, *A* and *B*, commit an equivalent robbery, and that the usual punishment for this crime is five years in prison. Suppose that *B* "gets off" this punishment by being declared mentally ill, and is transferred to a state mental institution. The liberal focusses on the possibility, say, that *B* may be released in two years by the State psychiatrist through being adjudged "cured" or "rehabilitated." But what if the psychiatrist *never* considers him cured, or does so only after a very long time? Then *B*, for the simple crime of theft, may face the horror of lifelong incarceration in a mental institution. Hence, the "liberal" concept of *indeterminate sentence*—of sentencing someone not for his objective crime but on the State's judgment of his psyche or spirit of cooperation—constitutes tyranny and dehumanization in its worst form. It is a tyranny, furthermore, which encourages the prisoner into

[8]Quoted in Maggie Scarf, "Dr. Thomas Szasz . . . ," *New York Times Magazine* (October 3, 1971), pp. 42, 45. Among other works, see Thomas S. Szasz, *Law, Liberty, and Psychiatry* (New York: Macmillan, 1963).

deceptive behavior to try to fool the State psychiatrist—whom he perceives quite correctly as his enemy—into thinking that he is "cured" so that he can get out of this incarceration. To call this process "therapy" or "rehabilitation" is surely cruel mockery of these terms. It is far more principled, as well as more truly humane, to treat every prisoner in accordance with objective criminal law.

6

Personal Liberty

Freedom of Speech

THERE ARE, OF COURSE, many problems of personal liberty which cannot be subsumed under the category of "involuntary servitude." Freedom of speech and press have long been treasured by those who confine themselves to being "civil libertarians"—"civil" meaning that economic freedom and the rights of private property are left out of the equation. But we have already seen that "freedom of speech" cannot be upheld as an absolute except as it is subsumed under the general rights of property of the individual (emphatically *including* property right in his own person). Thus, the man who shouts "fire" in a crowded theater has no right to do so because he is aggressing against the contractual property rights of the theater owner and of the patrons of the performance.

Aside from invasions of property, however, freedom of speech will necessarily be upheld to the uttermost by every libertarian. Freedom to say, print, and sell any utterance becomes an absolute right, in whatever area the speech or expression chooses to cover. Here, civil libertarians have a generally good record, and in the judiciary the late Justice Hugo Black was particularly notable in defending freedom of speech from government restriction on the basis of the First Amendment of the Constitution.

But there are areas in which even the most ardent civil libertarians

94

have been unfortunately fuzzy. What, for example, of "incitement to riot," in which the speaker is held guilty of a crime for whipping up a mob, which then riots and commits various actions and crimes against person and property? In our view, "incitement" can only be considered a crime if we deny every man's freedom of will and of choice, and assume that if *A* tells *B* and *C*: "You and him go ahead and riot!" that somehow *B* and *C* are then helplessly determined to proceed and commit the wrongful act. But the libertarian, who believes in freedom of the will, must insist that while it might be immoral or unfortunate for *A* to advocate a riot, that this is strictly in the realm of advocacy and should not be subject to legal penalty. Of course, if *A* also participates in the riot, then he himself becomes a rioter and is equally subject to punishment. Furthermore, if *A* is a boss in a criminal enterprise, and, as part of the crime, orders his henchmen: "You and him go and rob such and such a bank," then of course *A*, according to the law of accessories, becomes a participant or even leader in the criminal enterprise itself.

If advocacy should never be a crime, then neither should "conspiracy to advocate," for, in contrast to the unfortunate development of conspiracy law, "conspiring" (i.e., agreeing) to do something should never be more illegal than the act itself. (How, in fact, can "conspiracy" be defined except as an agreement by two or more people to do something that you, the definer, do not like?)[1]

Another difficult zone is the law of libel and slander. It has generally been held legitimate to restrict freedom of speech if that speech has the effect of either falsely or maliciously damaging the reputation of another person. What the law of libel and slander does, in short, is to argue a "property right" of someone in his own reputation. Yet someone's "reputation" is not and cannot be "owned" by him, since it is purely a function of the subjective feelings and attitudes held by other people. But since no one can ever truly "own" the mind and attitude of another, this means that no one can literally have a property right in his "reputation." A person's reputation fluctuates all the time, in accordance with the attitudes and opinions of the rest of the population. Hence, speech attacking someone cannot be an invasion of his property right and therefore should not be subject to restriction or legal penalty.

It is, of course, immoral to level false charges against another person,

---

[1]For a critique of the "clear and present danger" criterion as insufficient for drawing a clear line between advocacy and overt act, see Alexander Meiklejohn, *Political Freedom* (New York: Harper & Bros., 1960), pp. 29–50; and O. John Rogge, *The First and the Fifth* (New York: Thomas Nelson and Sons, 1960), pp. 88ff.

but once again, the *moral* and the *legal* are, for the libertarian, two very different categories.

Furthermore, pragmatically, if there were no laws of libel or slander, people would be much less willing to credit charges without full documentation than they are now. Nowadays, if a man is charged with some flaw or misdeed, the general reaction is to believe it, since if the charge were false, "Why doesn't he sue for libel?" The law of libel, of course, discriminates in this way against the poor, since a person with few financial resources is scarcely as ready to carry on a costly libel suit as a person of affluent means. Furthermore, wealthy people can now use the libel laws as a club against poorer persons, restricting perfectly legitimate charges and utterances under the threat of sueing their poorer enemies for libel. Paradoxically, then, a person of limited resources is more apt to suffer from libel—and to have his own speech restricted—in the present system than he would in a world without any laws against libel or defamation.

Fortunately, in recent years the laws against libel have been progressively weakened, so that one can now deliver vigorous and trenchant criticisms of public officials and of people in the public eye without fear of being subject to costly legal action or legal punishment.

Another action that should be completely free of restriction is the boycott. In a boycott, one or more people use their right of speech to urge, for whatever reasons—important or trivial—that other people cease to buy someone else's product. If, for example, several people organize a campaign—for whatever reason—to urge consumers to stop buying XYZ Beer, this is again purely advocacy, and, furthermore, advocacy of a perfectly legitimate act—*not* purchasing the beer. A successful boycott might be unfortunate for the producers of XYZ Beer, but this, again, is strictly within the realm of free speech and the rights of private property. The makers of XYZ Beer take their chances with the free choices of consumers, and consumers are entitled to listen and to be swayed by anyone they choose. Yet our labor laws have infringed upon the right of labor unions to organize boycotts against business firms. It is also illegal, under our banking laws, to spread rumors about the insolvency of a bank—an obvious case of the government's extending special privileges to banks by outlawing freedom of speech in opposition to their use.

A particularly thorny question is the whole matter of picketing and demonstrations. Freedom of speech implies, of course, freedom of assembly—the freedom to gather together and express oneself in concert with others. But the situation becomes more complex when the use of the *streets* is involved. It is clear that picketing is illegitimate when it is used—as it often is—to block access to a private building or factory, or when the pickets threaten violence against those who cross the picket line. It is also clear that sit-ins are an illegitimate invasion of private property. But even "peaceful picketing" is not clearly legitimate, for it is part of a wider problem: Who decides on the use of the streets? The problem stems from the fact that the streets are almost universally owned by (local) government. But the government, not being a private owner, lacks any criterion for allocating the use of its streets, so that any decision it makes will be arbitrary.

Suppose, for example, that the Friends of Wisteria wish to demonstrate and parade on behalf of Wisteria in a public street. The police ban the demonstration, claiming that it will clog the streets and disrupt traffic. Civil libertarians will automatically protest and claim that the "right of free speech" of the Wisteria demonstrators is being unjustly abridged. But the police, too, may have a perfectly legitimate point: the streets may well be clogged, and it is the government's responsibility to maintain the flow of traffic. How then decide? Whichever way the government decides, *some* group of taxpayers will be injured by the decision. If the government decides to allow the demonstration, the motorists or pedestrians will be injured; if it does not, then the Friends of Wisteria will suffer a loss. In either case, the very fact of government decision-making generates inevitable conflict over who shall, and who shall not among the taxpayers and citizens, use the governmental resource.

It is only the universal fact of government ownership and control of the streets that makes this problem insoluble and cloaks the true solution to it. The point is that *whoever* owns a resource will decide on how that resource is to be used. The owner of a press will decide what will be printed on that press. And the owner of the streets will decide how to allocate their use. In short, if the streets were privately owned and the Friends of Wisteria asked for the use of Fifth Avenue to demonstrate, it will be up to the owner of Fifth Avenue to decide whether to rent the street for demonstration use or to keep it clear for traffic. In a purely libertarian world, where all streets are privately owned, the various street owners will decide, at any given time, whether to rent out the street for demonstrations, whom to rent it to, and what price to charge. It would then be clear that what is involved is not a "free speech" or "free assembly" question at all, but a question of property rights: of the right of a group to offer to rent a street, and of the right of the street owner either to accept or reject the offer.

Freedom of Radio and Television

There is one important area of American life where no effective freedom of speech or the press does or can exist under the present system.
That is the entire field of radio and television. In this area, the federal
government, in the crucially important Radio Act of 1927, nationalized
the airwaves. In effect, the federal government took title to ownership
of all radio and television channels. It then presumed to grant licenses,
at its will or pleasure, for use of the channels to various privately owned
stations. On the one hand, the stations, since they receive the licenses
gratis, do not have to pay for the use of the scarce airwaves, as they
would on the free market. And so these stations receive a huge subsidy,
which they are eager to maintain. But on the other hand, the federal
government, as the licensor of the airwaves, asserts the right and the
power to regulate the stations minutely and continuously. Thus, over
the head of each station is the club of the threat of nonrenewal, or
even suspension, of its license. In consequence, the idea of freedom of
speech in radio and television is no more than a mockery. Every station
is grievously restricted, and forced to fashion its programming to the
dictates of the Federal Communications Commission. So every station
must have "balanced" programming, broadcast a certain amount of "public service" announcements, grant equal time to every political candidate
for the same office and to expressions of political opinion, censor "controversial" lyrics in the records it plays, etc. For many years, no station
was allowed to broadcast any editorial opinion at all; now, every opinion
must be balanced by "responsible" editorial rebuttals.

Because every station and every broadcaster must always look over
its shoulder at the FCC, free expression in broadcasting is a sham. Is
it any wonder that television opinion, when it is expressed at all on
controversial issues, tends to be blandly in favor of the "Establishment"?

The public has only put up with this situation because it has existed
since the beginning of large-scale commercial radio. But what would
we think, for example, if all newspapers were licensed, the licenses to
be renewable by a Federal Press Commission, and with newspapers
losing their licenses if they dare express an "unfair" editorial opinion,
or if they don't give full weight to public service announcements? Would
not this be an intolerable, not to say unconstitutional, destruction of
the right to a free press? Or consider if all book publishers had to be
licensed, and their licenses were not renewable if their book lists failed
to suit a Federal Book Commission? Yet what we would all consider
intolerable and totalitarian for the press and the book publishers is taken

for granted in a medium which is now the most popular vehicle for expression and education: radio and television. Yet the principles in both cases are exactly the same.

Here we see, too, one of the fatal flaws in the idea of "democratic socialism," i.e., the idea that the government should own all resources and means of production yet preserve and maintain freedom of speech and the press for all its citizens. An abstract constitution guaranteeing "freedom of the press" is meaningless in a socialist society. The point is that where the government owns all the newsprint, the paper, the presses, etc., the government—as owner—*must* decide how to allocate the newsprint and the paper, and what to print on them. Just as the government as street owner must make a decision how the street will be used, so a socialist government will have to decide how to allocate newsprint and all other resources involved in the areas of speech and press: assembly halls, machines, trucks, etc. Any government may profess its devotion to freedom of the press, yet allocate all of its newsprint only to its defenders and supporters. A free press is again a mockery; furthermore, why *should* a socialist government allocate any considerable amount of its scarce resources to antisocialists? The problem of genuine freedom of the press then becomes insoluble.

The solution for radio and television? Simple: Treat these media precisely the same way the press and book publishers are treated. For both the libertarian and the believer in the American Constitution the government should withdraw completely from any role or interference in all media of expression. In short, the federal government should denationalize the airwaves and give or sell the individual channels to private ownership. When private stations genuinely own their channels, they will be truly free and independent; they will be able to put on any programs they wish to produce, or that they feel their listeners want to hear; and they will be able to express themselves in whichever way they wish without fear of government retaliation. They will also be able to sell or rent the airwaves to whomever they wish, and in that way the users of the channels will no longer be artificially subsidized.

Furthermore, if TV channels become free, privately owned, and independent, the big networks will no longer be able to put pressure upon the FCC to outlaw the effective competition of pay-television. It is only because the FCC has outlawed pay-TV that it has not been able to gain a foothold. "Free TV" is, of course, not truly "free"; the programs are paid for by the advertisers, and the consumer pays by covering the advertising costs in the price of the product he buys. One might ask what difference it makes to the consumer whether he pays the advertising costs indirectly or pays directly for each program he buys. The difference is that these are not the same consumers for the same products. The television advertiser, for example, is always interested in (a) gaining the widest possible viewing market; and (b) in gaining those *particular* viewers who will be most susceptible to his message. Hence, the programs will all be geared to the lowest common denominator in the audience, and particularly to those viewers most susceptible to the message; that is, those viewers who do not read newspapers or magazines, so that the message will not duplicate the ads he sees there. As a result, free-TV programs tend to be unimaginative, bland, and uniform. Pay-TV would mean that each program would search for its own market, and many specialized markets for specialized audiences would develop— just as highly lucrative specialized markets have developed in the magazine and book publishing fields. The quality of programs would be higher and the offerings far more diverse. In fact, the menace of potential pay-TV competition must be great for the networks to lobby for years to keep it suppressed. But, of course, in a truly free market, both forms of television, as well as cable-TV and other forms we cannot yet envision, could and would enter the competition.

One common argument against private ownership of TV channels is that these channels are "scarce," and therefore have to be owned and parcelled out by the government. To an economist, this is a silly argument; *all* resources are scarce, in fact anything that has a price on the market commands that price precisely *because* it is scarce. We have to pay a certain amount for a loaf of bread, for shoes, for dresses *because* they are all scarce. If they were not scarce but superabundant like air, they would be free, and no one would have to worry about their production or allocation. In the press area, newsprint is scarce, paper is scarce, printing machinery and trucks are scarce, etc. The more scarce they are the higher the price they will command, and vice versa. Furthermore, and again pragmatically, there are far more television channels available than are now in use. The FCC's early decision to force stations into the VHF instead of the UHF zone created far more of a scarcity of channels than there needed to be.

Another common objection to private property in the broadcast media is that private stations would interfere with each other's broadcasts, and that such widespread interference would virtually prevent any programs from being heard or seen. But this is as absurd an argument for nationalizing the airwaves as claiming that since people *can* drive their cars over other people's land this means that all cars—or land— must be nationalized. The problem, in either case, is for the courts to demarcate property titles carefully enough so that any invasion of another's property will be clear-cut and subject to prosecution. In the case of land titles, this process is clear enough. But the point is that the courts can apply a similar process of staking out property rights in other areas—whether it be in airwaves, in water, or in oil pools. In the case of airwaves, the task is to find the technological unit—i.e., the place of transmission, the distance of the wave, and the technological width of a clear channel—and then to allocate property rights to this particular technological unit. If radio station WXYZ, for example, is assigned a property right in broadcasting on 1500 kilocycles, plus or minus a certain width of kilocycles, for 200 miles around Detroit, then any station which subsequently beams a program into the Detroit area on this wavelength would be subject to prosecution for interference with property rights. If the courts pursue their task of demarking and defending property rights, then there is no more reason to expect continual invasions of such rights in this area than anywhere else.

Most people believe that this is precisely the reason the airwaves were nationalized; that before the Radio Act of 1927, stations interfered with each other's signals and chaos ensued, and the federal government was finally forced to step in to bring order and make a radio industry feasible at last. But this is historical legend, not fact. The actual history is *precisely the opposite*. For when interference on the same channel began to occur, the injured party took the airwave aggressors into court, and the courts were beginning to bring order out of the chaos by very successfully applying the common law theory of property rights—in very many ways similar to the libertarian theory—to this new technological area. In short, the courts were beginning to assign property rights in the airwaves to their "homesteading" users. It was after the federal government saw the likelihood of this new extension of private property that it rushed in to nationalize the airwaves, using alleged chaos as the excuse.

To describe the picture a bit more fully, radio in the first years of the century was almost wholly a means of communication for ships—either ship-to-ship or ship-to-shore messages. The Navy Department was interested in regulating radio as a means of ensuring safety at sea, and the initial federal regulation, a 1912 act, merely provided that any radio station had to have a license issued by the Secretary of Commerce. No powers to regulate or to decide not to renew licenses were written into the law, however, and when public broadcasting began in the early 1920s, Secretary of Commerce Herbert Hoover attempted to regulate the stations. Court decisions in 1923 and 1926, however, struck down the government's power to regulate licenses, to fail to renew them, or even to decide on which wavelengths the stations should operate.[2] At about the same time, the courts were working out the concept of "homestead" private property rights in the airwaves, notably in the case of *Tribune Co.* v. *Oak Leaves Broadcasting Station* (Circuit Court, Cook County, Illinois, 1926). In this case the court held that the operator of an existing station had a property right, acquired by prior use, sufficient to enjoin a new station from using a radio frequency in any way so as to cause interference with the signals of the prior station.[3] And so order was being brought out of the chaos by means of the assignment of property rights. But it was precisely this development that the government rushed in to forestall.

The 1926 Zenith decision striking down the government's power to regulate or to fail to renew licenses, and forcing the Department of Commerce to issue licenses to any station that applied, produced a great boom in the broadcasting industry. Over two hundred new stations were created in the nine months after the decision. As a result, Congress rushed through a stopgap measure in July 1926 to *prevent* any property rights in radio frequencies, and resolved that all licenses should be limited to ninety days. By February 1927 the Congress passed the law establishing the Federal Radio Commission, which nationalized the airwaves and established powers similar to those of the current FCC. That the aim of the knowledgeable politicians was *not* to prevent chaos but to prevent private property in the airwaves as the solution to chaos is demonstrated by the legal historian H. P. Warner. Warner states that "grave fears were expressed by legislators, and those generally charged with the administration of communications . . . that government regulation of an effective sort might be permanently prevented through the accrual of property rights in licenses or means of access, and that thus franchises of the value of millions of dollars might be established for all time."[4] The net result, however, was to establish equally valuable franchises anyway, but in a monopolistic fashion through the largesse of the Federal Radio Commission and later FCC rather than through competitive homesteading.

Among the numerous direct invasions of freedom of speech exercised

[2]In the decisions *Hoover* v. *Intercity Radio Co.*, 286 Fed. 1003 (Appeals D.C., 1923); and *United States* v. *Zenith Radio Corp.*, 12 F. 2d 614 (N.D. Ill., 1926). See the excellent article by Ronald H. Coase, "The Federal Communications Commission," *Journal of Law and Economics* (October 1959), pp. 4–5.

[3]Coase, *ibid.*, p. 31n.

[4]Harry P. Warner, *Radio and Television Law* (1958), p. 540. Quoted in Coase, *op. cit.*, p. 32.

by the licensing power of the FRC and FCC, two cases will suffice. One was in 1931, when the FRC denied renewal of license to a Mr. Baker, who operated a radio station in Iowa. In denying renewal, the Commission said:

This Commission holds no brief for the Medical Associations and other parties whom Mr. Baker does not like. Their alleged sins may be at times of public importance, to be called to the attention of the public over the air in the right way. But this record discloses that Mr. Baker does not do so in any high-minded way. It shows that he continually and erratically over the air rides a personal hobby, his cancer cure ideas and his likes and dislikes of certain persons and things. Surely his infliction of all this on the listeners is not the proper use of a broadcasting license. Many of his utterances are vulgar, if not indeed indecent. Assuredly they are not uplifting or entertaining.[5]

Can we imagine the outcry if the federal government were to put a newspaper or a book publisher out of business on similar grounds?

A recent act of the FCC was to threaten nonrenewal of license of radio station KTRG in Honolulu, a major radio station in Hawaii. KTRG had been broadcasting libertarian programs for several hours a day for approximately two years. Finally, in late 1970, the FCC decided to open lengthy hearings moving toward nonrenewal of license, the threatened cost of which forced the owners to shut down the station permanently.[6]

Pornography

To the libertarian, the arguments between conservatives and liberals over laws prohibiting pornography are distressingly beside the point. The conservative position tends to hold that pornography is debasing and immoral and therefore should be outlawed. Liberals tend to counter that sex is good and healthy and that therefore pornography will only have good effects, and that depictions of violence—say on television, in movies, or in comic books—should be outlawed instead. Neither side deals with the crucial point: that the good, bad, or indifferent conse-

---

[5]Decisions of the FRC, Docket No. 967, June 5, 1931. Quoted in Coase, *op. cit.*, p. 9.

[6]The best and most fully elaborated portrayal of how private property rights could be assigned in radio and television is in A. DeVany *et al.*, "A Property System for Market Allocation of the Electromagnetic Spectrum: A Legal-Economic-Engineering Study," *Stanford Law Review* (June 1969). See also William H. Meckling, "National Communications Policy: Discussion," *American Economic Review, Papers and Proceedings* (May 1970), pp. 222–23. Since the DeVany article, the growth of community and cable television has further diminished the scarcity of frequencies and expanded the range of potential competition.

quences of pornography, while perhaps an interesting problem in its own right, is completely irrelevant to the question of whether or not it should be outlawed. The libertarian holds that it is not the business of the law—the use of retaliatory violence—to enforce anyone's conception of morality. It is not the business of the law—even if this were practically possible, which is, of course, most unlikely—to make anyone good or reverent or moral or clean or upright. This is for each individual to decide for himself. It is only the business of legal violence to defend people against the use of violence, to defend them from violent invasions of their person or property. But if the government presumes to outlaw pornography, it *itself* becomes the genuine outlaw—for it is invading the property rights of people to produce, sell, buy, or possess pornograpic material.

We do not pass laws to make people upright; we do not pass laws to force people to be kind to their neighbors or not to yell at the bus driver; we do not pass laws to force people to be honest with their loved ones. We do not pass laws to force them to eat X amount of vitamins per day. Neither is it the business of government, nor of any legal agency, to pass laws against the voluntary production or sale of pornography. Whether pornography is good, bad, or indifferent should be of no interest to the legal authorities.

The same holds true for the liberal bugbear of "the pornography of violence." Whether or not watching violence on television helps lead to actual crimes should not come under the purview of the State. To outlaw violent films because they *might* someday induce someone to commit a crime is a denial of man's free will, and a total denial, of course, of the right of those who will *not* commit crimes to see the film. But more important, it is no more justifiable—in fact, less so—to outlaw violent films for this reason than it would be, as we have noted, to lock up all teenage Negro males because they have a greater tendency to commit crime than the rest of the population.

It should be clear, too, that prohibition of pornography is an invasion of property right, of the right to produce, sell, buy, and own. Conservatives who call for the outlawing of pornography do not seem to realize that they are thereby violating the very concept of property rights they profess to champion. It is also a violation of freedom of the press, which, as we have seen, is really a subset of the general right of private property.

Sometimes it seems that the *beau ideal* of many conservatives, as well as of many liberals, is to put everyone into a cage and coerce him into doing what the conservatives or liberals believe to be the moral thing. They would of course be differently styled cages, but they would be cages just the same. The conservative would ban illicit sex, drugs, gambling, and impiety, and coerce everyone to act according to his version of moral and religious behavior. The liberal would ban films of violence, unesthetic advertising, football, and racial discrimination, and, at the extreme, place everyone in a "Skinner box" to be run by a supposedly benevolent liberal dictator. But the effect would be the same: to reduce everyone to a subhuman level and to deprive everyone of the most precious part of his or her humanity—the freedom to choose.

The irony, of course, is that by forcing men to be "moral"—i.e., to *act* morally—the conservative or liberal jailkeepers would in reality deprive men of the very *possibility* of being moral. The concept of "morality" makes no sense unless the moral act is freely chosen. Suppose, for example, that someone is a devout Muslim who is anxious to have as many people as possible bow to Mecca three times a day; to him let us suppose this is the highest moral act. But if he wields coercion to *force* everyone to bow to Mecca, he is thereby depriving everyone of the opportunity to be moral—to *choose freely* to bow to Mecca. Coercion deprives a man of the freedom to choose and, therefore, of the possibility of choosing morally.

The libertarian, in contrast to so many conservatives and liberals, does not want to place man in any cage. What he wants for everyone is freedom, the freedom to act morally or immorally, as each man shall decide.

Sex Laws

In recent years, liberals have fortunately been coming to the conclusion that "any act between two (or more) consenting adults" should be legal. It is unfortunate that the liberals have not yet widened this criterion from sex to trade and exchange, for if they ever would, they would be close to becoming full-scale libertarians. For the libertarian is precisely interested in legalizing all interrelations whatever between "consenting adults." Liberals have also begun to call for the abolition of "victimless crimes," which would be splendid if "victims" were defined with greater precision as victims of aggressive violence.

Since sex is a uniquely private aspect of life, it is particularly intolerable that governments should presume to regulate and legislate sexual behavior, yet of course this has been one of the State's favorite pastimes. Violent acts such as rape, of course, are to be classed as crimes in the same way as any other act of violence against persons.

Oddly enough, while voluntary sexual activities have often been rendered illegal and prosecuted by the State, accused rapists have been treated far more gently by the authorities than accused perpetrators of other forms of bodily assault. In many instances, in fact, the rape victim has been virtually treated as the guilty party by the law enforcement agencies—an attitude which is almost never taken toward victims of other crimes. Clearly, an impermissible sexual double standard has been at work. As the National Board of the American Civil Liberties Union declared in March 1977:

Sexual assault victims should be treated no differently from victims of other crimes. Sexual assault victims are often treated with skepticism and abuse at the hands of law enforcement and health services personnel. This treatment ranges from official disbelief and insensitivity to cruel and harsh probes of the victim's lifestyle and motivation. Such abrogation of responsibility by institutions meant to assist and protect victims of crime can only compound the trauma of the victim's original experience.

The double standard imposed by government can be remedied by removing rape as a special category of legal and judicial treatment, and of subsuming it under the general law of bodily assault. Whatever standards are used for judges' instructions to the jury, or for the admissibility of evidence, should be applied similarly in all these cases.

If labor and persons in general are to be free, then so should there be freedom for *prostitution*. Prostitution is a voluntary sale of a labor service, and the government has no right to prohibit or restrict such sales. It should be noted that many of the grimmer aspects of the streetwalking trade have been brought about by the outlawing of brothels. As long-lasting houses of prostitution operated by madams anxious to cultivate goodwill among customers over a long time span, brothels used to compete to provide high-quality service and build up their "brand name." The outlawing of brothels has forced prostitution into a "blackmarket," fly-by-night existence, with all the dangers and general decline in quality this always entails. Recently, in New York City, there has been a tendency for the police to crack down on prostitution with the excuse that the trade is no longer "victimless," since many prostitutes commit crimes against their customers. To outlaw trades that may attract crime, however, would in the same way justify prohibition because many fights take place in bars. The answer is not to outlaw the voluntary and truly lawful activity, but for the police to see to it that the genuine crimes do not get committed. It should be clear that advocacy of freedom for prostitution does not, for the libertarian, in the least imply advocacy of prostitution itself. In short, if a particularly puritanical government were to outlaw all cosmetics, the libertarian would call for legalizing cosmetics without in any sense implying that he favors—or for that matter, opposes—the use of cosmetics themselves. On the contrary, depending upon his personal ethics or esthetics, he might well agitate against the use of cosmetics after they become legalized; his attempt is always to persuade rather than to compel.

If sex should be free, then *birth control* should, of course, be free as well. It is unfortunately characteristic of our society, however, that scarcely has birth control been made legal when people—in this case liberals—arise to agitate for birth control being made *compulsory*. It is true, of course, that if my neighbor has a baby this may well affect me for good or ill. But, then, almost everything that anyone does may affect one or more people. To the libertarian, this is scarcely justification for using force, which may *only* be used to combat or restrain force itself. There is no right more personal, no freedom more precious, than for any woman to decide to have, or not to have, a baby, and it is totalitarian in the extreme for any government to presume to deny her that right. Besides, if any family has more children than it can support in comfort, the family itself will bear the main burden; hence, the almost universal result that the wish to preserve a treasured rise in living standards will induce a voluntary reduction of births by the families themselves.

This brings us to the more complex case of *abortion*. For the libertarian, the "Catholic" case against abortion, even if finally rejected as invalid, cannot be dismissed out of hand. For the essence of that case—not really "Catholic" at all in a theological sense—is that abortion destroys a human life and is therefore murder, and hence cannot be condoned. More than that, if abortion is truly murder, then the Catholic—or any other person who shares this view—cannot just shrug his shoulders and say that "Catholic" views should not be imposed upon non-Catholics. Murder is not an expression of religious preference; no sect, in the name of "freedom of religion," can or should get away with committing murder with the plea that its religion so commands. The vital question then becomes: Should abortion be considered as murder?

Most discussion of the issue bogs down in *minutiae* about *when* human life begins, when or if the fetus can be considered to be alive, etc. All this is really irrelevant to the issue of the *legality* (again, not necessarily the *morality*) of abortion. The Catholic antiabortionist, for example, declares that all that he wants for the fetus is the rights of any human being—i.e., the right not to be murdered. But there is more involved here, and this is the crucial consideration. If we are to treat the fetus as having the same rights as humans, then let us ask: What *human* has the right to remain, unbidden, as an unwanted parasite within some other human being's body? This is the nub of the issue: the absolute right of every person, and hence every woman, to the ownership of her own body. What the mother is doing in an abortion is causing an unwanted entity within her body to be ejected from it: If the fetus dies, this does not rebut the point that no being has a right to live, unbidden, as a parasite within or upon some person's body.

The common retort that the mother either originally wanted or at least was responsible for placing the fetus within her body is, again, beside the point. Even in the stronger case where the mother originally wanted the child, the mother, as the property owner in her own body, has the right to change her mind and to eject it.

If the State should not repress voluntary sexual activity, neither should it discriminate for or against either sex. "Affirmative action" decrees are an obvious way of compelling discrimination against males or other groups in employment, admissions, or wherever this implicit quota system is applied. But "protective" labor laws in regard to women insidiously pretend to favor women when they really discriminate against them by prohibiting them from working during certain hours or in certain occupations. Women are prevented by law from exercising their individual freedom of choice in deciding for themselves whether or not to enter these occupations or to work during these supposedly onerous hours. In this way, government prevents women from competing freely against men in these areas.

All in all, the 1978 Libertarian Party platform is trenchant and to the point in setting forth the libertarian position on governmental sex or other discrimination: "No individual rights should be denied or abridged by the laws of the United States or any state or locality on account of sex, race, color, creed, age, national origin, or sexual preference."

Wiretapping

Wiretapping is a contemptible invasion of privacy and of property right, and of course should be outlawed as an invasive act. Few, if any, people would condone private wiretapping. The controversy arises with those who maintain that the police should be able to tap the wires of persons they *suspect* as criminals. Otherwise, how would criminals be caught?

In the first place, from the pragmatic viewpoint, it is rare that wiretapping is effective in such "one-shot" crimes as bank robbery. Wiretapping is generally used in cases where the "business" is set up on a regularized and continuing basis—such as narcotics and gambling—and is therefore vulnerable to espionage and "bugging." Secondly, we remain with our contention that it is itself criminal to invade the property of anyone not yet convicted of a crime. It may well be true, for example, that if the government employed a ten-million man espionage force to spy upon and tap the wires of the entire population, the total amount of private crime would be reduced—just as it would if all ghetto residents or teenage males were promptly incarcerated. But what would this be compared to the mass crime that would thus be committed, legally and without shame, by the government itself?

There is one concession we might make to the police argument, but it is doubtful the police would be happy with the concession. It is proper to invade the property of a thief, for example, who has himself invaded to a far greater extent the property of others. Suppose the police decide that John Jones is a jewel thief. They tap his wires, and use this evidence to convict Jones of the crime. We might say that this tapping is legitimate, and should go unpunished: *provided*, however, that if Jones should prove *not* to be a thief, the police and the judges who may have issued the court order for the tap are now to be adjudged *criminals themselves* and sent to jail for their crime of unjust wiretapping. This reform would have two happy consequences: no policeman or judge would participate in wiretapping unless he was dead certain the victim is indeed a criminal; and the police and judges would at last join everyone else as equally subject to the rule of the criminal law. Certainly equality of liberty requires that the law applies to everyone; therefore any invasion of the property of a noncriminal by *anyone* should be outlawed, regardless of who committed the deed. The policeman who guessed wrong and thereby aggressed against a noncriminal should therefore be considered just as guilty as any "private" wiretapper.

Gambling

There are few laws more absurd and iniquitous than the laws against gambling. In the first place, the law, in its broadest sense, is clearly unenforceable. If every time Jim and Jack made a quiet bet on a football game, or on an election, or on virtually anything else, this were illegal, an enormous multimillion-man gestapo would be required to enforce such a law and to spy on everyone and ferret out every bet. Another large super-espionage force would then be needed to spy on the spies to make sure that they have not been bought off. Conservatives like to retort to such arguments—used against laws outlawing sexual practices, pornography, drugs, etc.—that the prohibition against murder is not fully enforceable either, but this is no argument for repeal of *that* law. This argument, however, ignores a crucial point: the mass of the public, making an instinctive libertarian distinction, abhors and condemns murder and does not engage in it; hence, the prohibition becomes broadly enforceable. But the mass of the public is not as convinced of the criminality of gambling, hence continues to engage in it, and the law—properly—becomes unenforceable.

Since the laws against quiet betting are clearly unenforceable, the authorities decide to concentrate on certain highly *visible* forms of gambling, and confine their activities to them: roulette, bookies, "numbers" betting—in short, on those areas where gambling is a fairly regularized activity. But then we have a peculiar and surely totally unsupportable kind of ethical judgment: roulette, horse betting, etc., are somehow morally evil and must be cracked down upon by the massed might of the police, whereas quiet betting is morally legitimate and need not be bothered.

In New York State, a particular form of imbecility developed over the years: until recent years, all forms of horse betting were illegal *except* those made at the tracks themselves. Why horse betting at Aqueduct or Belmont race track should be perfectly moral and legitimate while betting on the same race with your friendly neighborhood bookie should be sinful and bring down the awful majesty of the law defies the imagination. Unless, of course, if we consider the point of the law to force betters to swell the coffers of the tracks. Recently, a new wrinkle has developed. The City of New York has *itself* gone into the horse-betting business, and betting at city-owned stores is perfectly fine and proper, while betting with competing private bookies continues to be sinful and outlawed. Clearly, the point of the system is first to confer a special privilege upon the race tracks, and then upon the city's own betting installation. Various states are also beginning to finance their ever-growing expenditures through lotteries, which thus become conferred with the cloak of morality and respectability.

A standard argument for outlawing gambling is that, if the poor workman is allowed to gamble, he will improvidently blow his weekly paycheck and thereby render his family destitute. Aside from the fact that he can now spend his payroll on friendly betting, this paternalistic and dictatorial argument is a curious one. For it proves far too much: If we must outlaw gambling because the masses might spend too much of their substance, why should we not outlaw many other articles of mass consumption? After all, if a workman is determined to blow his paycheck, he has many opportunities to do so: he can improvidently spend too much on a TV set, a hi-fi, liquor, baseball equipment, and countless other goodies. The logic of prohibiting a man from gambling for his own or his family's good leads straight to that totalitarian cage, the cage in which Pappa Government tells the man exactly what to do, how to spend his money, how many vitamins he must ingest, and forces him to obey the State's dictates.

Narcotics and Other Drugs

The case for outlawing any product or activity is essentially the same twofold argument we have seen used to justify the compulsory commitment of mental patients: it will harm the person involved, or it will lead that person to commit crimes against others. It is curious that the general—and justified—horror of drugs has led the mass of the public to an irrational enthusiasm for outlawing them. The case against outlawing narcotic and hallucinogenic drugs is far weaker than the case against Prohibition, an experiment which the grisly era of the 1920s has hopefully discredited for all time. For while narcotics are undoubtedly more harmful than is alcohol, the latter can also be harmful, and outlawing something because it may harm the user leads straight down the logical garden path to our totalitarian cage, where people are prohibited from eating candy and are forced to eat yogurt "for their own good." But in the far more imposing argument about harm to others, alcohol is much more likely to lead to crimes, auto accidents, etc., than narcotics, which render the user preternaturally peaceful and passive. There is, of course, a very strong connection between addiction and crime, but the connection is the *reverse* of any argument for prohibition. Crimes are committed by addicts driven to theft by the high price of drugs caused by the outlawry itself! If narcotics were legal, the supply would greatly increase, the high costs of black markets and police payoffs would disappear, and the price would be low enough to eliminate most addict-caused crime.

This is not to argue, of course, for prohibition of alcohol; once again, to outlaw something which *might* lead to crime is an illegitimate and invasive assault on the rights of person and property, an assault which, again, would far more justify the immediate incarceration of all teenage males. Only the overt commission of a crime should be illegal, and the way to combat crimes committed under the influence of alcohol is to be more diligent about the crimes themselves, not to outlaw the alcohol. And this would have the further beneficial effect of reducing crimes *not* committed under the influence of alcohol.

Paternalism in this area comes not only from the right; it is curious that while liberals generally favor legalizing marijuana and sometimes of heroin, they seem to yearn to outlaw cigarettes, on the ground that cigarette smoking often causes cancer. Liberals have already managed to use federal control of television to outlaw cigarette advertising on that medium—and thereby to level a grave blow against the very freedom of speech liberals are supposed to cherish.

Once again: Every man has the right to choose. Propagandize against cigarettes as much as you want, but leave the individual free to run his own life. Otherwise, we may as well outlaw all sorts of possible carcinogenic agents—including tight shoes, improperly fitting false teeth, excessive exposure to the sun, as well as excessive intake of ice cream, eggs, and butter which might lead to heart disease. And, if such prohibitions prove unenforceable, again the logic is to place people in cages so that they will receive the proper amount of sun, the correct diet, properly fitting shoes, and so on.

Police Corruption

In the fall of 1971, the Knapp Commission focussed public attention on the problem of widespread police corruption in New York City. Midst the drama of individual cases, there is a danger of overlooking what is clearly the central problem, a problem of which the Knapp Commission itself was perfectly aware. In virtually every case of corruption, the policemen were involved in regularly functioning businesses which, by government fiat, had been declared illegal. And yet a vast number of people, by demanding these goods and services, have shown that they do not agree that such activities should be placed in the same category as murder, theft, or assault. Indeed, in practically no case did the "purchase" of the police involve these heinous crimes. In almost all cases, they consisted of the police looking the other way while legitimate, voluntary transactions took place.

The common law makes a vital distinction between a crime that is a *malum in se* and one that is merely a *malum prohibitum*. A *malum in se* is an act which the mass of the people instinctively feel is a reprehensible crime which should be punished. This coincides roughly with the libertarian's definition of a crime as an invasion of person or property: assault, theft, and murder. Other crimes are activities made into crimes by government edict: it is in this far more widely tolerated area that police corruption occurs.

In short, police corruption occurs in those areas where entrepreneurs supply voluntary services to consumers, but where the government has decreed that these services are illegal: narcotics, prostitution, and gambling. Where gambling, for example, is outlawed, the law places into the hands of the police assigned to the gambling detail the power to sell the privilege of engaging in the gambling business. In short, it is as if the police were empowered to issue special licenses to engage in these activities, and then proceeded to sell these unofficial but vital licenses at whatever price the traffic will bear. One policeman testified that, if the law were to be fully enforced, not a single construction site in New York City could continue functioning, so intricately did the government wrap construction sites in a web of trivial and impossible regulations. In short, whether consciously or not, the government proceeds as follows: first it outlaws a certain activity—drugs, gambling, construction, or whatever—then the governmental police sell to would-be entrepreneurs in the field the privilege of entering and continuing in business.

At best, the result of these actions is the imposition of higher cost, and more restricted output, of the activity than would have occurred in a free market. But the effects are still more pernicious. Often, what the policemen sell is not just permission to function, but what is in effect a privileged monopoly. In that case, a gambler pays off the police not just to continue in business but also to freeze out any competitors who might want to enter the industry. The consumers are then saddled with privileged monopolists, and are barred from enjoying the advantages of competition. It is no wonder, then, that when Prohibition was finally repealed in the early 1930s, the main opponents of repeal were, along with fundamentalist and Prohibitionist groups, the organized bootleggers, who had enjoyed special monopolistic privileges from their special arrangements with the police and other enforcement arms of government.

The way, then, to eliminate police corruption is simple but effective: abolish the laws against voluntary business activity and against all "victimless crimes." Not only would corruption be eliminated, but a large number of police would then be freed to operate against the *real* criminals, the aggressors against person and property. This, after all, is supposed to be the function of the police in the first place.

We should realize, then, that the problem of police corruption, as well as the broader question of government corruption in general, should be placed in a wider context. The point is that *given* the unfortunate and unjust laws prohibiting, regulating, and taxing certain activities, corruption is highly beneficial to society. In a number of countries, without corruption that nullified government prohibitions, taxes, and exactions, virtually no trade or industry would be carried on at all. Corruption greases the wheels of trade. The solution, then, is not to deplore corruption and redouble enforcement against it, but to abolish the crippling policies and laws of government that make corruption necessary.

Gun Laws

For most of the activities in this chapter, liberals tend to favor freedom of trade and activity while conservatives yearn for rigorous enforcement and maximum crackdowns against violators of the law. Yet, mysteriously, in the drive for gun laws the positions tend to be reversed. Every time a gun is used in a violent crime, liberals redouble their agitation for the severe restriction, if not prohibition of private ownership of guns, while conservatives oppose such restrictions on behalf of individual freedom.

If, as libertarians believe, every individual has the right to own his person and property, it then follows that he has the right to employ violence to defend himself against the violence of criminal aggressors. But for some odd reason, liberals have systematically tried to deprive innocent persons of the means for defending themselves against aggression. Despite the fact that the Second Amendment to the Constitution guarantees that "the right of the people to keep and bear arms shall not be infringed," the government has systematically eroded much of this right. Thus, in New York State, as in most other states, the Sullivan Law prohibits the carrying of "concealed weapons" without a license issued by the authorities. Not only has the carrying of guns been grievously restricted by this unconstitutional edict, but the government has extended this prohibition to almost any object that could possibly serve as a weapon—even those that could only be used for self-defense. As a result, potential victims of crime have been barred from carrying knives, tear-gas pens, or even hatpins, and people who have used such weapons in defending themselves against assault have themselves been prosecuted by the authorities. In the cities, this invasive prohibition against concealed weapons has in effect stripped victims of any possible self-defense against crime. (It is true that there is no official prohibition against carrying an *unconcealed* weapon, but a man in New York City who, several years ago, tested the law by walking the streets carrying a rifle was promptly arrested for "disturbing the peace.") Furthermore, victims are so hamstrung by provisions against "undue" force in self-defense that the criminal is automatically handed an enormous built-in advantage by the existing legal system.

It should be clear that no physical object is *in itself* aggressive; *any* object, whether it be a gun, a knife, or a stick, can be used for aggression, for defense, or for numerous other purposes unconnected with crime. It makes no more sense to outlaw or restrict the purchase and ownership of guns than it does to outlaw the possession of knives, clubs, hat-pins, or stones. And how are all of these objects to be outlawed, and if outlawed, how is the prohibition to be enforced? Instead of pursuing innocent people carrying or possessing various objects, then, the law should be concerned with combatting and apprehending real criminals.

There is, moreover, another consideration which reinforces our conclusion. If guns are restricted or outlawed, there is no reason to expect that determined criminals are going to pay much attention to the law. The criminals, then, will always be able to purchase and carry guns; it will only be their innocent victims who will suffer from the solicitous liberalism that imposes laws against guns and other weapons. Just as drugs, gambling, and pornography should be made legal, so too should guns and any other objects that might serve as weapons of self-defense.

In a notable article attacking control of handguns (the type of gun liberals most want to restrict), St. Louis University law professor Don B. Kates, Jr., chides his fellow liberals for not applying the same logic to guns that they use for marijuana laws. Thus, he points out that there are over fifty million handgun owners in America today, and that, based on polls and past experience, from two-thirds to over eighty percent of Americans would fail to comply with a ban on handguns. The inevitable result, as in the case of sex and marijuana laws, would be harsh penalties and yet highly selective enforcement—breeding disrespect for the law and law enforcement agencies. And the law would be enforced selectively against those people whom the authorities didn't like: "Enforcement becomes progressively more haphazard until at last the laws are used only against those who are unpopular with the police. We hardly need to be reminded of the odious search and seizure tactics police and government agents have often resorted to in order to trap violators of these laws." Kates adds that "if these arguments seem familiar, it is probably because they parallel the standard liberal argument against pot laws."[7]

Kates then adds a highly perceptive insight into this curious liberal blind spot. For:

Gun prohibition is the brainchild of white middle-class liberals who are oblivious to the situation of poor and minority people living in areas where the police have given up on crime control. Such liberals weren't upset about marijuana laws, either, in the fifties when the busts were confined to the ghettos. Secure in well-policed suburbs or high-security apartments guarded by Pinkertons (whom no one proposes to disarm), the oblivious liberal derides gun ownership as "an anachronism from the Old West."[8]

Kates further points out the demonstrated empirical value of self-defense armed with guns; in Chicago, for example, armed civilians justifiably killed three times as many violent criminals in the past five years as did the police. And, in a study of several hundred violent confrontations with criminals, Kates found the armed civilians to be more successful than the police: the civilians defending themselves captured, wounded, killed, or scared off criminals in 75% of the confrontations, whereas the police only had a 61% success rate. It is true that victims who resist robbery are more likely to be injured than those who remain passive. But Kates points out neglected qualifiers: (1) that resistance without a gun has been twice as hazardous to the victim than resistance with one, and (2) that the choice of resistance is up to the victim and his circumstances and values.

Avoiding injury will be paramount to a white, liberal academic with a comfortable bank account. It will necessarily be less important to the casual laborer or welfare recipient who is being robbed of the wherewithal to support his family

---

[7]Don B. Kates, Jr., "Handgun Control: Prohibition Revisited," *Inquiry* (December 5, 1977), p. 21. This escalation of harsh enforcement and despotic search-and-seizure methods is already here. Not only in Britain and numerous other countries, where indiscriminate searches for guns take place; in Malaysia, Rhodesia, Taiwan, and the Philippines, which impose the death penalty for possession of guns; but also in Missouri, where St. Louis police have conducted literally thousands of searches of blacks in recent years on the theory that any black person driving a recent-model car must have an illegal gun; and in Michigan, where nearly 70% of all firearms prosecutions have been thrown out by the appellate courts on grounds of illegal search procedures. And already a Detroit police official has advocated abolition of the Fourth Amendment so as to permit indiscriminate general searches for violations of a future handgun prohibition. *Ibid.*, p. 23.

[8]*Ibid.*, p. 21.

for a month—or to a black shopkeeper who can't get robbery insurance and will be literally run out of business by successive robberies.

And the 1975 national survey of handgun owners by the Decision Making Information organization found that the leading subgroups who own a gun *only* for self-defense include blacks, the lowest income groups, and senior citizens. "These are the people," Kates eloquently warns, "it is proposed we jail because they insist on keeping the only protection available for their families in areas in which the police have given up."[9]

What of historical experience? Have handgun bans really greatly lowered the degree of violence in society, as liberals claim? The evidence is precisely to the contrary. A massive study done at the University of Wisconsin concluded unequivocally in the fall of 1975 that "gun control laws have no individual or collective effect in reducing the rate of violent crime." The Wisconsin study, for example, tested the theory that ordinarily peaceful people will be irresistibly tempted to shoot their guns if available when tempers are being frayed. The study found *no correlation whatever* between rates of handgun ownership and rates of homicide when compared, state by state. Moreover, this finding is reinforced by a 1976 Harvard study of a Massachusetts law providing a mandatory minimum year in prison for anyone found possessing a handgun without a government permit. It turns out that, during the year 1975, this 1974 law did indeed considerably reduce the carrying of firearms and the number of assaults with firearms. But, lo and behold! the Harvard researchers found to their surprise that there was no corresponding reduction in any type of violence. That is,

As previous criminological studies have suggested, deprived of a handgun, a momentarily enraged citizen will resort to the far more deadly long gun. Deprived of all firearms, he will prove almost as deadly with knives, hammers, etc.

And clearly, "if reducing handgun ownership does not reduce homicide or other violence, a handgun ban is just one more diversion of police resources from real crime to victimless crime."[10]

[9] *Ibid.* The extremely harsh idea of jailing people for mere possession of handguns is not a farfetched straw man, but precisely the *beau ideal* of the liberal: the Massachusetts constitutional amendment, fortunately defeated overwhelmingly by the voters in 1977, provided for a *mandatory* minimum sentence of a year in prison for any person caught possessing a handgun.

[10] *Ibid.*, p. 22. Similarly in Britain, a 1971 Cambridge University study found that the British homicide rate, with handgun prohibition, has doubled in the last fifteen years. Furthermore, before the adoption of the handgun ban in 1920, the use of firearms in crime (when there were no gun restrictions at all) was far less than now.

Finally, Kates makes another intriguing point: that a society where peaceful citizens are armed is far more likely to be one where Good Samaritans who voluntarily go to the aid of victims of crime will flourish. But take away people's guns, and the public—disastrously for the victims—will tend to leave the matter to the police. Before New York State outlawed handguns, Good Samaritan instances were far more widespread than now. And, in a recent survey of Good Samaritan cases, no less than 81% of the Samaritans were owners of guns. If we wish to encourage a society where citizens come to the aid of neighbors in distress, we must not strip them of the actual power to do something about crime. Surely, it is the height of absurdity to disarm the peaceful public and *then*, as is quite common, to denounce them for "apathy" for failing to rush to the rescue of victims of criminal assault.

7
Education

Public and Compulsory Schooling

UNTIL THE LAST FEW YEARS there were few institutions in America that were held more sacred—especially by liberals—than the public school. Devotion to the public school had seized even those early Americans—such as Jeffersonians and Jacksonians—who were libertarian in most other respects. In recent years the public school was supposed to be a crucial ingredient of democracy, the fount of brotherhood, and the enemy of elitism and separateness in American life. The public school was the embodiment of the alleged right of every child to an education, and it was upheld as a crucible of understanding and harmony between men of all occupations and social classes who would rub elbows from an early age with all their neighbors.

Going hand in hand with the spread of public education have been *compulsory attendance laws,* which have forced all children up to a high—and continually increasing—minimum age, to attend either a public school or a private school certified as suitable by the state apparatus. In contrast to earlier decades, when a relatively small proportion of the population went to school in the higher grades, the entire mass of the population has thus been coerced by the government into spending a large portion of the most impressionable years of their lives in public institutions. We could easily have analyzed compulsory attendance laws in our chapter on involuntary servitude, for what institution is more evidently a vast system of incarceration? In recent years, Paul Goodman and other critics of education have trenchantly exposed the nation's public schools—and to a lesser extent their private appendages—as a vast prison system for the nation's youth, dragooning countless millions of unwilling and unadaptable children into the schooling structure. The New Left tactic of breaking into the high schools shouting "Jailbreak!" may have been absurd and ineffective, but it certainly expressed a great truth about the school system. For if we are to dragoon the entire youth population into vast prisons in the guise of "education," with teachers and administrators serving as surrogate wardens and guards, why should we not expect vast unhappiness, discontent, alienation, and rebellion on the part of the nation's youth? The only surprise should be that the rebellion was so long in coming. But now it is increasingly acknowledged that something is terribly wrong with America's proudest institution; that, especially in urban areas, the public schools have become cesspools of crime, petty theft, and drug addiction, and that little or no genuine education takes place amidst the warping of the minds and souls of the children.[1]

Part of the reason for this tyranny over the nation's youth is misplaced altruism on the part of the educated middle class. The workers, or the "lower classes," they felt, should have the opportunity to enjoy the schooling the middle classes value so highly. And if the parents or the children of the masses should be so benighted as to balk at this glorious opportunity set before them, well, then, a little coercion must be applied—"for their own good," of course.

A crucial fallacy of the middle-class school worshippers is confusion between formal schooling and *education* in general. Education is a lifelong process of learning, and learning takes place not only in school, but in all areas of life. When the child plays, or listens to parents or friends, or reads a newspaper, or works at a job, he or she is becoming *educated*. Formal schooling is only a small part of the educational process, and is really only suitable for formal subjects of instruction, particularly in the more advanced and systematic subjects. The elementary subjects, reading, writing, arithmetic and their corollaries, can easily be learned at home and outside the school.

Furthermore, one of the great glories of mankind is its diversity, the

[1]Thus, see Paul Goodman, *Compulsory Mis-education and the Community of Scholars* (New York: Vintage Press, 1964), and numerous works by Goodman, John Holt, Jonathan Kozol, Herbert Kohl, Ivan Illich, and many others.

fact that each individual is unique, with unique abilities, interests, and aptitudes. To coerce into formal schooling children who have neither the ability nor the interest in this area is a criminal warping of the soul and mind of the child. Paul Goodman has raised the cry that most children would be far better off if they were allowed to work at an early age, learn a trade, and begin to do that which they are most suited for. America was built by citizens and leaders, many of whom received little or no formal schooling, and the idea that one must have a high-school diploma—or nowadays, an A.B. degree—before he can begin to work and to live in the world is an absurdity of the current age. Abolish compulsory attendance laws and give children their head, and we will return to a nation of people far more productive, interested, creative, and happy. Many thoughtful opponents of the New Left and the youth rebellion have pointed out that much of the discontent of youth and their divorce from reality is due to the ever-longer period in which youth must remain at school, wrapped in a cocoon of dependence and irresponsibility. Well and good, but what is the main reason for this ever-lengthening cocoon? Clearly the whole system, and in particular the compulsory attendance laws, which preach that everyone must go perpetually to school—first to high school, now to college, and soon perhaps for a Ph.D. degree. It is the compulsion toward mass schooling that creates both the discontent and the ever-continuing shelter from the "real world." In no other nation and in no other age has this mania for mass schooling so taken hold.

It is remarkable that the old libertarian right and the New Left, from very different perspectives and using very different rhetoric, came to a similar perception of the despotic nature of mass schooling. Thus, Albert Jay Nock, the great individualist theorist of the 1920s and '30s, denounced the educational system for forcing the "ineducable" masses into the schools out of a vain egalitarian belief in the equal educability of every child. Instead of allowing those children with the needed aptitude and ability to go to school, all children are being coerced into schools for their own supposed good, and the result is a distortion of the lives of those not suited for school and the wrecking of proper schooling for the truly educable. Nock also perceptively criticized the conservatives who attacked "progressive education" for diluting educational standards by giving courses in automobile driving, basket weaving, or choosing a dentist. Nock pointed out that if you force a whole host of children who cannot absorb classical education into school, then you *have* to shift education in the direction of vocational training, suitable for the lowest common denominator. The fatal flaw is not progressive education, but the drive toward universal schooling to which progressivism was a makeshift response.[2]

Such New Left critics as John McDermott and Paul Goodman charge, for their part, that the middle class has been forcing working class children, many of them with completely different values and aptitudes, into a public school system designed to force these children into a middle-class mould. It should be clear that whether one favors one class or the other, one ideal of schooling or another, the substance of the criticism is very much the same: that a whole mass of children are being dragooned into an institution for which they have little interest or aptitude.

Indeed, if we look into the history of the drive for public schooling and compulsory attendance in this and other countries, we find at the root not so much misguided altruism as a conscious scheme to coerce the mass of the population into a mould desired by the Establishment. Recalcitrant minorities were to be forced into a majority mould; all citizens were to be inculcated in the civic virtues, notably and always including obedience to the State apparatus. Indeed, if the mass of the populace is to be educated in government schools, how could these schools *not* become a mighty instrument for the inculcation of obedience to the State authorities? Martin Luther, a leader in the first modern drive for compulsory State education, phrased the plea typically in his famous letter of 1524 to the rulers of Germany:

Dear rulers. . . . I maintain that the civil authorities are under obligation to compel the people to send their children to school. . . . If the government can compel such citizens as are fit for military service to bear spear and rifle, to mount ramparts, and perform other martial duties in time of war, how much more has it a right to the people to send their children to school, because in this case we are warring with the devil, whose object it is secretly to exhaust our cities and principalities. . . .[3]

Thus, for Luther, the State schools were to be an indispensable part of the "war with the devil," i.e., with Catholics, Jews, infidels, and competing Protestant sects. A modern admirer of Luther and of compulsory education was to remark that "the permanent and positive value of Luther's pronouncement of 1524 lies . . . in the hallowed associations which it established for Protestant Germany between the national religion and the educational duties of the individual and the state. Thus,

---

[2]Thus, see Albert Jay Nock, *The Theory of Education in the United States* (Chicago: Henry Regnery, 1949); and Nock, *Memoirs of a Superfluous Man* (New York: Harper & Bros., 1943).

[3]See John William Perrin, *The History of Compulsory Education in New England*, 1896.

doubtless, was created that healthy public opinion which rendered the principle of compulsory school attendance easy of acceptance in Prussia at a much earlier date than in England."[4]

The other great Protestant founder, John Calvin, was no less zealous in promoting mass public schooling, and for similar reasons. It is therefore not surprising that the earliest compulsory schooling in America was established by the Calvinist Puritans in Massachusetts Bay, those men who were so eager to plant an absolutist Calvinist theocracy in the New World. In June 1642, only a year after the Massachusetts Bay colony enacted its first set of laws, the colony established the first system of compulsory education in the English-speaking world. The law declared:

For as much as the good education of children is of singular behoof and benefit to any commonwealth, and whereas many parents and masters are too indulgent and negligent of their duty of that kind, it is ordered that the selectmen of every town . . . shall have a vigilant eye over their neighbors, to see first that none of them shall suffer so much barbarism in any of their families, as not to endeavor to teach, by themselves or others, their children and apprentices. . . .[5]

Five years later, Massachusetts Bay followed up this law with the establishment of public schools.

Thus, from the beginning of American history, the desire to mould, instruct, and render obedient the mass of the population was the major impetus behind the drive toward public schooling. In colonial days, public schooling was used as a device to suppress religious dissent, as well as to imbue unruly servants with the virtues of obedience to the State. It is typical, for example, that in the course of their suppression of the Quakers, Massachusetts and Connecticut forbade that despised sect from establishing their own schools. And Connecticut, in a vain attempt to suppress the "New Light" movement, in 1742 forbade that sect from establishing any of their own schools. Otherwise, the Connecticut authorities reasoned, the New Lights "may tend to train youth in ill principles and practices, and introduce such disorders as may be of fatal consequences to the public peace and weal of this colony."[6] It is hardly a coincidence that the only truly free colony in New England—

---

[4] A. E. Twentyman, "Education; Germany," *Encyclopaedia Britannica*, 14th Ed. (1929), VII, 999–1000.

[5] See Perrin, *op. cit.*

[6] See Merle Curti, *The Social Ideas of American Educators* (New York: Charles Scribner's Sons, 1935).

Rhode Island—was also the one colony in the area devoid of public schooling.

The motivation for public and compulsory schooling after Independence scarcely differed in essentials. Thus, Archibald D. Murphey, the father of the public school system in North Carolina, called for such schools as follows:

> . . . all the children will be taught in them. . . . In these schools the precepts of morality and religion should be inculcated, and habits of subordination and obedience be formed. . . . Their parents know not how to instruct them. . . . The state, in the warmth of her affection and solicitude for their welfare, must take charge of those children, and place them in school where their minds can be enlightened and their hearts can be trained to virtue.[7]

One of the most common uses of compulsory public schooling has been to oppress and cripple national ethnic and linguistic minorities or colonized peoples—to force them to abandon their own language and culture on behalf of the language and culture of the ruling groups. The English in Ireland and Quebec, and nations throughout Central and Eastern Europe and in Asia—all dragooned their national minorities into the public schools run by their masters. One of the most potent stimuli for discontent and rebellion by these oppressed peoples was the desire to rescue their language and heritage from the weapon of public schools wielded by their oppressors. Thus, the laissez-faire liberal Ludwig von Mises has written that, in linguistically mixed countries,

> . . . continued adherence to a policy of compulsory education is utterly incompatible with efforts to establish lasting peace. . . .
>
> The question of which language is to be made the basis of instruction assumes crucial importance. A decision one way or the other can, over the years, determine the nationality of a whole area. The school can alienate children from the nationality to which their parents belong and can be used as a means of oppressing whole nationalities. Whoever controls the schools has the power to injure other nationalities and to benefit his own.

Furthermore, Mises points out, the coercion inherent in rule by one nationality makes it impossible to solve the problem by formally allowing each parent to send his child to a school using a language of his own nationality.

> It is often not possible for an individual—out of regard for his means of livelihood—to declare himself openly for one or another nationality. Under a system of interventionism, it could cost him the patronage of customers belonging to

---

[7] *The Papers of Archibald D. Murphey* (Raleigh, N.C.: University of North Carolina Press, 1914), II, 53–54.

other nationalities or a job with an entrepreneur of a different nationality. . . . If one leaves to the parents the choice of the school to which they wish to send their children, then one exposes them to every conceivable form of political coercion. In all areas of mixed nationality, the school is a political prize of the highest importance. It cannot be deprived of its political character so long as it remains a public and compulsory institution. There is, in fact, only *one* solution: the state, the government, the laws must not in any way concern themselves with schooling or education. Public funds must not be used for such purposes. The rearing and instruction of youth must be left entirely to parents and to private associations and institutions.[8]

In fact, one of the major motivations of the legion of mid-nineteenth-century American "educational reformers" who established the modern public school system was precisely to use it to cripple the cultural and linguistic life of the waves of immigrants into America, and to mould them, as educational reformer Samuel Lewis stated, into "one people." It was the desire of the Anglo-Saxon majority to tame, channel, and restructure the immigrants, and in particular to smash the parochial school system of the Catholics, that formed the major impetus for educational "reform." The New Left critics who perceive the role of the public schools of today in crippling and moulding the minds of ghetto children are only grasping the current embodiment of a long-cherished goal held by the public school Establishment—by the Horace Manns and the Henry Barnards and the Calvin Stowes. It was Mann and Barnard, for example, who urged the use of the schools for indoctrination against the "mobocracy" of the Jacksonian movement. And it was Stowe, author of an admiring tract on the Prussian compulsory school system originally inspired by Martin Luther, who wrote of the schools in unmistakably Lutheran and military terms:

If a regard to the public safety makes it right for a government to compel the citizens to do military duty when the country is invaded, the same reason authorizes the government to compel them to provide for the education of their children. . . . A man has no more right to endanger the state by throwing upon it a family of ignorant and vicious children, than he has to give admission to the spies of an invading army.[9]

Forty years later, Newton Bateman, a leading educator, spoke of the State's "right of eminent domain" over the "minds and souls and bodies"

---

[8]Ludwig von Mises, *The Free and Prosperous Commonwealth* (Princeton, N.J.: D. Van Nostrand Co., 1962), pp. 114–15.

[9]Calvin E. Stowe, *The Prussian System of Public Instruction and its Applicability to the United States* (Cincinnati, 1830), pp. 61ff. On the elitist motivations of the educational reformers, see Michael B. Katz, *The Irony of Early School Reform* (Boston: Beacon Press, 1970).

of the nation's children: Education, he asserted, "cannot be left to the caprices and contingencies of individuals. . . ."[10]

The most ambitious attempt by the public school partisans to maximize their control over the nation's children came in Oregon during the early 1920s. The state of Oregon, unhappy even with allowing private schools certified by the state, passed a law on November 7, 1922, outlawing private schools and compelling all children to attend public school. Here was the culmination of the educationists' dream. At last, all children were to be forced into the "democratizing" mould of uniform education by the state authorities. The law, happily, was declared unconstitutional by the Supreme Court of the United States in 1925 *(Pierce v. Society of Sisters,* June 1, 1925). The Supreme Court declared that "the child is not the mere creature of the State," and asserted that the Oregon law clashed with the "fundamental theory of liberty upon which all governments in this Union repose." The public school fanatics never tried to go that far again. But it is instructive to realize what the forces were that attempted to outlaw all competing private education in the state of Oregon. For the spearheads of the law were *not,* as we might expect, liberal or progressive educators or intellectuals; the spearhead was the Ku Klux Klan, then strong in the northern states, which was eager to crush the Catholic parochial school system, and to force all Catholic and immigrant children into the neo-Protestantizing and "Americanizing" force of the public school. The Klan, it is interesting to note, opined that such a law was necessary for the "preservation of free institutions." It is well to ponder that the much-vaunted "progressive" and "democratic" public school system had its most ardent supporters in the most bigoted byways of American life, among people anxious to stamp out diversity and variety in America.[11]

Uniformity or Diversity?

While current educationists do not go as far as the Ku Klux Klan, it is important to realize that the very *nature* of the public school *requires* the imposition of uniformity and the stamping out of diversity and individuality in education.

For it is in the nature of any governmental bureaucracy to live by a set of rules, and to impose those rules in a uniform and heavy-handed

[10]Quoted in Edward C. Kirkland, *Dream and Thought in the Business Community, 1860–1900* (Chicago: Quadrangle Books, 1964), p. 54.

[11]See Lloyd P. Jorgenson, "The Oregon School Law of 1922: Passage and Sequel," *Catholic Historical Review* (October 1968), pp. 455–460.

manner. If it did not do so, and the bureaucrat were to decide individual cases ad hoc, he would then be accused, and properly so, of not treating each taxpayer and citizen in an equal and uniform manner. He would be accused of discrimination and of fostering special privilege. Furthermore, it is administratively more convenient for the bureaucrat to establish uniform rules throughout his jurisdiction. In contrast to the private, profit-making business, the government bureaucrat is neither interested in efficiency nor in serving his customers to the best of his ability. Having no need to make profits and sheltered from the possibility of suffering losses, the bureaucrat can and does disregard the desires and demands of his consumer-customers. His major interest is in "not making waves," and this he accomplishes by even-handedly applying a uniform set of rules, regardless of how inapplicable they may be in any given case.

The public school bureaucrat, for his part, is faced with a host of crucial and controversial decisions in deciding on the pattern of formal schooling in his area. He must decide: Should schooling be—traditional or progressive? free enterprise or socialistic? competitive or egalitarian? liberal arts or vocational? segregated or integrated? sex education or not? religious or secular? or various shades between these poles. The point is that *whatever* he decides, and even if he decides according to the wishes of the majority of the public, there will always be a substantial number of parents and children who will be totally deprived of the kind of education they desire. If the decision is for traditional discipline in the schools, then the more progressive-minded parents lose out, and vice versa; and the same is true for all the other critical decisions. The more that education becomes public, the more will parents and children be deprived of the education they feel they need. The more that education becomes public, the more will heavy-handed uniformity stamp out the needs and desires of individuals and minorities.

Consequently, the greater the sphere of public as opposed to private education, the greater the scope and intensity of conflict in social life. For if one agency is going to make the decision: sex education or no, traditional or progressive, integrated or segregated, etc., then it becomes particularly important to gain control of the government and to prevent one's adversaries from taking power themselves. Hence, in education as well as in all other activities, the more that government decisions replace private decision-making, the more various groups will be at each others' throats in a desperate race to see to it that the one and only decision in each vital area goes its own way.

Contrast the deprivation and intense social conflict inherent in government decision-making with the state of affairs on the free market. If education were strictly private, then each and every group of parents could and would patronize its own kind of school. A host of diverse schools would spring up to meet the varied structure of educational demands by parents and children. Some schools would be traditional, others progressive. Schools would range through the full traditional-progressive scale; some schools would experiment with egalitarian and gradeless education, others would stress the rigorous learning of subjects and competitive grading; some schools would be secular, others would emphasize various religious creeds; some schools would be libertarian and stress the virtues of free enterprise, others would preach various kinds of socialism.

Let us consider, for example, the structure of the magazine or book publishing industry today, remembering too that magazines and books are themselves an extremely important form of education. The magazine market, being roughly free, contains all manner of magazines to suit a wide variety of tastes and demands by consumers: there are nationwide, all-purpose magazines; there are liberal, conservative, and all manner of ideological journals; there are specialized scholarly publications; and there are a myriad of magazines devoted to special interests and hobbies like bridge, chess, hi-fi, etc. A similar structure appears in the free book market: there are wide-circulation books, books appealing to specialized markets, books of all ideological persuasions. Abolish public schools, and the free, varied, and diverse magazine and book markets would be parallelled by a similar kind of "school market." In contrast, if there were only one magazine for each city or state, think of the battles and conflicts that would rage: Should the magazine be conservative, liberal, or socialist; how much space should it devote to fiction or bridge, etc.? The pressures and conflicts would be intense, and no resolution would be satisfactory, for *any* decision would deprive countless numbers of people of what they want and require. What the libertarian is calling for, then, is not as *outré* as it might at first appear; what he is calling for is a school system as free and varied as most other educational media are today.

To focus again on other educational media, what then would we think of a proposal for the government, federal or state, to use the taxpayers' money to set up a nationwide chain of public magazines or newspapers, and then to compel all people, or all children, to read them? Further, what would we think of the government outlawing all other newspapers and magazines, or at the very least outlawing all newspapers or magazines that do not come up to certain "standards" of what a government commission thinks children ought to read? Such a proposal would surely be regarded with horror throughout the country, yet this is precisely the sort of regime that government has established in the schools. A compulsory public press would rightly be considered an invasion of the basic freedom of the press; is not scholastic freedom at least as important as press freedom? Aren't both vital media for public information and education, for free inquiry and search for the truth? In fact, the suppression of free schooling should be regarded with even greater horror than the suppression of a free press, since here the tender and unformed minds of children are more directly involved.

It is intriguing that at least some public school advocates have recognized the analogy between schooling and the press and have pursued their logic to the latter area. Thus, prominent in Boston politics in the 1780s and 1790s was the arch-Federalist "Essex Junto," a group of leading merchants and lawyers originally hailing from Essex County, Massachusetts. The Essexmen were particularly anxious for an extensive public school system in order to have the youth "taught the proper subordination." Essexman Stephen Higginson frankly declared that "the people must be taught to confide in and revere their rulers." And seeing with firm consistency that newspapers were as important a form of education as formal schooling, another leading Essex merchant and theoretician, Jonathan Jackson, denounced the free press for being necessarily subservient to its readership, and advocated a state-owned newspaper that could be independent of its readers and therefore inculcate the proper virtues into the citizenry.[12]

Professor E. G. West has also offered an instructive analogy between the provision of schooling and of food, surely an industry of at least an equal importance for children as well as adults. West writes:

Protection of a child against starvation or malnutrition is presumably just as important as protection against ignorance. It is difficult to envisage, however, that any government, in its anxiety to see that children have minimum standards of food and clothing, would pass laws for compulsory and universal eating, or that it should entertain measures which lead to increased taxes or rates in order to provide children's food, "free" at local authority kitchens or shops. It is still more difficult to imagine that most people would unquestioningly accept this system, especially where it had developed to the stage that for "administrative reasons" parents were allocated to those shops which happened to be nearest their homes. . . . Yet strange as such hypothetical measures may appear when

---

[12]See David Hackett Fischer, "The Myth of the Essex Junto," *William and Mary Quarterly* (April 1964), pp. 191–235. Also see Murray N. Rothbard, "Economic Thought: Comment," in D. T. Gilchrist, ed., *The Growth of the Seaport Cities, 1790–1825* (Charlottesville, Va.: University Press of Virginia, 1967), pp. 178–79.

applied to the provision of food and clothing they are nevertheless typical of . . . state education. . . .[13]

Several libertarian thinkers, from "left-" and "right"-wing ends of the libertarian spectrum, have delivered trenchant critiques of the totalitarian nature of compulsory public schooling. Thus, left-libertarian British critic Herbert Read:

Mankind is naturally differentiated into many types, and to press all these types into the same mold must inevitably lead to distortions and repressions. Schools should be of many kinds, following different methods and catering for different dispositions. It might be argued that even a totalitarian state must recognize this principle but the truth is that differentiation is an organic process, the spontaneous and roving associations of individuals for particular purposes. . . . The whole structure of education as the natural process we have envisaged, falls to pieces if we attempt to make that structure . . . artificial.[14]

And the great late-nineteenth-century individualist English philosopher Herbert Spencer asked:

For what is meant by saying that a government ought to educate the people? Why should they be educated? What is the education for? Clearly to fit the people for social life—to make them good citizens? And who is to say what are good citizens? The government: there is no other judge. And who is to say how these good citizens may be made? The government: there is no other judge. Hence the proposition is convertible into this—a government ought to mold children into good citizens. . . . It must first form for itself a definite conception of a pattern citizen; and having done this, must elaborate such system of discipline as seems best calculated to produce citizens after that pattern. This system of discipline it is bound to enforce to the uttermost. For if it does otherwise, it allows men to become different from what in its judgment they should become, and therefore fails in that duty it is charged to fulfill.[15]

And the twentieth-century American individualist writer Isabel Paterson declared:

Educational texts are necessarily selective, in subject matter, language, and point of view. Where teaching is conducted by private schools, there will be a considerable variation in different schools; the parents must judge what they want their children taught, by the curriculum offered. . . . Nowhere will there be any inducement to teach the "supremacy of the state as a compulsory philosophy." But every politically controlled educational system will inculcate the doctrine

[13]E. G. West, *Education and the State* (London: Institute of Economic Affairs, 1965), pp. 13–14.
[14]Herbert Read, *The Education of Free Men* (London: Freedom Press, 1944), pp. 27–28.
[15]Herbert Spencer, *Social Statics* (London: John Chapman, 1851), pp. 332–33.

of state supremacy sooner or later, whether as the divine right of kings, or the "will of the people" in "democracy." Once that doctrine has been accepted, it becomes an almost superhuman task to break the stranglehold of the political power over the life of the citizen. It has had his body, property, and mind in its clutches from infancy. An octopus would sooner release its prey.

A tax-supported, compulsory educational system is the complete model of the totalitarian state.[16]

As E. G. West indicated, bureaucratic convenience has invariably led the states to prescribe geographical public school districts, to place one school in each district, and then to force each public school child to attend school in the district closest to his residence. While in a free private school market most children would undoubtedly attend schools near their homes, the present system compels a monopoly of one school per district, and thereby coerces uniformity throughout each area. Children who, for whatever reason, would prefer to attend a school in another district are prohibited from doing so. The result is enforced geographic homogeneity, and it also means that the character of each school is completely dependent on its residential neighborhood. It is then inevitable that public schools, instead of being totally uniform, will be uniform *within* each district, and the composition of pupils, the financing of each school, and the quality of education will come to depend upon the values, the wealth, and the tax base, of each geographical area. The fact that wealthy school districts will have costlier and higher-quality teaching, higher teaching salaries, and better working conditions than the poorer districts, then becomes inevitable. Teachers will regard the better schools as the superior teaching posts, and the better teachers will gravitate to the better school districts, while the poorer ones must remain in the lower-income areas. Hence, the operation of district public schools inevitably results in the negation of the very egalitarian goal which is supposed to be a major aim of the public school system in the first place.

Moreover, if the residential areas are racially segregated, as they often tend to be, the result of a compulsory geographical monopoly is the compulsory racial segregation of the public schools. Those parents who prefer integrated schooling have to come up against the geographical monopoly system. Furthermore, just as some wag has said that nowadays "Whatever isn't prohibited is compulsory," the recent tendency of the public school bureaucrats has not been to institute voluntary busing of children to widen parental discretion, but to swing in the opposite direction and institute compulsory busing and compulsory racial integra-

[16]Isabel Paterson, *The God of the Machine* (New York: G. P. Putnam, 1943), pp. 257–58.

tion of the schools—often resulting in a grotesque transfer of children far from their homes. Once again, the typical government pattern: either compulsory segregation or compulsory integration. The voluntary way—leaving the decisions up to the individual parents involved—cuts across the grain of any State bureaucracy.

It is curious that recent movements for local parental control of public education have sometimes been called "extreme right-wing" and at other times "extreme left-wing," when the libertarian motivation has been precisely the same in either case. Thus, when parents have opposed the compulsory busing of their children to distant schools, the educational Establishment has condemned these movements as "bigoted" and "right-wing." But when, similarly, Negro parents—as in the case of Ocean Hill–Brownsville in New York City—have demanded local parental control of the school system, this drive in its turn has been condemned as "extreme left-wing" and "nihilistic." The most curious part of the affair is that the parents in both cases have failed to recognize their common desire for local parental control, and have themselves condemned the "bigots" or "militants" in the other group. Tragically, neither the local white nor black groups have recognized their common cause against the educational Establishment: against dictatorial control of their children's education by an educational bureaucracy which is trying to ram down their throats a form of schooling which *it* believes must be imposed upon the recalcitrant masses. One crucial task of libertarians is to highlight the common cause of all groups of parents against the State's educational tyranny. Of course, it must also be pointed out that parents can *never* get the State off their educational backs until the public school system is totally abolished and schooling becomes free once more.

The geographical nature of the public school system has also led to a coerced pattern of residential segregation, in income and consequently in race, throughout the country and particularly in the suburbs. As everyone knows, the United States since World War II has seen an expansion of population, not in the inner central cities, but in the surrounding suburban areas. As new and younger families have moved to the suburbs, by far the largest and growing burden of local budgets has been to pay for the public schools, which have to accommodate a young population with a relatively high proportion of children per capita. These schools invariably have been financed from growing property taxation, which largely falls on the suburban residences. This means that the wealthier the suburban family, and the more expensive its home, the greater will be its tax contribution for the local school. Hence, as the burden of school taxes increases steadily, the suburbanites try desperately to encourage an inflow of wealthy residents and expensive homes, and to *discourage* an inflow of poorer citizens. There is, in short, a break-even point of the price of a house beyond which a new family in a new house will more than pay for its children's education in its property taxes. Families in homes below that cost level will not pay enough in property taxes to finance their children's education and hence will throw a greater tax burden on the existing population of the suburb. Realizing this, suburbs have generally adopted rigorous zoning laws which prohibit the erection of housing below a minimum cost level—and thereby freeze out any inflow of poorer citizens. Since the proportion of Negro poor is far greater than white poor, this effectively also bars Negroes from joining the move to the suburbs. And since in recent years there has been an increasing shift of jobs and industry from the central city to the suburbs as well, the result is an increasing pressure of unemployment on the Negroes—a pressure which is bound to intensify as the job shift accelerates. The abolition of the public schools, and therefore of the school burden–property tax linkage, would go a long way toward removing zoning restrictions and ending the suburb as an upper middle-class-white preserve.

Burdens and Subsidies

The very existence of the public school system, furthermore, involves a complex network of coerced levies and subsidies, all of which are difficult to justify on any ethical grounds whatever. In the first place, public schools force those parents who wish to send their children to private schools to shoulder a double burden: they are coerced into subsidizing public school children, and they also have to pay for their own children's education. Only the evident breakdown of public education in the large cities has maintained a flourishing private school system there; in higher education, where the breakdown has not been as stark, private colleges are rapidly being put out of business by the competition from tax-subsidized free tuition and tax-financed higher salaries. Similarly, since public schools must constitutionally be secular, this means that religious parents must be forced to subsidize the secular public schools. While "separation of church and State" is a noble principle—and a subset of the libertarian principle of separating *everything* from the State—it is surely going too far in the other direction to force the religious to subsidize the nonreligious through State coercion.

The existence of the public school also means that unmarried and childless couples are coerced into subsidizing families with children. What is the ethical principle here? And now that population growth is no longer fashionable, consider the anomaly of liberal antipopulationists advocating a public school system that not only subsidizes families with children, but subsidizes them in *proportion to the number of children they have*. We need not subscribe to the full dimensions of the current antipopulation hysteria to question the wisdom of deliberately subsidizing the number of children per family by government action. This means, too, that poor single people and poor childless couples are forced to subsidize wealthy families with children. Does this make any ethical sense at all?

In recent years, the public school forces have promulgated the doctrine that "Every child has a right to an education," and therefore that the taxpayers should be coerced into granting that right. But this concept totally misconstrues the concept of "right." A "right," philosophically, must be something embedded in the nature of man and reality, something that can be preserved and maintained at any time and in any age. The "right" of self-ownership, of defending one's life and property, is clearly that sort of right: it can apply to Neanderthal cavemen, in modern Calcutta, or in the contemporary United States. Such a right is independent of time or place. But a "right to a job" or to "three meals a day" or to "twelve years of schooling" cannot be so guaranteed. Suppose that such things *cannot* exist, as was true in Neanderthal days or in modern Calcutta? To speak of a "right" as something which can only be fulfilled in modern industrial conditions is not to speak of a human, natural right at all. Furthermore, the libertarian "right" of self-ownership does not require the coercion of one set of people to provide such a "right" for another set. *Every* man can enjoy the right of self-ownership, without special coercion upon anyone. But in the case of a "right" to schooling, this can only be provided if other people are coerced into fulfilling it. The "right" to schooling, to a job, three meals, etc., is then not embedded in the nature of man, but requires for its fulfillment the existence of a group of exploited people who are coerced into providing such a "right."

Furthermore, the entire concept of a "right to education" should always be placed in the context that formal schooling is only a small fraction of any person's education in life. If every child really has a "right" to education, then why not a "right" to reading newspapers and magazines, and then why should not the government tax everyone to provide free public magazines for everyone who wishes to obtain them?

Professor Milton Friedman, an economist at the University of Chicago, has performed an important service in separating out money sums from various aspects of government subsidy, in education as well as in other areas. While Friedman unfortunately accepts the view that every child should have his schooling provided by the taxpayers, he points out the *non sequitur* in using this as an argument for public schools: It is quite feasible for the taxpayer to subsidize every child's education without having any public schools whatsoever![17] In Friedman's now famous "voucher plan," the government would give to every parent a voucher entitling him to pay a certain amount of tuition for each child, in *any school* of the parent's choice. The voucher plan would continue the tax-financed provision of education for every child, yet enable the abolition of the vast monopolistic, inefficient, dictatorial public school bureaucracy. The parent could then send his child to any sort of private school that he wished, and the range of choice for every parent and child would then be maximized. The child could then go to any type of school—progressive or traditional, religious or secular, free enterprise or socialistic—the parent desired. The monetary subsidy would then be totally separated from the government's actual provision of schooling through a public school system.

While the Friedman plan would be a great improvement over the present system in permitting a wider range of parental choice and enabling the abolition of the public school system, the libertarian finds many grave problems yet remaining. In the first place, the immorality of coerced subsidy for schooling would still continue in force. Secondly, it is inevitable that the power to subsidize brings with it the power to regulate and control: The government is not about to hand out vouchers for *any* kind of schooling whatever. Clearly, then, the government would only pay vouchers for private schools *certified* as fitting and proper by the State, which means detailed control of the private schools by the government—control over their curriculum, methods, form of financing, etc. The power of the State over private schools, through its power to certify or not to certify for vouchers, will be even greater than it is now.[18]

Since the Oregon case, the public school advocates have never gone so far as to abolish private schools, but these schools remain regulated and confined in numerous ways. Each state, for example, provides that

[17]Milton Friedman, *Capitalism and Freedom* (Chicago: University of Chicago Press, 1962), pp. 85–107.

[18]For a libertarian critique of the voucher scheme, see George Pearson, *Another Look at Education Vouchers* (Wichita, Kan.: Center for Independent Education).

every child must be educated in schools it certifies, which again coerces the schools into a curricular mould desired by the government. In order to "qualify" as certified private schools, all sorts of pointless and costly regulations have to be fulfilled, by the school as well as by the teacher, who must often take a host of meaningless "education" courses in order to be deemed qualified to teach. Many fine private schools are now operating technically "illegally," because they refuse to conform to the often stultifying government requirements. Perhaps the gravest injustice is that, in most states, parents are prohibited from teaching their children themselves, since the state will not agree that they constitute a proper "school." There are a vast number of parents who are more than qualified to teach their children themselves, particularly the elementary grades. Furthermore, they are more qualified than any outside party to judge the abilities and the required pacing of each child, and to gear education to the individual needs and abilities of each child. No formal school, confined to uniform classrooms, can perform that sort of service.

"Free" schools, whether current public schools or future vouchered schools, are of course not *really* free; someone, that is, the taxpayers, must pay for the educational services involved. But with service severed from payment, there tends to be an oversupply of children into the schools (apart from the compulsory attendance laws which have the same effect), and a lack of interest by the child in the educational service for which his family does not have to pay. As a result, a large number of children unsuitable for or uninterested in school who would be better off either at home or working, are dragooned into going to school and into staying there far longer than they should. The resulting mania for mass schooling has led to a mass of discontented and imprisoned children, along with the general view that everyone *has* to finish high school (or even college) to be worthy of being employed. Adding to this pressure has been the hysterical growth of "antidropout" propaganda in the mass media. Part of this development is the fault of business, for employers are quite happy to have their labor force trained, not by the employers or on the job, but at the expense of the hapless taxpayer. How much of the burgeoning of mass public schooling is a means by which employers foist the cost of training their workers upon the taxpayers at large?

One would expect that this training, being without cost to employers, will be highly expensive, inefficient, and far too lengthy. There is in fact increasing evidence that a vast amount of current schooling is not needed for productive employment. As Arthur Stinchcombe asks:

Is there anything that a high school can teach which employers of manual labor would be willing to pay for, if it were learned well? In general, the answer is no. Neither physical abilities nor reliability, the two main variables of interest in employers of manual labor, are much influenced by schooling. Employers concerned with securing reliable workers may require high school diplomas as evidence of good discipline. Otherwise they can train workers better and cheaper than a high school can, on the job.[19]

And, as Professor Banfield points out, most job skills are learned on the job anyway.[20]

The relative uselessness of the public school system for training manual labor is demonstrated by the fascinating work of MIND, a private educational service now operated by the Corn Products Refining Company of Greenwich, Connecticut. MIND deliberately chose high-school dropouts who were unskilled for manual jobs, and in a few short weeks, using intensive training and teaching machines, was able to teach these dropouts basic skills and typing, and place them in corporate jobs. Ten years of public schooling had taught these youngsters less than a few weeks of private, job-oriented training! Allowing youngsters to drop out from enforced dependency into becoming independent and self-supporting could only have immeasurable benefits for the youngsters themselves and for the rest of society.

There is considerable evidence linking compulsory attendance laws with the growing problem of juvenile delinquency, particularly in frustrated older children. Thus, Stinchcombe found that rebellious and delinquent behavior is "largely a reaction to the school itself"; and the British Crowther Committee found that when in 1947 the minimum school-leaving age was raised by the government from fourteen to fifteen, there was an immediate and sharp increase in the delinquencies committed by the newly incarcerated fourteen-year-olds.[21]

Part of the blame for compulsory attendance and mass public schooling must also be laid at the door of the labor unions which, in order to reduce competition from young, adolescent workers, try to force the youth out of the labor market and into educational institutions for as long a time as possible. Thus, both labor unions and employers exert powerful pressure for compulsory schooling and therefore for the nonemployment of most of the nation's youth.

[19]Arthur L. Stinchcombe, *Rebellion in a High School* (Chicago: Quadrangle Books, 1964), p. 180. Quoted in Edward C. Banfield, *The Unheavenly City* (Boston: Little, Brown & Co., 1970), p. 136.
[20]Banfield, *ibid.*, p. 292.
[21]See Banfield, *ibid.*, pp. 149ff.

Higher Education

With the exception of the effects of compulsory attendance laws, the same strictures we have levelled against public schools can also be directed against public higher education, with one noteworthy addition. There is increasing evidence that, certainly in the case of public higher education, the coerced subsidy is largely in the direction of forcing poorer citizens to subsidize the education of the wealthier! There are three basic reasons: the tax structure for schools is not particularly "progressive," i.e., does not tax the wealthier in greater proportion; the kids going to college generally have wealthier parents than the kids who do not; and the kids going to college will, as a result, acquire a higher lifetime working income than those who do not go. Hence a net redistribution of income from the poorer to the richer via the public college! Where is the ethical justification here?

Professors Weisbrod and Hansen have already demonstrated this redistribution effect in their studies of public higher education in Wisconsin and California. They found, for example, that the average family income of Wisconsinites without children in Wisconsin state universities was $6,500 in 1964–1965, while the average family income of families *with* children at the University of Wisconsin was $9,700. In California the respective figures were $7,900 and $12,000, and the subsidy disparity was even greater because the tax structure was much less "progressive" in the latter state. Douglas Windham found a similar redistribution effect from poorer to wealthier in the state of Florida. Hansen and Weisbrod concluded, from their California study:

. . . on the whole, the effect of these subsidies is to promote greater rather than less inequality among people of various social and economic backgrounds by making available substantial subsidies that lower income families are either not eligible for or cannot make use of because of other conditions and constraints associated with their income position.

What we have found true in California—an exceedingly unequal distribution of subsidies provided through public higher education—quite probably is even more true for other states. No state has such an extensive system of local Junior Colleges as does California, and for this reason, no state has such a large percentage of its high school graduates going on to public higher education. As a result we can be rather confident that California has a smaller percentage of its young people receiving a zero subsidy than do other states.[22]

[22]W. Lee Hansen and Burton A. Weisbrod, *Benefits, Costs, and Finance of Public Higher Education* (Chicago: Markham Pub. Co., 1969), p. 78. On Wisconsin and its comparison with California, see W. Lee Hansen, "Income Distribution Effects of Higher Education," *American Economic Review, Papers and Proceedings* (May 1969), pp. 335–40. On the general

Furthermore, the states, in addition to putting private colleges into financial jeopardy by their unfair, tax-subsidized competition, enforce strict controls on private higher education through various regulations. Thus, in New York State, no one can establish any institution called a "college" or "university" unless he posts a $500,000 bond with the state of New York. Clearly, this severely discriminates against small, poorer educational institutions, and effectively keeps them out of higher education. Also, the regional associations of colleges, through their power of "accreditation," can effectively put any college that does not conform to Establishment canons of curriculum or financing out of business. For example, these associations strictly refuse to accredit *any* college, no matter how excellent its instruction, that is proprietary or profit making, rather than trustee-governed. Since proprietary colleges, having a far greater incentive to be efficient and to serve the consumer, will tend to be more successful financially, this discrimination places another heavy economic burden on private higher education. In recent years, the successful Marjorie Webster Junior College in Washington, D.C., was almost put out of business by the refusal of its regional association to grant it accreditation. While one might say that the regional associations are private and not public, they work hand in hand with the federal government, which, for example, refuses to provide the usual scholarships or GI benefits to unaccredited colleges.[23]

Governmental discrimination against proprietary colleges (and other institutions, as well) does not stop at accreditation and scholarships. The entire income tax structure discriminates against them even more severely. By exempting trustee-run organizations from income taxes and by levying heavy taxes on profit-making institutions, the federal and state governments cripple and repress what could be the most efficient and solvent form of private education. The libertarian solution to this inequity, of course, is *not* to place equal burdens on the trustee colleges, but to remove the tax burdens on the proprietary schools. The libertarian ethic is not to impose equal slavery on everyone, but to arrive at equal freedom.

Trustee governance is, in general, a poor way to run any institution. In the first place, in contrast to profit-making firms, partnerships, or corporations, the trustee-run firm is not fully owned by *anyone*. The

---

problem of redistribution from poorer to richer in the modern "welfare state," see Leonard Ross, "The Myth that Things are Getting Better," *New York Review of Books* (Aug. 12, 1971), pp. 7–9.

[23]On the Marjorie Webster Junior College case, see James D. Koerner, "The Case of Marjorie Webster," *The Public Interest* (Summer, 1970), pp. 40–64.

trustees *cannot* make profits from successful operation of the organization, so there is no incentive to be efficient, or to serve the firm's customers properly. As long as the college or other organization does not suffer excessive deficits it can peg along at a low level of performance. Since the trustees cannot make profits by bettering their service to customers, they tend to be lax in their operations. Furthermore, they are hobbled in financial efficiency by the terms of their charters; for example, the trustees of a college are forbidden from saving their institution by converting part of the campus into a commercial enterprise—say a profit-making parking lot.

The short-changing of the customers is aggravated in the case of current trustee-colleges, where the students pay only a small fraction of the cost of their education, the major part being financed by subsidy or endowment. The usual market situation, where the producers sell the product and the consumers pay the full amount, is gone, and the disjunction between service and payment leads to an unsatisfactory state of affairs for everyone. The consumers, for example, feel that the managers are calling the tune. In contrast, as one libertarian remarked at the height of the student riots of the late 1960s, "nobody sits in at Berlitz." Furthermore, the fact that the "consumers" are really the governments, foundations, or alumni who pay the largest share of the bill, means that higher education inevitably gets skewed in the direction of their demands rather than toward the education of students. As Professors Buchanan and Devletoglou state:

The interposition of the government between the universities and their student-consumers has created a situation in which universities cannot meet demand and tap directly resources for satisfying student-consumer preferences. In order to get resources, universities have to compete with other tax-financed activities (armed forces, lower schools, welfare programs, and so forth). In the process, student-consumer demand is neglected, and the resulting student unrest provides the ingredients for the chaos we observe. . . . The mounting dependence on governmental financial support, as this has been translated into the institution of free tuition, may itself be one significant source of current unrest.[24]

The libertarian prescription for our educational mess can, then, be summed up simply: Get the government out of the educational process. The government has attempted to indoctrinate and mould the nation's youth through the public school system, and to mould the future leaders through State operation and control of higher education. Abolition of

[24]James M. Buchanan and Nicos E. Devletoglou, *Academia in Anarchy: An Economic Diagnosis* (New York: Basic Books, 1970), pp. 32–33.

compulsory attendance laws would end the schools' role as prison custodians of the nation's youth, and would free all those better off outside the schools for independence and for productive work. The abolition of the public schools would end the crippling property tax burden and provide a vast range of education to satisfy all the freely exercised needs and demands of our diverse and varied population. The abolition of government schooling would end the unjust coerced subsidy granted to large families, and, often, toward the upper classes and against the poor. The miasma of government, of moulding the youth of America in the direction desired by the State, would be replaced by freely chosen and voluntary actions—in short, by a genuine and truly free education, both in and out of formal schools.

8

Welfare and the Welfare State

Why the Welfare Crisis?

ALMOST EVERYONE, regardless of ideology, agrees that there is something terribly wrong with the accelerating, runaway welfare system in the United States, a system in which an ever-increasing proportion of the population lives as idle, compulsory claimants on the production of the rest of society. A few figures and comparisons will sketch in some of the dimensions of this galloping problem. In 1934, in the middle of the greatest depression in American history, at a nadir of our economic life, total government social welfare expenditures were $5.8 billion, of which direct welfare payments ("public aid") amounted to $2.5 billion. In 1976, after four decades of the greatest boom in American history, at a time when we had reached the status of having the highest standard of living in the history of the world with a relatively low level of unemployment, government social welfare expenditures totalled $331.4 billion, of which direct welfare amounted to $48.9 billion. In short, total social welfare spending rose by the enormous sum of 5614% in these four decades, and direct welfare aid increased by 1856%. Or, put another way, social welfare spending increased by an average of 133.7% per year during this 1934–1976 period, while direct welfare aid increased by 44.2% per annum.

If we concentrate further on direct welfare, we find that spending stayed about the same from 1934 to 1950, and then took off into the stratosphere along with the post–World War II boom. In the years from 1950 to 1976, in fact, welfare aid increased by the huge sum of 84.4% per year.

Now some of these enormous increases can be accounted for by inflation, which diluted the value and purchasing power of the dollar. If we correct all the figures for inflation by putting them in terms of "constant 1958 dollars" (i.e., where each dollar has roughly the same purchasing power that the dollar could command in 1958), then the relevant figures become as follows: 1934—total social welfare spending, $13.7 billion; direct welfare aid, $5.9 billion. In 1976—total social welfare spending, $247.7 billion; direct welfare aid, $36.5 billion.

Even if we correct the figures for inflation, then, social welfare spending by the government rose by the vast amount of 1798%, or 42.8% per year over these forty-two years, while direct welfare aid rose 519%, or 12.4% per annum. Furthermore, if we look at the figures for 1950 and for 1976 for direct welfare aid, corrected for inflation, we find that welfare spending went up, during the intervening boom years, by 1077%, or 41.4% per annum.

If we adjust the figures still further to correct for population growth (total American population was 126 million in 1934, 215 million in 1976), then we still get an almost tenfold increase in total social welfare expenditures (from $108 to $1152 per capita in constant 1958 dollars), and a more than tripling of direct public aid (from $47 in 1934 to $170 per capita in 1976).

A few more comparisons: from 1955 to 1976—years of great prosperity—the total number of people on welfare quintupled, from 2.2 to 11.2 million. From 1952 to 1970, the population of children eighteen years old and younger increased by 42%; the number on welfare, however, increased by 400%. The total population remained static, yet the number of welfare recipients in New York City jumped from 330,000 in 1960 to 1.2 million in 1971. Clearly, a welfare crisis is upon us.[1]

The crisis is shown to be far greater if we include in "welfare payments" all social welfare aids to the poor. Thus, federal "aid to the poor" nearly tripled from 1960 to 1969, leaping from $9.5 billion to $27.7 billion. State and local social welfare expenditures zoomed from $3.3 billion in 1935 to $46 billion, a 1300% increase! Total social welfare expend-

[1]The *Statistical Abstract of the United States,* in its various annual editions, has the basic data for the nation. For the local figures and some earlier analysis, see Henry Hazlitt, *Man vs. the Welfare State* (New Rochelle, N.Y.: Arlington House, 1969), pp. 59–60.

itures for 1969, federal, state, and local, amounted to a staggering $73.7 billion.

Most people think of being on welfare as a process external to the welfare clients themselves, as almost a natural disaster (like a tidal wave or volcanic eruption) that occurs beyond and despite the will of the people on welfare. The usual dictum is that "poverty" is the cause of individuals or families being on welfare. But on whatever criterion one wants to define poverty, on the basis of any chosen income level, it is undeniable that the number of people or families below that "poverty line" has been steadily *decreasing* since the 1930s, not vice versa. Thus, the extent of poverty can scarcely account for the spectacular growth in the welfare clientele.

The solution to the puzzle becomes clear once one realizes that the number of welfare recipients has what is called in economics a "positive supply function"; in other words, that when the *incentives* to go on welfare rise, the welfare rolls will lengthen, and that a similar result will occur if the *disincentives* to go on welfare become weaker. Oddly enough, nobody challenges this finding in any *other* area of the economy. Suppose, for example, that someone (whether the government or a dotty billionaire is not important here) offers an extra $10,000 to everyone who will work in a shoe factory. Clearly, the supply of eager workers in the shoe business will multiply. The same will happen when *dis*incentives are reduced, e.g., if the government promises to relieve every shoe worker from paying income taxes. If we begin to apply the same analysis to welfare clientele as to all other areas of economic life, the answer to the welfare puzzle becomes crystal-clear.

What, then, are the important incentives/disincentives for going on welfare, and how have they been changing? Clearly, an extremely important factor is the relation between the income to be gained on welfare, *as compared with* the income to be earned from productive work. Suppose, to put it simply, that the "average," or going wage (very roughly, the wage open to an "average" worker), in a certain area is $7,000 a year. Suppose, also, that the income to be obtained from welfare is $3,000 a year. This means that the average net gain to be made from working (before taxes) is $4,000 a year. Suppose now that the welfare payments go up to $5,000 (or, alternatively, that the average wage is reduced to $5,000). The differential—the *net* gain to be made from working—has now been cut in half, reduced from $4,000 to $2,000 a year. It stands to reason that the result will be an enormous increase in the welfare rolls (which will increase still more when we consider that the $7,000 workers will have to pay higher taxes in order to support a swollen and virtually nontaxpaying welfare clientele). We would then expect that if—as, of course, has been the case—welfare payment levels have been rising faster than average wages, an increasing number of people will flock to the welfare rolls. This effect will be still greater if we consider that, of course, not everyone earns the "average"; it will be the "marginal" workers, the ones earning below the average, who will flock to the welfare rolls. In our example, if the welfare payment rises to $5,000 a year, what can we expect to happen to the workers making $4,000? $5,000? or even $6,000? The $5,000-a-year man who previously earned a net of $2,000 higher than the welfare client now finds that his differential has been reduced to zero, that he is making no more— even *less* after taxes!—than the welfare client kept in idleness by the state. Is it any wonder that he will begin to flock to the welfare bonanza?

Specifically, during the period between 1952 and 1970, when the welfare rolls quintupled from 2 to 10 million, the average monthly benefit of a welfare family more than doubled, from $82 to $187, an increase of almost 130% at a time when consumer prices were rising by only 50%. Furthermore, in 1968, the Citizens Budget Commission of New York City compared the ten states in the Union having the fastest rise in welfare rolls with the ten states enjoying the lowest rate of growth. The Commission found that the average monthly welfare benefit in the ten fastest-growing states was twice as high as in the ten slowest states. (Monthly welfare payments per person averaged $177 in the former group of states, and only $88 in the latter.)[2]

Another example of the impact of high welfare payments and of their relation to wages available from working was cited by the McCone Commission investigating the Watts riot of 1965. The Commission found that a job at the minimum wage paid about $220 a month, out of which had to come such work-related expenses as clothing and transportation. In contrast, the average welfare family in the area received from $177 to $238 a month, out of which no work-related expenses had to be deducted.[3]

Another powerful factor in swelling the welfare rolls is the increasing

[2]See Roger A. Freeman, "The Wayward Welfare State," *Modern Age* (Fall, 1971), pp. 401–02. In a detailed state-by-state study, Professors Brehm and Saving estimated that over 60% of the number of welfare clients in each state in 1951 could be accounted for by the level of welfare payments in that state; by the end of the '50s, the percentage had increased to over 80%. C. T. Brehm and T. R. Saving, "The Demand for General Assistance Payments," *American Economic Review* (December 1964), pp. 1002–1018.

[3]Governor's Commission on the Los Angeles Riots, *Violence in the City—An End or a Beginning?* December 2, 1965, p. 72; quoted in Edward C. Banfield, *The Unheavenly City* (Boston: Little, Brown & Co., 1970), p. 288.

disappearance of the various sturdy disincentives for going on welfare. The leading disincentive has always been the stigma that every person on the welfare dole used to feel, the stigma of being parasitic and living off production instead of contributing to production. This stigma has been socially removed by the permeating values of modern liberalism; furthermore, the government agencies and social workers themselves have increasingly rolled out the red carpet to welcome and even urge people to get on welfare as quickly as possible. The "classical" view of the social worker was to help people to help themselves, to aid people in achieving and maintaining their independence and to stand on their own feet. For welfare clients, the aim of social workers used to be to help them get *off* the welfare rolls as quickly as possible. But now social workers have the opposite aim: to try to get as many people *on* welfare as possible, to advertise and proclaim their "rights." The result has been a continuing easing of eligibility requirements, a reduction in red tape, and the withering away of the enforcing of residency, work, or even income requirements for being on the dole. Anyone who suggests, however faintly, that welfare recipients should be required to accept employment and get off the dole is considered a reactionary moral leper. And with the old stigma increasingly removed, people now tend more and more to move rapidly toward welfare instead of shrinking from it. Irving Kristol has trenchantly written of the "welfare explosion" of the 1960s:

This "explosion" was created—in part intentionally, in larger part unwittingly by public officials and public employees who were executing public policies as part of a "War on Poverty." And these policies had been advocated and enacted by many of the same people who were subsequently so bewildered by the "welfare explosion." Not surprisingly it took them a while to realize that the problem they were trying to solve was the problem they were creating.

Here . . . are the reasons behind the "welfare explosion" of the 1960s:

1. The number of poor people who are eligible for welfare will increase as one elevates the official definitions of "poverty" and "need." The War on Poverty elevated these official definitions; therefore, an increase in the number of "eligibles" automatically followed.
2. The number of eligible poor who actually apply for welfare will increase as welfare benefits go up—as they did throughout the 1960s. When welfare payments (and associated benefits, such as Medicaid and food stamps) compete with low wages, many poor people will rationally prefer welfare. In New York City today, as in many other large cities, welfare benefits not only compete with low wages; they outstrip them.

3. The reluctance of people actually eligible for welfare to apply for it—a reluctance based on pride or ignorance or fear—will diminish if any organized campaign is instituted to "sign them up." Such a campaign was successfully launched in the 1960s by (a) various community organizations sponsored and financed by the Office of Economic Opportunity, (b) the Welfare Rights Movement, and (c) the social work profession, which was now populated by college graduates who thought it their moral duty to help people get on welfare—instead of, as used to be the case, helping them get off welfare. In addition, the courts cooperated by striking down various legal obstacles (for example, residence requirements). . . .

Somehow, the fact that more poor people are on welfare, receiving more generous payments, does not seem to have made this country a nice place to live—not even for the poor on welfare, whose condition seems not noticeably better than when they were poor and off welfare. Something appears to have gone wrong; a liberal and compassionate social policy has bred all sorts of unanticipated and perverse consequences.[4]

The spirit that used to animate the social work profession was a far different—and a libertarian—one. There were two basic principles: (a) that all relief and welfare payments should be voluntary, by private agencies, rather than by the coercive levy of government; and (b) that the object of giving should be to help the recipient become independent and productive as soon as possible. Of course, in ultimate logic, (b) follows from (a), since no private agency is able to tap the virtually unlimited funds that can be mulcted from the long-suffering taxpayer. Since private aid funds are strictly limited, there is therefore no room for the idea of welfare "rights" as an unlimited and permanent claim on the production of others. As a further corollary of the limitation on funds, the social workers also realized that there was no room for aid to malingerers, those who refused to work, or who used the aid as a racket; hence came the concept of the "deserving" as against the "undeserving" poor. Thus, the nineteenth-century laissez-faire English agency, the Charity Organisation Society, included among the undeserving poor ineligible for aid those who did not need relief, impostors, and the man whose "condition is due to improvidence or thriftlessness, and there is no hope of being able to make him independent of charitable . . . assistance in the future."[5]

English laissez-faire liberalism, even though it generally accepted

[4]Irving Kristol, "Welfare: The best of intentions, the worst of results," *Atlantic Monthly* (August 1971), p. 47.

[5]Charity Organisation Society, *15th Annual Report*, 1883, p. 54; quoted in Charles Loch Mowat, *The Charity Organisation Society*, 1869-1913 (London: Methuen & Co., 1961), p. 35.

"Poor Law" governmental welfare, insisted that there be a strong disincentive effect: not only strict eligibility rules for assistance, but also making the workhouse conditions unpleasant enough to insure that workhouse relief would be a strong deterrent rather than an attractive opportunity. For the "undeserving poor," those responsible for their own fate, abuse of the relief system could only be curbed by "making it as distasteful as possible to the applicants; that is, by insisting (as a general rule) on a labour test or residence in a workhouse."[6]

While a strict deterrent is far better than an open welcome and a preachment about the recipients' "rights," the libertarian position calls for the complete abolition of governmental welfare and reliance on private charitable aid, based as it necessarily will be on helping the "deserving poor" on the road to independence as rapidly as possible. There was, after all, little or no governmental welfare in the United States until the Depression of the 1930s, and yet—in an era of a far lower general standard of living—there was no mass starvation in the streets. A highly successful private welfare program in the present-day is the one conducted by the three-millon-member Mormon Church. This remarkable people, hounded by poverty and persecution, emigrated to Utah and nearby states in the nineteenth century, and by thrift and hard work raised themselves to a general level of prosperity and affluence. Very few Mormons are on welfare; Mormons are taught to be independent, self-reliant, and to shun the public dole. Mormons are devout believers and have therefore successfully internalized these admirable values. Furthermore, the Mormon Church operates an extensive private welfare plan for its members—based, again, on the principle of helping their members toward independence as rapidly as possible.

Note, for example, the following principles from the "Welfare Plan" of the Mormon Church. "Ever since its organization in 1830, the Church has encouraged its members to establish and maintain their economic independence; it has encouraged thrift and fostered the establishment of employment-creating industries; it has stood ready at all times to help needy faithful members." In 1936, the Mormon Church developed a "Church Welfare Plan, . . . a system under which the curse of idleness would be done away with, the evils of a dole abolished, and independence, industry, thrift and self-respect be once more established amongst our people. The aim of the Church is to help the people to help themselves. Work is to be enthroned as the ruling principle of the lives of

[6]Charity Organisation Society, *2nd Annual Report*, 1870, p. 5; quoted in Mowat, *ibid.*, p. 36.

our Church membership."[7] Mormon social workers in the program are instructed to act accordingly: "Faithful to this principle, welfare workers will earnestly teach and urge Church members to be self-sustaining to the full extent of their powers. No true Latter-Day Saint will, while physically able, voluntarily shift from himself the burden of his own support. So long as he can, under the inspiration of the Almighty and with his own labors, he will supply himself with the necessities of life."[8] The immediate objectives of the welfare program are to: "1. Place in gainful employment those who are able to work. 2. Provide employment within the Welfare Program, in so far as possible, for those who cannot be placed in gainful employment. 3. Acquire the means with which to supply the needy, for whom the Church assumes responsibility, with the necessities of life."[9] Insofar as possible, this program is carried on in small, decentralized, grass-roots groups: "Families, neighbors, quorums and wards and other Church organizational units may find it wise and desirable to form small groups for extending mutual help one to the other. Such groups may plant and harvest crops, process foods, store food, clothing and fuel, and carry out other projects for their mutual benefit."[10]

Specifically, the Mormon bishops and priesthood quorums are enjoined to aid their brethren to self-help: "In his temporal administrations the bishop looks at every able-bodied needy person as a purely temporary problem, caring for him until he can help himself. The priesthood quorum must look at its needy member as a continuing problem until not alone his temporal needs are met but his spiritual ones also. As a concrete example—a bishop extends help while the artisan or craftsman is out of work and in want; a priesthood quorum assists in establishing him in work and tries to see that he becomes fully self-supporting and active in his priesthood duties." Concrete rehabilitation activities for needy members enjoined upon the priesthood quorums include: "1. Placing quorum members and members of their families in permanent jobs. In some instances through trade school training, apprenticeships, and in other ways, quorums have assisted their quorum members to qualify themselves for better jobs. 2. Assisting quorum members and their families to get established in businesses of their own. . . . "[11]

[7] *Welfare Plan of the Church of Jesus Christ of Latter-Day Saints* (The General Church Welfare Committee, 1960), p. 1.

[8] *Ibid.*, p. 4.

[9] *Ibid.*, p. 4.

[10] *Ibid.*, p. 5.

[11] *Ibid.*, p. 19.

The prime objective of the Mormon Church is to find jobs for their needy. To this end, "The finding of suitable jobs, under the Welfare Program, is a major responsibility of priesthood quorum members. They and members of the Relief Society should be constantly on the alert for employment opportunities. If every member of the ward welfare committee does well his or her work in this respect, most of the unemployed will be placed in gainful employment at the group or ward level."[12] Other members are rehabilitated as self-employed, the church may aid with a small loan, and the member's priesthood quorum may guarantee repayment from its funds. Those Mormons who cannot be placed in jobs or rehabilitated as self-employed "are to be given, in so far as possible, work at productive labor on Church properties. . . ." The Church is insistent on work by the recipient as far as possible: "It is imperative that people being sustained through the bishops storehouse program work to the extent of their ability, thus earning what they receive. . . . Work of an individual on welfare projects should be considered as temporary rather than permanent employment. It should nevertheless continue so long as assistance is rendered to the individual through the bishops storehouse program. In this way the spiritual welfare of people will be served as their temporal needs are supplied. Feelings of diffidence will be removed. . . ."[13] Failing other work, the bishop may assign welfare recipients to aid individual members who are in need of help, the aided members reimbursing the Church at prevailing wage rates. In general, in return for their assistance, the welfare recipients are expected to make whatever contributions they can to the Church welfare program, either in funds, produce, or by their labor.[14]

Complementary to this comprehensive system of private aid on the principle of fostering independence, the Mormon Church sternly discourages its members from going on public welfare. "It is requested that local Church officers stress the importance of each individual, each family and each Church community becoming self-sustaining and independent of public relief." And: "To seek and accept direct public relief all too often invites the curse of idleness and fosters the other evils of dole. It destroys one's independence, industry, thrift and self-respect."[15]

There is no finer model than the Mormon Church for a private, voluntary, rational, individualistic welfare program. Let government welfare be abolished, and one would expect that numerous such pro-

[12] *Ibid.*, p. 22.
[13] *Ibid.*, p. 25.
[14] *Ibid.*, pp. 25, 46.
[15] *Ibid.*, pp. 46, 48.

grams for rational mutual aid would spring up throughout the country.

The inspiring example of the Mormon Church is a demonstration that the major determinant of who or how many people go on public welfare is their cultural and moral values rather than their level of income. Another example is the group of Albanian-Americans in New York City.

Albanian-Americans are an extremely poor group, and in New York they are almost invariably poor slum dwellers. Statistics are scanty, but their average income is undoubtedly lower than that of the more highly publicized blacks and Puerto Ricans. Yet there is not a single Albanian-American on welfare. Why? Because of their pride and independence. As one of their leaders stated: "Albanians do not beg, and to Albanians, taking welfare is like begging in the street."[16]

A similar case is the decaying, poor, largely Polish-American and almost totally Catholic community of Northside, in Brooklyn, New York. Despite the low incomes, blight, and old and deteriorating housing in the area, there are virtually no welfare recipients in this community of 15,000. Why? Rudolph J. Stobierski, president of the Northside Community Development Council, supplied the answer: "They consider welfare an insult."[17]

In addition to the impact of religion and ethnic differences on values, Professor Banfield, in his brilliant book, *The Unheavenly City*, has demonstrated the importance of what he calls "upper-class" or "lower-class" culture in influencing the values of their members. The definitions of "class" in Banfield are not strictly income or status levels, but they tend to overlap strongly with these more common definitions. His definitions of class center on the different attitudes toward the present and the future: upper- and middle-class members tend to be future-oriented, purposeful, rational, and self-disciplined. Lower-class people, on the other hand, tend to have a strong present-orientation, are capricious, hedonistic, purposeless, and therefore unwilling to pursue a job or a career with any consistency. People with the former values therefore *tend* to have higher incomes and better jobs, and lower-class people *tend* to be poor, jobless, or on welfare. In short, the economic fortunes of people tend over the long run to be their own internal responsibility, rather than to be determined—as liberals always insist—by external factors. Thus, Banfield quotes Daniel Rosenblatt's findings on the lack of interest in medical care due to the "general lack of future orientation" among the urban poor:

[16] *New York Times*, April 13, 1970.
[17] Nadine Brozan, in *New York Times*, February 14, 1972.

For example, regular checkups of automobiles to detect incipient defects are not in the general value system of the urban poor. In similar fashion, household objects are often worn out and discarded rather than repaired at an early stage of disintegration. Installment buying is easily accepted without an awareness of the length of payments.

The body can be seen as simply another class of objects to be worn out but not repaired. Thus, teeth are left without dental care; later there is often small interest in dentures, whether free or not. In any event, false teeth may be little used. Corrective eye examinations, even for those people who wear glasses, are often neglected—regardless of clinic facilities. It is as though the middle class thinks of the body as a machine to be preserved and kept in perfect running order whether through prosthetic devices, rehabilitation, cosmetic surgery, or perpetual treatment, whereas the poor think of the body as having a limited span of utility: to be enjoyed in youth and then, with age and decrepitude, to be suffered and endured stoically.[18]

Banfield points out, furthermore, that lower-class death rates are, and have been for generations, far higher than for upper-class persons. Much of the differential is caused not by poverty or low incomes per se, as much as by the values or culture of the lower-class citizens. Thus, prominent and particularly lower-class causes of death are alcoholism, narcotics addiction, homicide, and venereal disease. Infant mortality has also been far higher among the lower classes, ranging up to two and three times that of upper groups. That this is due to cultural values rather than to income level may be seen in Banfield's comparison of turn-of-the-century Irish immigrants with Russian Jewish immigrants in New York City. The Irish immigrants were, in those days, generally present-minded and "lower class" in attitudes, while the Russian Jews, though living in overcrowded tenements and on an income level probably lower than the Irish, were unusually future-minded, purposive, and "upper class" in their values and attitudes. At the turn of the century, the life expectancy at the age of ten of an Irish immigrant was only thirty-eight years, whereas for the Russian Jewish immigrant it was more than fifty years. Furthermore, whereas in 1911–1916, in a study of seven cities, the infant mortality was over three times as high for the lowest as compared to the highest income groups, the Jewish infant mortality was extremely low.[19]

[18]Daniel Rosenblatt, "Barriers to Medical Care for the Urban Poor," in A. Shostak and W. Gomberg, eds., *New Perspectives on Poverty* (Englewood Cliffs, N.J.: Prentice-Hall, 1965), pp. 72–73; quoted in Banfield, *The Unheavenly City*, pp. 286–87.

[19]See Banfield, *op. cit.*, pp. 210–16, 303. Infant mortality comparisons can be found in O. W. Anderson, "Infant Mortality and Social and Cultural Factors: Historical Trends and Current Patterns," in E. G. Jaco, ed., *Patients, Physicians, and Illness* (New York: The

As in illness or mortality, so in unemployment—which obviously has a close relation to both poverty and welfare. Banfield cites the findings of Professor Michael J. Piore on the essential "unemployability" of many or most of the persistently low-income unemployed. Piore discovered that their difficulty was not so much in finding or learning the skills for steady, well-paying jobs as in the lack of personal fibre in sticking to such jobs. These people are inclined to high absenteeism, leaving their jobs without notice, being insubordinate, and sometimes stealing from the employer.[20] Furthermore, Peter Doeringer's study of the Boston "ghetto" labor market in 1968 found that about 70% of job applicants referred by neighborhood employment centers received job offers—but that over half of these offers were rejected, and of those accepted only about 40% of the new workers kept their jobs for as long as one month. Doeringer concluded: "Much of the ghetto unemployment appears to be a result of work instability rather than job scarcity."[21]

It is highly instructive to compare the descriptions of this common refusal of the lower-class unemployed to engage in steady work by the frostily disapproving Professor Banfield and by the highly approving leftist sociologist Alvin Gouldner. Banfield: "Men accustomed to a street-corner style of life, to living off women on welfare, and to 'hustling' are seldom willing to accept the dull routines of the 'good' job."[22] Pondering the lack of success of welfare workers in luring these men "away from a life of irresponsibility, sensuality, and freewheeling aggression," Gouldner proclaims that they judge the proferred bargain to be unattractive: "Give up promiscuous sex, give up freely expressed aggression, and wild spontaneity . . . and you, or your children, may be admitted to the world of three square meals a day, to a high school or perhaps even a college education, to the world of charge accounts, of secure

---

Free Press, 1958), pp. 10–22; the seven cities study is in R. M. Woodbury, *Causal Factors in Infant Mortality: A Statistical Study Based on Investigation in Eight Cities*, U.S. Children's Bureau Publication #142 (Washington, D.C.: U.S. Govt. Printing Office, 1925), p. 157. On Irish and Jewish life expectancy see James J. Walsh, "Irish Mortality in New York and Pennsylvania," *Studies: An Irish Quarterly Review* (December 1921), p. 632. On the necessity for changing values and life styles in order to reduce infant mortality, see C. V. Willie and W. B. Rothney, "Racial, Ethnic and Income Factors in the Epidemiology of Neonatal Mortality," *American Sociological Review* (August 1962), p. 526.

[20]Michael J. Piore, "Public and Private Responsibilities in On-the-Job Training of Disadvantaged Workers," M.I.T. Dept. of Economics Working Paper #23, June 1968. Cited in Banfield, *op. cit.*, pp. 105, 285.

[21]Peter B. Doeringer, *Ghetto Labor Markets—Problems and Programs*, Harvard Institute of Economic Research, Discussion Paper #33, June 1968, p. 9; quoted in Banfield, *op. cit.*, pp. 112, 285–86.

[22]Banfield, *ibid.*, p. 105. Also p. 112.

jobs and respectability."[23] The interesting point is that from both ends of the ideological spectrum both Banfield and Gouldner agree on the essential nature of this process, despite their contrasting value judgments on it: that much of persistent lower-class unemployment, and hence poverty, is voluntary on the part of the unemployed themselves.

Gouldner's attitude is typical of liberals and leftists in the present day: that it is shameful to try to foist, even noncoercively, "bourgeois" or "middle-class values" on the gloriously spontaneous and "natural" lower-class culture. Fair enough, perhaps; but then don't expect—or call upon—those same hard-working bourgeoisie to be coerced into supporting and subsidizing those very parasitic values of idleness and irresponsibility which they abhor—and which are clearly dysfunctional for the survival of any society. If people wish to be "spontaneous," let them do so on their own time and with their own resources, and let them then take the consequences of this decision, and not use State coercion to force the hard-working and "unspontaneous" to bear those consequences instead. In short, abolish the welfare system.

If the major problem with the lower-class poor is irresponsible present-mindedness, and if it takes the inculcation of "bourgeois" future-minded values to get people off welfare and dependency (*pace* the Mormons), then at the very least these values should be encouraged and not discouraged in society. The left-liberal attitudes of social workers discourage the poor directly by fostering the idea of welfare as a "right" and as a moral claim upon production. Furthermore, the easy availability of the welfare check obviously promotes present-mindedness, unwillingness to work, and irresponsibility among the recipients—thus perpetuating the vicious cycle of poverty-welfare. As Banfield puts it, "there is perhaps no better way to make converts to present-mindedness than to give a generous welfare check to everyone."[24]

Generally, in their attacks on the welfare system conservatives have focussed on the ethical and moral evils of coercively mulcting the taxpayers to support the idle, while the leftist critics have concentrated on the demoralization of the welfare "clients" through their dependency on the largesse of the State and its bureaucracy. Actually, both sets of criticisms are right; there is no contradiction between them. We have seen that voluntary programs such as those of the Mormon Church are keenly alive to this problem. And in fact, earlier laissez-faire critics

[23]Alvin W. Gouldner, "The Secrets of Organizations," in *The Social Welfare Forum,* Proceedings of the National Conference on Social Welfare (New York: Columbia University Press, 1963), p. 175; quoted in Banfield, *op. cit.,* pp. 221–22, 305.

[24]Banfield, *op. cit.,* p. 221.

of the dole were just as concerned with the demoralization as with the coercion over those forced to pay for welfare.

Thus, the nineteenth-century English laissez-faire advocate Thomas Mackay declared that welfare reform "consists in a re-creation and development of the arts of independence." He called "not for more philanthropy, but rather for more respect for the dignity of human life, and more faith in its ability to work out its own salvation." And Mackay poured his scorn on the advocates of greater welfare, on "the vicarious philanthropist who, in a reckless race after a cheap popularity, uses the rate [tax] extorted from his neighbors to multiply the occasions of stumbling set before the . . . crowd who are only too ready to fall into dependence. . . ."[25] Mackay added that the "legal endowment of destitution" implied by the welfare system "introduces a most dangerous and at times demoralising influence into our social arrangements. Its real necessity is by no means proved. Its apparent necessity arises mainly from the fact that the system has created its own dependent population."[26] Elaborating on the theme of dependence, Mackay observed that "the bitterest element in the distress of the poor arises, not from mere poverty, but from the feeling of dependence which must of necessity be an ingredient in every measure of public relief. This feeling cannot be removed, but is rather intensified by liberal measures of public relief."[27]

Mackay concluded that "the only way in which the legislator or the administrator can promote the reduction of pauperism is by abolishing or restricting the legal endowments provided for pauperism. The country can have, there is no doubt of it, exactly as many paupers as it chooses to pay for. Abolish or restrict that endowment . . . and new agencies are called into activity, man's natural capacity for independence, the natural ties of relationship and friendship, and under this head I would include private as distinguished from public charity. . . ."[28]

The Charity Organisation Society, England's leading private charity agency in the late nineteenth century, operated precisely on this principle of aid to foster self-help. As Mowat, the historian of the Society notes: "The C.O.S. embodied an idea of charity which claimed to reconcile the divisions in society, to remove poverty and to produce a happy, self-reliant community. It believed that the most serious aspect of poverty was the degradation of the character of the poor man or woman.

[25]Thomas Mackay, *Methods of Social Reform* (London: John Murray, 1896), p. 13.
[26]*Ibid.*, pp. 38–39.
[27]*Ibid.*, pp. 259–60.
[28]*Ibid.*, pp. 268–69.

Indiscriminate charity only made things worse; it demoralised. True charity demanded friendship, thought, the sort of help that would restore a man's self-respect and his ability to support himself and his family."[29]

Perhaps one of the grimmest consequences of welfare is that it actively discourages self-help by crippling the financial incentive for rehabilitation. It has been estimated that, on the average, every dollar invested by handicapped persons in their own rehabilitation brings them from $10 to $17 in the present value of increased future earnings. But this incentive is crippled by the fact that, by becoming rehabilitated, they will lose their welfare relief, Social Security disability payments, and workmen's compensation. As a result, most of the disabled decide not to invest in their own rehabilitation.[30] Many people, moreover, are by now familiar with the crippling disincentive effects of the Social Security system, which—in glaring contrast to all private insurance funds—cuts off payments if the recipient should be brazen enough to work and earn an income after age 62.

In these days, when most people look askance at population growth, few antipopulationists have focussed on another unfortunate effect of the welfare system: Since welfare families are paid proportionately to the number of their children, the system provides an important subsidy for the production of more children. Furthermore, the people being induced to have more children are precisely those who can afford it least; the result can only be to perpetuate their dependence on welfare, and, in fact, to develop generations who are permanently dependent on the welfare dole.

In recent years, there has been a great deal of agitation for the government to supply day-care centers to care for children of working mothers. Allegedly the market has failed to supply this much needed service.

Since the market is in the business of meeting urgent consumer demands, however, the question to ask is *why* the market seems to have failed in this particular case. The answer is that the government has ringed the supply of day-care service with a network of onerous and costly legal restrictions. In short: while it is perfectly legal to deposit one's children with a friend or relative, no matter who the person is or the condition of his apartment, or to hire a neighbor who will be taking care of one or two children, let the friend or neighbor become

---

[29]Mowat, *op. cit.*, pp. 1–2.

[30]Estelle James, "Review of *The Economics of Vocational Rehabilitation,*" *American Economic Review* (June 1966), p. 642; also see Yale Brozen, "Welfare Without the Welfare State," *The Freeman* (December 1966), pp. 50–51.

a slightly bigger business, and the State cracks down with a vengeance. Thus, the State will generally insist that such day-care centers be licensed and will refuse to grant the license unless registered nurses are in attendance at all times, minimal playground facilities are available, and the facility is of a minimum size. There will be all sorts of other absurd and costly restrictions which the government does not bother to impose on friends, relatives, and neighbors—or, indeed, on mothers themselves. Remove these restrictions, and the market will go to work to meet the demand.

For the past thirteen years the poet Ned O'Gorman has been operating a successful, privately financed day-care center in Harlem on a shoestring, but he is in danger of being put out of business by bureaucratic restrictions imposed by the New York City government. While the city admits the "dedication and effectiveness" of O'Gorman's center, The Storefront, it is threatening fines and ultimately the coercive closing of the center unless he has a state-certified social worker present whenever there are five or more children in attendance. As O'Gorman indignantly remarks:

Why on earth should I be forced to hire someone with a piece of paper that says they've studied social work and are qualified to run a day-care center? If I'm not qualified after thirteen years in Harlem, then who is?[31]

The example of day care demonstrates an important truth about the market: if there seems to be a shortage of supply to meet an evident demand, then look to government as the cause of the problem. Give the market its head, and there will be no shortages of day-care centers, just as there are no shortages of motels, of washing machines, of TV sets, or of any of the other accoutrements of daily living.

Burdens and Subsidies of the Welfare State

Does the modern welfare state really help the poor? The commonly held notion, the idea that has propelled the welfare state and maintained it in being, is that the welfare state redistributes income and wealth from the rich to the poor: the progressive tax system takes money from the rich while numerous welfare and other services distribute the money to the poor. But even liberals, the great advocates and abettors of the welfare state, are beginning to realize that every part and aspect of this idea is merely a cherished myth. Government contracts, notably of the military, funnel tax funds into the pockets of favored corporations

[31]"Poet and Agency at Odds Over His Day-Care Center," *New York Times* (April 17, 1978), p. B2.

and well-paid industrial workers. Minimum wage laws tragically gener-
ate unemployment, especially so among the poorest and least skilled
or educated workers—in the South, among teenage Negroes in the ghet-
toes, and among the vocationally handicapped. Because a minimum
wage, of course, does not guarantee any worker's employment; it only
prohibits, by force of law, anyone from being employed at the wage
which would pay his employer to hire him. It therefore compels unemployment. Economists have demonstrated that raises in the federal minimum wage have created the well-known Negro-white teenage employment gap, and have driven the rate of male Negro teenage unemployment
from an early postwar rate of about 8% to what is now well over 35%—
an unemployment rate among teenage Negroes that is far more catastrophic than the massive general unemployment rate of the 1930s (20–
25%).[32]

We have already seen how State higher education redistributes income
from poorer to wealthier citizens. A host of government licensing restrictions, permeating occupation after occupation, exclude poorer and less
skilled workers from these jobs. It is becoming recognized that urban
renewal programs, supposedly designed to aid the slum housing of the
poor, in fact demolish their housing and force the poor into more
crowded and less available housing, all for the benefit of wealthier subsidized tenants, construction unions, favored real estate developers, and
downtown business interests. Unions, once the pampered favorites of
liberals, are now generally seen to use their governmental privileges
to exclude poorer and minority-group workers. Farm price supports,
jacked ever higher by the federal government, mulct the taxpayers in
order to push food prices higher and higher, thereby injuring particularly the poor consumers and helping—*not* poor farmers, but the wealthy
farmers commanding a large amount of acreage. (Since farmers are paid
per pound or per bushel of product, the support program largely benefits
the wealthy farmers; in fact, since farmers are often paid *not* to produce,
the resulting taking of acreage out of production causes severe unemployment among the poorest segment of the farm population—the farm tenants and farm workers.) Zoning laws in the burgeoning suburbs of the
United States serve to keep out the poorer citizens by legal coercion,
very often Negroes who are attempting to move out of the inner cities
to follow increasing job opportunities in the suburbs. The U.S. Postal

[32]Among numerous studies, see Yale Brozen and Milton Friedman, *The Minimum Wage:
Who Pays?* (Washington, D.C.: Free Society Association, April 1966); and John M. Peterson
and Charles T. Stewart, Jr., *Employment Effects of Minimum Wage Rates* (Washington, D.C.:
American Enterprise Institute, August 1969).

Service charges high monopoly rates on the first-class mail used by the general public in order to subsidize the distribution of newspapers and magazines. The FHA subsidizes the mortgages of well-to-do homeowners. The Federal Bureau of Reclamation subsidizes irrigation water to well-to-do farmers in the West, thereby depriving the urban poor of water and forcing them to pay higher water charges. The Rural Electrification Administration and the Tennessee Valley Authority subsidize electric service to well-to-do farmers, suburbanites, and corporations. As Professor Brozen sardonically observes: "Electricity for poverty-stricken corporations such as the Aluminum Corporation of America and the DuPont Company is subsidized by the tax-free status of the Tennessee Valley Authority (27 percent of the price of electricity goes to pay the taxes imposed on privately operated utilities)."[33] And the government regulation monopolizes and cartelizes much of industry, thereby driving up prices to consumers and restricting production, competitive alternatives, or improvements in products (e.g., railroad regulation, public utility regulation, airline regulation, oil proration laws). Thus, the Civil Aeronautics Board allocates airline routes to favored companies and keeps out and even drives out of business smaller competitors. State and federal oil proration laws provide for absolute maximum limits on crude oil production, thereby driving up oil prices, prices that are further kept up by import restrictions. And government throughout the country grants an absolute monopoly in each area to gas, electric, and telephone companies, thus protecting them from competition, and sets their rates in order to guarantee them a fixed profit. Everywhere and in every area the story is the same: a systematic mulcting of the mass of the population by the "welfare state."[34]

Most people believe that the American tax system basically taxes the rich far more than it taxes the poor and is therefore a method of redistributing income from higher to lower income classes. (There are, of course, many *other* kinds of redistribution, e.g., from the taxpayers to Lockheed or General Dynamics.) But even the federal income tax, which everybody assumes to be "progressive" (taxing the rich far more than the poor, with the middle classes in between), does not really work that way when we take into account other aspects of this tax. For example, the

[33]Brozen, "Welfare Without the Welfare State," pp. 48–49.

[34]In addition to Brozen, *op. cit.*, see Yale Brozen, "The Untruth of the Obvious," *The Freeman* (June 1968), pp. 328–40. See also Yale Brozen, "The Revival of Traditional Liberalism," *New Individualist Review* (Spring, 1965), pp. 3–12; Sam Peltzman, "CAB: Freedom from Competition," *New Individualist Review* (Spring, 1963), pp. 16–23; Martin Anderson, *The Federal Bulldozer* (Cambridge: MIT Press, 1964). An introduction to the oil price story is Hendrik S. Houthakker, "No Use for Controls," *Barrons* (Nov. 8, 1971), pp. 7–8.

Social Security tax is blatantly and starkly "regressive," since it is a soak-the-poor-and-middle-class tax: a person making the base income ($8,000) pays fully as much Social Security tax—and the amount is rising every year—as someone making $1,000,000 a year. Capital gains, mostly accruing to wealthy stockholders and owners of real estate, pay far less than income taxes; private trusts and foundations are tax exempt, and interest earned on state and municipal government bonds is also exempt from the federal income tax. We wind up with the following estimate of what percentage of income is paid, overall, by each "income class" in federal taxes:

1965

Income Classes	Percent of Income Paid in Federal Tax
Under $2,000	19
$2,000–$4,000	16
$4,000–$6,000	17
$6,000–$8,000	17
$8,000–$10,000	18
$10,000–$15,000	19
Over $15,000	32
AVERAGE	22

If federal taxes are scarcely "progressive," the impact of state and local taxes is almost fiercely regressive. Property taxes are (a) proportional, (b) hit only owners of real estate, and (c) depend on the political vagaries of local assessors. Sales and excise taxes hit the poor more than anyone else. The following is the estimate of the percentage of income extracted, overall, by state and local taxes:

1965

Income Classes	Percent of Income Paid in State and Local Taxes
Under $2,000	25
$2,000–$4,000	11
$4,000–$6,000	10
$6,000–$8,000	9
$8,000–$10,000	9
$10,000–$15,000	9
Over $15,000	7
AVERAGE	9

Following are the combined estimates for the total impact of taxation—federal, state, and local—on income classes:

1965

Income Classes	Percent of Income Paid in All Taxes[35]
Under $2,000	44
$2,000–$4,000	27
$4,000–$6,000	27
$6,000–$8,000	26
$8,000–$10,000	27
$10,000–$15,000	27
Over $15,000	38
AVERAGE	31

Still more recent (1968) estimates of the total impact of taxes on all levels of government amply confirm the above, while also showing a far greater relative rise in the three years of the tax burden on the lowest income groups:

1968

Income Classes	Percent of Income Paid in All Taxes[36]
Under $2,000	50
$2,000–$4,000	35
$4,000–$6,000	31
$6,000–$8,000	30
$8,000–$10,000	29
$10,000–$15,000	30
$15,000–$25,000	30
$25,000–$50,000	33
$50,000 and over	45

Many economists try to mitigate the impact of these telltale figures by saying that the people in the "Under $2,000" category, for example, receive more in welfare and other "transfer" payments than they pay out in taxes; but of course this ignores the vital fact that the *same* people

[35]For the estimates, see Joseph A. Pechman, "The Rich, the Poor, and the Taxes They Pay," *Public Interest* (Fall, 1969), p. 33.
[36]R. A. Herriott and H. P. Miller, "The Taxes We Pay," *The Conference Board Record* (May 1971), p. 40.

in each category are *not* the welfare receivers *and* the taxpayers. The latter group is socked heavily in order to subsidize the former. In short, the poor (and the middle class) are taxed in order to pay for the subsidized public housing of *other* poor—*and* middle-income groups. And it is the working poor who are socked a staggering amount to pay for the subsidies of the welfare poor.

There is plenty of income redistribution in this country: to Lockheed, to welfare recipients, and so on and on . . . , but the "rich" are not being taxed to pay for the "poor." The redistribution is *within* income categories; some poor are forced to pay for other poor.

Other tax estimates confirm this chilling picture. The Tax Foundation, for example, estimates that federal, state, and local taxes extract 34% of the overall income of those who make less than $3,000 a year.[37]

The object of this discussion is not, of course, to advocate a "really" progressive income tax structure, a real soaking of the rich, but to point out that the modern welfare state, highly touted as soaking the rich to subsidize the poor, does no such thing. In fact, soaking the rich would have disastrous effects, not just for the rich but for the poor and middle classes themselves. For it is the rich who provide a proportionately greater amount of saving, investment capital, entrepreneurial foresight, and financing of technological innovation that has brought the United States to by far the highest standard of living—for the mass of the people—of any country in history. Soaking the rich would not only be profoundly immoral, it would drastically penalize the very virtues: thrift, business foresight, and investment, that have brought about our remarkable standard of living. It would truly be killing the goose that lays the golden eggs.

What Can Government Do?

What, then, *can* the government do to help the poor? The only correct answer is also the libertarian answer: Get out of the way. Let the government get out of the way of the productive energies of all groups in the population, rich, middle class, and poor alike, and the result will be an enormous increase in the welfare and the standard of living of everyone, and most particularly of the poor who are the ones supposedly helped by the miscalled "welfare state."

[37]See William Chapman, "Study Shows Taxes Hit Poor," *New York Post* (February 10, 1971), p. 46; *U.S. News* (December 9, 1968); Rod Manis, *Poverty: A Libertarian View* (Los Angeles: Rampart College, n.d.); Yale Brozen, "Welfare Without the Welfare State," *op. cit.*

There are four major ways in which the government can get out of the way of the American people. First, it can abolish—or at the very least drastically reduce—the level of all taxation, taxation which cripples productive energies, savings, investment, and technological advance. In fact, the creation of jobs and increase of wage rates resulting from abolishing these taxes would benefit the lower-income groups *more* than anyone else. As Professor Brozen points out: "With less attempt to use state power to compress the inequality in the distribution of income, inequality would diminish more rapidly. Low wage rates would rise more rapidly with a higher rate of saving and capital formation, and inequality would diminish with the rise in income of wage earners."[38] The best way to help the poor is to slash taxes and allow savings, investment, and creation of jobs to proceed unhampered. As Dr. F. A. Harper pointed out years ago, productive investment is the "greatest economic charity." Wrote Harper:

According to one view, sharing a crust of bread is advocated as the method of charity. The other advocates savings and tools for the production of additional loaves of bread, which is the greatest economic charity.

The two views are in conflict because the two methods are mutually exclusive in absorbing one's time and means in all the choices he makes day by day. . . .

The reason for the difference in view really stems from different concepts about the nature of the economic world. The former view stems from the belief that the total of economic goods is a constant. The latter view is built on the belief that expansion in production is possible without any necessary limit.

The difference between the two views is like the difference between a two- and three-dimensional perspective of production. The two-dimensional size is fixed at any instant of time, but the third dimension and therefore the size of the total is expandable without limit by savings and tools. . . .

All the history of mankind denies that there is a fixed total of economic goods. History further reveals that savings and expansion of tools constitute the only way to any appreciable increase.[39]

The libertarian writer Isabel Paterson put the case eloquently:

As between the private philanthropist and the private capitalist acting as such, take the case of the truly needy man, who is not incapacitated, and suppose that the philanthropist gives him food and clothes and shelter—when he has used them, he is just where he was before, except that he may have acquired the habit of dependence. But suppose someone with no benevolent motive what-

[38]Brozen, "Welfare Without the Welfare State," p. 47.

[39]F. A. Harper, "The Greatest Economic Charity," in M. Sennholz, ed., *On Freedom and Free Enterprise* (Princeton, N.J.: D. Van Nostrand, 1956), p. 106.

ever, simply wanting work done for his own reasons, should hire the needy man for a wage. The employer has not done a good deed. Yet the condition of the employed man has actually been changed. What is the vital difference between the two actions?

It is that the unphilanthropic employer has brought the man he employed *back into the production line*, on the great circuit of energy; whereas the philanthropist can only divert energy in such manner that there can be no return into production, and therefore less likelihood of the object of his benefaction finding employment. . . .

If the full role of *sincere* philanthropists were called, from the beginning of time, it would be found that all of them together by their strictly philanthropic activities have never conferred upon humanity one-tenth of the benefit derived from the normally self-interested efforts of Thomas Alva Edison, to say nothing of the greater minds who worked out the scientific principles which Edison applied. Innumerable speculative thinkers, inventors, and organizers, have contributed to the comfort, health, and happiness of their fellow men—because that was not their objective.[40]

Second, and as a corollary to a drastic reduction or abolition of taxation, would come an equivalent reduction in government expenditures. No longer would scarce economic resources be siphoned off into wasteful and unproductive expenditures: into the multibillion dollar space program, public works, the military-industrial complex, or whatever. Instead, these resources would be available to produce goods and services desired by the mass of the consuming population. The outpouring of goods and services would provide new and better goods to the consumers at far lower prices. No longer would we suffer the inefficiencies and the injury to productivity of government subsidies and contracts. Furthermore, the diversion of most of the nation's scientists and engineers to wasteful military and other governmental research and expenditure would be released for peaceful and productive activities and inventions benefitting the nation's consumers.[41]

Third, if the government also cut out the numerous ways in which it taxes the poorer to subsidize the wealthier, such as we have named above (higher education, farm subsidies, irrigation, Lockheed, etc.), this

---

[40]Isabel Paterson, *The God of the Machine* (New York: G. P. Putnam's Sons, 1943), pp. 248–50.

[41]On the massive diversion of scientists and engineers to government in recent years, see H. L. Nieburg, *In the Name of Science* (Chicago: Quadrangle, 1966); on the inefficiencies and misallocations of the military-industrial complex, see Seymour Melman, ed., *The War Economy of the United States* (New York: St. Martin's Press, 1971).

in itself would stop the government's deliberate exactions upon the poor. By ceasing to tax the poorer in order to subsidize the richer, the government would aid the poor by removing its burdens from their productive activity.

Finally, one of the most significant ways in which the government could aid the poor is by removing its own direct roadblocks from their productive energies. Thus, minimum wage laws disemploy the poorest and least productive members of the population. Government privileges to trade unions enable them to keep the poorer and minority-group workers from productive and high-wage employment. And licensing laws, the outlawing of gambling, and other government restrictions prevent the poor from starting small businesses and creating jobs on their own. Thus, the government has everywhere clamped onerous restrictions on peddling, ranging from outright prohibition to heavy license fees. Peddling was the classic path by which immigrants, poor and lacking capital, were able to become entrepreneurs and eventually to become big businessmen. But now this route has been cut off—largely to confer monopoly privileges on each city's retail stores, who fear that they would lose profits if faced with the highly mobile competition of street peddlers.

Typical of how government has frustrated the productive activities of the poor is the case of the neurosurgeon Dr. Thomas Matthew, founder of the black self-help organization NEGRO, which floats bonds to finance its operations. In the mid-1960s, Dr. Matthew, over the opposition of the New York City government, established a successful interracial hospital in the black section of Jamaica, Queens. He soon found, however, that public transportation in Jamaica was so abysmal that transportation service was totally inadequate for the hospital's patients and staff. Finding bus service inadequate, Dr. Matthew purchased a few busses and established a regular bus service in Jamaica, service that was regular, efficient, and successful. The problem was that Dr. Matthew did not have a city license to operate a bus line—that privilege is reserved to inefficient but protected monopolies. The ingenious Dr. Matthew, discovering that the city did not allow any unlicensed busses to charge fares, made his bus service free, except that any riders who wished could buy a 25¢ company bond instead whenever they rode the busses.

So successful was the Matthew bus service that he proceeded to establish another bus line in Harlem; but it was at this point, in early 1968, that the New York City government took fright and cracked down. The government went to court and put both lines out of business for operating without licenses.

A few years later, Dr. Matthew and his colleagues seized an unused

building in Harlem owned by the city government. (The New York
City government is the city's biggest "slumlord," owning as it does a
vast amount of useful buildings abandoned because of nonpayment of
high property taxes and rotting away, rendered useless and uninhab-
itable.) In this building, Dr. Matthew established a low-cost hospital—
at a time of soaring hospital costs and scarcity of hospital space. The
city finally succeeded in putting this hospital, too, out of business, claiming "fire violations." Again and again, in area after area, the role of
government has been to thwart the economic activities of the poor. It
is no wonder that when Dr. Matthew was asked by a white official of
the New York City government how it could best aid Negro self-help
projects, Matthew replied: "Get out of our way, and let us try something."

Another example of how government functions occurred a few years
ago, when the federal and New York City governments loudly proclaimed that they would rehabilitate a group of thirty-seven buildings
in Harlem. But instead of following the usual practice of private industry
and awarding rehabilitation contracts on each house individually, the
government instead awarded one contract on the entire thirty-seven
building package. By doing so, the government made sure that small,
black-owned construction firms would not be able to bid, and so the
prize contract naturally went to a large white-owned company. Still
another example: In 1966, the federal Small Business Administration
proudly proclaimed a program for encouraging new black-owned small
business. But the government put certain key restrictions on its loans.
First, it decided that any borrower must be "at the poverty level." Now
since the very poor are not apt to be setting up their own businesses,
this restriction ruled out many small businesses by owners with moder-
ately low incomes—just the ones likely to be small entrepreneurs. To
top this, the New York SBA added a further restriction: All blacks
seeking such loans must "prove a real need in their community" for
filling a recognizable "economic void"—the need and the void to be
proved to the satisfaction of remote bureaucrats far from the actual
economic scene.[42]

A fascinating gauge of whether or to what extent government is helping or hurting the poor in the "welfare state" is provided by an unpublished study by the Institute for Policy Studies of Washington, D.C.
An inquiry was made on the estimated flow of government money (fed-

---

[42]On the Matthew and Small Business Administration cases, see Jane Jacobs, *The Economy
of Cities* (New York: Random House, 1969), pp. 225–28.

eral and district) *into* the low-income Negro ghetto of Shaw-Cardozo in Washington, D.C., as compared to the *outflow* that the area pays in taxes to the government. In fiscal 1967, the Shaw-Cardozo area had a population of 84,000 (of whom 79,000 were black) with a median family income of $5,600 per year. Total earned personal income for the residents of the area for that year amounted to $126.5 million. The value of total government benefits flowing into the district (ranging from welfare payments to the estimated expenditure on public schools) during fiscal 1967 was estimated at $45.7 million. A generous subsidy, amounting to almost 40% of total Shaw-Cardozo income? Perhaps, but against this we have to offset the total outflow of taxes from Shaw-Cardozo, best estimated at $50.0 million—a net *outflow* from this low-income ghetto of $4.3 million! Can it still be maintained that abolition of the entire massive, unproductive welfare state structure would hurt the poor?[43]

Government could then best help the poor—and the rest of society— by getting out of the way: by removing its vast and crippling network of taxes, subsidies, inefficiencies, and monopoly privileges. As Professor Brozen summed up his analysis of the "welfare state":

The state has typically been a device for producing affluence for a few at the expense of many. The market has produced affluence for many with little cost even to a few. The state has not changed its ways since Roman days of bread and circuses for the masses, even though it now pretends to provide education and medicine as well as free milk and performing arts. It still is the source of monopoly privilege and power for the few behind its facade of providing welfare for the many—welfare which would be more abundant if politicians would not expropriate the means they use to provide the illusion that they care about their constituents.[44]

The Negative Income Tax

Unfortunately, the recent trend—embraced by a wide spectrum of advocates (with unimportant modifications) from President Nixon to Milton Friedman on the right to a large number on the left—is to abolish the current welfare system *not* in the direction of freedom but toward its very opposite. This new trend is the "guaranteed annual income" or "negative income tax," or President Nixon's "Family Assistance Plan." Citing the inefficiencies, inequities, and red tape of the present

---

[43]Data adapted from an unpublished study by Earl F. Mellor, "Public Goods and Services: Costs and Benefits, A Study of the Shaw-Cardozo Area of Washington, D.C." (presented to the Institute for Policy Studies, Washington, D.C., October 31, 1969).

[44]Brozen, "Welfare Without the Welfare State," p. 52.

system, the guaranteed annual income would make the dole easy, "efficient," and automatic: The income tax authorities will pay money each year to families earning below a certain base income—this automatic dole to be financed, of course, by taxing working families making *more* than the base amount. Estimated costs of this seemingly neat and simple scheme are supposed to be only a few billion dollars per year.

But there is an extremely important catch: the costs are estimated *on the assumption* that everyone—the people on the universal dole as well as those financing it—will continue to work to the same extent as before. But this assumption begs the question. For the chief problem is the enormously crippling disincentive effect the guaranteed annual income will have on taxpayer and recipient alike.

The one element that saves the present welfare system from being an utter disaster is precisely the red tape and the stigma involved in going on welfare. The welfare recipient still bears a psychic stigma, even though weakened in recent years, and he still has to face a typically inefficient, impersonal, and tangled bureaucracy. But the guaranteed annual income, *precisely* by making the dole efficient, easy, and automatic, will remove the major obstacles, the major disincentives, to the "supply function" for welfare, and will lead to a massive flocking to the guaranteed dole. Moreover, everyone will now consider the new dole as an automatic "right" rather than as a privilege or gift, and all stigma will be removed.

Suppose, for example, that $4,000 per year is declared the "poverty line," and that everyone earning income below that line receives the difference from Uncle Sam automatically as a result of filling out his income tax return. Those making zero income will receive $4,000 from the government, those making $3,000 will get $1,000, and so on. It seems clear that there will be no real reason for *anyone* making less than $4,000 a year to keep on working. Why should he, when his nonworking neighbor will wind up with the same income as himself? In short, the net income from working will then be zero, and the entire working population below the magic $4,000 line will quit work and flock to its "rightful" dole.

But this is not all; what of the people making either $4,000, or slightly or even moderately above that line? The man making $4,500 a year will soon find that the lazy slob next door who refuses to work will be getting his $4,000 a year from the federal government; his own *net* income from forty hours a week of hard work will be only $500 a year. So he will quit work and go on the negative-tax dole. The same will undoubtedly hold true for those making $5,000 a year, etc.

The baleful process is not over. As all the people making below $4,000 and even considerably above $4,000 leave work and go on the dole, the total dole payments will skyrocket enormously, and they can only be financed by taxing *more* heavily the higher income folk who will continue to work. But then *their* net, after-tax incomes will fall sharply, until many of *them* will quit work and go on the dole too. Let us contemplate the man making $6,000 a year. He is, at the outset, faced with a net income from working of only $2,000, and if he has to pay, let us say, $500 a year to finance the dole of the nonworkers, his net after-tax income will be only $1,500 a year. If he then has to pay *another* $1,000 to finance the rapid expansion of others on the dole, his net income will fall to $500 and he will go on the dole. Thus, the logical conclusion of the guaranteed annual income will be a vicious spiral into disaster, heading toward the logical and impossible goal of virtually no one working, and everyone on the dole.

In addition to all this, there are some important extra considerations. In practice, of course, the dole, once set at $4,000, will not remain there; irresistible pressure by welfare clients and other pressure groups will inexorably raise the base level every year, thereby bringing the vicious spiral and economic disaster that much closer. In practice, too, the guaranteed annual income will *not*, as in the hopes of its conservative advocates, *replace* the existing patchwork welfare system; it will simply be added *on top of* the existing programs. This, for example, is precisely what happened to the states' old-age relief programs. The major talking point of the New Deal's federal Social Security program was that it would efficiently *replace* the then existing patchwork old-age relief programs of the states. In practice, of course, it did no such thing, and old-age relief is far higher now than it was in the 1930s. An ever-rising Social Security structure was simply placed on top of existing programs. In practice, finally, President Nixon's sop to conservatives that able-bodied recipients of the new dole would be forced to work is a patent phony. They would, for one thing, only have to find "suitable" work, and it is the universal experience of state unemployment relief agencies that almost no "suitable" jobs are ever found.[45]

The various schemes for a guaranteed annual income are no genuine

[45]For a brilliant theoretical critique of the guaranteed annual income, negative income tax, and Nixon schemes, see Hazlitt, *Man vs. Welfare State*, pp. 62–100. For a definitive and up-to-date empirical critique of all guaranteed annual income plans and experiments, including President Carter's welfare reform scheme, see Martin Anderson, *Welfare: the Political Economy of Welfare Reform in the United States* (Stanford, Calif.: Hoover Institution, 1978).

replacement for the universally acknowledged evils of the welfare system; they would only plunge us still more deeply into those evils. The only workable solution is the libertarian one: the abolition of the welfare dole in favor of freedom and voluntary action for all persons, rich and poor alike.

9

Inflation and
the Business Cycle:
The Collapse of
the Keynesian Paradigm

UNTIL THE YEARS 1973–1974, the Keynesians who had formed the ruling economic orthodoxy since the late 1930s had been riding high, wide, and handsome.[1] Virtually everyone had accepted the Keynesian view that there is something in the free-market economy that makes it subject to swings of under- and overspending (in practice, the Keynesian concern is almost exclusively with alleged *under*spending), and that hence it is the function of the government to compensate for this market defect. The government was to compensate for this alleged imbalance by manipulating its spending and deficits (in practice, to increase them). Guiding this vital "macroeconomic" function of government, of course, was to be a board of Keynesian economists (the "Council of Economic Advisors"), who would be able to "fine-tune" the economy so as to prevent either inflation or recession, and to regulate the proper amount of total spending so as to insure continuing full employment without inflation.

It was in 1973–1974 that even the Keynesians finally realized that something was very, very wrong with this confident scenario, that it was time to go back in confusion to their drawing boards. For not only

[1]Keynesians are creators of "macroeconomics" and disciples of Lord Keynes, the wealthy and charismatic Cambridge University economist whose *General Theory of Employment, Interest, and Money* (New York: Harcourt Brace, 1936) is the cornerstone of Keynesian economics.

had forty-odd years of Keynesian fine-tuning *not* eliminated a chronic inflation that had set in with World War II, but it was in those years that inflation escalated temporarily into double-digit figures (to about 13% per annum). Not only that, it was also in 1973–1974 that the United States plunged into its deepest and longest recession since the 1930s (it would have been called a "depression" if the term hadn't long since been abandoned as impolitic by economists). This curious phenomenon of a vaunting inflation occurring *at the same time* as a steep recession was simply *not supposed to happen* in the Keynesian view of the world. Economists had always known that *either* the economy is in a boom period, in which case prices are rising, *or else* the economy is in a recession or depression marked by high unemployment, in which case prices are falling. In the boom, the Keynesian government was supposed to "sop up excess purchasing power" by increasing taxes, according to the Keynesian prescription—that is, it was supposed to take spending out of the economy; in the recession, on the other hand, the government was supposed to increase its spending and its deficits, in order to pump spending into the economy. But if the economy should be in an inflation *and* a recession with heavy unemployment *at the same time*, what in the world was government supposed to do? How could it step on the economic accelerator *and* brake at the same time?

As early as the recession of 1958, things had started to work peculiarly; for the first time, in the midst of a recession, consumer goods prices rose, if only slightly. It was a cloud no bigger than a man's hand, and it seemed to give Keynesians little to worry about.

Consumer prices, again, rose in the recession of 1966, but this was such a mild recession that no one worried about that either. The sharp inflation of the recession of 1969–1971, however, was a considerable jolt. But it took the steep recession that began in the midst of the double-digit inflation of 1973–1974 to throw the Keynesian economic establishment into permanent disarray. It made them realize that not only had fine-tuning failed, not only was the supposedly dead and buried cycle still with us, but now the economy was in a state of chronic inflation and getting worse—and it was also subject to continuing bouts of recession: of inflationary recession, or "stagflation." It was not only a new phenomenon, it was one that could not be explained, that could not even *exist*, in the theories of economic orthodoxy.

And the inflation appeared to be getting worse: approximately 1–2% per annum in the Eisenhower years, up to 3–4% during the Kennedy era, to 5–6% in the Johnson administration, then up to about 13% in 1973–1974, and then falling "back" to about 6%, but only under the hammer blows of a steep and prolonged depression (approximately 1973–1976).

There are several things, then, which need almost desperately to be explained: (1) Why the chronic and accelerating inflation? (2) Why an inflation even during deep depressions? And while we are at it, it would be important to explain, if we could, (3) Why the business cycle at all? Why the seemingly unending round of boom and bust?

Fortunately, the answers to these questions are at hand, provided by the tragically neglected "Austrian School" of economics and its theory of the money and business cycle, developed in Austria by Ludwig von Mises and his follower Friedrich A. Hayek and brought to the London School of Economics by Hayek in the early 1930s. Actually, Hayek's Austrian business cycle theory swept the younger economists in Britain precisely because it alone offered a satisfactory explanation of the Great Depression of the 1930s. Such future Keynesian leaders as John R. Hicks, Abba P. Lerner, Lionel Robbins, and Nicholas Kaldor in England, as well as Alvin Hansen in the United States, had been Hayekians only a few years earlier. Then, Keynes's *General Theory* swept the boards after 1936 in a veritable "Keynesian Revolution," which arrogantly proclaimed that no one before it had presumed to offer any explanation whatever of the business cycle or of the Great Depression. It should be emphasized that the Keynesian theory did *not* win out by carefully debating and refuting the Austrian position; on the contrary, as often happens in the history of social science, Keynesianism simply became the new fashion, and the Austrian theory was not refuted but only ignored and forgotten.

For four decades, the Austrian theory was kept alive, unwept, unhonored, and unsung by most of the world of economics: only Mises (at NYU) and Hayek (at Chicago) themselves and a few followers still clung to the theory. Surely it is no accident that the current renaissance of Austrian economics has coincided with the phenomenon of stagflation and its consequent shattering of the Keynesian paradigm for all to see. In 1974 the first conference of Austrian School economists in decades was held at Royalton College in Vermont. Later that year, the economics profession was astounded by the Nobel Prize being awarded to Hayek. Since then, there have been notable Austrian conferences at the University of Hartford, at Windsor Castle in England, and at New York University, with even Hicks and Lerner showing signs of at least partially returning to their own long-neglected position. Regional conferences have been held on the East Coast, on the West Coast, in the Middle West, and in the Southwest. Books are being published in this field, and, perhaps most important, a number of extremely able graduate students and young professors devoted to Austrian economics have emerged and will undoubtedly be contributing a great deal in the future.

Money and Inflation

What, then, does this resurgent Austrian theory have to say about our problem?[2] The first thing to point out is that inflation is not ineluctably built into the economy, nor is it a prerequisite for a growing and thriving world. During most of the nineteenth century (apart from the years of the War of 1812 and the Civil War), prices were falling, *and yet* the economy was growing and industrializing. Falling prices put no damper whatsoever on business or economic prosperity.

Thus, falling prices are apparently the *normal* functioning of a growing market economy. So how is it that the very idea of steadily falling prices is so counter to our experience that it seems a totally unrealistic dreamworld? Why, since World War II, have prices gone up continuously, and even swiftly, in the United States and throughout the world? Before that point, prices had gone up steeply during World War I and World War II; in between, they fell slightly despite the great boom of the 1920s, and then fell steeply during the Great Depression of the 1930s. In short, apart from wartime experiences, the idea of inflation as a peacetime norm really arrived after World War II.

The favorite explanation of inflation is that greedy businessmen persist in putting up prices in order to increase their profits. But surely the quotient of business "greed" has not suddenly taken a great leap forward since World War II. Weren't businesses equally "greedy" in the nineteenth century and up to 1941? So why was there no inflation trend then? Moreover, if businessmen are so avaricious as to jack up prices 10% per year, why do they stop there? Why do they wait; why don't they raise prices by 50%, or double or triple them immediately? *What holds them back?*

A similar flaw rebuts another favorite explanation of inflation: that unions insist on higher wage rates, which in turn leads businessmen

---

[2]A brief introduction to Austrian business cycle theory can be found in Murray N. Rothbard, *Depressions: Their Cause and Cure* (Lansing, Mich.: Constitutional Alliance, March 1969). The theory is set forth and then applied to the Great Depression of 1929–1933, and also used briefly to explain our current stagflation, in Rothbard, *America's Great Depression*, 3rd ed. (Kansas City, Kans.: Sheed and Ward, 1975).

The best source for the Austrian theory of money is still its original work: Ludwig von Mises, *Theory of Money and Credit*, 3rd ed. (Irvington-on Hudson, N.Y.: Foundation for Economic Education, 1971). For an introduction, see Rothbard, *What Has Government Done to Our Money?* 2nd ed. (Los Angeles: Libertarian Publishers, 1974).

to raise prices. Apart from the fact that inflation appeared as long ago as ancient Rome and long before unions arrived on the scene, and apart from the lack of evidence that union wages go up faster than nonunion or that prices of unionized products rise faster than of nonunionized, a similar question arises: Why don't businesses raise their prices *anyway?* What is it that permits them to raise prices by a certain amount, but *not* by more? If unions are that powerful, and businesses that responsive, why don't wages and prices rise by 50%, or 100%, per year? *What holds them back?*

A government-inspired TV propaganda campaign a few years ago got a bit closer to the mark: consumers were blamed for inflation by being too "piggy," by eating and spending too much. We have here at least the beginning of an explanation of what holds businesses or unions back from demanding still higher prices: consumers won't pay them. Coffee prices zoomed upward a few years ago; a year or two later they fell sharply because of consumer resistance—to some extent from a flashy consumer "boycott"—but more importantly from a shift in consumer buying habits away from coffee and toward lower-priced substitutes. So a limit on consumer demand holds them back.

But this pushes the problem one step backward. For if consumer demand, as seems logical, is limited at any given time, how come it keeps going up, year after year, and validating or permitting price and wage increases? And if it can go up by 10%, what keeps it from going up by 50%? In short, what enables consumer demand to keep going up, year after year, and yet keeps it from going up any further?

To go any further in this detective hunt we must analyze the meaning of the term "price." What exactly *is* a price? The price of any given quantity of a product is the amount of money the buyer must spend on it. In short, if someone must spend seven dollars on ten loaves of bread, then the "price" of those ten loaves is seven dollars, or, since we usually express price per unit of product, the price of bread is seventy cents per loaf. So there are two sides to this exchange: the buyer with money and the seller with bread. It should be clear that the interaction of both sides brings about the ruling price in the market. In short, if more bread comes onto the market, the price of bread will be bid down (increased supply lowers the price); while, on the other hand, if the bread buyers have more money in their wallets, the price of bread will be bid higher (increased demand raises the price).

We have now found the crucial element that limits and holds back the amount of consumer demand and hence the price: the amount of money in the consumers' possession. If the money in their pockets increases by 20%, then the limitation on their demand is relaxed by 20%, and, other things remaining equal, prices will tend to rise by 20% as well. We have found the crucial factor: the stock or the supply of money.

If we consider prices across-the-board for the entire economy, then the crucial factor is the total stock or supply of money in the whole economy. In fact, the importance of the money supply in analyzing inflation may be seen in extending our treatment from the bread or coffee market to the overall economy. For *all* prices are determined inversely by the supply of the good and directly by the demand for it. But the supplies of goods are, in general, going up year after year in our still growing economy. So that, from the point of view of the supply side of the equation, most prices should be falling, and we should right now be experiencing a nineteenth-century-style steady fall in prices ("deflation"). If chronic inflation were due to the supply side—to activities by producers such as business firms or unions—then the supply of goods overall would necessarily be *falling*, thereby raising prices. But since the supply of goods is manifestly increasing, the source of inflation must be the demand side—and the dominant factor on the demand side, as we have indicated, is the total supply of money.

And, indeed, if we look at the world past and present, we find that the money supply has been going up at a rapid pace. It rose in the nineteenth century, too, but at a much slower pace, far slower than the increase of goods and services; but, since World War II, the increase in the money supply—both here and abroad—has been much faster than in the supply of goods. Hence, inflation.

The crucial question then becomes who, or what, controls and determines the money supply, and keeps increasing its amount, especially in recent decades? To answer this question, we must first consider how money arises to begin with in the market economy. For money first arises on the market as individuals begin to choose one or several useful commodities to act as a money: the best money-commodities are those that are in high demand; that have a high value per unit-weight; that are durable, so they can be stored a long time, mobile, so they can be moved readily from one place to another, and easily recognizable; and that can be readily divisible into small parts without losing their value. Over the centuries, various markets and societies have chosen a large number of commodities as money: from salt to sugar to cowrie shells to cattle to tobacco down to cigarettes in POW camps during World War II. But over all these centuries, two commodities have always won out in the competitive race to become moneys when they have been available: gold and silver.

Metals always circulate by their weight—a *ton* of iron, a *pound* of copper, etc.—and their prices are reckoned in terms of these units of weight. Gold and silver are no exception. Every one of the modern currency units originated as units of weight of either gold or silver. Thus, the British unit, the "pound sterling," is so named because it originally meant simply *one pound of silver.* (To see how the pound has lost value in the centuries since, we should note that the pound sterling is now worth two-fifths of an *ounce* of silver on the market. This is the effect of British inflation—of the *debasement* of the value of the pound.) The "dollar" was originally a Bohemian coin consisting of an ounce of silver. Later on, the "dollar" came to be defined as one-twentieth of an ounce of gold.

When a society or a country comes to adopt a certain commodity as a money, and its unit of weight then becomes the unit of currency— the unit of reckoning in everyday life—then that country is said to be on that particular commodity "standard." Since markets have universally found gold or silver to be the best standards whenever they are available, the natural course of these economies is to be on the gold or silver standard. In that case, the supply of gold is determined by market forces: by the technological conditions of supply, the prices of other commodities, etc.

From the beginning of market adoption of gold and silver as money, the State has been moving in to seize control of the money-supply function, the function of determining and creating the supply of money in the society. It should be obvious why the State should want to do so: this would mean seizing control over the money supply from the market and turning it over to a group of people in charge of the State apparatus. Why they should want to do so is clear: here would be an alternative to taxation which the victims of a tax always consider onerous.

For now the rulers of the State can simply create their own money and spend it or lend it out to their favorite allies. None of this was easy until the discovery of the art of printing; after that, the State could contrive to change the definition of the "dollar," the "pound," the "mark," etc., from units of weight of gold or silver into simply the *names* for pieces of paper printed by the central government. Then that government could print them costlessly and virtually ad lib, and then spend or lend them out to its heart's content. It took centuries for this complex movement to be completed, but now the stock and the issuance of money is totally in the hands of every central government. The consequences are increasingly visible all around us.

Consider what would happen if the government should approach one group of people—say the Jones family—and say to them: "Here, we give you the absolute and unlimited power to print dollars, to determine the number of dollars in circulation. And you will have an absolute monopoly power: anyone else who presumes to use such power will be jailed for a long, long time as an evil and subversive counterfeiter. We hope you use this power wisely." We can pretty well predict what the Jones family will do with this newfound power. At first, it will use the power slowly and carefully, to pay off its debts, perhaps buy itself a few particularly desired items; but then, habituated to the heady wine of being able to print their own currency, they will begin to use the power to the hilt, to buy luxuries, reward their friends, etc. The result will be continuing and even accelerated increases in the money supply, and therefore continuing and accelerated inflation.

But this is precisely what governments—all governments—*have* done. Except that instead of granting the monopoly power to counterfeit to the Jones or other families, government has "granted" the power to *itself.* Just as the State arrogates to itself a monopoly power over legalized kidnapping and calls it *conscription;* just as it has acquired a monopoly over legalized robbery and calls it *taxation;* so, too, it has acquired the monopoly power to counterfeit and calls it increasing the supply of dollars (or francs, marks, or whatever). Instead of a gold standard, instead of a money that emerges from and whose supply is determined by the free market, we are living under a fiat paper standard. That is, the dollar, franc, etc., are simply pieces of paper with such names stamped upon them, issued at will by the central government—by the State apparatus.

Furthermore, since the interest of a counterfeiter is to print as much money as he can get away with, so too will the State print as much money as *it* can get away with, just as it will employ the power to tax in the same way: to extract as much money as it can without raising too many howls of protest.

Government control of money supply is inherently inflationary, then, for the same reason that *any* system in which a group of people obtains control over the printing of money is bound to be inflationary.

The Federal Reserve and Fractional Reserve Banking

Inflating by simply printing more money, however, is now considered old-fashioned. For one thing, it is too *visible;* with a lot of high-denomination bills floating around, the public might get the troublesome idea that the cause of the unwelcome inflation is the government's printing of all the bills—and the government might be stripped of that power. Instead, governments have come up with a much more complex and sophisticated, and much less visible, means of doing the same thing: of organizing increases in the money supply to give themselves more money to spend and to subsidize favored political groups. The idea was this: instead of stressing the printing of money, retain the paper dollars or marks or francs as the basic money (the "legal tender"), and then pyramid on top of that a mysterious and invisible, but no less potent, "checkbook money," or bank demand deposits. The result is an inflationary engine, controlled by government, which no one but bankers, economists, and government central bankers understands—and designedly so.

First, it must be realized that the entire commercial banking system, in the United States or elsewhere, is under the total control of the central government—a control that the banks welcome, for it permits them to create money. The banks are under the complete control of the central bank—a government institution—a control stemming largely from the central bank's compulsory monopoly over the printing of money. In the United States, the Federal Reserve System performs this central banking function. The Federal Reserve ("the Fed") then permits the commercial banks to pyramid bank demand deposits ("checkbook money") on top of their own "reserves" (deposits at the Fed) by a multiple of approximately 6 : 1. In other words, if bank reserves at the Fed increase by $1 billion, the banks can and do pyramid their deposits by $6 billion— that is, the banks create $6 billion worth of new money.

Why do bank demand deposits constitute the major part of the money supply? Officially, they are not money or legal tender in the way that Federal Reserve Notes are money. But they constitute a promise by a bank that it will redeem its demand deposits in cash (Federal Reserve Notes) anytime that the depositholder (the owner of the "checking account") may desire. The point, of course, is that the banks *don't have* the money; they cannot, since they owe six times their reserves, which are their own checking account at the Fed. The public, however, is induced to trust the banks by the penumbra of soundness and sanctity laid about them by the Federal Reserve System. For the Fed can and does bail out banks in trouble. If the public understood the process and descended in a storm upon the banks demanding their money, the Fed, in a pinch, if it wanted, could always *print* enough money to tide the banks over.

The Fed, then, controls the rate of monetary inflation by adjusting the multiple (6 : 1) of bank money creation, or, more importantly, by determining the total amount of bank reserves. In other words, if the Fed wishes to increase the total money supply by $6 billion, instead of actually printing the $6 billion, it will contrive to increase bank reserves by $1 billion, and then leave it up to the banks to create $6 billion of new checkbook money. The public, meanwhile, is kept ignorant of the process or of its significance.

How do the banks create new deposits? Simply by lending them out in the process of creation. Suppose, for example, that the banks receive the $1 billion of new reserves; the banks will lend out $6 billion and create the new deposits in the course of making these new loans. In short, when the commercial banks lend money to an individual, a business firm, or the government, they are *not* relending existing money that the public laboriously had saved and deposited in their vaults—as the public usually believes. They lend out new demand deposits that they create in the course of the loan—and they are limited only by the "reserve requirements," by the required maximum multiple of deposit to reserves (e.g., 6 : 1). For, after all, they are not printing paper dollars or digging up pieces of gold; they are simply issuing deposit or "checkbook" claims upon themselves for cash—claims which they wouldn't have a prayer of honoring if the public as a whole should ever rise up at once and demand such a settling of their accounts.

How, then, does the Fed contrive to determine (almost always, to *increase*) the total reserves of the commercial banks? It can and does *lend* reserves to the banks, and it does so at an artificially cheap rate (the "rediscount rate"). But still, the banks do not like to be heavily in debt to the Fed, and so the total loans outstanding from the Fed to the banks is never very high. By far the most important route for the Fed's determining of total reserves is little known or understood by the public: the method of "open market purchases." What this simply means is that the Federal Reserve Bank goes out into the open market and buys an asset. Strictly, it doesn't matter what kind of an asset the Fed buys. It could, for example, be a pocket calculator for twenty dollars. Suppose that the Fed buys a pocket calculator from XYZ Electronics for twenty dollars. The Fed acquires a calculator; but the important point for our purposes is that XYZ Electronics acquires a check for twenty dollars from the Federal Reserve Bank. Now, the Fed is not open to checking accounts from private citizens, only from banks and the federal government itself. XYZ Electronics, therefore, can only do one thing with its twenty-dollar check: deposit it at its own bank, say the Acme Bank. At this point, another transaction takes place: XYZ gets an increase of twenty dollars in its checking account, in its "demand deposits." In return, Acme Bank gets a check, made over to itself, from the Federal Reserve Bank.

Now, the first thing that has happened is that XYZ's money stock has gone up by twenty dollars—its newly increased account at the Acme Bank—and nobody else's money stock has changed at all. So, at the end of this initial phase—phase I—the money supply has increased by twenty dollars, the same amount as the Fed's purchase of an asset. If one asks, where did the Fed get the twenty dollars to buy the calculator, then the answer is: it created the twenty dollars *out of thin air* by simply writing out a check upon itself. No one, neither the Fed nor anyone else, *had* the twenty dollars before it was created in the process of the Fed's expenditure.

But this is not all. For now the Acme Bank, to its delight, finds it has a check on the Federal Reserve. It rushes to the Fed, deposits it, and acquires an increase of $20 in its reserves, that is, in its "demand deposits with the Fed." Now that the banking system has an increase in $20, it can and does expand credit, that is, create more demand deposits in the form of loans to business (or to consumers or government), until the total increase in checkbook money is $120. At the end of phase II, then, we have an increase of $20 in bank reserves generated by Fed purchase of a calculator for that amount, an increase in $120 in bank demand deposits, and an increase of $100 in bank loans to business or others. The total money supply has increased by $120, of which $100 was created by the banks in the course of lending out checkbook money to business, and $20 was created by the Fed in the course of buying the calculator.

In practice, of course, the Fed does not spend much of its time buying haphazard assets. Its purchases of assets are so huge in order to inflate the economy that it must settle on a regular, highly liquid asset. In practice, this means purchases of U.S. government bonds and other U.S. government securities. The U.S. government bond market is huge and highly liquid, and the Fed does not have to get into the political conflicts that would be involved in figuring out which private stocks or bonds to purchase. For the government, this process also has the happy consequence of helping to prop up the government security market, and keep up the price of government bonds.

Suppose, however, that some bank, perhaps under the pressure of its depositors, might have to cash in some of its checking account reserves in order to acquire hard currency. What would happen to the Fed then, since its checks had created new bank reserves out of thin air? Wouldn't it be forced to go bankrupt or the equivalent? No, because the Fed has a monopoly on the printing of cash, and it could—and would— simply redeem its demand deposit by printing whatever Federal Reserve Notes are needed. In short, if a bank came to the Fed and demanded $20 in cash for its reserve—or, indeed, if it demanded $20 million—all the Fed would have to do is print that amount and pay it out. As we can see, being able to print its own money places the Fed in a uniquely enviable position.

So here we have, at long last, the key to the mystery of the modern inflationary process. It is a process of continually expanding the money supply through continuing Fed purchases of government securities on the open market. Let the Fed wish to increase the money supply by $6 billion, and it will purchase government securities on the open market to a total of $1 billion (if the money multiplier of demand deposits/ reserves is 6 : 1), and the goal will be speedily accomplished. In fact, week after week, even as these lines are being read, the Fed goes into the open market in New York and purchases whatever amount of government bonds it has decided upon, and thereby helps decide upon the amount of monetary inflation.

The monetary history of this century has been one of repeated loosening of restraints on the State's propensity to inflate, the removal of one check after another until now the government is able to inflate the money supply, and therefore prices, at will. In 1913, the Federal Reserve System was created to enable this sophisticated pyramiding process to take place. The new system permitted a large expansion of the money supply, and of inflation to pay for war expenditures in World War I. In 1933, another fateful step was taken: the United States government took the country off the gold standard, that is, dollars, while still legally defined in terms of a weight of gold, were no longer redeemable in gold. In short, before 1933, there was an important shackle upon the Fed's ability to inflate and expand the money supply: Federal Reserve Notes themselves were payable in the equivalent weight of gold.

There is, of course, a crucial difference between gold and Federal Reserve Notes. The government cannot create new gold at will. Gold has to be dug, in a costly process, out of the ground. But Federal Reserve Notes can be issued at will, at virtually zero cost in resources. In 1933, the United States government removed the gold restraint on its inflationary potential by shifting to fiat money: to making the paper dollar itself the standard of money, with government the monopoly supplier of dollars. It was going off the gold standard that paved the way for the mighty U.S. money and price inflation during and after World War II.

But there was still one fly in the inflationary ointment, one restraint left on the U.S. government's propensity for inflation. While the United States had gone off gold domestically, it was still pledged to redeem any paper dollars (and ultimately bank dollars) held by foreign governments in gold should they desire to do so. We were, in short, still on a restricted and aborted form of gold standard *internationally*. Hence, as the United States inflated the money supply and prices in the 1950s and 1960s, the dollars and dollar claims (in paper and checkbook money) piled up in the hands of European governments. After a great deal of economic finagling and political arm-twisting to induce foreign governments not to exercise their right to redeem dollars in gold, the United States, in August 1971, declared national bankruptcy by repudiating its solemn contractual obligations and "closing the gold window." It is no coincidence that this tossing off of the last vestige of gold restraint upon the governments of the world was followed by the double-digit inflation of 1973–1974, and by similar inflation in the rest of the world.

We have now explained the chronic and worsening inflation in the contemporary world and in the United States: the unfortunate product of a continuing shift in this century from gold to government-issued paper as the standard money, and of the development of central banking and the pyramiding of checkbook money on top of inflated paper currency. Both interrelated developments amount to one thing: the seizure of control over the money supply by government.

If we have explained the problem of inflation, we have not yet examined the problem of the business cycle, of recessions, and of inflationary recession or stagflation. Why the business cycle, and why the new mysterious phenomenon of stagflation?

Bank Credit and the Business Cycle

The business cycle arrived in the Western world in the latter part of the eighteenth century. It was a curious phenomenon, because there seemed to be no reason for it, and indeed it had not existed before. The business cycle consisted of a regularly recurring (though not strictly periodical) series of booms and busts, of inflationary periods marked by increased business activity, higher employment, and higher prices followed sharply by recessions or depressions marked by declining business activity, higher unemployment, and price declines; and then, after a term of such recession, recovery takes place and the boom phase begins again.

A priori, there is no reason to expect this sort of cyclical pattern of economic activity. There will be cyclical waves in specific types of activity, of course; thus, the cycle of the seven-year locust will cause a seven-year cycle in locust-fighting activity, in the production of antilocust sprays and equipment, etc. But there is no reason to expect boom-bust cycles in the overall economy. In fact, there is reason to expect just the opposite; for usually the free market works smoothly and efficiently, and especially with no massive cluster of error such as becomes evident when boom turns suddenly to bust and severe losses are incurred. And indeed, before the late eighteenth century there were no such overall cycles. Generally, business went along smoothly and evenly until a sudden interruption occurred: a wheat famine would cause a collapse in an agricultural country; the king would seize most of the money in the hands of financiers, causing a sudden depression; a war would disrupt trading patterns. In each of these cases, there was a specific blow to trade brought about by an easily identifiable, one-shot cause, with no need to search further for explanation.

So why the new phenomenon of the business cycle? It was seen that the cycle occurred in the most economically advanced areas of each country: in the port cities, in the areas engaged in trade with the most advanced world centers of production and activity. Two different and vitally important phenomena began to emerge on a significant scale in Western Europe during this period, precisely in the most advanced centers of production and trade: industrialization and commercial banking. The commercial banking was the same sort of "fractional reserve" banking we have analyzed above, with London the site of the world's first central bank, the Bank of England, which originated at the turn of the eighteenth century. By the nineteenth century, in the new discipline of economics and among financial writers and commentators, two types of theories began to emerge in an attempt to explain the new and unwelcome phenomenon: those focussing the blame on the existence of industry, and those centering upon the banking system. The former, in sum, saw the responsibility for the business cycle to lie deep within the free-market economy—and it was easy for such economists to call either for the abolition of the market (e.g., Karl Marx) or for its drastic control and regulation by the government in order to alleviate the cycle (e.g., Lord Keynes). On the other hand, those economists who saw the fault to lie in the fractional reserve banking system placed the blame outside the market economy and onto an area—money and banking—which even English classical liberalism had never taken away from tight government control. Even in the nineteenth century, then, blaming the banks meant essentially blaming government for the boom-bust cycle.

We cannot go into details here on the numerous fallacies of the schools of thought that blame the market economy for the cycles; suffice it to say that these theories cannot explain the rise in prices in the boom or the fall in the recession, or the massive cluster of error that emerges suddenly in the form of severe losses when the boom turns to bust.

The first economists to develop a cycle theory centering on the money and banking system were the early nineteenth-century English classical economist David Ricardo and his followers, who developed the "monetary theory" of the business cycle.[3] The Ricardian theory went somewhat as follows: the fractional-reserve banks, spurred and controlled by the government and its central bank, expand credit. As credit is expanded and pyramided on top of paper money and gold, the money supply (in the form of bank deposits or, in that historical period, bank notes) expands. The expansion of the money supply raises prices and sets the inflationary boom into motion. As the boom continues, fueled by the pyramiding of bank notes and deposits on top of gold, domestic prices also increase. But this means that domestic prices will be higher, and still higher, than the prices of imported goods, so that imports will increase and exports to foreign lands will decline. A deficit in the balance of payments will emerge and widen, and it will have to be paid for by gold flowing out of the inflating country and into the hard-money countries. But as gold flows out, the expanding money and banking pyramid will become increasingly top-heavy, and the banks will find themselves in increasing danger of going bankrupt. Finally, the government and banks will have to stop their expansion, and, to save themselves, the banks will have to contract their bank loans and checkbook money.

The sudden shift from bank credit expansion to contraction reverses the economic picture and bust quickly follows boom. The banks must pull in their horns, and businesses and economic activity suffer as the pressure mounts for debt repayment and contraction. The fall in the supply of money, in turn, leads to a general fall in prices ("deflation"). The recession or depression phase has arrived. However, as the money supply and prices fall, goods again become more competitive with foreign products and the balance of payments reverses itself, with a surplus replacing the deficit. Gold flows into the country, and, as bank notes and deposits contract on top of an expanding gold base, the condition of the banks becomes much sounder, and recovery gets under way.

The Ricardian theory had several notable features: It accounted for the behavior of prices by focussing on changes in the supply of bank

[3]For the analysis of the remainder of this chapter, see Rothbard, *Depressions: Their Cause and Cure*, pp. 13–26.

money (which indeed always increased in booms and declined in busts). It also accounted for the behavior of the balance of payments. And, moreover, it linked the boom and the bust, so that the bust was seen to be the consequence of the preceding boom. And not only the consequence, but the salutary means of adjusting the economy to the unwise intervention that created the inflationary boom.

In short, for the first time, the bust was seen to be neither a visitation from hell nor a catastrophe generated by the inner workings of the industrialized market economy. The Ricardians realized that the major evil was the preceding inflationary boom caused by government intervention in the money and banking system, and that the recession, unwelcome though its symptoms may be, is really the necessary adjustment process by which that interventionary boom gets washed out of the economic system. The depression is the process by which the market economy adjusts, throws off the excesses and distortions of the inflationary boom, and reestablishes a sound economic condition. The depression is the unpleasant but necessary reaction to the distortions and excesses of the previous boom.

Why, then, does the business cycle recur? Why does the next boom-and-bust cycle always begin? To answer that, we have to understand the motivations of the banks and the government. The commercial banks live and profit by expanding credit and by creating a new money supply; so they are naturally inclined to do so, "to monetize credit," if they can. The government also wishes to inflate, both to expand its own revenue (either by printing money or so that the banking system can finance government deficits) and to subsidize favored economic and political groups through a boom and cheap credit. So we know why the initial boom began. The government and the banks had to retreat when disaster threatened and the crisis point had arrived. But as gold flows into the country, the condition of the banks becomes sounder. And when the banks have pretty well recovered, they are then in the confident position to resume their natural tendency of inflating the supply of money and credit. And so the *next* boom proceeds on its way, sowing the seeds for the *next* inevitable bust.

Thus, the Ricardian theory also explained the continuing recurrence of the business cycle. But two things it did not explain. First, and most important, it did not explain the massive cluster of error that businessmen are suddenly seen to have made when the crisis hits and bust follows boom. For businessmen are trained to be successful forecasters, and it is not like them to make a sudden cluster of grave error that forces them to experience widespread and severe losses. Second, another important feature of every business cycle has been the fact that both booms and busts have been much more severe in the "capital goods industries" (the industries making machines, equipment, plant or industrial raw materials) than in consumer goods industries. And the Ricardian theory had no way of explaining this feature of the cycle.

The Austrian, or Misesian, theory of the business cycle built on the Ricardian analysis and developed its own "monetary overinvestment" or, more strictly, "monetary malinvestment" theory of the business cycle. The Austrian theory was able to explain not only the phenomena explicated by the Ricardians, but also the cluster of error and the greater intensity of capital goods' cycles. And, as we shall see, it is the only one that can comprehend the modern phenomenon of stagflation.

Mises begins as did the Ricardians: government and its central bank stimulate bank credit expansion by purchasing assets and thereby increasing bank reserves. The banks proceed to expand credit and hence the nation's money supply in the form of checking deposits (private bank notes having virtually disappeared). As with the Ricardians, Mises sees that this expansion of bank money drives up prices and causes inflation.

But, as Mises pointed out, the Ricardians understated the unfortunate consequences of bank credit inflation. For something even more sinister is at work. Bank credit expansion not only raises prices, it also artificially lowers the rate of interest, and thereby sends misleading signals to businessmen, causing them to make unsound and uneconomic investments.

For, on the free and unhampered market, the interest rate on loans is determined solely by the "time preferences" of all the individuals that make up the market economy. For the essence of any loan is that a "present good" (money which can be used at present) is being exchanged for a "future good" (an IOU which can be used at some point in the future). Since people always prefer having money right now to the present *prospect* of getting the same amount of money at some point in the future, present goods always command a premium over future goods in the market. That premium, or "agio," is the interest rate, and its height will vary according to the degree to which people prefer the present to the future, i.e., the degree of their time preferences.

People's time preferences also determine the extent to which people will save and invest for future use, as compared to how much they will consume now. If people's time preferences should fall, i.e., if their degree of preference for present over future declines, then people will tend to consume less now and save and invest more; at the same time, and for the same reason, the rate of interest, the rate of time-discount, will also fall. Economic growth comes about largely as the result of falling rates of time preference, which bring about an increase in the proportion of saving and investment to consumption, as well as a falling rate of interest.

But what happens when the rate of interest falls *not* because of voluntary lower time preferences and higher savings on the part of the public, but from government interference that promotes the expansion of bank credit and bank money? For the new checkbook money created in the course of bank loans to business will come onto the market as a supplier of loans, and will therefore, at least initially, lower the rate of interest. What happens, in other words, when the rate of interest falls artificially, due to intervention, rather than naturally, from changes in the valuations and preferences of the consuming public?

What happens is trouble. For businessmen, seeing the rate of interest fall, will react as they always must to such a change of market signals: they will invest more in capital goods. Investments, particularly in lengthy and time-consuming projects, which *previously* looked unprofitable, now seem profitable because of the fall in the interest charge. In short, businessmen react as they would have if savings had *genuinely* increased: they move to invest those supposed savings. They expand their investment in durable equipment, in capital goods, in industrial raw material, and in construction, as compared with their direct production of consumer goods.

Thus, businesses happily borrow the newly expanded bank money that is coming to them at cheaper rates; they use the money to invest in capital goods, and eventually this money gets paid out in higher wages to workers in the capital goods industries. The increased business demand bids up labor costs, but businesses think they will be able to pay these higher costs because they have been fooled by the government-and-bank intervention in the loan market and by its vitally important tampering with the interest-rate signal of the marketplace—the signal that determines how many resources will be devoted to the production of capital goods and how many to consumer goods.

Problems surface when the workers begin to spend the new bank money that they have received in the form of higher wages. For the time preferences of the public have not *really* gotten lower; the public doesn't *want* to save more than it has. So the workers set about to consume most of their new income, in short, to reestablish their old consumer/saving proportions. This means that they now redirect spending in the economy back to the consumer goods industries, and that they don't save and invest enough to buy the newly produced machines, capital equipment, industrial raw materials, etc. This lack of enough saving-and-investment to buy all the new capital goods at expected and existing prices reveals itself as a sudden, sharp depression in the capital goods industries. For once the consumers reestablish their desired consumption/investment proportions, it is thus revealed that business had invested too much in capital goods (hence the term *"monetary overinvestment theory"*), and had also underinvested in consumer goods. Business had been seduced by the governmental tampering and artificial lowering of the rate of interest, and acted as if more savings were available to invest than were really there. As soon as the new bank money filtered through the system and the consumers reestablish their old time-preference proportions, it became clear that there were not enough savings to buy all the producers' goods, and that business had misinvested the limited savings available ("monetary malinvestment theory"). Business had overinvested in capital goods and underinvested in consumer goods.

The inflationary boom thus leads to distortions of the pricing and production system. Prices of labor, raw materials, and machines in the capital goods industries are bid up too high during the boom to be profitable once the consumers are able to reassert their old consumption/investment preferences. The "depression" is thus seen—even more than in the Ricardian theory—as the necessary and healthy period in which the market economy sloughs off and liquidates the unsound, uneconomic investments of the boom, and reestablishes those proportions between consumption and investment that are truly desired by the consumers. The depression is the painful but necessary process by which the free market rids itself of the excesses and errors of the boom and reestablishes the market economy in its function of efficient service to the mass of consumers. Since the prices of factors of production (land, labor, machines, raw materials) have been bid too high in the capital goods industries during the boom, this means that these prices must be allowed to fall in the recession until proper market proportions of prices and production are restored.

Put another way, the inflationary boom will not only increase prices in general, it will also distort relative prices, will distort relations of one type of price to another. In brief, inflationary credit expansion will raise all prices; but prices and wages in the capital goods industries will go up faster than the prices of consumer goods industries. In short, the boom will be more intense in the capital goods than in the consumer goods industries. On the other hand, the essence of the depression adjustment period will be to lower prices and wages in the capital goods industries relative to consumer goods, in order to induce resources to move back from the swollen capital goods to the deprived consumer goods industries. All prices will fall because of the contraction of bank credit, but prices and wages in capital goods will fall more sharply than in consumer goods. In short, both the boom and the bust will be more intense in the capital than in the consumer goods industries. Hence, we have explained the greater intensity of business cycles in the former type of industry.

There seems to be a flaw in the theory, however; for, since workers receive the increased money in the form of higher wages fairly rapidly, and then begin to reassert their desired consumer/investment proportions, how is it that booms go on for years without facing retribution: without having their unsound investments revealed or their errors caused by bank tampering with market signals made evident? In short, why does it take so long for the depression adjustment process to begin its work? The answer is that the booms would indeed be very short-lived (say, a few months) *if* the bank credit expansion and the subsequent pushing of interest rates below the free-market level were just a one-shot affair. But the crucial point is that the credit expansion is *not* one shot. It proceeds on and on, never giving the consumers the chance to reestablish their preferred proportions of consumption and saving, never allowing the rise in cost in the capital goods industries to catch up to the inflationary rise in prices. Like the repeated doping of a horse, the boom is kept on its way and ahead of its inevitable comeuppance by repeated and accelerating doses of the stimulant of bank credit. It is only when bank credit expansion must finally stop or sharply slow down, either because the banks are getting shaky or because the public is getting restive at the continuing inflation, that retribution finally catches up with the boom. As soon as credit expansion stops, the piper must be paid, and the inevitable readjustments must liquidate the unsound over-investments of the boom and redirect the economy more toward consumer goods production. And, of course, the longer the boom is kept going, the greater the malinvestments that must be liquidated, and the more harrowing the readjustments that must be made.

Thus, the Austrian theory accounts for the massive cluster of error (overinvestments in capital goods industries suddenly revealed as such by the stopping of the artificial stimulant of credit expansion) and for the greater intensity of boom and bust in the capital goods than in the consumer goods industries. Its explanation for the recurrence, for the inauguration of the next boom, is similar to the Ricardian; once the liquidations and bankruptcies are undergone, and the price and production adjustments completed, the economy and the banks begin to recover, and the banks can set themselves to return to their natural and desired course of credit expansion.

What of the Austrian explanation—the only proferred explanation—of stagflation? How is it that, in recent recessions, prices continue to go up? We must amend this first by pointing out that it is particularly *consumer goods* prices that continue to rise during recessions, and that confound the public by giving them the worst of both worlds at the same time: high unemployment *and* increases in the cost of living. Thus, during the most recent 1974–1976 depression, consumer goods prices rose rapidly, but wholesale prices remained level, while industrial raw material prices fell rapidly and substantially. So how is it that the cost of living continues to rise in current recessions?

Let us go back and examine what happened to prices in the "classic," or old-fashioned boom-bust cycle (pre–World War II vintage). In the booms the money supply went up, prices in general therefore went up, but the prices of capital goods rose by *more* than consumer goods, drawing resources out of consumer and into capital goods industries. In short, abstracting from general price increases, *relative to each other*, capital goods prices *rose* and consumer prices *fell* in the boom. What happened in the bust? The opposite situation: the money supply went down, prices in general therefore fell, but the prices of capital goods fell by *more* than consumer goods, drawing resources back out of capital goods into consumer goods industries. In short, abstracting from general price declines, *relative to each other*, capital goods prices *fell* and consumer prices *rose* during the bust.

The Austrian point is that this scenario in relative prices in boom and bust is *still* taking place unchanged. During the booms, capital goods prices still rise and consumer goods prices still fall relative to each other, and vice versa during the recession. The difference is that a new monetary world has arrived, as we have indicated earlier in this chapter. For now that the gold standard has been eliminated, the Fed can and does increase the money supply *all the time*, whether it be boom or recession. There hasn't been a contraction of the money supply since the early 1930s, and there is not likely to be another in the foreseeable future. So now that the money supply *always* increases, prices in general are *always* going up, sometimes more slowly, sometimes more rapidly.

In short, in the classic recession, consumer goods prices were always going up relative to capital goods. Thus, if consumer goods prices fell by 10% in a particular recession, and capital goods prices fell by 30%, consumer prices were *rising* substantially in relative terms. But, from the point of view of the consumer, the fall in the cost of living was

highly welcome, and indeed was the blessed sugarcoating on the pill
of recession or depression. Even in the Great Depression of the 1930s,
with very high rates of unemployment, the 75–80% of the labor force
still employed enjoyed bargain prices for their consumer goods.

But now, with Keynesian fine-tuning at work, the sugarcoating has
been removed from the pill. Now that the supply of money—and hence
general prices—is *never* allowed to fall, the rise in relative consumer
goods prices during a recession will hit the consumer as a visible rise
in nominal prices as well. His cost of living now goes up in a depression,
and so he reaps the worst of both worlds; in the classical business cycle,
before the rule of Keynes and the Council of Economic Advisors, he
at least had to suffer only one calamity at a time.

What then are the policy conclusions that arise rapidly and easily
from the Austrian analysis of the business cycle? They are the precise
opposite from those of the Keynesian establishment. For, since the virus
of distortion of production and prices stems from inflationary bank credit
expansion, the Austrian prescription for the business cycle will be: First,
if we are in a boom period, the government and its banks must cease
inflating immediately. It is true that this cessation of artificial stimulant
will inevitably bring the inflationary boom to an end, and will inaugurate
the inevitable recession or depression. But the longer the government
delays this process, the harsher the necessary readjustments will have
to be. For the sooner the depression readjustment is gotten over with,
the better. This also means that the government must never try to delay
the depression process; the depression must be allowed to work itself
out as quickly as possible, so that real recovery can begin. This means,
too, that the government must particularly avoid any of the interventions
so dear to Keynesian hearts. It must never try to prop up unsound
business situations; it must never bail out or lend money to business
firms in trouble. For doing so will simply prolong the agony and convert
a sharp and quick depression phase into a lingering and chronic disease.
The government must never try to prop up wage rates or prices, especially in the capital goods industries; doing so will prolong and delay
indefinitely the completion of the depression adjustment process. It will
also cause indefinite and prolonged depression and mass unemployment
in the vital capital goods industries. The government must not try to
inflate again in order to get out of the depression. For even if this reinfla-
tion succeeds (which is by no means assured), it will only sow greater
trouble and more prolonged and renewed depression later on. The government must do nothing to encourage consumption, and it must not
increase its own expenditures, for this will further increase the social

consumption/investment ratio—when the only thing that could speed up the adjustment process is to lower the consumption/savings ratio so that more of the currently unsound investments will become validated and become economic. The only way the government can aid in this process is to lower its own budget, which will increase the ratio of investment to consumption in the economy (since government spending may be regarded as consumption spending for bureaucrats and politicians).

Thus, what the government should do, according to the Austrian analysis of the depression and the business cycle, is absolutely nothing. It should stop its *own* inflating, and then it should maintain a strict hands-off, laissez-faire policy. Anything it does will delay and obstruct the adjustment processes of the market; the less it does, the more rapidly will the market adjustment process do its work and sound economic recovery ensue.

The Austrian prescription for a depression is thus the diametric opposite of the Keynesian: it is for the government to keep absolute hands off the economy, and to confine itself to stopping its own inflation, and to cutting its own budget.

It should be clear that the Austrian analysis of the business cycle meshes handsomely with the libertarian outlook toward government and a free economy. Since the State would always like to inflate and to interfere in the economy, a libertarian prescription would stress the importance of absolute separation of money and banking from the State. This would involve, at the very least, the abolition of the Federal Reserve System and the return to a commodity money (e.g., gold or silver) so that the money-unit would once again be a unit of weight of a market-produced commodity rather than the name of a piece of paper printed by the State's counterfeiting apparatus.

10

The Public Sector, I: Government in Business

PEOPLE TEND TO FALL into habits and into unquestioned ruts, especially in the field of government. On the market, in society in general, we expect and accommodate rapidly to change, to the unending marvels and improvements of our civilization. New products, new life styles, new ideas are often embraced eagerly. But in the area of government we follow blindly in the path of centuries, content to believe that whatever has been must be right. In particular, government, in the United States and elsewhere, for centuries and seemingly from time immemorial has been supplying us with certain essential and necessary services, services which nearly everyone concedes are important: defense (including army, police, judicial, and legal), firefighting, streets and roads, water, sewage and garbage disposal, postal service, etc. So identified has the State become in the public mind with the provision of these services that an attack on State financing *appears* to many people as an attack on the service itself. Thus if one maintains that the State should not supply court services, and that private enterprise on the market could supply such service more efficiently as well as more morally, people tend to think of this as denying the importance of courts themselves.

The libertarian who wants to replace government by private enterprises in the above areas is thus treated in the same way as he would be if the government had, for various reasons, been supplying shoes as a tax-financed monopoly from time immemorial. If the government and only the government had had a monopoly of the shoe manufacturing and retailing business, how would most of the public treat the libertarian who now came along to advocate that the government get out of the shoe business and throw it open to private enterprise? He would undoubtedly be treated as follows: people would cry, "How could you? You are opposed to the public, and to poor people, wearing shoes! And *who* would supply shoes to the public if the government got out of the business? Tell us that! Be constructive! It's easy to be negative and smart-alecky about government; but tell us *who* would supply shoes? Which people? How many shoe stores would be available in each city and town? How would the shoe firms be capitalized? How many brands would there be? What material would they use? What lasts? What would be the pricing arrangements for shoes? Wouldn't regulation of the shoe industry be needed to see to it that the product is sound? And who would supply the poor with shoes? Suppose a poor person didn't have the money to buy a pair?"

These questions, ridiculous as they seem to be and are with regard to the shoe business, are just as absurd when applied to the libertarian who advocates a free market in fire, police, postal service, or any other government operation. The point is that the advocate of a free market in *anything* cannot provide a "constructive" blueprint of such a market in advance. The essence and the glory of the free market is that individual firms and businesses, competing on the market, provide an ever-changing orchestration of efficient and progressive goods and services: continually improving products and markets, advancing technology, cutting costs, and meeting changing consumer demands as swiftly and as efficiently as possible. The libertarian economist can try to offer a few guidelines on how markets *might* develop where they are now prevented or restricted from developing; but he can do little more than point the way toward freedom, to call for government to get out of the way of the productive and ever-inventive energies of the public as expressed in voluntary market activity. No one can predict the number of firms, the size of each firm, the pricing policies, etc., of any future market in any service or commodity. We just know—by economic theory and by historical insight—that such a free market will do the job infinitely better than the compulsory monopoly of bureaucratic government.

How will the poor pay for defense, fire protection, postal service, etc., can basically be answered by the counter-question: how do the poor pay for *anything* they now obtain on the market? The difference is that we know that the free private market will supply these goods and services far more cheaply, in greater abundance, and of far higher quality than monopoly government does today. Everyone in society would benefit, and *especially* the poor. And we also know that the mammoth tax burden to finance these and other activities would be lifted from the shoulders of everyone in society, including the poor.

We have seen above that the universally acknowledged pressing problems of our society are all wrapped up in government operations. We have also seen that the enormous social conflicts entwined in the public school system would all disappear when each group of parents was allowed to finance and support whichever education it preferred for their children. The grave inefficiencies and the intense conflicts are all inherent in government operation. If the government, for example, provides monopoly services (e.g., in education or in water supply), then whichever decisions the government makes are coercively imposed on the hapless minority—whether it is a question of educational policies for the schools (integration or segregation, progressive or traditional, religious or secular, etc.), or even for the kind of water to be sold (e.g., fluoridated or unfluoridated). It should be clear that no such fierce arguments occur where each group of consumers can purchase the goods or services they demand. There are no battles between consumers, for example, over what kind of newspapers should be printed, churches established, books printed, records marketed, or automobiles manufactured. Whatever is produced on the market reflects the diversity as well as the strength of consumer demand.

On the free market, in short, the consumer is king, and any business firm that wants to make profits and avoid losses tries its best to serve the consumer as efficiently and at as low a cost as possible. In a government operation, in contrast, everything changes. *Inherent in all government operation is a grave and fatal split between service and payment,* between the providing of a service and the payment for receiving it. The government bureau does not get its income as does the private firm, from serving the consumer well or from consumer purchases of its products exceeding its costs of operation. No, the government bureau acquires its income from mulcting the long-suffering taxpayer. Its operations therefore become inefficient, and costs zoom, since government bureaus need not worry about losses or bankruptcy; they can make up their losses by additional extractions from the public till. Furthermore, the consumer, instead of being courted and wooed for his favor, becomes a mere annoyance to the government, someone who is "wasting" the *government's* scarce resources. In government operations, the consumer is treated like an unwelcome intruder, an interference in the quiet enjoyment by the bureaucrat of his steady income.

Thus, if consumer demand should increase for the goods or services of any private business, the private firm is delighted; it woos and welcomes the new business and expands its operations eagerly to fill the new orders. Government, in contrast, generally meets this situation by sourly urging or even ordering consumers to "buy" less, and allows shortages to develop, along with deterioration in the quality of its service. Thus, the increased consumer use of government streets in the cities is met by aggravated traffic congestion and by continuing denunciations and threats against people who drive their own cars. The New York City administration, for example, is continually threatening to outlaw the use of private cars in Manhattan, where congestion has been most troublesome. It is only government, of course, that would ever think of bludgeoning consumers in this way; it is only government that has the audacity to "solve" traffic congestion by forcing private cars (or trucks or taxis or whatever) off the road. According to this principle, of course, the "ideal" solution to traffic congestion is simply to outlaw all vehicles!

But this sort of attitude toward the consumer is not confined to traffic on the streets. New York City, for example, has suffered periodically from a water "shortage." Here is a situation where, for many years, the city government has had a compulsory monopoly of the supply of water to its citizens. Failing to supply enough water, and failing to price that water in such a way as to clear the market, to equate supply and demand (which private enterprise does automatically), New York's response to water shortages has always been to blame *not* itself, but the consumer, whose sin has been to use "too much" water. The city administration could only react by outlawing the sprinkling of lawns, restricting use of water, and demanding that people drink less water. In this way, government transfers its own failings to the scapegoat user, who is threatened and bludgeoned instead of being served well and efficiently.

There has been similar response by government to the ever-accelerating crime problem in New York City. Instead of providing efficient police protection, the city's reaction has been to force the innocent citizen to stay out of crime-prone areas. Thus, after Central Park in Manhattan became a notorious center for muggings and other crime in the night hours, New York City's "solution" to the problem was to impose a curfew, banning use of the park in those hours. In short, if an innocent citizen wants to stay in Central Park at night, it is he who is arrested for disobeying the curfew; it is, of course, easier to arrest him than to rid the park of crime.

In short, while the long-held motto of private enterprise is that "the customer is always right," the implicit maxim of government operation is that the customer is always to be blamed.

Of course, the political bureaucrats have a standard response to the mounting complaints of poor and inefficient service: "The taxpayers must give us more money!" It is not enough that the "public sector," and its corollary in taxation, has been growing far more rapidly in this century than the national income. It is not enough that the flaws and headaches of government operation have multiplied along with the increased burden of the government budget. We are supposed to pour still more money down the governmental rathole!

The proper counter-argument to the political demand for more tax money is the question: "How is it that private enterprise doesn't have these problems?" How is it that hi-fi manufacturers or photocopy companies or computer firms or whatever do not have trouble finding capital to expand their output? Why don't *they* issue manifestoes denouncing the investing public for not providing *them* with more money to serve consumer needs? The answer is that consumers pay for the hi-fi sets or the photocopy machines or the computers, and that investors, as a result, know that they can make money by investing in those businesses. On the private market, firms that successfully serve the public find it easy to obtain capital for expansion; inefficient, unsuccessful firms do not, and eventually have to go out of business. But there is no profit-and-loss mechanism in *government* to induce investment in efficient operations and to penalize and drive the inefficient or obsolete ones out of business. There are no profits or losses in government operations inducing either expansion or contraction of operations. In government, then, no one truly "invests," and no one can insure that successful operations will expand and unsuccessful ones disappear. In contrast, government must raise its "capital" by literally conscripting it through the coercive mechanism of taxation.

Many people, including some government officials, think that these problems could be solved if only "government were run like a business." The government then sets up a pseudocorporate monopoly, run by government, which is supposed to set affairs on a "business basis." This has been done, for example, in the case of the Post Office—now the U.S. "Postal Service"—and in the case of the ever-crumbling and decaying New York City Transit Authority.[1] The "corporations" are enjoined

---

[1]For a critique of the Post Office and the Postal Service, see John Haldi, *Postal Monopoly* (Washington, D.C.: American Enterprise Institute for Public Policy Research, 1974).

to end their chronic deficits and are allowed to float bonds on the bond market. It is true that direct users then would be taking some of the burden off the mass of taxpayers, which include users and nonusers alike. But there are fatal flaws inherent in any government operation which cannot be avoided by this pseudobusiness device. In the first place, government service is always a monopoly or semimonopoly. Often, as in the case of the Postal Service or the Transit Authority, it is a compulsory monopoly—all or nearly all private competition is outlawed. The monopoly means that government service will be far more costly, higher priced, and poorer in quality than would be the case in the free market. Private enterprise gains a profit by cutting costs as much as it can. Government, which cannot go bankrupt or suffer losses in any case, need not cut costs; protected from competition as well as losses, it need only cut its service or simply raise prices. A second fatal flaw is that, try as it may, a government corporation can *never* be run as a business because its *capital* continues to be conscripted from the taxpayer. There is no way of avoiding that; the fact that the government corporation may raise bonds on the market still rests on the ultimate power of taxation to redeem these bonds.

Finally, there is another critical problem inherent in any government operation of a business. One of the reasons that private firms are models of efficiency is because the free market establishes prices which permit them to *calculate*, to figure out what their costs are and therefore what they must do to make profits and avoid losses. It is through this price system, as well as through the motivation to increase profits and avoid losses, that goods and services are properly allocated in the market among all the intricate branches and areas of production that make up the modern industrial "capitalist" economy. It is economic calculation that makes this marvel possible; in contrast, central planning, such as is attempted under socialism, is deprived of accurate pricing, and therefore *cannot* calculate costs and prices. This is the major reason that central socialist planning has increasingly proved to be a failure as the communist countries have become industrialized. It is because central planning cannot determine prices and costs with any accuracy that the communist countries of Eastern Europe have been moving rapidly away from socialist planning and toward a free-market economy.

If central planning, then, thrusts the economy into hopeless calculational chaos, and into irrational allocations and production operations, the advance of government activities inexorably introduces ever greater *islands* of such chaos into the economy, and makes calculation of costs and rational allocation of production resources more and more difficult.

As government operations expand and the market economy withers, the calculational chaos becomes more and more disruptive and the economy increasingly unworkable.

The ultimate libertarian program may be summed up in one phrase: the *abolition* of the public sector, the conversion of all operations and services performed by the government into activities performed voluntarily by the private-enterprise economy. Let us now turn from general considerations of government as contrasted with private activity to some of the major areas of government operation and how they could be performed by the free-market economy.

11

The Public Sector, II: Streets and Roads

Protecting the Streets

ABOLITION OF THE PUBLIC SECTOR means, of course, that *all* pieces of land, all land areas, including streets and roads, would be owned privately, by individuals, corporations, cooperatives, or any other voluntary groupings of individuals and capital. The fact that all streets and land areas would be private would by itself solve many of the seemingly insoluble problems of private operation. What we need to do is to reorient our thinking to consider a world in which all land areas are privately owned.

Let us take, for example, police protection. How would police protection be furnished in a totally private economy? *Part* of the answer becomes evident if we consider a world of totally private land and street ownership. Consider the Times Square area of New York City, a notoriously crime-ridden area where there is little police protection furnished by the city authorities. Every New Yorker knows, in fact, that he lives and walks the streets, and not only Times Square, virtually in a state of "anarchy," dependent solely on the normal peacefulness and good will of his fellow citizens. Police protection in New York is minimal, a fact dramatically revealed in a recent week-long police strike when, lo and behold!, crime in no way increased from its normal state when the police are supposedly alert and on the job. At any rate, suppose that the Times Square area, including the streets, was privately owned, say by the "Times Square Merchants Association." The merchants would know full well, of course, that if crime was rampant in their area, if muggings and holdups abounded, then their customers would fade away and would patronize competing areas and neighborhoods. Hence, it would be to the economic interest of the merchants' association to supply efficient and plentiful police protection, so that customers would be attracted to, rather than repelled from, their neighborhood. Private business, after all, is always trying to attract and keep its customers. But what good would be served by attractive store displays and packaging, pleasant lighting and courteous service, if the customers may be robbed or assaulted if they walk through the area?

The merchants' association, furthermore, would be induced, by their drive for profits and for avoiding losses, to supply not only sufficient police protection but also courteous and pleasant protection. Governmental police have not only no incentive to be efficient or worry about their "customers'" needs; they also live with the ever-present temptation to wield their power of force in a brutal and coercive manner. "Police brutality" is a well-known feature of the police system, and it is held in check only by remote complaints of the harassed citizenry. But if the private merchants' police should yield to the temptation of brutalizing the merchants' customers, those customers will quickly disappear and go elsewhere. Hence, the merchants' association will see to it that its police are courteous as well as plentiful.

Such efficient and high-quality police protection would prevail throughout the land, throughout all the private streets and land areas. Factories would guard their street areas, merchants their streets, and road companies would provide safe and efficient police protection for their toll roads and other privately owned roads. The same would be true for residential neighborhoods. We can envision two possible types of private street ownership in such neighborhoods. In one type, all the landowners in a certain block might become the joint *owners* of that block, let us say as the "85th St. Block Company." This company would then provide police protection, the costs being paid either by the homeowners directly or out of tenants' rent if the street includes rental apartments. Again, homeowners will of course have a direct interest in seeing that their block is safe, while landlords will try to attract tenants by supplying safe streets in addition to the more usual services such as heat, water, and janitorial service. To ask *why* landlords should provide safe streets in the libertarian, fully private society is just as silly as asking *now* why they should provide their tenants with heat or hot water. The force of competition and of consumer demand would make them supply such services. Furthermore, whether we are considering homeowners or rental housing, in *either case* the capital value of the land and the house will be a function of the safety of the street as well as of the other well-known characteristics of the house and the neighborhood. Safe and well-patrolled streets will raise the value of the landowners' land and houses in the same way as well-tended houses do; crime-ridden streets will lower the value of the land and houses as surely as dilapidated housing itself does. Since landowners always prefer higher to lower market values for their property, there is a built-in incentive to provide efficient, well-paved, and safe streets.

Another type of private street-ownership in residential areas might be private street companies, which would own only the streets, not the houses or buildings on them. The street companies would then charge landowners for the service of maintaining, improving, and policing their streets. Once again, safe, well-lit, and well-paved streets will induce landowners and tenants to flock to those streets; unsafe, badly lit and badly maintained streets will drive those owners and users away. A happy and flourishing use of the streets by landlords and automobiles will raise the profits and stock values of the street companies; an unhappy and decaying regard for streets by their owners will drive the users away and lower the profits and the stock values of the private street companies. Hence, the street-owning companies will do their best to provide efficient street service, including police protection, to secure happy users; they will be driven to do this by their desire to make profits and to increase the value of their capital, and by their equally active desire not to suffer losses and erosion of their capital. It is infinitely better to rely on the pursuit of economic interest by landowners or street companies than to depend on the dubious "altruism" of bureaucrats and government officials.

At this point in the discussion, someone is bound to raise the question: If streets are owned by street companies, and granting that they generally would aim to please their customers with maximum efficiency, what if some kooky or tyrannical street owner should suddenly decide to block access to his street to an adjoining homeowner? How could the latter get in or out? Could he be blocked permanently, or be charged an enormous amount to be allowed entrance or exit? The answer to this question is the same as to a similar problem about land-ownership: Suppose that everyone owning homes surrounding someone's property would suddenly not allow him to go in or out? The answer is that everyone, in purchasing homes or street service in a libertarian society, would make sure that the purchase or lease contract provides full access for whatever term of years is specified. With this sort of "easement" provided in advance by contract, no such sudden blockade would be allowed, since it would be an invasion of the property right of the landowner.

There is of course nothing new or startling in the *principle* of this envisioned libertarian society. We are already familiar with the energizing effects of inter-location and inter-transportation competition. For example, when the private railroads were being built throughout the nation in the nineteenth century, the railroads and their competition provided a remarkable energizing force for developing their respective areas. Each railroad tried its best to induce immigration and economic development in its area in order to increase its profits, land values, and value of its capital; and each hastened to do so, lest people and markets leave their area and move to the ports, cities, and lands served by competing railroads. The same principle would be at work if all streets and roads were private as well. Similarly, we are already familiar with police protection provided by private merchants and organizations. *Within* their property, stores provide guards and watchmen; banks provide guards; factories employ watchmen; shopping centers retain guards, etc. The libertarian society would simply extend this healthy and functioning system to the *streets* as well. It is scarcely accidental that there are far more assaults and muggings on the *streets* outside stores than in the stores themselves; this is because the stores are supplied with watchful private guards while on the streets we must all rely on the "anarchy" of government police protection. Indeed, in various blocks of New York City there has already arisen in recent years, in response to the galloping crime problem, the hiring of private guards to patrol the blocks by voluntary contributions of the landlords and homeowners on that block. Crime on these blocks has already been substantially reduced. The problem is that these efforts have been halting and inefficient because those streets are not *owned* by the residents, and hence there is no effective mechanism for gathering the capital to provide efficient protection on a permanent basis. Furthermore, the patrolling street guards cannot legally be armed because they are not on their owners' property, and they cannot, as store or other property owners can, challenge anyone acting in a suspicious but not yet criminal manner. They cannot, in short, do the things, financially or administratively, that *owners* can do with their property.

Furthermore, police paid for by the landowners and residents of a block or neighborhood would not only end police brutality against customers; this sytem would end the current spectacle of police being considered by many communities as alien "imperial" colonizers, there not to serve but to oppress the community. In America today, for example, we have the general rule in our cities of black areas patrolled by police hired by central urban governments, governments that are perceived to be alien to the black communities. Police supplied, controlled, and paid for by the residents and landowners of the communities themselves would be a completely different story; they would be supplying, and perceived to be supplying, services to their customers rather than coercing them on behalf of an alien authority.

A dramatic contrast of the merits of public vs. private protection is provided by one block in Harlem. On West 135th Street between Seventh and Eighth Avenues is the station house of the 82nd Precinct of the New York City Police Department. Yet the august presence of the station house did not prevent a rash of night robberies of various stores on the block. Finally, in the winter of 1966, fifteen merchants on the block banded together to hire a guard to walk the block all night; the guard was hired from the Leroy V. George protection company to provide the police protection not forthcoming from their property taxes.[1]

The most successful and best organized private police forces in American history have been the railway police, maintained by many railroads to prevent injury or theft to passengers or freight. The modern railway police were founded at the end of World War I by the Protection Section of the American Railway Association. So well did they function that by 1929 freight claim payments for robberies had declined by 93%. Arrests by the railway police, who at the time of the major study of their activities in the early 1930s totalled 10,000 men, resulted in a far higher percentage of convictions than earned by police departments, ranging from 83% to 97%. Railway police were armed, could make normal arrests, and were portrayed by an unsympathetic criminologist as having a widespread reputation for good character and ability.[2]

---

[1]See William C. Wooldridge, *Uncle Sam the Monopoly Man* (New Rochelle, N.Y.: Arlington House, 1970), pp. 111ff.

[2]See Wooldridge, *op. cit.*, pp. 115–17. The criminological study was made by Jeremiah P. Shalloo, *Private Police* (Philadelphia: Annals of the American Academy of Political and Social Science, 1933). Wooldridge comments that Shalloo's reference to the good reputation of the railway police "contrasts with the present status of many big-city public forces; sanctions against misconduct are so ineffective or roundabout that they may as well not exist, however rhetorically comforting the forces' status as servants of the people may be." Wooldridge, *op. cit.*, p. 117.

Street Rules

One of the undoubted consequences of all land areas in the country being owned by private individuals and companies would be a greater richness and diversity of American neighborhoods. The character of the police protection and the rules applied by the private police would depend on the wishes of the landowners or street owners, the owners of the given area. Thus, suspicious residential neighborhoods would insist that any people or cars entering the area have a prior appointment with a resident, or else be approved by a resident with a phone call from the gate. In short, the same rules for street property would be applied as are now often applied in private apartment buildings or family estates. In other, more raffish areas, everyone would be permitted to enter at will, and there might be varying degrees of surveillance in between. Most probably commercial areas, anxious not to rebuff customers, would be open to all. All this would give full scope to the desires and values of the residents and owners of all the numerous areas in the country.

It might be charged that all this will allow freedom "to discriminate" in housing or use of the streets. There is no question about that. Fundamental to the libertarian creed is every man's right to choose who shall enter or use his own property, provided of course that the other person is willing.

"Discrimination," in the sense of choosing favorably or unfavorably in accordance with whatever criteria a person may employ, is an integral part of freedom of choice, and hence of a free society. But of course in the free market any such discrimination is costly, and will have to be paid for by the property owner concerned.

Suppose, for example, that someone in a free society is a landlord of a house or a block of houses. He *could* simply charge the free market rent and let it go at that. But then there are risks; he may choose to discriminate against renting to couples with young children, figuring that there is substantial risk of defacing his property. On the other hand, he may well choose to charge extra rent to compensate for the higher risk, so that the free-market rent for such families will tend to be higher than otherwise. This, in fact, will happen in most cases on the free market. But what of personal, rather than strictly economic, "discrimination" by the landlord? Suppose, for example, that the landlord is a great admirer of six-foot Swedish-Americans, and decides to rent his apartments only to families of such a group. In the free society it would be fully in his right to do so, but he would clearly suffer a large monetary loss as a result. For this means that he would have to turn away tenant after tenant in an endless quest for very tall Swedish-Americans. While this may be considered an extreme example, the effect is exactly the same, though differing in degree, for any sort of personal discrimination in the marketplace. If, for example, the landlord dislikes redheads and determines not to rent his apartments to them, he will suffer losses, although not as severely as in the first example.

In any case, anytime anyone practices such "discrimination" in the free market, he must bear the costs, either of losing profits or of losing services as a consumer. If a consumer decides to boycott goods sold by people he does not like, whether the dislike is justified or not, he then will go without goods or services which he otherwise would have purchased.

All property owners, then, in a free society, would set down the rules for use of, or admission to, their property. The more rigorous the rules the fewer the people who will engage in such use, and the property owner will then have to balance rigor of admission as against loss of income. A landlord might "discriminate," for example, by insisting, as George Pullman did in his "company town" in Illinois in the late nineteenth century, that all his tenants appear at all times dressed in jacket and tie; he might do so, but it is doubtful that many tenants would elect to move into or remain in such a building or development and the landlord would suffer severe losses.

The principle that property is administered by its owners also provides the rebuttal to a standard argument for government intervention in the economy. The argument holds that "after all, the government sets down traffic rules—red and green lights, driving on the right-hand side, maximum speed limits, etc. Surely everyone must admit that traffic would degenerate into chaos if not for such rules. Therefore, why should government not intervene in the rest of the economy as well?" The fallacy here is not that traffic should be regulated; of course such rules are necessary. But the crucial point is that such rules will always be laid down by whoever owns and therefore administers the roads. Government has been laying down traffic rules because it is the government that has always owned and therefore run the streets and roads; in a libertarian society of private ownership the *private* owners would lay down the rules for the use of their roads.

However, might not the traffic rules be "chaotic" in a purely free society? Wouldn't some owners designate red for "stop," others green or blue, etc.? Wouldn't some roads be used on the right-hand side and others on the left? Such questions are absurd. Obviously, it would be to the interest of all road owners to have uniform rules in these matters, so that road traffic could mesh smoothly and without difficulty. Any maverick road owner who insisted on a left-hand drive or green for "stop" instead of "go" would soon find himself with numerous accidents, and the disappearance of customers and users. The private railroads in nineteenth-century America faced similar problems and solved them harmoniously and without difficulty. Railroads allowed each other's cars on their tracks; they inter-connected with each other for mutual benefit; the gauges of the different railroads were adjusted to be uniform; and uniform regional freight classifications were worked out for 6,000 items. Furthermore, it was the railroads and not government that took the initiative to consolidate the unruly and chaotic patchwork of time zones that had existed previously. In order to have accurate scheduling and timetables, the railroads *had* to consolidate; and in 1883 they agreed to consolidate the existing fifty-four time zones across the country into the four which we have today. The New York financial paper, the *Commercial and Financial Chronicle*, exclaimed that "the laws of trade and the instinct for self-preservation effect reforms and improvements that all the legislative bodies combined could not accomplish."[3]

Pricing Streets and Roads

If, in contrast, we examine the performance of governmental streets and highways in America, it is difficult to see how private ownership could pile up a more inefficient or irrational record. It is now widely recognized, for example, that federal and state governments, spurred by the lobbying of automobile companies, oil companies, tire companies, and construction contractors and unions, have indulged in a vast over-expansion of highways. The highways grant gross subsidies to the users and have played the major role in killing railroads as a viable enterprise. Thus, trucks can operate on a right-of-way constructed and maintained by the taxpayer, while railroads had to build and maintain their own trackage. Furthermore, the subsidized highway and road programs led to an overexpansion of automobile-using suburbs, the coerced bulldozing of countless homes and businesses, and an artificial burdening of the central cities. The cost to the taxpayer and to the economy has been enormous.

[3]See Edward C. Kirkland, *Industry Comes of Age: Business, Labor, and Public Policy, 1860–1897* (New York: Holt, Rinehart, and Winston, 1961), pp. 48–50.

Particularly subsidized has been the urban auto-using commuter, and it is precisely in the cities where traffic congestion has burgeoned along with this subsidy to overaccumulation of their traffic. Professor William Vickrey of Columbia University has estimated that urban expressways have been built at a cost of from 6 cents to 27 cents per vehicle-mile, while users pay in gasoline and other auto taxes only about 1 cent per vehicle-mile. The general taxpayer rather than the motorist pays for maintenance of urban streets. Furthermore, the gasoline tax is paid *per mile* regardless of the particular street or highway being used, and regardless of the time of day of the ride. Hence, when highways are financed from the general gasoline tax fund, the users of the low-cost rural highways are being taxed in order to subsidize the users of the far higher-cost urban expressways. Rural highways typically cost only 2 cents per vehicle-mile to build and maintain.[4]

In addition, the gasoline tax is scarcely a rational pricing system for the use of the roads, and no private firms would ever price the use of roads in that way. Private business prices its goods and services to "clear the market," so that supply equals demand, and there are neither shortages nor goods going unsold. The fact that gasoline taxes are paid per mile regardless of the road means that the more highly demanded urban streets and highways are facing a situation where the *price* charged is far below the free-market price. The result is enormous and aggravated traffic congestion on the heavily traveled streets and roads, especially in rush hours, and a virtually unused network of roads in rural areas. A rational pricing system would at the same time maximize profits for road owners and always provide clear streets free of congestion. In the current system, the government holds the price to users of congested roads extremely low and far below the free-market price; the result is a chronic shortage of road space reflected in traffic congestion. The government has invariably tried to meet this growing problem not by rational pricing but by building still more roads, socking the taxpayer for yet greater subsidies to drivers, and thereby making the shortage still worse. Frantically increasing the supply while holding the price of use far below the market simply leads to chronic and aggravated congestion.[5] It is like a dog chasing a mechanical rabbit. Thus, the *Washington Post* has traced the impact of the federal highway program in the nation's capital:

[4]From an unpublished study by William Vickrey, "Transit Fare Increases a Costly Revenue."

[5]For similar results of irrational pricing of runway service by government-owned air-

Washington's Capital Beltway was one of the first major links in the system to be completed. When the last section was opened in the summer of 1964, it was hailed as one of the finest highways ever built.

It was expected to (a) relieve traffic congestion in downtown Washington by providing a bypass for north-south traffic and (b) knit together the suburban counties and cities ringing the capital.

What the Beltway actually became was (a) a commuter highway and local traffic circulator and (b) the cause of an enormous building boom that accelerated the flight of the white and the affluent from the central city.

Instead of relieving traffic congestion, the Beltway has increased it. Along with I-95, 70-S, and I-66, it has made it possible for commuters to move farther and farther from their downtown jobs.

It has also led to relocation of government agencies and retail and service firms from downtown to the suburbs, putting the jobs they create out of reach of many inner city dwellers.[6]

What would a rational pricing system, a system instituted by private road owners, look like? In the first place, highways would charge tolls, especially at such convenient entrances to cities as bridges and tunnels, but not as is charged now. For example, toll charges would be much higher at rush-hour and other peak-hour traffic (e.g., Sundays in the summer) than in off-hours. In a free market, the greater demand at peak hours would lead to higher toll charges, until congestion would be eliminated and the flow of traffic steady. But people *have* to go to work, the reader will ask? Surely, but they don't *have* to go in their own cars. Some commuters will give up altogether and move back to the city; others will go in car pools; still others will ride in express

---

ports, see Ross D. Eckert, *Airports And Congestion* (Washington, D.C.: American Enterprise Institute for Public Policy Research, 1972).

[6]Hank Burchard, "U.S. Highway System: Where to Now?," *Washington Post* (November 29, 1971). Or, as John Dyckman puts it: "in motoring facilities . . . additional accommodation creates additional traffic. The opening of a freeway designed to meet existing demand may eventually increase that demand until congestion on the freeway increases the travel time to what it was before the freeway existed." John W. Dyckman, "Transportation in Cities," in A. Schreiber, P. Gatons, and R. Clemmer, eds., *Economics of Urban Problems; Selected Readings* (Boston: Houghton Mifflin, 1971), p. 143. For an excellent analysis of how increased supply cannot end congestion when pricing is set far below market price, see Charles O. Meiburg, "An Economic Analysis of Highway Services," *Quarterly Journal of Economics* (November 1963), pp. 648–56.

busses or trains. In this way, use of the roads at peak hours would be restricted to those most willing to pay the market-clearing price for their use. Others, too, will endeavor to shift their times of work so as to come in and leave at staggered hours. Weekenders would also drive less or stagger their hours. Finally, the higher profits to be earned from, say, bridges and tunnels, will lead private firms to build more of them. Road building will be governed not by the clamor of pressure groups and users for subsidies, but by the efficient demand and cost calculations of the marketplace.

While many people can envision the working of private *highways*, they boggle at the thought of private urban streets. How would *they* be priced? Would there be toll gates at every block? Obviously not, for such a system would be clearly uneconomic, prohibitively costly to the owner and driver alike. In the first place, the street owners will price *parking* far more rationally than at present. They will price parking on congested downtown streets very heavily, in response to the enormous demand. And contrary to common practice nowadays, they will charge proportionately far *more* rather than less for longer, all-day parking. In short, the street owners will try to induce rapid turnover in the congested areas. All right for parking; again, this is readily understandable. But what about *driving* on congested urban streets? How could this be priced? There are numerous possible ways. In the first place the downtown street owners might require anyone driving on their streets to buy a license, which could be displayed on the car as licenses and stickers are now. But, furthermore, they might require anyone driving at peak hours to buy and display an extra, very costly license. There are other ways. Modern technology may make feasible the requirement that all cars equip themselves with a meter, a meter which will not only click away per mile, but may speed up in a predetermined manner on congested streets and roads at peak hours. Then the car owner could receive a bill at the end of the month. A similar plan was set forth a decade ago by Professor A. A. Walters:

The particular administrative instruments which might be used include . . . special mileometers (similar to those used by taxis). . . . The special mileometers would record mileage when the "flag" is up and a charge would be levied on this mileage. This would be suitable for large urban areas such as New York, London, Chicago, etc. "Flag-up" streets could be specified for certain hours of the day. Vehicles might be allowed to travel on those streets without a special mileometer provided that they bought and displayed a daily "sticker." The occasional traffic on "sticker" authority would have been charged more than the maximum amount paid by those on mileometer authority. The supervision of the scheme would be fairly simple. Cameras could be set up to record those cars without sticker or flag, and a suitable fine could be levied for contravention.[7]

Professor Vickrey has also suggested that TV cameras at the intersections of the most congested streets could record the license numbers of all cars, with motorists sent a bill each month in proportion to all the times that they crossed the intersection. Alternatively, he proposed that each car could be equipped with the Oxford electronic metering device; each car would then emit its own unique signal which would be picked up by the device placed at the given intersection.[8]

In any case, the problem of rational pricing for streets and highways would be an easy one for private enterprise and modern technology to solve. Businessmen on the free market have readily solved far more difficult problems; all that is needed is to allow them the room to function.

If all transportation were set completely free, if the roads, airlines, railroads, and waterways were freed of their labyrinthine networks of subsidies, controls, and regulations in a purely private system, how would the consumers allocate their transportation dollars? Would we return to railroad travel, for example? The best estimates of cost and demand for transportation predict that railroads would become the main staple for long-haul freight, airlines for long-range passenger service, trucks for short-haul freight, and busses for public commuter travel. While railroads, in short, would stage a comeback for long-haul freight, they would not be revivified for much passenger service. In recent years, many liberals who have become disenchanted with the overbuilding of highways have been calling for massive discouragement of highway use, and the subsidizing and building of subways and commuter railways on a vast scale for urban traffic. But these grandiose schemes ignore the enormous expense and waste that would be involved. For even if

[7]Professor Walters adds that with a suitably large application of the mileometer method, the cost of each mileometer could probably be reduced to about $10. A. A. Walters, "The Theory and Measurement of Private and Social Cost of Highway Congestion," *Econometrica* (October 1961), p. 684. Also see Meiburg, *op. cit.*, p. 652; Vickrey, *op. cit.*; Dyckman, "Transportation in Cities," *op. cit.*, pp. 135–51; John F. Kain, "A Re-appraisal of Metropolitan Transport Planning," in Schreiber, Gatons, and Clemmer, *op. cit.*, pp. 152–66; John R. Meyer, "Knocking Down the Straw Men," in B. Chinitz, ed., *City and Suburb* (Englewood Cliffs, N.J.: Prentice-Hall, 1964), pp. 85–93; and James C. Nelson, "The Pricing of Highway, Waterway, and Airway Facilities," *American Economic Review, Papers and Proceedings* (May 1962), pp. 426–32.

[8]Douglass C. North and Roger LeRoy Miller, *The Economics of Public Issues* (New York: Harper & Row, 1971), p. 72.

many of these highways should not have been built, they are *there*, and it would be folly not to take advantage of them. In recent years, some intelligent transportation economists have raised their voices against the massive waste involved in constructing new rapid transit railroads (such as in the San Francisco Bay area) and have called instead for making use of the existing highways through employing express busses for commuting.[9]

It is not difficult to envision a network of private, unsubsidized and unregulated railroads and airlines; but could there be a system of private roads? Could such a system be at all feasible? One answer is that private roads have worked admirably in the past. In England before the eighteenth century, for example, roads, invariably owned and operated by local governments, were badly constructed and even more badly maintained. These public roads could never have supported the mighty Industrial Revolution that England experienced in the eighteenth century, the "revolution" that ushered in the modern age. The vital task of improving the almost impassable English roads was performed by private turnpike companies, which, beginning in 1706, organized and established the great network of roads which made England the envy of the world. The owners of these private turnpike companies were generally landowners, merchants, and industrialists in the area being served by the road, and they recouped their costs by charging tolls at selected tollgates. Often the collection of tolls was leased out for a year or more to individuals selected by competitive bids at auction. It was these private roads that developed an internal market in England, and that greatly lowered the costs of transport of coal and other bulky material. And since it was mutually beneficial for them to do so, the turnpike companies linked up with each other to form an interconnected road network throughout the land—all a result of private enterprise in action.[10]

As in England, so in the United States a little later in time. Faced again with virtually impassable roads built by local governmental units, private companies built and financed a great turnpike network throughout the northeastern states, from approximately 1800 to 1830. Once again, private enterprise proved superior in road building and ownership to the backward operations of government. The roads were built and operated by private turnpike corporations, and tolls were charged to the

---

[9]See for example the works of Meyer and Kain cited above, as well as Meyer, Kain, and Wohl, *The Urban Transportation Problem* (Cambridge: Harvard University Press, 1965).

[10]See T. S. Ashton, *An Economic History of England: the 18th Century* (New York: Barnes and Noble, 1955), pp. 78–90. See the same source, pp. 72–90, for the mighty network of private canals built throughout England during the same period.

users. Again, the turnpike companies were largely financed by merchants and property owners along the routes, and they voluntarily linked themselves into an interconnected network of roads. And these turnpikes constituted the first really good roads in the United States.[11]

[11]See George Rogers Taylor, *The Transportation Revolution, 1815–1860* (New York: Rinehart & Co., 1951), pp. 22–28. Also see W. C. Wooldridge, *Uncle Sam the Monopoly Man,* pp. 128–36.

12

The Public Sector,
III: Police, Law,
and the Courts

Police Protection

THE MARKET AND PRIVATE ENTERPRISE do exist, and so most people can readily envision a free market in most goods and services. Probably the most difficult single area to grasp, however, is the abolition of government operations in the service of protection: police, the courts, etc.— the area encompassing defense of person and property against attack or invasion. How could private enterprise and the free market possibly provide *such* service? How could police, legal systems, judicial services, law enforcement, prisons—how could these be provided in a free market? We have already seen how a great deal of police protection, at the least, could be supplied by the various owners of streets and land areas. But we now need to examine this entire area systematically.

In the first place, there is a common fallacy, held even by most advocates of laissez-faire, that the government must supply "police protection," as if police protection were a single, absolute entity, a fixed quantity of something which the government supplies to all. But in actual fact there is no absolute commodity called "police protection" any more than there is an absolute single commodity called "food" or "shelter." It is true that everyone pays taxes for a seemingly fixed quantity of protection, but this is a myth. In actual fact, there are almost infinite degrees of all sorts of protection. For any given person or business, the police can provide everything from a policeman on the beat who patrols once a night, to two policemen patrolling constantly on each block, to cruising patrol cars, to one or even several round-the-clock personal bodyguards. Furthermore, there are many other decisions the police must make, the complexity of which becomes evident as soon as we look beneath the veil of the myth of absolute "protection." How shall the police allocate their funds which are, of course, always limited as are the funds of all other individuals, organizations, and agencies? How much shall the police invest in electronic equipment? fingerprinting equipment? detectives as against uniformed police? patrol cars as against foot police, etc?

The point is that the government has no rational way to make these allocations. The government only knows that it has a limited budget. Its allocations of funds are then subject to the full play of politics, boondoggling, and bureaucratic inefficiency, with no indication at all as to whether the police department is serving the consumers in a way responsive to their desires or whether it is doing so efficiently. The situation would be different if police services were supplied on a free, competitive market. In that case, consumers would pay for whatever degree of protection they wish to purchase. The consumers who just want to see a policeman once in a while would pay less than those who want continuous patrolling, and far less than those who demand twenty-four-hour bodyguard service. On the free market, protection would be supplied in proportion and in whatever way that the consumers wish to pay for it. A drive for efficiency would be insured, as it always is on the market, by the compulsion to make profits and avoid losses, and thereby to keep costs low and to serve the highest demands of the consumers. Any police firm that suffers from gross inefficiency would soon go bankrupt and disappear.

One big problem a government police force must always face is: what laws *really* to enforce? Police departments are theoretically faced with the absolute injunction, "enforce all laws," but in practice a limited budget forces them to allocate their personnel and equipment to the most urgent crimes. But the absolute dictum pursues them and works against a rational allocation of resources. On the free market, what would be enforced is whatever the customers are willing to pay for. Suppose, for example, that Mr. Jones has a precious gem he believes might soon be stolen. He can ask, and pay for, round-the-clock police protection at whatever strength he may wish to work out with the police company. He might, on the other hand, also have a private road on his estate he doesn't want many people to travel on—but he might not *care* very much about trespassers on that road. In that case, he won't devote any police resources to protecting the road. As on the market in general, it is up to the comsumer—and since all of us are consumers this means each person individually decides how much and what kind of protection he wants and is willing to buy.

All that we have said about landowners' police applies to private police in general. Free-market police would not only be efficient, they would have a strong incentive to be courteous and to refrain from brutality against either their clients or their clients' friends or customers. A private Central Park would be guarded efficiently in order to maximize park revenue, rather than have a prohibitive curfew imposed on innocent— and paying—customers. A free market in police would reward efficient and courteous police protection to customers and penalize any falling off from this standard. No longer would there be the current disjunction between service and payment inherent in all government operations, a disjunction which means that police, like all other government agencies, acquire their revenue, not voluntarily and competitively from consumers, but from the taxpayers coercively.

In fact, as government police have become increasingly inefficient, consumers have been turning more and more to private forms of protection. We have already mentioned block or neighborhood protection. There are also private guards, insurance companies, private detectives, and such increasingly sophisticated equipment as safes, locks, and closed-circuit TV and burglar alarms. The President's Commission on Law Enforcement and the Administration of Justice estimated in 1969 that government police cost the American public $2.8 billion a year, while it spends $1.35 billion on private protection service and another $200 million on equipment, so that private protection expenses amounted to over half the outlay on government police. These figures should give pause to those credulous folk who believe that police protection is somehow, by some mystic right or power, necessarily and forevermore an attribute of State sovereignty.[1]

Every reader of detective fiction knows that private insurance detectives are far more efficient than the police in recovering stolen property. Not only is the insurance company impelled by economics to serve the consumer—and thereby try to avoid paying benefits—but the major focus of the insurance company is very different from that of the police. The police, standing as they do for a mythical "society," are primarily interested in catching and punishing the criminal; restoring the stolen

---

[1]See Wooldridge, *op. cit.*, pp. 111ff.

loot to the victim is strictly secondary. To the insurance company and its detectives, on the other hand, the prime concern is recovery of the loot, and apprehension and punishment of the criminal is secondary to the prime purpose of aiding the victim of crime. Here we see again the difference between a private firm impelled to serve the customer-victim of crime and the public police, which is under no such economic compulsion.

We cannot blueprint a market that exists only as an hypothesis, but it is reasonable to believe that police service in the libertarian society would be supplied by the landowners or by insurance companies. Since insurance companies would be paying benefits to victims of crime, it is highly likely that they would supply police service as a means of keeping down crime and hence their payment of benefits. It is certainly likely in any case that police service would be paid for in regular monthly premiums, with the police agency—whether insurance company or not—called on whenever needed.

This supplies what should be the first simple answer to a typical nightmare question of people who first hear about the idea of a totally private police: "Why, that means that if you're attacked or robbed you have to rush over to a policeman and start dickering on how much it will cost to defend you." A moment's reflection should show that no service is supplied in this way on the free market. Obviously, the person who wants to be protected by Agency A or Insurance Company B will pay regular premiums rather than wait to be attacked before buying protection. "But suppose an emergency occurs and a Company A police-man sees someone being mugged; will he stop to ask if the victim has bought insurance from Company A?" In the first place, this sort of street crime will be taken care of, as we noted above, by the police hired by whoever owns the street in question. But what of the unlikely case that a neighborhood does not have street police, and a policeman of Company A happens to see someone being attacked? Will he rush to the victim's defense? That, of course, would be up to Company A, but it is scarcely conceivable that private police companies would not cultivate goodwill by making it a policy to give free aid to victims in emergency situations and perhaps ask the rescued victim for a voluntary donation afterward. In the case of a homeowner being robbed or at-tacked, then of course he will call on whichever police company he has been using. He will call Police Company A rather than "the police" he calls upon now.

Competition insures efficiency, low price, and high quality, and there is no reason to assume *a priori*, as many people do, that there is something divinely ordained about having only *one* police agency in a given geographical area. Economists have often claimed that the production of certain goods or services is a "natural monopoly," so that more than one private agency could not long survive in a given area. Perhaps, although only a totally free market could decide the matter once and for all. Only the market can decide what and how many firms, and of what size and quality, can survive in active competition. But there is no reason to suppose in advance that police protection is a "natural monopoly." After all, insurance companies are not; and if we can have Metropolitan, Equitable, Prudential, etc., insurance companies coexisting side by side, why not Metropolitan, Equitable, and Prudential police protection companies? Gustave de Molinari, the nineteenth-century French free-market economist, was the first person in history to contemplate and advocate a free market for police protection.[2] Molinari estimated that there would eventually turn out to be several private police agencies side by side in the cities, and one private agency in each rural area. Perhaps—but we must realize that modern technology makes much more feasible branch offices of large urban firms in even the most remote rural areas. A person living in a small village in Wyoming, therefore, could employ the services of a local protection company, *or* he might use a nearby branch office of the Metropolitan Protection Company.

"But how could a poor person afford private protection he would have to pay for instead of getting free protection, as he does now?" There are several answers to this question, one of the most common criticisms of the idea of totally private police protection. One is: that this problem of course applies to *any* commodity or service in the libertarian society, not just the police. But isn't protection necessary? Perhaps, but then so is food of many different kinds, clothing, shelter, etc. Surely these are at least as vital if not more so than police protection, and yet almost nobody says that *therefore* the government must nationalize food, clothing, shelter, etc., and supply these free as a compulsory monopoly. Very poor people would be supplied, in general, by private charity, as we saw in our chapter on welfare. Furthermore, in the specific case of police there would undoubtedly be ways of voluntarily supplying free police protection to the indigent—either by the police companies themselves for goodwill (as hospitals and doctors do now) or by special "police aid" societies that would do work similar to "legal aid" societies

[2]Cf. Gustave de Molinari, *The Production of Security* (New York: Center for Libertarian Studies, 1977).

today. (Legal aid societies voluntarily supply free legal counsel to the indigent in trouble with the authorities.)

There are important supplementary considerations. As we have seen, police service is *not* "free"; it is paid for by the taxpayer, and the taxpayer is very often the poor person himself. He may very well be paying more in taxes for police now than he would in fees to private, and far more efficient, police companies. Furthermore, the police companies would be tapping a mass market; with the economies of such a large-scale market, police protection would undoubtedly be much cheaper. No police company would wish to price itself out of a large chunk of its market, and the cost of protection would be no more prohibitively expensive than, say, the cost of insurance today. (In fact, it would tend to be much cheaper than current insurance, because the insurance industry today is heavily regulated by government to keep out low-cost competition.)

There is a final nightmare which most people who have contemplated private protection agencies consider to be decisive in rejecting such a concept. Wouldn't the agencies always be clashing? Wouldn't "anarchy" break out, with perpetual conflicts between police forces as one person calls in "his" police while a rival calls in "his"?

There are several levels of answers to this crucial question. In the first place, since there would be no overall State, no central or even single local government, we would *at least* be spared the horror of inter-State wars, with their plethora of massive, superdestructive, and now nuclear, weapons. As we look back through history, isn't it painfully clear that the number of people killed in isolated neighborhood "rumbles" or conflicts is as nothing to the total mass devastation of inter-State wars? There are good reasons for this. To avoid emotionalism, let us take two hypothetical countries: "Ruritania" and "Walldavia." If both Ruritania and Walldavia were dissolved into a libertarian society, with no government and innumerable private individuals, firms, and police agencies, the only clashes that *could* break out would be local, and the weaponry would necessarily be strictly limited in scope and devastation. Suppose that in a Ruritanian city two police agencies clash and start shooting it out. At worst, they could *not* use mass bombing or nuclear destruction or germ warfare, since they themselves would be blown up in the holocaust. It is the slicing off of territorial areas into single, governmental monopolies that leads to mass destruction—for *then* if the single monopoly government of Walldavia confronts its ancient rival, the government of Ruritania, each can wield weapons of mass destruction and even nuclear warfare because it will be the "other guy" and the "other country" they will hurt. Furthermore, now that every person is a subject of a monopoly government, in the eyes of every other government he becomes irretrievably *identified* with "his" government. The citizen of France is identified with "his" government, and therefore if another government attacks France, it will attack the citizenry as well as the government of France. But if Company A battles with Company B, the *most* that can happen is that the respective customers of each company may be dragged into the battle—but *no one else.* It should be evident, then, that *even* if the worst happened, and a libertarian world would indeed become a world of "anarchy," we would *still* be much better off than we are now, at the mercy of rampant, "anarchic" nation-states, each possessing a fearsome monopoly of weapons of mass destruction. We must never forget that we are all living, and always have lived, in a world of "international anarchy," in a world of coercive nation-states unchecked by any overall world government, and there is no prospect of this situation changing.

A libertarian world, then, even if anarchic, would *still* not suffer the brutal wars, the mass devastation, the A-bombing, that our State-ridden world has suffered for centuries. Even if local police clash continually, there would be no more Dresdens, no more Hiroshimas.

But there is far more to be said. We should never concede that this local "anarchy" would be likely to occur. Let us separate the problem of police clashes into distinct and different parts: honest disagreements, and the attempt of one or more police forces to become "outlaws" and to extract funds or impose their rule by coercion. Let us assume for a moment that the police forces will be honest, and that they are only riven by honest clashes of opinion; we will set aside for a while the problem of outlaw police. Surely one of the very important aspects of protection service the police can offer their respective customers is quiet protection. Every consumer, every buyer of police protection, would wish above all for protection that is efficient and quiet, with no conflicts or disturbances. Every police agency would be fully aware of this vital fact. To assume that police would continually clash and battle with each other is absurd, for it ignores the devastating effect that this chaotic "anarchy" would have on the business of all the police companies. To put it bluntly, such wars and conflicts would be bad—very bad—for business. Therefore, on the free market, the police agencies would all see to it that there would be no clashes between them, and that all conflicts of opinion would be ironed out in private courts, decided by private judges or arbitrators.

To get more specific: in the first place, as we have said, clashes would be minimal because the street owner would have his guards, the store-keeper his, the landlord his, and the homeowner his own police company. Realistically, in the everyday world, there would be little room for direct clashes between police agencies. But suppose, as will sometimes occur, two neighboring home owners get into a fight, each accuses the other of initiating assault or violence, and each calls on his own police company, should they happen to subscribe to different companies. What then? Again, it would be pointless and economically as well as physically self-destructive for the two police companies to start shooting it out. Instead, every police company, to remain in business at all, would announce as a *vital part* of its service, the use of private courts or arbitrators to decide who is in the wrong.

The Courts

Suppose, then, that the judge or arbitrator decides Smith was in the wrong in a dispute, and that he aggressed against Jones. If Smith accepts the verdict, then, whatever damages or punishment is levied, there is no problem for the theory of libertarian protection. But what if he does *not* accept it? Or suppose another example: Jones is robbed. He sets his police company to do detective work in trying to track down the criminal. The company decides that a certain Brown is the criminal. Then what? If Brown acknowledges his guilt, then again there is no problem and judicial punishment proceeds, centering on forcing the criminal to make restitution to the victim. But, again, what if Brown denies his guilt?

These cases take us out of the realm of police protection and into another vital area of protection: *judicial* service, i.e., the provision, in accordance with generally accepted procedures, of a method of trying as best as one can to determine *who* is the criminal, or *who* is the breaker of contracts, in any sort of crime or dispute. Many people, even those who acknowledge that there could be privately competitive police service supplied on a free market, balk at the idea of totally private courts. How in the world could *courts* be private? How would courts employ force in a world without government? Wouldn't eternal conflicts and "anarchy" *then* ensue?

In the first place, the monopoly courts of government are subject to the same grievous problems, inefficiencies, and contempt for the consumer as any other government operation. We all know that judges, for example, are *not* selected according to their wisdom, probity, or efficiency in serving the consumer, but are political hacks chosen by the political process. Furthermore, the courts are monopolies; if, for example, the courts in some town or city should become corrupt, venal, oppressive, or inefficient, the citizen at present has no recourse. The aggrieved citizen of Deep Falls, Wyoming, must be governed by the local Wyoming court or not at all. In a libertarian society, there would be many courts, many judges to whom he could turn. Again, there is no reason to assume a "natural monopoly" of judicial wisdom. The Deep Falls citizen could, for example, call upon the local branch of the Prudential Judicial Company.

How would courts be financed in a free society? There are many possibilities. Possibly, each individual would subscribe to a court service, paying a monthly premium, and then calling upon the court if he is in need. Or, since courts will probably be needed much less frequently than policemen, he may pay a fee whenever he chooses to use the court, with the criminal or contract-breaker eventually recompensing the victim or plaintiff. Or, in still a third possibility, the courts may be hired by the police agencies to settle disputes, *or* there may even be "vertically integrated" firms supplying *both* police and judicial service: the Prudential Judicial Company might have a police and a judicial division. Only the market will be able to decide which of these methods will be most appropriate.

We should all be more familiar with the increasing use of private arbitration, even in our present society. The government courts have become so clogged, inefficient, and wasteful that more and more parties to disputes are turning to private arbitrators as a cheaper and far less time-consuming way of settling their disputes. In recent years, private arbitration has become a growing and highly successful profession. Being voluntary, furthermore, the rules of arbitration can be decided rapidly by the parties themselves, without the need for a ponderous, complex legal framework applicable to all citizens. Arbitration therefore permits judgments to be made by people expert in the trade or occupation concerned. Currently, the American Arbitration Association, whose motto is "The Handclasp is Mightier than the Fist," has 25 regional offices throughout the country, with 23,000 arbitrators. In 1969, the Association conducted over 22,000 arbitrations. In addition, the insurance companies adjust over 50,000 claims a year through voluntary arbitration. There is also a growing and successful use of private arbitrators in automobile accident claim cases.

It might be protested that, while performing an ever greater proportion of judicial functions, the private arbitrators' decisions are still enforced by the courts, so that once the disputing parties agree on an arbitrator, his decision becomes legally binding. This is true, but it was *not* the case before 1920, and the arbitration profession grew at as rapid a rate from 1900 to 1920 as it has since. In fact, the modern arbitration movement began in full force in England during the time of the American Civil War, with merchants increasingly using the "private courts" provided by voluntary arbitrators, even though the decisions were not legally binding. By 1900, voluntary arbitration began to take hold in the United States. In fact, in medieval England, the entire structure of merchant law, which was handled clumsily and inefficiently by the government's courts, grew up in private merchants' courts. The merchants' courts were purely voluntary arbitrators, and the decisions were not legally binding. How, then, were they successful?

The answer is that the merchants, in the Middle Ages and down to 1920, relied solely on ostracism and boycott by the other merchants in the area. In other words, should a merchant refuse to submit to arbitration or ignore a decision, the other merchants would publish this fact in the trade, and would refuse to deal with the recalcitrant merchant, bringing him quickly to heel. Wooldridge mentions one medieval example:

Merchants made their courts work simply by agreeing to abide by the results. The merchant who broke the understanding would not be sent to jail, to be sure, but neither would he long continue to be a merchant, for the compliance exacted by his fellows, and their power over his goods, proved if anything more effective than physical coercion. Take John of Homing, who made his living marketing wholesale quantities of fish. When John sold a lot of herring on the representation that it conformed to a three-barrel sample, but which, his fellow merchants found, was actually mixed with "sticklebacks and putrid herring," he made good the deficiency on pain of economic ostracism.[3]

In modern times, ostracism became even more effective, and it included the knowledge that anyone who ignored an arbitrator's award could never again avail himself of an arbitrator's services. Industrialist Owen D. Young, head of General Electric, concluded that the moral censure of other businessmen was a far more effective sanction than legal enforcement. Nowadays, modern technology, computers, and credit ratings would make such nationwide ostracism even more effective than it has ever been in the past.

Even if purely voluntary arbitration is sufficient for commercial disputes, however, what of frankly criminal activities: the mugger, the rapist, the bank robber? In these cases, it must be admitted that ostracism would probably not be sufficient—even though it would also include,

[3]Wooldridge, *op. cit.*, p. 96. Also see pp. 94–110.

we must remember, refusal of private street owners to allow such criminals in their areas. For the criminal cases, then, courts and legal enforcement become necessary.

How, then, would the courts operate in the libertarian society? In particular, how could they *enforce* their decisions? In all their operations, furthermore, they must observe the critical libertarian rule that no physical force may be used against anyone who has not been convicted as a criminal—otherwise, the users of such force, whether police or courts, would be themselves liable to be convicted as aggressors if it turned out that the person they had used force against was innocent of crime. In contrast to statist systems, no policeman or judge could be granted special immunity to use coercion beyond what anyone else in society could use.

Let us now take the case we mentioned before. Mr. Jones is robbed, his hired detective agency decides that one Brown committed the crime, and Brown refuses to concede his guilt. What then? In the first place, we must recognize that there is at present no overall world court or world government enforcing its decrees; yet while we live in a state of "international anarchy" there is little or no problem in disputes between private citizens of two countries. Suppose that right now, for example, a citizen of Uruguay claims that he has been swindled by a citizen of Argentina. Which court does he go to? He goes to his own, i.e., the victim's or the plaintiff's court. The case proceeds in the Uruguayan court, and its decision is honored by the Argentinian court. The same is true if an American feels he has been swindled by a Canadian, and so on. In Europe after the Roman Empire, when German tribes lived side by side and in the same areas, if a Visigoth felt that he had been injured by a Frank, he took the case to his own court, and the decision was generally accepted by the Franks. Going to the plaintiff's court is the rational libertarian procedure as well, since the victim or plaintiff is the one who is aggrieved, and who naturally takes the case to his own court. So, in our case, Jones would go to the Prudential Court Company to charge Brown with theft.

It is possible, of course, that Brown is also a client of the Prudential Court, in which case there is no problem. The Prudential's decision covers both parties, and becomes binding. But one important stipulation is that no coercive subpoena power can be used against Brown, because he must be considered innocent until he is convicted. But Brown would be served with a voluntary subpoena, a notice that he is being tried on such and such a charge and inviting him or his legal representative to appear. If he does not appear, then he will be tried *in absentia*, and this will obviously be less favorable for Brown since his side of the case will not be pleaded in court. If Brown is declared guilty, then the court and its marshals will employ force to seize Brown and exact whatever punishment is decided upon—a punishment which obviously will focus first on restitution to the victim.

What, however, if Brown does not recognize the Prudential Court? What if he is a client of the Metropolitan Court Company? Here the case becomes more difficult. What will happen then? First, victim Jones pleads his case in the Prudential Court. If Brown is found innocent, this ends the controversy. Suppose, however, that defendant Brown is found guilty. If he does nothing, the court's judgment proceeds against him. Suppose, however, Brown then takes the case to the Metropolitan Court Company, pleading inefficiency or venality by Prudential. The case will then be heard by Metropolitan. If Metropolitan also finds Brown guilty, this too ends the controversy and Prudential will proceed against Brown with dispatch. Suppose, however, that Metropolitan finds Brown innocent of the charge. Then what? Will the two courts and their arms-wielding marshals shoot it out in the streets?

Once again, this would clearly be irrational and self-destructive behavior on the part of the courts. An essential part of their judicial service to their clients is the provision of just, objective, and peacefully functioning decisions—the best and most objective way of arriving at the truth of who committed the crime. Arriving at a decision and then allowing chaotic gunplay would scarcely be considered valuable judicial service by their customers. Thus, an essential part of any court's service to its clients would be an appeals procedure. In short, every court would agree to abide by an appeals trial, as decided by a voluntary arbitrator to whom Metropolitan and Prudential would now turn. The appeals judge would make his decision, and the result of this third trial would be treated as binding on the guilty. The Prudential court would then proceed to enforcement.

An appeals court! But isn't this setting up a compulsory monopoly government once again? No, because there is nothing in the system that requires any one person or court to be the court of appeal. In short, in the United States at present the Supreme Court is established as *the* court of final appeal, so the Supreme Court judges become the final arbiters regardless of the wishes of plaintiff or defendant alike. In contrast, in the libertarian society the various competing private courts could go to *any* appeals judge they think fair, expert, and objective. No single appeals judge or set of judges would be foisted upon society by coercion.

How would the appeals judges be financed? There are many possible ways, but the most likely is that they will be paid by the various original courts who would charge their customers for appeals services in their premiums or fees.

But suppose Brown insists on another appeals judge, and yet another? Couldn't he escape judgment by appealing ad infinitum? Obviously, in *any* society legal proceedings cannot continue indefinitely; there must be *some* cutoff point. In the present statist society, where government monopolizes the judicial function, the Supreme Court is arbitrarily designated as the cutoff point. In the libertarian society, there would also have to be an agreed-upon cutoff point, and since there are only two parties to any crime or dispute—the plaintiff and the defendant—it seems most sensible for the legal code to declare that *a decision arrived at by any two courts* shall be binding. This will cover the situation when both the plaintiff's and the defendant's courts come to the same decision, as well as the situation when an appeals court decides on a disagreement between the two original courts.

The Law and the Courts

It is now clear that there will have to be a legal code in the libertarian society. How? How can there be a legal code, a system of law *without* a government to promulgate it, an appointed system of judges, or a legislature to vote on statutes? To begin with, is a legal code consistent with libertarian principles?

To answer the last question first, it should be clear that a legal code is necessary to lay down precise guidelines for the private courts. If, for example, Court A decides that all redheads are inherently evil and must be punished, it is clear that such decisions are the reverse of libertarian, that such a law would constitute an invasion of the rights of redheads. Hence, any such decision would be *illegal* in terms of libertarian principle, and could not be upheld by the rest of society. It then becomes necessary to have a legal code which would be generally accepted, and which the courts would pledge themselves to follow. The legal code, simply, would insist on the libertarian principle of no aggression against person or property, define property rights in accordance with libertarian principle, set up rules of evidence (such as currently apply) in deciding who are the wrongdoers in any dispute, and set up a code of maximum punishment for any particular crime. Within the framework of such a code, the particular courts would compete on the most efficient procedures, and the market would then decide whether judges, juries, etc., are the most efficient methods of providing judicial services.

Are such stable and consistent law codes possible, with only competing judges to develop and apply them, and without government or legislature? Not only are they *possible*, but over the years the best and most successful parts of our legal system were developed precisely in this manner. Legislatures, as well as kings, have been capricious, invasive, and inconsistent. They have only introduced anomalies and despotism into the legal system. In fact, the government is no more qualified to develop and apply law than it is to provide any other service; and just as religion has been separated from the State, and the economy can be separated from the State, so can every other State function, including police, courts, *and* the law itself!

As indicated above, for example, the entire law merchant was developed, not by the State or in State courts, but by private merchant courts. It was only much later that government took over mercantile law from its development in merchants' courts. The same occurred with admiralty law, the entire structure of the law of the sea, shipping, salvages, etc. Here again, the State was not interested, and its jurisdiction did not apply to the high seas; so the shippers themselves took on the task of not only applying, but working out the whole structure of admiralty law in their own private courts. Again, it was only later that the government appropriated admiralty law into its own courts.

Finally, the major body of Anglo-Saxon law, the justly celebrated *common law*, was developed over the centuries by competing judges applying time-honored principles rather than the shifting decrees of the State. These principles were not decided upon arbitrarily by any king or legislature; they grew up over centuries by applying rational—and very often libertarian—principles to the cases before them. The idea of following precedent was developed, *not* as a blind service to the past, but because all the judges of the past had made their decisions in applying the generally accepted common law principles to specific cases and problems. For it was universally held that the judge did not *make* law (as he often does today); the judge's task, his expertise, was in *finding* the law in accepted common law principles, and then applying that law to specific cases or to new technological or institutional conditions. The glory of the centuries-long development of the common law is testimony to their success.

The common law judges, furthermore, functioned very much like private arbitrators, as experts in the law to whom private parties went with their disputes. There was no arbitrarily imposed "supreme court" whose decision would be binding, nor was precedent, though honored, considered as *automatically* binding either. Thus, the libertarian Italian jurist Bruno Leoni has written:

. . . courts of judicature could not easily enact arbitrary rules of their own in England, as they were never in a position to do so directly, that is to say, in the usual, sudden, widely ranging and imperious manner of legislators. Moreover, there were so many courts of justice in England and they were so jealous of one another that even the famous principle of the binding precedent was not openly recognized as valid by them until comparatively recent times. Besides, they could never decide anything that had not been previously brought before them by private persons. Finally, comparatively few people used to go before the courts to ask from them the rules deciding their cases.[4]

And on the absence of "supreme courts":

. . . it cannot be denied that the lawyers' law or the judiciary law may tend to acquire the characteristics of legislation, including its undesirable ones, whenever jurists or judges are entitled to decide ultimately on a case. . . . In our time the mechanism of the judiciary in certain countries where "supreme courts" are established results in the imposition of the personal views of the members of these courts, or of a majority of them, on all the other people concerned whenever there is a great deal of disagreement between the opinion of the former and the convictions of the latter. But . . . this possibility, far from being necessarily implied in the nature of lawyers' law or of judiciary law, is rather a deviation from it. . . .[5]

Apart from such aberrations, the imposed personal views of the judges were kept to a minimum: (a) by the fact that judges could only make decisions when private citizens brought cases to them; (b) each judge's decisions applied only to the particular case; and (c) because the decisions of the common-law judges and lawyers always considered the precedents of the centuries. Furthermore, as Leoni points out, in contrast to legislatures or the executive, where dominant majorities or pressure groups ride roughshod over minorities, judges, by their very position, are constrained to hear and weigh the arguments of the two contending parties in each dispute. "Parties are *equal* as regards the judge, in the sense that they are free to produce arguments and evidence. They do not constitute a group in which dissenting minorities give way to triumphant majorities. . . ." And Leoni points out the analogy between this process and the free-market economy: "Of course, arguments may be stronger or weaker, but the fact that every party can produce them is comparable

[4]Bruno Leoni, *Freedom and the Law* (Los Angeles: Nash Publishing Co., 1972), p. 87.
[5]*Ibid.*, pp. 23–24.

to the fact that everybody can individually compete with everybody else in the market in order to buy and sell."[6]

Professor Leoni found that, in the *private law* area, the ancient Roman judges operated in the same way as the English common law courts:

The Roman jurist was a sort of scientist; the objects of his research were the solutions to cases that citizens submitted to him for study, just as industrialists might today submit to a physicist or to an engineer a technical problem concerning their plants or their production. Hence, private Roman law was something to be described or to be discovered, not something to be enacted—a world of things that were there, forming part of the common heritage of all Roman citizens. Nobody enacted that law; nobody could change it by any exercise of his personal will. . . . This is the long-run concept or, if you prefer, the Roman concept, of the certainty of the law.[7]

Finally, Professor Leoni was able to use his knowledge of the operations of ancient and common law to answer the vital question: In a libertarian society, "who will appoint the judges . . . to let them perform the task of defining the law?" His answer is: the *people* themselves, people who would go to the judges with the greatest reputation of expertise and wisdom in knowing and applying the basic common legal principles of the society:

In fact, it is rather immaterial to establish in advance who will appoint the judges, for, in a sense, everybody could do so, as happens to a certain extent when people resort to private arbiters to settle their own quarrels. . . . For the appointment of judges is not such a special problem as would be, for example, that of "appointing" physicists or doctors or other kinds of learned and experienced people. The emergence of good professional people in any society is only apparently due to official appointments, if any. It is, in fact, based on a widespread consent on the part of clients, colleagues, and the public at large—a consent without which no appointment is really effective. Of course, people can be wrong about the true value chosen as being worthy, but these difficulties in their choice are inescapable in any kind of choice.[8]

Of course, in the future libertarian society, the basic legal code would not rely on blind custom, much of which could well be antilibertarian. The code would have to be established on the basis of acknowledged libertarian principle, of nonaggression against the person or property of others; in short, on the basis of reason rather than on mere tradition,

[6] *Ibid.*, p. 188.
[7] *Ibid.*, pp. 84–85.
[8] *Ibid.*, p. 183.

however sound its general outlines. Since we have a body of common law principles to draw on, however, the task of reason in correcting and amending the common law would be far easier than trying to construct a body of systematic legal principles *de novo* out of the thin air.

The most remarkable historical example of a society of libertarian law and courts, however, has been neglected by historians until very recently. And this was also a society where not only the courts and the law were largely libertarian, but where they operated within a purely *state-less* and libertarian society. This was ancient Ireland—an Ireland which persisted in this libertarian path for roughly a thousand years until its brutal conquest by England in the seventeenth century. And, in contrast to many similarly functioning primitive tribes (such as the Ibos in West Africa, and many European tribes), preconquest Ireland was not in any sense a "primitive" society: it was a highly complex society that was, for centuries, the most advanced, most scholarly, and most civilized in all of Western Europe.

For a thousand years, then, ancient Celtic Ireland had no State or anything like it. As the leading authority on ancient Irish law has written: "There was no legislature, no bailiffs, no police, no public enforcement of justice. . . . There was no trace of State-administered justice."[9]

How then was justice secured? The basic political unit of ancient Ireland was the *tuath*. All "freemen" who owned land, all professionals, and all craftsmen, were entitled to become members of a *tuath*. Each *tuath's* members formed an annual assembly which decided all common policies, declared war or peace on other *tuatha*, and elected or deposed their "kings." An important point is that, in contrast to primitive tribes, no one was stuck or bound to a given *tuath*, either because of kinship or of geographical location. Individual members were free to, and often did, secede from a *tuath* and join a competing *tuath*. Often, two or more *tuatha* decided to merge into a single, more efficient unit. As Professor Peden states, "the *tuath* is thus a body of persons voluntarily united for socially beneficial purposes and the sum total of the landed properties of its members constituted its territorial dimension."[10] In short, they did not have the modern State with its claim to sovereignty over a given (usually expanding) territorial area, divorced from the landed property rights of its subjects; on the contrary, *tuatha* were voluntary associa-

---

[9]Quoted in the best introduction to ancient, anarchistic Irish institutions, Joseph R. Peden, "Property Rights in Celtic Irish Law," *Journal of Libertarian Studies*, 1 (Spring 1977), p. 83; see also pp. 81–95. For a summary, see Peden, "Stateless Societies: Ancient Ireland," *The Libertarian Forum* (April 1971), pp. 3–4.

[10]Peden, "Stateless Societies," p. 4.

tions which only comprised the landed properties of its voluntary members. Historically, about 80 to 100 *tuatha* coexisted at any time throughout Ireland.

But what of the elected "king"? Did *he* constitute a form of State ruler? Chiefly, the king functioned as a religious high priest, presiding over the worship rites of the *tuath*, which functioned as a voluntary religious, as well as a social and political, organization. As in pagan, pre-Christian, priesthoods, the kingly function was hereditary, this practice carrying over to Christian times. The king was elected by the *tuath* from within a royal kin-group (the *derbfine*), which carried the hereditary priestly function. *Politically*, however, the king had strictly limited functions: he was the military leader of the *tuath*, and he presided over the *tuath* assemblies. But he could only conduct war or peace negotiations as agent of the assemblies; and he was in no sense sovereign and had no rights of administering justice over *tuath* members. He could not legislate, and when he himself was party to a lawsuit, he had to submit his case to an independent judicial arbiter.

Again, how, then, was law developed and justice maintained? In the first place, the law itself was based on a body of ancient and immemorial custom, passed down as oral and then written tradition through a class of professional jurists called the *brehons*. The brehons were in no sense public, or governmental, officials; they were simply selected by parties to disputes on the basis of their reputations for wisdom, knowledge of the customary law, and the integrity of their decisions. As Professor Peden states:

. . . the professional jurists were consulted by parties to disputes for advice as to what the law was in particular cases, and these same men often acted as arbitrators between suitors. They remained at all times private persons, not public officials; their functioning depended upon their knowledge of the law and the integrity of their judicial reputations.[11]

Furthermore, the brehons had *no connection whatsoever* with the individual *tuatha* or with their kings. They were completely private, national in scope, and were used by disputants throughout Ireland. Moreover, and this is a vital point, in contrast to the system of private Roman lawyers, the brehon was all there was; there were no other judges, no "public" judges of any kind, in ancient Ireland.

It was the brehons who were schooled in the law, and who added glosses and applications to the law to fit changing conditions. Further-

[11] *Ibid.*

more, there was no monopoly, in any sense, of the brehon jurists; instead, several competing schools of jurisprudence existed and competed for the custom of the Irish people.

How were the decisions of the brehons enforced? Through an elaborate, voluntarily developed system of "insurance," or sureties. Men were linked together by a variety of surety relationships by which they guaranteed one another for the righting of wrongs, and for the enforcement of justice and the decisions of the brehons. In short, the brehons themselves were not involved in the enforcement of decisions, which rested again with private individuals linked through sureties. There were various types of surety. For example, the surety would guarantee with his own property the payment of a debt, and then join the plaintiff in enforcing a debt judgment if the debtor refused to pay. In that case, the debtor would have to pay double damages: one to the original creditor, and another as compensation to his surety. And this system applied to all offences, aggressions and assaults as well as commercial contracts; in short, it applied to all cases of what we would call "civil" and "criminal" law. All criminals were considered to be "debtors" who owed restitution and compensation to their victims, who thus became their "creditors." The victim would gather his sureties around him and proceed to apprehend the criminal or to proclaim his suit publicly and demand that the defendant submit to adjudication of their dispute with the brehons. The criminal might then send his own sureties to negotiate a settlement or agree to submit the dispute to the brehons. If he did not do so, he was considered an "outlaw" by the entire community; he could no longer enforce any claim of his own in the courts, and he was treated to the opprobrium of the entire community.[12]

There were occasional "wars," to be sure, in the thousand years of Celtic Ireland, but they were minor brawls, negligible compared to the devastating wars that racked the rest of Europe. As Professor Peden points out, "without the coercive apparatus of the State which can through taxation and conscription mobilize large amounts of arms and manpower, the Irish were unable to sustain any large scale military force in the field for any length of time. Irish wars . . . were pitiful brawls and cattle raids by European standards."[13]

---

[12]Professor Charles Donahue of Fordham University has maintained that the secular part of ancient Irish law was not simply haphazard tradition; that it was consciously rooted in the Stoic conception of *natural law*, discoverable by man's reason. Charles Donahue, "Early Celtic Laws" (unpublished paper, delivered at the Columbia University Seminar in the History of Legal and Political Thought, Autumn, 1964), pp. 13ff.

[13]Peden, "Stateless Societies," p. 4.

Thus, we have indicated that it is perfectly possible, in theory and historically, to have efficient and courteous police, competent and learned judges, and a body of systematic and socially accepted law—and none of these things being furnished by a coercive government. Government—claiming a compulsory monopoly of protection over a geographical area, and extracting its revenues by force—can be separated from the entire field of protection. Government is no more necessary for providing vital protection service than it is necessary for providing anything else. And we have not stressed a crucial fact about government: that its compulsory monopoly over the weapons of coercion has led it, over the centuries, to infinitely more butcheries and infinitely greater tyranny and oppression than any decentralized, private agencies could possibly have done. If we look at the black record of mass murder, exploitation, and tyranny levied on society by governments over the ages, we need not be loath to abandon the Leviathan State and . . . try freedom.

Outlaw Protectors

We have saved for the last this problem: What if police or judges and courts should be venal and biased—what if they should bias their decisions, for example, in favor of particularly wealthy clients? We have shown how a libertarian legal and judicial system could work on the purely free market, assuming honest differences of opinion—but what if one or more police or courts should become, in effect, outlaws? What then?

In the first place, libertarians do not flinch from such a question. In contrast to such utopians as Marxists or left-wing anarchists (anarcho-communists or anarcho-syndicalists), libertarians do *not* assume that the ushering in of the purely free society of their dreams will also bring with it a new, magically transformed Libertarian Man. We do not assume that the lion will lie down with the lamb, or that no one will have criminal or fraudulent designs upon his neighbor. The "better" that people will be, of course, the better *any* social system will work, in particular the less work *any* police or courts will have to do. But no such assumption is made by libertarians. What we assert is that, given any particular degree of "goodness" or "badness" among men, the purely libertarian society will be at once the most moral and the most efficient, the least criminal and the most secure of person or property.

Let us first consider the problem of the venal or crooked judge or court. What of the court which favors its own wealthy client in trouble? In the first place, any such favoritism will be highly unlikely, given the rewards and sanctions of the free market economy. The very life of the court, the very livelihood of a judge, will depend on his reputation for integrity, fair-mindedness, objectivity, and the quest for truth in every case. This is his "brand name." Should word of any venality leak out, he will immediately lose clients and the courts will no longer have customers; for even those clients who may be criminally inclined will scarcely sponsor a court whose decisions are no longer taken seriously by the rest of society, or who themselves may well be in jail for dishonest and fraudulent dealings. If, for example, Joe Zilch is accused of a crime or breach of contract, and he goes to a "court" headed by his brother-in-law, no one, least of all other, honest courts will take this "court's" decision seriously. It will no longer be considered a "court" in the eyes of anyone but Joe Zilch and his family.

Contrast this built-in corrective mechanism to the present-day government courts. Judges are appointed or elected for long terms, up to life, and they are accorded a monopoly of decision-making in their particular area. It is almost impossible, except in cases of gross corruption, to do anything about venal decisions of judges. Their power to make and to enforce their decisions continues unchecked year after year. Their salaries continue to be paid, furnished under coercion by the hapless taxpayer. But in the totally free society, any suspicion of a judge or court will cause their customers to melt away and their "decisions" to be ignored. This is a far more efficient system of keeping judges honest than the mechanism of government.

Furthermore, the temptation for venality and bias would be far less for another reason: business firms in the free market earn their keep, *not* from wealthy customers, but from a mass market by consumers. Macy's earns its income from the mass of the population, not from a few wealthy customers. The same is true of Metropolitan Life Insurance today, and the same would be true of any "Metropolitan" court system tomorrow. It would be folly indeed for the courts to risk the loss of favor by the bulk of its customers for the favors of a few wealthy clients. But contrast the present system, where judges, like all other politicians, may be beholden to wealthy contributors who finance the campaigns of their political parties.

There is a myth that the "American System" provides a superb set of "checks and balances," with the executive, the legislature, and the courts all balancing and checking one against the other, so that power cannot unduly accumulate in one set of hands. But the American "checks and balances" system is largely a fraud. For each one of these institutions is a coercive monopoly in its area, and all of them are part of one government, headed by one political party at any given time. Furthermore, at best there are only two parties, each one close to the other in ideology and personnel, often colluding, and the actual day-to-day business of government headed by a civil service bureaucracy that *cannot* be displaced by the voters. Contrast to these mythical checks and balances the *real* checks and balances provided by the free-market economy! What keeps A&P honest is the competition, actual and potential, of Safeway, Pioneer, and countless other grocery stores. What keeps them honest is the ability of the consumers to cut off their patronage. What would keep the free-market judges and courts honest is the lively possibility of heading down the block or down the road to *another* judge or court if suspicion should descend on any particular one. What would keep them honest is the lively possibility of their customers cutting off their business. These are the *real*, active checks and balances of the free-market economy and the free society.

The same analysis applies to the possibility of a private police force becoming outlaw, of using their coercive powers to exact tribute, set up a "protection racket" to shake down their victims, etc. Of course, such a thing *could* happen. But, in contrast to present-day society, there would be immediate checks and balances available; there would be *other* police forces who could use their weapons to band together to put down the aggressors against their clientele. If the Metropolitan Police Force should become gangsters and exact tribute, then the rest of society could flock to the Prudential, Equitable, etc., police forces who could band together to put them down. And this contrasts vividly with the State. If a group of gangsters should capture the State apparatus, with its monopoly of coercive weapons, there is nothing at present that can stop them—short of the immensely difficult process of revolution. In a libertarian society there would be no need for a massive revolution to stop the depredation of gangster-States; there would be a swift turning to the honest police forces to check and put down the force that had turned bandit.

And, indeed, what is the State anyway but organized banditry? What is taxation but theft on a gigantic, unchecked, scale? What is war but mass murder on a scale impossible by private police forces? What is conscription but mass enslavement? Can anyone envision a private police force getting away with a tiny fraction of what States get away with, and do habitually, year after year, century after century?

There is another vital consideration that would make it almost impossible for an outlaw police force to commit anything like the banditry that modern governments practice. One of the crucial factors that permits governments to do the monstrous things they habitually do is the sense of *legitimacy* on the part of the stupefied public. The average citizen may not like—may even strongly object to—the policies and exactions of his government. But he has been imbued with the idea—carefully indoctrinated by centuries of governmental propaganda—that the government is his legitimate sovereign, and that it would be wicked or mad to refuse to obey its dictates. It is this sense of legitimacy that the State's intellectuals have fostered over the ages, aided and abetted by all the trappings of legitimacy: flags, rituals, ceremonies, awards, constitutions, etc. A bandit gang—*even if all* the police forces conspired together into one vast gang—could never command such legitimacy. The public would consider them purely bandits; their extortions and tributes would never be considered legitimate though onerous "taxes," to be paid automatically. The public would quickly resist these illegitimate demands and the bandits would be resisted and overthrown. Once the public had tasted the joys, prosperity, freedom, and efficiency of a libertarian, State-less society, it would be almost impossible for a State to fasten itself upon them once again. Once freedom has been fully enjoyed, it is no easy task to force people to give it up.

But *suppose*—just suppose—that despite all these handicaps and obstacles, despite the love for their new-found freedom, despite the inherent checks and balances of the free market, suppose *anyway* that the State manages to reestablish itself. What then? Well, then, all that would have happened is that we would have a State once again. We would be no worse off than we are now, with our current State. *And*, as one libertarian philosopher has put it, "at least the world will have had a glorious holiday." Karl Marx's ringing promise applies far more to a libertarian society than to communism: In trying freedom, in abolishing the State, we have nothing to lose and everything to gain.

National Defense

We come now to what is usually the final argument against the libertarian position. Every libertarian has heard a sympathetic but critical listener say: "All right, I see how this system could be applied successfully to local police and courts. But how could a libertarian society defend us against the Russians?"

There are, of course, several dubious assumptions implied in such a question. There is the assumption that the Russians are bent upon military invasion of the United States, a doubtful assumption at best. There is the assumption that any such desire would still remain after the United

States had become a purely libertarian society. This notion overlooks the lesson of history that wars result from conflicts between nation-states, each armed to the teeth, each direly suspicious of attack by the other. But a libertarian America would clearly not be a threat to anyone, not because it had no arms but because it would be dedicated to no aggression against anyone, or against any country. Being no longer a nation-state, which is inherently threatening, there would be little chance of any country attacking us. One of the great evils of the nation-state is that each State is able to identify all of its subjects with itself; hence in any inter-State war, the innocent civilians, the subjects of each country, are subject to aggression from the enemy State. But in a libertarian society there would be no such identification, and hence very little chance of such a devastating war. Suppose, for example, that our outlaw Metropolitan Police Force has initiated aggression not only against Americans but also against Mexicans. If Mexico had a government, then clearly the Mexican government would know full well that Americans in general were not implicated in the Metropolitan's crimes, and had no symbiotic relationship with it. If the Mexican police engaged in a punitive expedition to punish the Metropolitan force, they would not be at war with Americans in general—as they would be now. In fact, it is highly likely that other American forces would join the Mexicans in putting down the aggressor. Hence, the idea of inter-State war against a libertarian country or geographical area would most likely disappear.

There is, furthermore, a grave philosophical error in the very posing of this sort of question about the Russians. When we contemplate *any* sort of new system, whatever it may be, we must *first* decide whether we want to see it brought about. In order to decide whether we *want* libertarianism or communism, or left-wing anarchism, or theocracy, or any other system, we must first assume that it has been established, and *then* consider whether the system could work, whether it could remain in existence, and just how efficient such a system would be. We have shown, I believe, that a libertarian system, once instituted, could work, be viable, and be at once far more efficient, prosperous, moral, and free than any other social system. But we have said nothing about how to *get* from the present system to the ideal; for these are two totally separate questions: the question of what *is* our ideal goal, and of the strategy and tactics of how to get from the present system *to* that goal. The Russian question mixes these two levels of discourse. It assumes, *not* that libertarianism has been established everywhere throughout the globe, but that for some reason it has been established *only* in America and nowhere else. But why assume this? Why not first assume that it has been established *everywhere* and see whether we like it? After all, the libertarian philosophy is an eternal one, not bound to time or place. We advocate liberty for everyone, everywhere, not just in the United States. If someone agrees that a world libertarian society, once established, is the best that he can conceive, that it would be workable, efficient, and moral, then let him *become* a libertarian, let him join us in accepting liberty as our ideal goal, and *then* join us further in the separate—and obviously difficult—task of figuring out how to bring this ideal about.

If we do move on to strategy, it is obvious that the larger an area in which liberty is first established the *better* its chances for survival, and the better its chance to resist any violent overthrow that may be attempted. If liberty is established instantaneously throughout the world, then there will of course be *no* problem of "national defense." *All* problems will be local police problems. If, however, only Deep Falls, Wyoming, becomes libertarian while the rest of America and the world remain statist, its chances for survival will be very slim. If Deep Falls, Wyoming, declares its secession from the United States government and establishes a free society, the chances are great that the United States—given its historical ferocity toward secessionists—would quickly invade and crush the new free society, and there is little that *any* Deep Falls police force could do about it. Between these two polar cases, there is an infinite continuum of degrees, and obviously, the larger the area of freedom, the better it could withstand any outside threat. The "Russian question" is therefore a matter of strategy rather than a matter of deciding on basic principles and on the goal toward which we wish to direct our efforts.

But after all this is said and done, let us take up the Russian question anyway. Let us assume that the Soviet Union would really be hell-bent on attacking a libertarian population within the present boundaries of the United States (clearly, there would no longer be a United States government to form a single nation-state). In the first place, the form and quantity of defense expenditures would be decided upon by the American consumers themselves. Those Americans who favor Polaris submarines, and fear a Soviet threat, would subscribe toward the financing of such vessels. Those who prefer an ABM system would invest in such defensive missiles. Those who laugh at such a threat or those who are committed pacifists would not contribute to any "national" defense service at all. Different defense theories would be applied in proportion to those who agree with, and support, the various theories being offered. Given the enormous waste in all wars and defense preparations in all countries throughout history, it is certainly not beyond the bounds of reason to propose that private, voluntary defense efforts would be far more efficient than government boondoggles. Certainly these efforts would be infinitely more moral.

But let us assume the worst. Let us assume that the Soviet Union at last invades and conquers the territory of America. What then? We have to realize that the Soviet Union's difficulties will have only just begun. The main reason a conquering country can rule a defeated country is that the latter has an existing State apparatus to transmit and enforce the victor's orders onto a subject population. Britain, though far smaller in area and population, was able to rule India for centuries because it could transmit British orders to the ruling Indian princes, who in turn could enforce them on the subject population. But in those cases in history where the conquered *had* no government, the conquerors found rule over the conquered extremely difficult. When the British conquered West Africa, for example, they found it extremely difficult to govern the Ibo tribe (later to form Biafra) because that tribe was essentially libertarian, and had no ruling government of tribal chiefs to transmit orders to the natives. And perhaps the major reason it took the English centuries to conquer ancient Ireland is that the Irish had no State, and that there was therefore no ruling governmental structure to keep treaties, transmit orders, etc. It is for this reason that the English kept denouncing the "wild" and "uncivilized" Irish as "faithless," because they would not keep treaties with the English conquerors. The English could never understand that, lacking any sort of State, the Irish warriors who concluded treaties with the English could *only* speak for themselves; they could never commit any other group of the Irish population.[14]

Furthermore, the occupying Russians' lives would be made even more difficult by the inevitable eruption of guerrilla warfare by the American population. It is surely a lesson of the twentieth century—a lesson first driven home by the successful American revolutionaries against the mighty British Empire—that no occupying force can long keep down a native population determined to resist. If the giant United States, armed with far greater productivity and firepower, could not succeed against a tiny and relatively unarmed Vietnamese population, how in the world could the Soviet Union succeed in keeping down the American people? No Russian occupation soldier's life would be safe from the

---

[14]Peden, "Stateless Societies," p. 3; also see Kathleen Hughes, introduction to A. Jocelyn Otway-Ruthven, *A History of Medieval Ireland* (New York: Barnes & Noble, 1968).

wrath of a resisting American populace. Guerrilla warfare has proved to be an irresistible force precisely because it stems, not from a dictatorial central government, but from the people themselves, fighting for their liberty and independence against a foreign State. And surely the anticipation of this sea of troubles, of the enormous costs and losses that would inevitably follow, would stop well in advance even a hypothetical Soviet government bent on military conquest.

13

Conservation, Ecology, and Growth

Liberal Complaints

LEFT-LIBERAL INTELLECTUALS are often a wondrous group to behold. In the last three or four decades, not a very long time in human history, they have, like whirling dervishes, let loose a series of angry complaints against free-market capitalism. The curious thing is that each of these complaints has been contradictory to one or more of their predecessors. But contradictory complaints by liberal intellectuals do not seem to faze them or serve to abate their petulance—even though it is often the very same intellectuals who are reversing themselves so rapidly. And these reversals seem to make no dent whatever in their self-righteousness or in the self-confidence of their position.

Let us consider the record of recent decades:

1. In the late 1930s and early 1940s, the liberal intellectuals came to the conclusion that capitalism was suffering from inevitable "secular stagnation," a stagnation imposed by the slowing down of population growth, the end of the old Western frontier, and by the supposed fact that no further inventions were possible. All this spelled eternal stagnation, permanent mass unemployment, and therefore the need for socialism, or thoroughgoing State planning, to replace free-market capitalism. This on the threshold of the greatest boom in American history!

2. During the 1950s, despite the great boom in postwar America, the

liberal intellectuals kept raising their sights; the cult of "economic growth" now entered the scene. To be sure, capitalism was growing, but it was not growing fast enough. Therefore free-market capitalism must be abandoned, and socialism or government intervention must step in and force-feed the economy, must build investments and compel greater saving in order to maximize the rate of growth, even if we don't *want* to grow that fast. Conservative economists such as Colin Clark attacked this liberal program as "growthmanship."

3. Suddenly, John Kenneth Galbraith entered the liberal scene with his best-selling *The Affluent Society* in 1958. And just as suddenly, the liberal intellectuals reversed their indictments. The trouble with capitalism, it now appeared, was that it had grown *too much;* we were no longer stagnant, but *too well off,* and man had lost his spirituality amidst supermarkets and automobile tail fins. What was necessary, then, was for government to step in, either in massive intervention or as socialism, and tax the consumers heavily in order to reduce their bloated affluence.

4. The cult of excess affluence had its day, to be superseded by a contradictory worry about poverty, stimulated by Michael Harrington's *The Other America* in 1962. Suddenly, the problem with America was not excessive affluence, but increasing and grinding poverty—and, once again, the solution was for the government to step in, plan mightily, and tax the wealthy in order to lift up the poor. And so we had the War on Poverty for several years.

5. Stagnation; deficient growth; overaffluence; overpoverty; the intellectual fashions changed like ladies' hemlines. Then, in 1964, the happily short-lived Ad Hoc Committee on the Triple Revolution issued its then-famous manifesto, which brought us and the liberal intellectuals full circle. For two or three frenetic years we were regaled with the idea that America's problem was not stagnation but the exact reverse: in a few short years all of America's production facilities would be automated and cybernated, incomes and production would be enormous and superabundant, *but* everyone would be automated out of a job. Once again, free-market capitalism would lead to permanent mass unemployment, which could *only* be remedied—you guessed it!—by massive State intervention or by outright socialism. For several years, in the mid-1960s, we thus suffered from what was justly named the "Automation Hysteria."[1]

---

[1]Ironically, the conservative economist Dr. George Terborgh, who had written the major refutation of the stagnation thesis a generation earlier *(The Bogey of Economic Maturity* [1945]), now wrote the leading refutation of the new wave, *The Automation Hysteria* (1966).

6. By the late 1960s it was clear to everyone that the automation hysterics had been dead wrong, that automation was proceeding at no faster a pace than old-fashioned "mechanization," and indeed that the 1969 recession was causing a falling off in the rate of increase of productivity. One hears no more about automation dangers nowadays; we are now in the seventh phase of liberal economic flip-flops.

7. Affluence is again excessive, and, in the name of conservation, ecology, and the increasing scarcity of resources, free-market capitalism is growing much too fast. State planning, or socialism, must, of course, step in to abolish all growth and bring about a zero-growth society and economy—in order to avoid negative growth, or retrogression, sometime in the future! We are now back to a super-Galbraithian position, to which has been added scientific jargon about effluents, ecology, and "spaceship earth," as well as a bitter assault on technology itself as being an evil polluter. Capitalism has brought about technology, growth—including population growth, industry, and pollution—and government is supposed to step in and eradicate these evils.

It is not at all unusual, in fact, to find the same people now holding a contradictory blend of positions 5 and 7 and maintaining *at one and the same time* that (a) we are living in a "post-scarcity" age where we no longer need private property, capitalism, or material incentives to production; *and* (b) that capitalist greed is depleting our resources and bringing about imminent worldwide scarcity. The liberal answer to both, or indeed to all, of these problems turns out, of course, to be the same: socialism or state planning to replace free-market capitalism. The great economist Joseph Schumpeter put the whole shoddy performance of liberal intellectuals into a nutshell a generation ago: "Capitalism stands its trial before judges who have the sentence of death in their pockets. They are going to pass it, whatever the defense they may hear; the only success victorious defense can possibly produce is a change in the indictment."[2] And so, the charges, the indictments, may change and contradict previous charges—but the answer is always and wearily the same.

The Attack on Technology and Growth

The fashionable attack on growth and affluence is palpably an attack by comfortable, contented upper-class liberals. Enjoying a material con-

[2]Joseph A. Schumpeter, *Capitalism, Socialism, and Democracy* (New York: Harper & Bros., 1942), p. 144.

tentment and a living standard undreamt of by even the wealthiest men of the past, it is easy for upper-class liberals to sneer at "materialism," and to call for a freeze on all further economic advance.[3] For the mass of the world's population still living in squalor such a cry for the cessation of growth is truly obscene; but even in the United States, there is little evidence of satiety and superabundance. Even the upper-class liberals themselves have not been conspicuous for making a bonfire of their salary checks as a contribution to their war on "materialism" and affluence.

The widespread attack on technology is even more irresponsible. If technology were to be rolled back to the "tribe" and to the preindustrial era, the result would be mass starvation and death on a universal scale. The vast majority of the world's population is dependent for its very survival on modern technology and industry. The North American continent was able to accommodate approximately one million Indians in the days before Columbus, all living on a subsistence level. It is now able to accommodate several hundred million people, all living at an infinitely higher living standard—and the reason is modern technology and industry. Abolish the latter and we will abolish the people as well. For all one knows, to our fanatical antipopulationists this "solution" to the population question may be a good thing, but for the great majority of us, this would be a draconian "final solution" indeed.

The irresponsible attack on technology is another liberal flip-flop: it comes from the same liberal intellectuals who, thirty-odd years ago, were denouncing capitalism for not putting modern technology to full use in the service of State planning and were calling for absolute rule by a modern "technocratic" elite. Yet now the very same intellectuals who not so long ago were yearning for a technocratic dictatorship over

---

[3]Cf. the interpretation in William Tucker, "Environmentalism and the Leisure Class," *Harper's* (December 1977), pp. 49–56, 73–80.

Fortunately, black groups are beginning to understand the significance of liberal antigrowth ideology. In January 1978, the board of directors of the National Association for the Advancement of Colored People opposed President Carter's energy program and called for the deregulation of oil and natural gas prices. Explaining the NAACP's new position, chairman of the board Margaret Bush Wilson declared:

"We are concerned about the slow growth policy of President Carter's energy plan. The issue is what kind of energy policy will lend itself to . . . a viable expansive economy, one that is not restrictive, because under slow growth blacks suffer more than anyone else."

Paul Delaney, "NAACP in Major Dispute on Energy View," *New York Times* (January 30, 1978).

all of our lives are now trying to deprive us of the vital fruits of technology itself.

Yet the various contradictory phases of liberal thought never completely die; and many of the same antitechnologists, in a 180-degree reversal of the automation hysteria, are *also* confidently forecasting technological stagnation from now on. They cheerily predict a gloomy future for mankind by assuming that technology will stagnate, and not continue to improve and accelerate. This is the technique of pseudoscientific forecasting of the widely touted antigrowth Club of Rome Report. As Passell, Roberts, and Ross write in their critique of the report, "If the telephone company were restricted to turn-of-the-century technology 20 million operators would be needed to handle today's volume of calls. Or, as British editor Norman Macrae has observed, "an extrapolation of the trends of the 1880s would show today's cities buried under horse manure."[4] Or, further:

While the team's [Club of Rome's] model hypothesizes exponential growth for industrial and agricultural needs, it places arbitrary, nonexponential, limits on the technical progress that might accommodate these needs. . . .

The Rev. Thomas Malthus made a similar point two centuries ago without benefit of computer printouts. . . . Malthus argued that people tend to multiply exponentially, while the food supply at best increases at a constant rate. He expected that starvation and war would periodically redress the balance. . . .

But there is no particular criterion beyond myopia on which to base that speculation. Malthus was wrong; food capacity has kept up with population. While no one knows for certain, technical progress shows no sign of slowing down. The best econometric estimates suggest that it is indeed growing exponentially.[5]

What we need is more economic growth, not less; more and better technology, and not the impossible and absurd attempt to scrap technology and return to the primitive tribe. Improved technology and greater capital investment will lead to higher living standards for all and provide greater material comforts, as well as the leisure to pursue and enjoy the "spiritual" side of life. There is precious little culture or civilization available for people who must work long hours to eke out a subsistence living. The real problem is that productive capital investment is being siphoned off by taxes, restrictions, and government contracts for unproductive and wasteful government expenditures, including military and

---

[4]D. Meadows, *et al.*, *The Limits to Growth* (New York: Universe Books, 1972); P. Passell, M. Roberts, and L. Ross, "Review of *The Limits to Growth*," *New York Times Book Review* (April 2, 1972), p. 10.

[5]Passell, Roberts, and Ross, *op. cit.*, p. 12.

space boondoggling. Furthermore, the precious technical resource of scientists and engineers is being ever more intensively diverted to government, instead of to "civilian" consumer production. What we need is for government to get out of the way, remove its incubus of taxation and expenditures from the economy, and allow productive and technical resources once again to devote themselves fully to increasing the well-being of the mass of consumers. We need growth, higher living standards, and a technology and capital equipment that meet consumer wants and demands; but we can only achieve these by removing the incubus of statism and allowing the energies of all of the population to express themselves in the free-market economy. We need an economic and technological growth that emerges freely, as Jane Jacobs has shown, from the free-market economy, and not the distortions and wastes imposed upon the world economy from the liberal force-feeding of the 1950s. We need, in short, a truly free-market, libertarian economy.

Conservation of Resources

As we have mentioned, the selfsame liberals who claim that we have entered the "postscarcity" age and are in no further need of economic growth, are in the forefront of the complaint that "capitalist greed" is destroying our scarce natural resources. The gloom-and-doom soothsayers of the Club of Rome, for example, by simply extrapolating current trends of resource use, confidently predict the exhaustion of vital raw materials within forty years. But confident—and completely faulty— predictions of exhaustion of raw materials have been made countless times in recent centuries.

What the soothsayers have overlooked is the vital role that the free-market economic mechanism plays in conserving, and adding to, natural resources. Let us consider, for example, a typical copper mine. Why has copper ore not been exhausted long before now by the inexorable demands of our industrial civilization? Why is it that copper miners, once they have found and opened a vein of ore, do not mine all the copper immediately; why, instead, do they conserve the copper mine, add to it, and extract the copper gradually, from year to year? Because the mine owners realize that, for example, if they triple *this year's* production of copper they may indeed triple this year's income, *but* they will also be depleting the mine, and therefore the *future* income they will be able to derive from it. On the market, this loss of future income is immediately reflected in the monetary value—the price—of the mine as a whole. This monetary value, reflected in the selling price of the mine, and then of individual shares of mining stock, is based on the expected future income to be earned from the production of the copper; any depletion of the mine, then, will lower the value of the mine and hence the price of the mining stock. Every mine owner, then, has to weigh the advantages of immediate income from copper production against the loss in the "capital value" of the mine as a whole, and hence against the loss in the value of his shares.

The mine owners' decisions are determined by their expectations of future copper yields and demands, the existing and expected rates of interest, etc. Suppose, for example, that copper is expected to be rendered obsolete in a few years by a new synthetic metal. In that case, copper mine owners will rush to produce more copper now when it is more highly valued, and save less for the future when it will have little value—thereby benefitting the consumers and the economy as a whole by producing copper now when it is more intensely needed. But, on the other hand, if a copper shortage is expected in the future, mine owners will produce less now and wait to produce more later when copper prices are higher—thereby benefitting society by producing more in the future when it will be needed more intensely. Thus, we see that the market economy contains a marvelous built-in mechanism whereby the decisions of resource owners on present as against future production will benefit not only their own income and wealth, but the mass of consumers and the economy as a whole.

But there is much more to this free-market mechanism: Suppose that a growing shortage of copper is now expected in the future. The result is that more copper will be withheld now and saved for future production. The price of copper now will rise. The increase in copper prices will have several "conserving" effects. In the first place, the higher price of copper is a signal to the users of copper that it is scarcer and more expensive; the copper users will then conserve the use of this more expensive metal. They will use less copper, substituting cheaper metals or plastics; and copper will be conserved more fully and saved for those uses for which there is no saisfactory substitute. Moreover, the greater cost of copper will stimulate (a) a rush to find new copper ores; and (b) a search for less expensive substitutes, perhaps by new technological discoveries. Higher prices for copper will also stimulate campaigns for saving and recycling the metal.This price mechanism of the free market is precisely the reason that copper, and other natural resources, have not disappeared long ago. As Passell, Roberts, and Ross say in their critique of the Club of Rome:

Natural resource reserves and needs in the model are calculated [in] . . . the absence of prices as a variable in the "Limits" projection of how resources will be used. In the real world, rising prices act as an economic signal to conserve scarce resources, providing incentives to use cheaper materials in their place, stimulating research efforts on new ways to save on resource inputs, and making renewed exploration attempts more profitable.[6]

In fact, in contrast to the gloom-and-doomers, raw material and natural resource prices have remained low, and have generally declined relative to other prices. To liberal and Marxist intellectuals, this is usually a sign of capitalist "exploitation" of the underdeveloped countries which are often the producers of the raw materials. But it is a sign of something completely different, of the fact that natural resources have not been growing scarcer but more abundant; hence their relatively lower cost. The development of cheap substitutes, e.g., plastics, synthetic fibres, has kept natural resources cheap and abundant. And in a few decades we can expect that modern technology will develop a remarkably cheap source of energy—nuclear fusion—a development which will automatically yield a great abundance of raw materials for the work that will be needed.

The development of synthetic materials and of cheaper energy highlights a vital aspect of modern technology the doom-sayers overlook: that technology and industrial production *create* resources which had never existed as effective resources. For example, before the development of the kerosene lamp and especially the automobile, petroleum was not a resource but an unwanted waste, a giant liquid black "weed." It was only the development of modern industry that converted petroleum *into* a useful resource. Furthermore, modern technology, through improved geological techniques and through the incentives of the market, has been *finding* new petroleum reserves at a rapid rate.

Predictions of imminent exhaustion of resources, as we have noted, are nothing new. In 1908, President Theodore Roosevelt, calling a Governors' Conference on natural resources, warned of their "imminent exhaustion." At the same conference, steel industrialist Andrew Carnegie predicted the exhaustion of the Lake Superior iron range by 1940, while railroad magnate James J. Hill forecast the exhaustion of much of our timber resources in ten years. Not only that: Hill even predicted an imminent shortage of wheat production in the United States, in a country where we are still grappling with the wheat *surpluses* generated by

[6]Passell, Roberts, and Ross, *op. cit.*, p. 12.

our farm subsidy program. Current forecasts of doom are made on the same basis: a grievous underweighting of the prospects of modern technology and an ignorance of the workings of the market economy.[7]

It is true that several particular natural resources have suffered, in the past and now, from depletion. But in each case the reason has not been "capitalist greed"; on the contrary, the reason has been the *failure* of government to allow private property in the resource—in short, a failure to pursue the logic of private property rights far enough.

One example has been timber resources. In the American West and in Canada, most of the forests are owned, not by private owners but by the federal (or provincial) government. The government then *leases* their use to private timber companies. In short, private property is permitted only in the annual *use* of the resource, but not in the forest, the resource, itself. In this situation, the private timber company does not own the capital value, and therefore does not have to worry about depletion of the resource itself. The timber company has no economic incentive to conserve the resource, replant trees, etc. Its only incentive is to cut as many trees as quickly as possible, since there is no economic value to the timber company in maintaining the capital value of the forest. In Europe, where private ownership of forests is far more common, there is little complaint of destruction of timber resources. For wherever private property is allowed in the forest itself, it is to the benefit of the owner to preserve and restore tree growth while he is cutting timber, so as to avoid depletion of the forest's capital value.[8]

Thus, in the United States, a major culprit has been the Forest Service of the U.S. Department of Agriculture, which owns forests and leases annual rights to cut timber, with resulting devastation of the trees. In contrast, private forests such as those owned by large lumber firms like Georgia-Pacific and U.S. Plywood scientifically cut and reforest their trees in order to maintain their future supply.[9]

Another unhappy consequence of the American government's failure

[7]On these mistaken forecasts, see Thomas B. Nolan, "The Inexhaustible Resource of Technology," in H. Jarrett, ed., *Perspectives on Conservation* (Baltimore: Johns Hopkins Press, 1958), pp. 49-66.

[8]On timber, and on conservation generally, see Anthony Scott, *Natural Resources: The Economics of Conservation* (Toronto: University of Toronto Press, 1955), pp. 121-25 and *passim*.

On ways in which the federal government itself has been destroying rather than conserving timber resources, from highway building to the indiscriminate dams and other projects of the Army Corps of Engineers, see Edwin G. Dolan, TANSTAAFL (New York: Holt, Rinehart & Winston, 1971), p. 96.

[9]See Robert Poole, Jr., "Reason and Ecology," in D. James, ed., *Outside, Looking In* (New York: Harper & Row, 1972), pp. 250-51.

to allow private property in a resource was the destruction of the Western grasslands in the late nineteenth century. Every viewer of "Western" movies is familiar with the mystique of the "open range" and the often violent "wars" among cattlemen, sheepmen, and farmers over parcels of ranch land. The "open range" was the failure of the federal government to apply the policy of homesteading to the changed conditions of the drier climate west of the Mississippi. In the East, the 160 acres granted free to homesteading farmers on government land constituted a viable technological unit for farming in a wetter climate. But in the dry climate of the West, no successful cattle or sheep ranch could be organized on a mere 160 acres. But the federal government refused to expand the 160-acre unit to allow the "homesteading" of larger cattle ranches. Hence, the "open range," on which private cattle and sheep owners were able to roam unchecked on government-owned pasture land. But this meant that no one owned the pasture, the land itself; it was therefore to the economic advantage of every cattle or sheep owner to graze the land and use up the grass as quickly as possible, otherwise the grass would be grazed by some other sheep or cattle owner. The result of this tragically shortsighted refusal to allow private property in grazing land itself was an overgrazing of the land, the ruining of the grassland by grazing too early in the season, and the failure of anyone to restore or replant the grass—anyone who bothered to restore the grass would have had to look on helplessly while someone else grazed his cattle or sheep. Hence the overgrazing of the West, and the onset of the "dust bowl." Hence also the illegal attempts by numerous cattlemen, farmers, and sheepmen to take the law into their own hands and fence off the land into private property—and the range wars that often followed.

Professor Samuel P. Hays, in his authoritative account of the conservation movement in America, writes of the range problem:

Much of the Western livestock industry depended for its forage upon the "open" range, owned by the federal government, but free for anyone to use. . . . Congress had never provided legislation regulating grazing or permitting stockmen to acquire range lands. Cattle and sheepmen roamed the public domain. . . . Cattlemen fenced range for their exclusive use, but competitors cut the wire. Resorting to force and violence, sheepherders and cowboys "solved" their disputes over grazing lands by slaughtering rival livestock and murdering rival stockmen. . . . Absence of the most elementary institutions of property law created confusion, bitterness, and destruction.

Amid this turmoil the public range rapidly deteriorated. Originally plentiful and lush, the forage supply was subjected to intense pressure by increasing use. . . . The public domain became stocked with more animals than the range could support. Since each stockman feared that others would beat him to the available forage, he grazed early in the year and did not permit the young grass to mature and reseed. Under such conditions the quality and quantity of available forage rapidly decreased; vigorous perennials gave way to annuals and annuals to weeds.[10]

Hays concludes that public-domain range lands may have been depleted by over two-thirds by this process, as compared to their virgin condition.

There is a vitally important area in which the absence of private property in the resource has been and is causing, not only depletion of resources, but also a complete failure to develop vast potential resources. This is the potentially enormously productive *ocean* resource. The oceans are in the international public domain, i.e., no person, company, or even national government is allowed property rights in parts of the ocean. As a result, the oceans have remained in the same primitive state as was the land in the precivilized days before the development of agriculture. The way of production for primitive man was "hunting-and-gathering": the hunting of wild animals and the gathering of fruits, berries, nuts, and wild seeds and vegetables. Primitive man worked passively *within* his environment instead of acting to transform it; hence he just lived off the land without attempting to remould it. As a result, the land was unproductive, and only a relatively few tribesmen could exist at a bare subsistence level. It was only with the development of agriculture, the farming of the soil, and the transformation of the land through farming that productivity and living standards could take giant leaps forward. And it was only with agriculture that civilization could begin. But to permit the development of agriculture there had to be private property rights, first in the fields and crops, and then in the land itself.

With respect to the ocean, however, we are still in the primitive, unproductive hunting and gathering stage. Anyone can capture fish in the ocean, or extract its resources, but only on the run, only as hunters and gatherers. No one can *farm* the ocean, no one can engage in *aquaculture*. In this way we are deprived of the use of the immense fish and mineral resources of the seas. For example, if anyone tried to farm the sea and to increase the productivity of the fisheries by fertilizers, he would immediately be deprived of the fruits of his efforts because he could not keep other fishermen from rushing in and seizing the fish.

[10]Samuel P. Hays, *Conservation and the Gospel of Efficiency* (Cambridge: Harvard University Press, 1959), pp. 50-51. See also E. Louise Peffer, *The Closing of the Public Domain* (Stanford: Stanford University Press, 1951), pp. 22-31, and *passim*.

And so no one tries to fertilize the oceans as the land is fertilized. Furthermore, there is no economic incentive—in fact, there is every *disincentive*—for anyone to engage in technological research in the ways and means of improving the productivity of the fisheries, or in extracting the mineral resources of the oceans. There will only be such incentive when property rights in parts of the ocean are as fully allowed as property rights in the land. Even now there is a simple but effective technique that could be used for increasing fish productivity: parts of the ocean could be fenced off electronically, and through this readily available electronic fencing, fish could be segregated by size. By preventing big fish from eating smaller fish, the production of fish could be increased enormously. And if private property in parts of the ocean were permitted, a vast flowering of *aquaculture* would create and multiply ocean resources in numerous ways we cannot now even foresee.

National governments have tried vainly to cope with the problem of fish depletion by placing irrational and uneconomic restrictions on the total size of the catch, or on the length of the allowable season. In the cases of salmon, tuna, and halibut, technological methods of fishing have thereby been kept primitive and unproductive by unduly shortening the season and injuring the quality of the catch and by stimulating overproduction—and underuse during the year—of the fishing fleets. And of course such governmental restrictions do nothing at all to stimulate the growth of aquaculture. As Professors North and Miller write:

Fishermen are poor because they are forced to use inefficient equipment and to fish only a small fraction of the time [by the governmental regulations] and of course there are far too many of them. The consumer pays a much higher price for red salmon than would be necessary if efficient methods were used. Despite the ever-growing intertwining bonds of regulations, the preservation of the salmon run is still not assured.

The root of the problem lies in the current non-ownership arrangement. It is not in the interests of any individual fisherman to concern himself with perpetuation of the salmon run. Quite the contrary: It is rather in his interests to catch as many fish as he can during the season.[11]

In contrast, North and Miller point out that private property rights in the ocean, under which the owner would use the least costly and most efficient technology *and* preserve and make productive the resource itself, is now more feasible than ever: "The invention of modern elec-

[11]Douglass C. North and Roger LeRoy Miller, *The Economics of Public Issues* (New York: Harper & Row, 1971), p. 107.

tronic sensing equipment has now made the policing of large bodies of water relatively cheap and easy."[12]

The growing international conflicts over parts of the ocean only further highlight the importance of private property rights in this vital area. For as the United States and other nations assert their sovereignty 200 miles from their shores, and as private companies and governments squabble over areas of the ocean; and as trawlers, fishing nets, oil drillers, and mineral diggers war over the same areas of the ocean—property rights become increasingly and patently more important. As Francis Christy writes:

. . . coal is mined in shafts below the sea floor, oil is drilled from platforms fixed to the bottom rising above the water, minerals can be dredged from the surface of the ocean bed . . . sedentary animals are scraped from the bed on which telephone cables may lie, bottom feeding animals are caught in traps or trawls, mid-water species may be taken by hook and line or by trawls which occasionally interfere with submarines, surface species are taken by net and harpoon, and the surface itself is used for shipping as well as the vessels engaged in extracting resources.[13]

This growing conflict leads Christy to predict that "the seas are in a stage of transition. They are moving from a condition in which property rights are almost nonexistent to a condition in which property rights of some form will become appropriated or made available." Eventually, concludes Christy, "as the sea's resources become more valuable, exclusive rights will be acquired."[14]

Pollution

All right: Even if we concede that full private property in resources and the free market will conserve and create resources, and do it far

---

[12] *Ibid.*, p. 108. Also see James A. Crutchfield and Giulio Pontecorvo, *The Pacific Salmon Fisheries: A Study of Irrational Conservation* (Baltimore: Johns Hopkins Press, 1969). On a similar situation in the tuna industry, see Francis T. Christy, Jr., "New Dimensions for Transnational Marine Resources," *American Economic Review, Papers and Proceedings* (May 1970), p. 112; and on the Pacific halibut industry, see James A. Crutchfield and Arnold Zellner, *Economic Aspects of the Pacific Halibut Industry* (Washington, D.C.: U.S. Dept. of the Interior, 1961). For an imaginative proposal for private property in parts of the ocean even before the advent of electronic fencing, see Gordon Tullock, *The Fisheries—Some Radical Proposals* (Columbia, S.C.: University of South Carolina Bureau of Business and Economic Research, 1962).

[13] Christy, *loc. cit.*, p. 112.

[14] *Ibid.*, pp. 112-113. For a definitive discussion, economic, technological, and legal, of the

better than government regulation, what of the problem of pollution? Wouldn't we be suffering aggravated pollution from unchecked "capitalist greed"?

There is, first of all, this stark empirical fact: Government ownerhip, even socialism, has proved to be no solution to the problem of pollution. Even the most starry-eyed proponents of government planning concede that the poisoning of Lake Baikal in the Soviet Union is a monument to heedless industrial pollution of a valuable natural resource. But there is far more to the problem than that. Note, for example, the two crucial areas in which pollution has become an important problem: the air and the waterways, particularly the rivers. But these are precisely two of the vital areas in society in which private property has not been permitted to function.

First, the rivers. The rivers, and the oceans too, are generally owned by the government; private property, certainly complete private property, has not been permitted in the water. In essence, then, government owns the rivers. But government ownership is not true ownership, because the government officials, while able to control the resource, cannot themselves reap their capital value on the market. Government officials cannot sell the rivers or sell stock in them. Hence, they have no economic incentive to preserve the purity and value of the rivers. Rivers are, then, in the economic sense, "unowned"; therefore government officials have permitted their corruption and pollution. Anyone has been able to dump polluting garbage and wastes in the waters. But consider what would happen if private firms were able to own the rivers and the lakes. If a private firm owned Lake Erie, for example, then anyone dumping garbage in the lake would be promptly sued in the courts for their aggression against private property and would be forced by the courts to pay damages and to cease and desist from any further aggression. Thus, only private property rights will insure an end to pollution-invasion of resources. Only because the rivers are unowned is there no owner to rise up and defend his precious resource from attack. If, in contrast, anyone should dump garbage or pollutants into a lake which is privately owned (as are many smaller lakes), he would not be permitted to do so for very long—the owner would come roaring to its defense.[15] As Professor Dolan writes:

entire problem of the ocean and ocean fisheries, see Francis T. Christy, Jr., and Anthony Scott, *The Common Wealth in Ocean Fisheries* (Baltimore: Johns Hopkins Press, 1965).

[15]Existing "appropriation" law in the Western states already provides the basis for full "homesteading" private property rights in the rivers. For a full discussion, see Jack Hirshleifer, James C. DeHaven, and Jerome W. Milliman, *Water Supply; Economics, Technology, and Policy* (Chicago: University of Chicago Press, 1960), Chapter IX.

With a General Motors owning the Mississippi River, you can be sure that stiff effluent charges would be assessed on industries and municipalities along its banks, and that the water would be kept clean enough to maximize revenues from leases granted to firms seeking rights to drinking water, recreation, and commercial fishing.[16]

If government as owner has allowed the pollution of the rivers, government has also been the single major active polluter, especially in its role as municipal sewage disposer. There already exist low-cost chemical toilets which can burn off sewage without polluting air, ground, or water; but who will invest in chemical toilets when local governments will dispose of sewage free to their customers?

This example points up a problem similar to the case of the stunting of aquaculture technology by the absence of private property: if governments as owners of the rivers permit pollution of water, then industrial technology will—and has—become a water-polluting technology. If production processes are allowed to pollute the rivers unchecked by their owners, then that is the sort of production technology we will have.

If the problem of water pollution can be cured by private property rights in water, how about air pollution? How can libertarians possibly come up with a solution for this grievous problem? Surely, there can't be private property in the *air?* But the answer is: yes, there can. We have already seen how radio and TV frequencies can be privately owned. So could channels for airlines. Commercial airline routes, for example, could be privately owned; there is no need for a Civil Aeronautics Board to parcel out—and restrict—routes between various cities. But in the case of air pollution we are dealing not so much with private property *in the air* as with protecting private property in one's lungs, fields, and orchards. The vital fact about air pollution is that the polluter sends unwanted and unbidden pollutants—from smoke to nuclear fallout to sulfur oxides—*through* the air and into the lungs of innocent victims, as well as onto their material property. All such emanations which injure person or property constitute aggression against the private property of the victims. Air pollution, after all, is just as much aggression as committing arson against another's property or injuring him physically. Air pollution that injures others is aggression pure and simple. The

---

[16]Edwin G. Dolan, "Capitalism and the Environment," *Individualist* (March 1971), p. 3.

major function of government—of courts and police—is to stop aggression; instead, the government has failed in this task and has failed grievously to exercise its defense function against air pollution.

It is important to realize that this failure has *not* been a question purely of ignorance, a simple time lag between recognizing a new technological problem and facing up to it. For if some of the modern pollutants have only recently become known, factory smoke and many of its bad effects have been known ever since the Industrial Revolution, known to the extent that the American courts, during the late—and as far back as the early—nineteenth century made the deliberate decision to allow property rights to be violated by industrial smoke. To do so, the courts had to—and did—systematically change and weaken the defenses of property right embedded in Anglo-Saxon common law. Before the mid and late nineteenth century, any injurious air pollution was considered a tort, a nuisance against which the victim could sue for damages and against which he could take out an injunction to cease and desist from any further invasion of his property rights. But during the nineteenth century, the courts systematically altered the law of negligence and the law of nuisance to *permit* any air pollution which was not unusually greater than any similar manufacturing firm, one that was not more extensive than the customary practice of fellow polluters.

As factories began to arise and emit smoke, blighting the orchards of neighboring farmers, the farmers would take the manufacturers to court, asking for damages and injunctions against further invasion of their property. But the judges said, in effect, "Sorry. We *know* that industrial smoke (i.e., air pollution) invades and interferes with your property rights. But there is something *more important* than mere property rights: and that is public policy, the 'common good.' And the common good decrees that industry is a good thing, industrial progress is a good thing, and therefore your mere private property rights must be overridden on behalf of the general welfare." And now all of us are paying the bitter price for this overriding of private property, in the form of lung disease and countless other ailments. And all for the "common good"![17]

That this principle has guided the courts during the air age as well may be seen by a decision of the Ohio courts in *Antonik* v. *Chamberlain* (1947). The residents of a suburban area near Akron sued to enjoin the

[17]See E. F. Roberts, "Plead the Ninth Amendment!" *Natural History* (August–September 1970), pp. 18ff. For a definitive history and analysis of the change in the legal system toward growth and property rights in the first half of the nineteenth century, see Morton J. Horwitz, *The Transformation of American Law, 1780–1860* (Cambridge: Harvard University Press, 1977).

defendants from operating a privately owned airport. The grounds were invasion of property rights through excessive noise. Refusing the injunction, the court declared:

> In our business of judging in this case, while sitting as a court of equity, we must not only weigh the conflict of interests between the airport owner and the nearby landowners, but we must further recognize the public policy of the generation in which we live. We must recognize that the establishment of an airport . . . is of great concern to the public, and if such an airport is abated, or its establishment prevented, the consequences will be not only a serious injury to the owner of the port property but may be a serious loss of a valuable asset to the entire community.[18]

To cap the crimes of the judges, legislatures, federal and state, moved in to cement the aggression by prohibiting victims of air pollution from engaging in "class action" suits against polluters. Obviously, if a factory pollutes the atmosphere of a city where there are tens of thousands of victims, it is impractical for each victim to sue to collect his particular damages from the polluter (although an *injunction* could be used effectively by one small victim). The common law, therefore, recognizes the validity of "class action" suits, in which one or a few victims can sue the aggressor not only on their own behalf, but on behalf of the entire *class* of similar victims. But the legislatures systematically outlawed such class action suits in pollution cases. For this reason, a victim may successfully sue a polluter who injures him individually, in a one-to-one "private nuisance" suit. But he is prohibited by law from acting against a mass polluter who is injuring a large number of people in a given area! As Frank Bubb writes, "It is as if the government were to tell you that it will (attempt to) protect you from a thief who steals only from you, but it will not protect you if the thief also steals from everyone else in the neighborhood . . ."[19]

Noise, too, is a form of air pollution. Noise is the creation of sound waves which go through the air and then bombard and invade the property and persons of others. Only recently have physicians begun to investigate the damaging effects of noise on the human physiology. Again, a libertarian legal system would permit damage and class action suits and injunctions against excessive and damaging noise: against "noise pollution."

[18]Quoted in Milton Katz, *The Function of Tort Liability in Technology Assessment* (Cambridge: Harvard University Program on Technology and Society, 1969), p. 610.

[19]Frank Bubb, "The Cure for Air Pollution," *The Libertarian Forum* (April 15, 1970), p. 1. Also see Dolan, TANSTAAFL, pp. 37–39.

The remedy against air pollution is therefore crystal clear, and it has nothing to do with multibillion-dollar palliative government programs at the expense of the taxpayers which do not even meet the real issue. The remedy is simply for the courts to return to their function of defending person and property rights against invasion, and therefore to enjoin anyone from injecting pollutants into the air. But what of the propollution defenders of industrial progress? And what of the increased costs that would have to be borne by the consumer? And what of our present polluting technology?

The argument that such an injunctive prohibition against pollution would add to the costs of industrial production is as reprehensible as the pre–Civil War argument that the abolition of slavery would add to the costs of growing cotton, and that therefore abolition, however morally correct, was "impractical." For this means that the polluters are able to impose all of the high costs of pollution upon those whose lungs and property rights they have been allowed to invade with impunity.

Furthermore, the cost and technology argument overlooks the vital fact that if air pollution is allowed to proceed with impunity, there continues to be no economic incentive to develop a technology that will *not* pollute. On the contrary, the incentive would continue to cut, as it has for a century, precisely the other way. Suppose, for example, that in the days when automobiles and trucks were first being used, the courts had ruled as follows: "Ordinarily, we would be opposed to trucks invading people's lawns as an invasion of private property, and we would insist that trucks confine themselves to the roads, regardless of traffic congestion. But trucks are vitally important to the public welfare, and therefore we decree that trucks should be allowed to cross any lawns they wish provided they believe that this would ease their traffic problems." If the courts had ruled in this way, then we would now have a transportation system in which lawns would be systematically desecrated by trucks. And any attempt to stop this would be decried in the name of modern transportation needs! The point is that this is precisely the way that the courts ruled on air pollution—pollution which is far more damaging to all of us than trampling on lawns. In this way, the government gave the green light, from the very start, to a polluting technology. It is no wonder then that this is precisely the kind of technology we have. The only remedy is to force the polluting invaders to stop their invasion, and thereby to redirect technology into nonpolluting or even antipolluting channels.

Already, even at our necessarily primitive stage in antipollution tech-

nology, techniques have been developed to combat air and noise pollution. Mufflers can be installed on noisy machines that emit sound waves
precisely contra-cyclical to the waves of the machines, and thereby can
cancel out these racking sounds. Air wastes can even now be recaptured
as they leave the chimney and be recycled to yield products useful to
industry. Thus, sulfur dioxide, a major noxious air pollutant, can be
captured and recycled to produce economically valuable sulfuric acid.[20]
The highly polluting spark ignition engine will either have to be "cured"
by new devices or replaced altogether by such nonpolluting engines
as diesel, gas turbine, or steam, or by an electric car. And, as libertarian
systems engineer Robert Poole, Jr., points out, the costs of installing
the non- or antipolluting technology would then "ultimately be borne
by the consumers of the firms' products, i.e., by those who *choose* to
associate with the firm, rather than being passed on to innocent third
parties in the form of pollution (or as taxes)."[21]

Robert Poole cogently defines pollution "as the transfer of harmful
matter or energy to the person or property of another, without the
latter's consent."[22] The libertarian—and the only complete—solution
to the problem of air pollution is to use the courts and the legal structure
to combat and prevent such invasion. There are recent signs that the
legal system is beginning to change in this direction: new judicial decisions and repeal of laws disallowing class action suits. But this is only
a beginning.[23]

Among conservatives—in contrast to libertarians—there are two ultimately similar responses to the problem of air pollution. One response,
by Ayn Rand and Robert Moses among others, is to deny that the problem exists, and to attribute the entire agitation to leftists who want to
destroy capitalism and technology on behalf of a tribal form of socialism.
While part of this charge may be correct, denial of the very existence
of the problem is to deny science itself and to give a vital hostage to
the leftist charge that defenders of capitalism "place property rights
above human rights." Moreover, a defense of air pollution does *not even*
defend property rights; on the contrary, it puts these conservatives'
stamp of approval on those industrialists who are trampling upon the
property rights of the mass of the citizenry.

A second, and more sophisticated, conservative response is by such
free-market economists as Milton Friedman. The Friedmanites concede

[20]See Jane Jacobs, *The Economy of Cities* (New York: Random House, 1969), pp. 109ff.
[21]Poole, *op. cit.*, pp. 251–52.
[22]Poole, *op. cit.*, p. 245.
[23]Thus, see Dolan, TANSTAAFL, p. 39, and Katz, *passim.*

the existence of air pollution but propose to meet it, *not* by a defense of property rights, but rather by a supposedly utilitarian "cost-benefit" calculation by government, which will then make and enforce a "social decision" on *how much* pollution to allow. This decision would then be enforced either by licensing a given amount of pollution (the granting of "pollution rights"), by a graded scale of taxes against it, or by the taxpayers paying firms *not* to pollute. Not only would these proposals grant an enormous amount of bureaucratic power to government in the name of safeguarding the "free market"; they would continue to override property rights in the name of a collective decision enforced by the State. This is far from any genuine "free market," and reveals that, as in many other economic areas, it is impossible to *really* defend freedom and the free market without insisting on defending the rights of private property. Friedman's grotesque dictum that those urban inhabitants who don't wish to contract emphysema should move to the country is starkly reminiscent of Marie Antoinette's famous "Let them eat cake"—and reveals a lack of sensitivity to human or property rights. Friedman's statement, in fact, is of a piece with the typically conservative, "If you don't like it here, leave," a statement that implies that the government rightly owns the entire land area of "here," and that anyone who objects to its rule must therefore leave the area. Robert Poole's libertarian critique of the Friedmanite proposals offers a refreshing contrast:

Unfortunately, it is an example of the most serious failing of the conservative economists: nowhere in the proposal is there any mention of *rights*. This is the same failing that has undercut advocates of capitalism for 200 years. Even today, the term "laissez-faire" is apt to bring forth images of eighteenth century English factory towns engulfed in smoke and grimy with soot. The early capitalists agreed with the courts that smoke and soot were the "price" that must be paid for the benefits of industry. . . . Yet laissez-faire without rights is a contradiction in terms; the laissez-faire position is based on and derived from man's rights, and can endure only when rights are held inviolable. Now, in an age of increasing awareness of the environment, this old contradiction is coming back to haunt capitalism.

It is *true* that air is a scarce resource [as the Friedmanites say], but one must then ask *why* it is scarce. If it is scarce because of a systematic violation of rights, then the solution is not to raise the price of the status quo, thereby sanctioning the rights-violations, but to assert the rights and demand that they be protected. . . . When a factory discharges a great quantity of sulfur dioxide molecules that enter someone's lungs and cause pulmonary edema, the factory owners have aggressed against him as much as if they had broken his leg. The point must be emphasized because it is vital to the libertarian laissez-faire position. A laissez-faire polluter is a contradiction in terms and must be identified as such. A libertarian society would be a *full-liability* society, where everyone is fully responsible for his actions and any harmful consequences they might cause.[24]

In addition to betraying its presumed function of defending private property, government has contributed to air pollution in a more positive sense. It was not so long ago that the Department of Agriculture conducted mass sprayings of DDT by helicopter over large areas, overriding the wishes of individual objecting farmers. It *still* continues to pour tons of poisonous and carcinogenic insecticides all over the South, in an expensive and vain attempt to eradicate the fire ant.[25] And the Atomic Energy Commission has poured radioactive wastes into the air and into the ground by means of atomic testing. Municipal power and water plants, and the plants of licensed monopoly utility companies, mightily pollute the atmosphere. One of the major tasks of the State in this area is therefore to stop its *own* poisoning of the atmosphere.

Thus, when we peel away the confusions and the unsound philosophy of the modern ecologists, we find an important bedrock case against the existing system; but the case turns out to be not against capitalism, private property, growth, or technology per se. It is a case against the failure of government to allow and to defend the rights of private property against invasion. If property rights were to be defended fully, against private and governmental invasion alike, we would find here, as in other areas of our economy and society, that private enterprise and modern technology would come to mankind not as a curse but as its salvation.

[24]Poole, *op. cit.*, pp. 252–53. Friedman's dictum can be found in Peter Maiken, "Hysterics Won't Clean Up Pollution," *Human Events* (April 25, 1970), pp. 13, 21–23. A fuller presentation of the Friedmanite position may be found in Thomas D. Crocker and A. J. Rogers III, *Environmental Economics* (Hinsdale, Ill.: Dryden Press, 1971); and similar views may be found in J. H. Dales, *Pollution, Property, and Prices* (Toronto: University of Toronto Press, 1968), and Larry E. Ruff, "The Economic Common Sense of Pollution," *Public Interest* (Spring, 1970), pp. 69–85.

[25]Glenn Garvin, "Killing Fire Ants With Carcinogens," *Inquiry* (February 6, 1978), pp. 7–8.

14

War and Foreign Policy

"Isolationism," Left and Right

"ISOLATIONISM" WAS COINED as a smear term to apply to opponents of American entry into World War II. Since the word was often applied through guilt-by-association to mean pro-Nazi, "isolationist" took on a "right wing" as well as a generally negative flavor. If not actively pro-Nazi, "isolationists" were at the very least narrow-minded ignoramuses ignorant of the world around them, in contrast to the sophisticated, worldly, *caring* "internationalists" who favored American crusading around the globe. In the last decade, of course, antiwar forces have been considered "leftists," and interventionists from Lyndon Johnson to Jimmy Carter and their followers have constantly tried to pin the "isolationist" or at least "neoisolationist" label on today's left wing.

Left or right? During World War I, opponents of the war were bitterly attacked, just as now, as "leftists," even though they included in their ranks libertarians and advocates of laissez-faire capitalism. In fact, the major center of opposition to the American war with Spain and the American war to crush the Philippine rebellion at the turn of the century was laissez-faire liberals, men like the sociologist and economist William Graham Sumner, and the Boston merchant Edward Atkinson, who founded the "Anti-Imperialist League." Furthermore, Atkinson and Sumner were squarely in the great tradition of the classical English liberals of the eighteenth and nineteenth centuries, and in particular such laissez-faire "extremists" as Richard Cobden and John Bright of the "Manchester School." Cobden and Bright took the lead in vigorously opposing every British war and foreign political intervention of their era, and for his pains Cobden was known not as an "isolationist" but as the "International Man."[1] Until the smear campaign of the late 1930s, opponents of war were considered the true "internationalists," men who opposed the aggrandizement of the nation-state and favored peace, free trade, free migration, and peaceful cultural exchanges among peoples of all nations. Foreign intervention is "international" only in the sense that war is international: coercion, whether the threat of force or the outright movement of troops, will always cross frontiers between one nation and another.

"Isolationism" has a right-wing sound; "neutralism" and "peaceful coexistence" sound leftish. But their essence is the same: opposition to war and political intervention between countries. This has been the position of antiwar forces for two centuries, whether they were the classical liberals of the eighteenth and nineteenth centuries, the "leftists" of World War I and the Cold War, or the "rightists" of World War II. In very few cases have these antiinterventionists favored literal "isolation": what they have generally favored is political nonintervention in the affairs of other countries, coupled with economic and cultural internationalism in the sense of peaceful freedom of trade, investment, and interchange between the citizens of all countries. And this is the essence of the libertarian position as well.

Limiting Government

Libertarians favor the abolition of all States everywhere, and the provision of legitimate functions now supplied poorly by governments (police, courts, etc.) by means of the free market. Libertarians favor liberty as a natural human right, and advocate it not only for Americans but for all peoples. In a purely libertarian world, therefore, there would *be no* "foreign policy" because there would be no States, no governments with a monopoly of coercion over particular territorial areas. But since we live in a world of nation-states, and since this system is hardly likely to disappear in the near future, what is the attitude of libertarians toward foreign policy in the current State-ridden world?

[1]See William H. Dawson, *Richard Cobden and Foreign Policy* (London: George Allen and Unwin, 1926).

Pending the dissolution of States, libertarians desire to *limit*, to whittle down, the area of government power in all directions and as much as possible. We have already demonstrated how this principle of "de-statizing" might work in various important "domestic" problems, where the goal is to push back the role of government and to allow the voluntary and spontaneous energies of free persons full scope through peaceful interaction, notably in the free-market economy. In foreign affairs, the goal is the same: to keep government from interfering in the affairs of other governments or other countries. Political "isolationism" and peaceful coexistence—refraining from acting upon other countries—is, then, the libertarian counterpart to agitating for laissez-faire policies at home. The idea is to shackle government from acting abroad just as we try to shackle government at home. Isolationism or peaceful coexistence is the foreign policy counterpart of severely limiting government at home.

Specifically, the entire land area of the world is now parcelled out among various States, and each land area is ruled by a central government with monopoly of violence over that area. In relations between States, then, the libertarian goal is to keep each of these States from extending their violence to other countries, so that each State's tyranny is *at least* confined to its own bailiwick. For the libertarian is interested in reducing as much as possible the area of State aggression against all private individuals. The only way to do this, in international affairs, is for the people of each country to pressure their own State to confine its activities to the area it monopolizes and not to attack other States or aggress against their subjects. In short, the objective of the libertarian is to confine any existing State to as small a degree of invasion of person and property as possible. And this means the total avoidance of war. The people under each State should pressure "their" respective States not to attack one another, or, if a conflict should break out, to withdraw from it as quickly as physically possible.

Let us assume, for the moment, a world with two hypothetical countries: Graustark and Belgravia. Each is ruled by its own State. What happens if the government of Graustark invades the territory of Belgravia? From the libertarian point of view two evils immediately occur. First, the Graustark Army begins to slaughter innocent Belgravian civilians, persons who are not implicated in whatever crimes the Belgravian government might have committed. War, then, is mass murder, and this massive invasion of the right to life, of self-ownership, of numbers of people is not only a crime but, for the libertarian, the ultimate crime. Second, since all governments obtain their revenue from the thievery of coercive taxation, any mobilization and launching of troops inevitably involve an increase in tax-coercion in Graustark. For both reasons—because inter-State wars inevitably involve both mass murder and an increase in tax-coercion, the libertarian opposes war. Period.

It was not always thus. During the Middle Ages, the scope of wars was far more limited. Before the rise of modern weapons, armaments were so limited that governments could—and often *did*—strictly confine their violence to the *armies* of the rival governments. It is true that tax-coercion increased, but at least there was no mass murder of the innocents. Not only was firepower low enough to confine violence to the armies of the contending sides, but in the premodern era there was no central nation-state that spoke inevitably in the name of all inhabitants of a given land area. If one set of kings or barons fought another, it was not felt that everyone in the area must be a dedicated partisan. Moreover, instead of mass conscript armies enslaved to their respective rulers, armies were small bands of hired mercenaries. Often, a favorite sport for the populace was to observe a battle from the safety of the town ramparts, and war was regarded as something of a sporting match. But with the rise of the centralizing State and of modern weapons of mass destruction, the slaughter of civilians, as well as conscript armies, have become a vital part of inter-State warfare.

Suppose that despite possible libertarian opposition, war has broken out. Clearly, the libertarian position should be that, so long as the war continues, the scope of assault upon innocent civilians must be diminished as much as possible. Old-fashioned international law had two excellent devices to accomplish this goal: the "laws of war," and the "laws of neutrality" or "neutrals' rights." The laws of neutrality were designed to keep any war confined to the warring States themselves, without attacks upon nonwarring States and, particularly, aggression against the peoples of other nations. Hence the importance of such ancient and now almost forgotten American principles as "freedom of the seas" or severe limitations upon the rights of warring States to blockade neutral trade with the enemy country. In short, the libertarian tries to induce neutral States to *remain* neutral in any inter-State conflict, and to induce the warring States to observe fully the rights of neutral citizens. The "laws of war," for their part, were designed to limit as much as possible the invasion by warring States of the rights of civilians in their respective countries. As the British jurist F. J. P. Veale put it:

The fundamental principle of this code was that hostilities between civilized peoples must be limited to the armed forces actually engaged. . . . It drew a distinction between combatants and non-combatants by laying down that the sole business of the combatants is to fight each other and, consequently, that non-combatants must be excluded from the scope of military operations.[2]

In the modified form of prohibiting the bombardment of all cities not in the front line, this rule held in Western European wars in recent centuries until Britain launched the strategic bombing of civilians in World War II. Now, of course, the entire concept is scarcely remembered, since the very nature of modern nuclear warfare rests upon the annihilation of civilians.

To return to our hypothetical Graustark and Belgravia, suppose that Graustark has invaded Belgravia, and that a third government, Walldavia, now leaps into the war in order to defend Belgravia against "Graustarkian aggression." Is this action justifiable? Here, indeed, is the germ of the pernicious twentieth-century theory of "collective security"— the idea that when one government "aggresses" against another, it is the moral obligation of the other governments of the world to band together to defend the "victimized" State.

There are several fatal flaws in this concept of collective security against "aggression." One is that when Walldavia, or any other States, leap into the fray they are themselves expanding and compounding the extent of the aggression, because they are (1) unjustly slaughtering masses of Graustarkian civilians, and (2) increasing tax-coercion over Walldavian citizens. Furthermore, (3) in this age when States and subjects are closely identifiable, Walldavia is thereby leaving Walldavian civilians open to retaliation by Graustarkian bombers or missiles. Thus, entry into the war by the Walldavian government puts into jeopardy the very lives and properties of Walldavian citizens which the government is *supposed* to be protecting. Finally, (4) conscription-enslavement of Walldavian citizens will usually intensify.

If this kind of "collective security" should really be applied on a world-wide scale, with all the "Walldavias" rushing into every local conflict and escalating them, every local skirmish would soon be raised into a global conflagration.

There is another crucial flaw in the collective security concept. The idea of entering a war in order to stop "aggression" is clearly an analogy from aggression by one *individual* upon another. Smith is seen to be beating up Jones—aggressing against him. Nearby police then rush to the defense of the victim Jones; they are using "police action" to stop

[2]F. J. P. Veale, *Advance to Barbarism* (Appleton, Wisc.: C. C. Nelson Publishing Co., 1953), p. 58.

aggression. It was in pursuit of this myth, for example, that President Truman persisted in referring to American entry into the Korean war as a "police action," a collective UN effort to repel "aggression."

But "aggression" only makes sense on the individual Smith-Jones level, as does the very term "police action." These terms make no sense whatever on an inter-State level. First, we have seen that governments entering a war thereby become aggressors themselves against innocent civilians; indeed, become mass murderers. The *correct* analogy to individual action would be: Smith beats up Jones, the police rush in to help Jones, and in the course of trying to apprehend Smith, the police bomb a city block and murder thousands of people, or spray machine-gun fire into an innocent crowd. *This* is a far more accurate analogy, for that is what a warring government does, and in the twentieth century it does so on a monumental scale. But any police agency that behaves this way *itself* becomes a criminal aggressor, often far more so than the original Smith who began the affair.

But there is yet another fatal flaw in the analogy with individual aggression. When Smith beats up Jones or steals his property we can identify Smith as an aggressor upon the personal or property right of his victim. But when the Graustarkian State invades the territory of the Belgravian State, it is impermissible to refer to "aggression" in an analogous way. For the libertarian, no government has a just claim to any property or "sovereignty" right in a given territorial area. The Belgravian State's claim to its territory is therefore totally different from Mr. Jones' claim to his property (although the latter might also, on investigation, turn out to be the illegitimate result of theft). No State has any legitimate property; all of its territory is the result of some kind of aggression and violent conquest. Hence the Graustarkian State's invasion is necessarily a battle between two sets of thieves and aggressors: the only problem is that innocent civilians on both sides are being trampled upon.

Aside from this general caveat on governments, the so-called "aggressor" State often has a quite plausible claim on its "victim"; plausible, that is, within the context of the nation-state system. Suppose that Graustark has crossed the Belgravian border because Belgravia had, a century earlier, invaded Graustark and seized its northeastern provinces. The inhabitants of these provinces are culturally, ethnically, and linguistically Graustarkian. Graustark now invades in order to be reunited at last with its fellow Graustarkians. In this situation, by the way, the libertarian, while condemning both governments for making war and killing civilians, would have to side with Graustark as having the more just, or the less unjust, claim. Let us put it this way: In the unlikely event that the two countries could return to premodern warfare, with (a) weapons limited so that no civilians were injured in their persons or property; (b) volunteer rather than conscript armies; and also (c) financing by voluntary methods instead of taxation; the libertarian could then, given our context, side unreservedly with Graustark.

Of all the recent wars, none has come closer—though not completely so—to satisfying these three criteria for a "just war" than the Indian war of late 1971 for the liberation of Bangla Desh. The government of Pakistan had been created as a last terrible legacy of Imperial Britain to the Indian subcontinent. In particular, the nation of Pakistan consisted of imperial rule by the Punjabis of West Pakistan over the more numerous and productive Bengalis of East Pakistan (and also over the Pathans of the North-West Frontier). The Bengalis had long been yearning for independence from their imperial oppressors; in early 1971, parliament was suspended as a result of Bengali victory in the elections; from then on, Punjabi troops systematically slaughtered the civilian Bengal population. Indian entry into the conflict aided the popular Bengali resistance forces of the Mukhti Bahini. While taxes and conscription were, of course, involved, the Indian armies did not use their weapons against Bengali civilians; on the contrary, here was a genuine revolutionary war of the Bengali public *against* a Punjabi occupying State. Only Punjabi soldiers were on the receiving end of Indian bullets.

This example points up another characteristic of warfare: that revolutionary guerrilla war *can be* far more consistent with libertarian principles than any inter-State war. By the very nature of their activities, guerrillas defend the civilian population *against* the depredations of a State; hence, guerrillas, inhabiting as they do the same country as the enemy State, *cannot* use nuclear or other weapons of mass destruction. Further: since guerrillas rely for victory on the support and aid of the civilian population, they *must*, as a basic part of their strategy, spare civilians from harm and pinpoint their activities solely against the State apparatus and its armed forces. Hence, guerrilla war returns us to the ancient and honorable virtue of pinpointing the enemy and sparing innocent civilians. And guerrillas, as part of their quest for enthusiastic civilian support, often refrain from conscription and taxation and rely on voluntary support for men and materiel.

The libertarian qualities of guerrilla warfare reside only on the revolutionary side; for the counterrevolutionary forces of the State, it is quite a different story. While the State cannot go to the length of "nuking" its own subjects, it does, of necessity, rely primarily on campaigns of mass terror: killing, terrorizing, and rounding up the mass of civilians. Since guerrillas, to be successful, must be supported by the bulk of the population, the State, in order to wage its war, must concentrate on destroying that population, or must herd masses of civilians into concentration camps in order to separate them from their guerrilla allies. This tactic was used by the Spanish general, "Butcher" Weyler, against the Cuban rebels in the 1890s, was continued by the American troops in the Philippines, and by the British in the Boer War, and continues to be used down to the recent ill-fated "strategic hamlet" policy in South Vietnam.

The libertarian foreign policy, then, is *not* a pacifist policy. We do not hold, as do the pacifists, that no individual has the right to use violence in defending himself against violent attack. What we *do* hold is that no one has the right to conscript, tax, or murder others, or to use violence against others in order to defend himself. Since all States exist and have their being in aggression against their subjects and in the acquiring of their present territory, and since inter-State wars slaughter innocent civilians, such wars are always unjust—although some may be more unjust than others. Guerrilla warfare against States at least has the potential for meeting libertarian requirements by pinpointing the guerrilla's battle against State officials and armies, and by their use of voluntary methods to staff and finance their struggle.

American Foreign Policy

We have seen that libertarians have as their prime responsibility the focussing on the invasions and aggressions of their *own* State. The libertarians of Graustark must center their attentions on attempting to limit and whittle down the Graustark State, the Walldavian libertarians must try to check the Walldavian State, and so on. In foreign affairs, the libertarians of every country must press *their* government to refrain from war and foreign intervention, and to withdraw from any war in which they may be engaged. If for no other reason, then, libertarians in the United States must center their critical attention on the imperial and warlike activities of their own government.

But there are still other reasons for libertarians here to focus upon the invasions and foreign interventions of the United States. For empirically, taking the twentieth century as a whole, the single most warlike, most interventionist, most imperialist government has been the United States. Such a statement is bound to shock Americans, subject as we have been for decades to intense propaganda by the Establishment on the invariable saintliness, peaceful intentions, and devotion to justice of the American government in foreign affairs.

The expansionist impulse of the American State began to take increasing hold in the late nineteenth century, leaping boldly overseas with America's war against Spain, dominating Cuba, grabbing Puerto Rico and the Philippines, and brutally suppressing a Filipino rebellion for independence. The imperial expansion of the United States reached full flower in World War I, when President Woodrow Wilson's leap into the fray prolonged the war and the mass slaughter, and unwittingly bred the grisly devastation that led directly to the Bolshevik triumph in Russia and the Nazi victory in Germany. It was Wilson's particular genius to supply a pietistic and moralistic cloak for a new American policy of worldwide intervention and domination, a policy of trying to mould every country in the American image, suppressing radical or Marxist regimes on the one hand and old-fashioned monarchist governments on the other. It was Woodrow Wilson who was to fix the broad features of American foreign policy for the rest of this century. Almost every succeeding President has considered himself a Wilsonian and followed his policies. It was no accident that both Herbert Hoover and Franklin D. Roosevelt—so long thought of as polar opposites—played important roles in America's first global crusade of World War I, and that both men harked back to their experience in World War I intervention and planning as the guideposts for their future foreign and domestic policies. And it was one of Richard Nixon's first acts as President to place Woodrow Wilson's picture upon his desk.

In the name of "national self-determination" and "collective security" against aggression, the American government has consistently pursued a goal and a policy of world domination and of the forcible suppression of any rebellion against the status quo anywhere in the world. In the name of combatting "aggression" everywhere—of being the world's "policeman"—it has itself become a great and continuing aggressor.

Anyone who balks at such a description of American policy should simply consider what the typical American reaction is to *any* domestic or foreign crisis anywhere on the globe, even at some remote site that cannot by any stretch of the imagination be considered a direct or even indirect threat to the lives and security of the American people. The military dictator of "Bumblestan" is in danger; perhaps his subjects are tired of being exploited by him and his colleagues. The United States then becomes gravely concerned; articles by journalists friendly to the State Department or the Pentagon spread the alarm about what might happen to the "stability" of Bumblestan and its surrounding area if the dictator should be toppled. For it so happens that he is a "pro-American" or "pro-Western" dictator: that is, he is one of "ours" instead of "theirs." Millions or even billions of dollars' worth of military and economic aid are then rushed by the United States to prop up the Bumblestani field marshal. If "our" dictator is saved, then a sigh of relief is heaved, and congratulations are passed around at the saving of "our" State. The continuing or intensified oppression of the American taxpayer and of the Bumblestanian citizens are, of course, not considered in the equation. Or if it should happen that the Bumblestani dictator may fall, hysteria might hit the American press and officialdom for the moment. But then, after a while, the American people seem to be able to live their lives after "losing" Bumblestan about as well as before—perhaps even better, if it means a few billion less in foreign aid extracted from them to prop up the Bumblestani State.

If it is understood and expected, then, that the United States will try to impose its will on every crisis everywhere in the world, then this is clear indication that America is the great interventionary and imperial power. The one place where the United States does not now attempt to work its will is the Soviet Union and the Communist countries—but, of course, it has tried to do so in the past. Woodrow Wilson, along with Britain and France, tried for several years to crush bolshevism in the cradle, with American and Allied troops being sent to Russia to aid the Czarist ("White") forces in trying to defeat the Reds. After World War II, the United States tried its best to oust the Soviets from Eastern Europe, and succeeded in pushing them out of Azerbaijan in northwestern Iran. It also helped the British to crush a Communist regime in Greece. The United States tried its best to maintain Chiang Kai-shek's dictatorial rule in China, flying many of Chiang's troops northward to occupy Manchuria as the Russians pulled out after World War II; and it continues to prevent the Chinese from occupying their offshore islands, Quemoy and Matsu. After virtually installing the dictator Batista in Cuba, the United States tried desperately to oust the Communist Castro regime, by actions ranging from the CIA-engineered Bay of Pigs invasion to CIA-Mafia attempts to assassinate Castro.

Of all America's recent wars, certainly the most traumatic for Americans and their attitude toward foreign policy was the Vietnam war. America's imperial war in Vietnam was, indeed, a microcosm of what has been tragically wrong with American foreign policy in this century. American intervention in Vietnam did not begin, as most people believe, with Kennedy or Eisenhower or even Truman. It began no later than the date when the American government, under Franklin Roosevelt, on November 26, 1941, delivered a sharp and insulting ultimatum to Japan to get its armed forces out of China and Indochina, from what would later be Vietnam. This U.S. ultimatum set the stage inevitably for Pearl Harbor. Engaged in a war in the Pacific to oust Japan from the Asian continent, the United States and its OSS (predecessor to the CIA) favored and aided Ho Chi Minh's Communist-run national resistance movement against the Japanese. After World War II, the Communist Viet Minh was in charge of all northern Vietnam. But then France, previously the imperial ruler of Vietnam, betrayed its agreement with Ho and massacred Viet Minh forces. In this double cross, France was aided by Britain and the United States.

When the French lost to the reconstituted Viet Minh guerrilla movement under Ho, the United States endorsed the Geneva agreement of 1954, under which Vietnam was to be quickly reunited as one nation. For it was generally recognized that the postwar occupation divisions of the country into North and South were purely arbitrary and merely for military convenience. But, having by trickery managed to oust the Viet Minh from the southern half of Vietnam, the United States proceeded to break the Geneva agreement and to replace the French and their puppet Emperor Bao Dai by its own clients, Ngo Dinh Diem and his family, who were installed in dictatorial rule over South Vietnam. When Diem became an embarrassment, the CIA engineered a coup to assassinate Diem and replace him with another dictatorial regime. To suppress the Viet Cong, the Communist-led national independence movement in the South, the United States rained devastation on South and North Vietnam alike—bombing and murdering a million Vietnamese and dragging half a million American soldiers into the quagmires and jungles of Vietnam.

Throughout the tragic Vietnamese conflict, the United States maintained the fiction that it was a war of "aggression" by the Communist North Vietnamese State against a friendly and "pro-Western" (whatever that term may mean) South Vietnamese State which had called for our aid. Actually, the war was really a doomed but lengthy attempt by an imperial United States to suppress the wishes of the great bulk of the Vietnamese population and to maintain unpopular client dictators in the southern half of the country, by virtual genocide if necessary.

Americans are not accustomed to applying the term "imperialism" to the actions of the U.S. government, but the word is a particularly apt one. In its broadest sense, *imperialism* may be defined as aggression by State A against the people of country B, followed by the subsequent coercive maintenance of such foreign rule. In our example above, the permanent rule by the Graustark State over formerly northeastern Belgravia would be an example of such imperialism. But imperialism does not have to take the form of direct rule over the foreign population. In the twentieth century, the indirect form of "neoimperialism" has increasingly replaced the old-fashioned direct kind; it is more subtle and less visible but no less effective a form of imperialism. In this situation, the imperial State rules the foreign population through its effective control over native client-rulers. This version of modern Western imperialism has been trenchantly defined by the libertarian historian Leonard Liggio:

The imperialist power of the Western countries . . . imposed on the world's peoples a double or reinforced system of exploitation—imperialism—by which the power of the Western governments maintains the local ruling class in exchange for the opportunity to superimpose Western exploitation upon existing exploitation by local states.[3]

This view of America as a long-time imperial world power has taken hold among historians in recent years as the result of compelling and scholarly work by a distinguished group of New Left revisionist historians inspired by Professor William Appleman Williams. But this was also the view of conservative as well as classical liberal "isolationists" during World War II and in the early days of the Cold War.[4]

Isolationist Criticisms

The last antiinterventionist and antiimperialist thrust of the old conservative and classical liberal isolationists came during the Korean War.

[3]Leonard P. Liggio, *Why the Futile Crusade?* (New York: Center for Libertarian Studies, 1978), p. 3.

[4]For "New Left" revisionists, see, in addition to Williams himself, the work of Gabriel Kolko, Lloyd Gardner, Stephen E. Ambrose, N. Gordon Levin, Jr., Walter LaFeber, Robert F. Smith, Barton Bernstein, and Ronald Radosh. Coming to similar conclusions from far different revisionist traditions were Charles A. Beard and Harry Elmer Barnes, the libertarian James J. Martin, and classical liberals John T. Flynn and Garet Garrett.

Ronald Radosh, in his *Prophets on the Right: Profiles of Conservative Critics of American Globalism* (New York: Simon & Schuster, 1975), has appreciatively portrayed the conservative isolationist opposition to American intervention in World War II. In numerous articles and in his *Not to the Swift: The Old Isolationists in the Cold War Era* (Lewisburg, Pa.: Bucknell University Press, 1979), Justus D. Doenecke has carefully and sympathetically analyzed the sentiment of World War II isolationists in confronting the early Cold War. A call for a common antiinterventionist and antiimperialist movement by Left and Right can be found in Carl Oglesby and Richard Shaull, *Containment and Change* (New York: Macmillan, 1967). For an annotated bibliography of the writings of isolationists, see Doenecke, *The Literature of Isolationism* (Colorado Springs, Colo.: Ralph Myles, 1972).

Conservative George Morgenstern, chief editorial writer of the *Chicago Tribune* and author of the first revisionist book on Pearl Harbor, published an article in the right-wing Washington weekly *Human Events*, which detailed the grisly imperialist record of the United States government from the Spanish-American War down to Korea. Morgenstern noted that the "exalted nonsense" by which President McKinley had justified the war against Spain was "familiar to anyone who later attended the evangelical rationalizations of Wilson for intervening in the European war, of Roosevelt promising the millennium, . . . of Eisenhower treasuring the 'crusade in Europe' that somehow went sour, or of Truman, Stevenson, Paul Douglas or the New York *Times* preaching the holy war in Korea."[5]

In a widely noted speech at the height of the American defeat in North Korea at the hands of the Chinese in late 1950, conservative isolationist Joseph P. Kennedy called for U.S. withdrawal from Korea. Kennedy proclaimed that "I naturally opposed Communism but I said if portions of Europe or Asia wish to go Communistic or even have Communism thrust upon them, we cannot stop it." The result of the Cold War, the Truman Doctrine, and the Marshall Plan, Kennedy charged, was disaster—a failure to purchase friends and a threat of land war in Europe or Asia. Kennedy warned that:

. . . half of this world will never submit to dictation by the other half. . . . What business is it of ours to support French colonial policy in Indo-China or to achieve Mr. Syngman Rhee's concepts of democracy in Korea? Shall we now send the Marines into the mountains of Tibet to keep the Dalai Lama on his throne?

Economically, Kennedy added, we have been burdening ourselves with unnecessary debts as a consequence of Cold War policy. If we continue to weaken our economy "with lavish spending either on foreign nations or in foreign wars, we run the danger of precipitating another 1932 and of destroying the very system which we are trying to save."

Kennedy concluded that the only rational alternative for America is to scrap the Cold War foreign policy altogether: "to get out of Korea," and out of Berlin and Europe. The United States could not possibly contain Russian armies if they chose to march through Europe, and if

[5]George Morgenstern, "The Past Marches On," *Human Events* (April 22, 1953). The revisionist work on Pearl Harbor was Morgenstern, *Pearl Harbor: Story of a Secret War* (New York: Devin-Adair, 1947). For more on the conservative isolationists and their critique of the Cold War, see Murray N. Rothbard, "The Foreign Policy of the Old Right," *Journal of Libertarian Studies* (Winter 1978).

Europe should then turn Communist, Communism "may break of itself as a unified force. . . . The more people that it will have to govern, the more necessary it becomes for those who govern to justify themselves to those being governed. The more peoples that are under its yoke, the greater are the possibilities of revolt." And here, at a time when cold warriors were forecasting a world Communist monolith as an eternal fact of life, Joseph Kennedy cited Marshall Tito as pointing the way for the eventual breakup of the Communist world: thus, "Mao in China is not likely to take his orders from Stalin. . . ."

Kennedy realized that "this policy will, of course, be criticized as appeasement. [But] . . . is it appeasement to withdraw from unwise commitments. . . . If it is wise in our interest not to make commitments that endanger our security, and this is appeasement, then I am for appeasement." Kennedy concluded that "the suggestions I make [would] conserve American lives for American ends, not waste them in the freezing hills of Korea or on the battlescarred plains of Western Germany."[6]

One of the most trenchant and forceful attacks on American foreign policy to emerge from the Korean War was leveled by the veteran classical liberal journalist, Garet Garrett. Garrett began his pamphlet, *The Rise of Empire* (1952), by declaring, "We have crossed the boundary that lies between Republic and Empire." Explicitly linking this thesis with his notable pamphlet of the 1930s, *The Revolution Was*, which had denounced the advent of executive and statist tyranny within the republican form under the New Deal, Garrett once more saw a "revolution within the form" of the old constitutional republic. Garrett, for example, called Truman's intervention in Korea without a declaration of war a "usurpation" of congressional power.

In his pamphlet, Garrett adumbrated the criteria, the hallmarks for the existence of Empire. The first is the dominance of the executive power, a dominance reflected in the President's unauthorized intervention in Korea. The second is the subordination of domestic to foreign policy; the third, the "ascendancy of the military mind"; the fourth, a "system of satellite nations"; and the fifth, "a complex of vaunting and fear," a vaunting of unlimited national might combined with a continuing fear, fear of the enemy, of the "barbarian," and of the unreliability of the satellite allies. Garrett found each one of these criteria to apply fully to the United States.

Having discovered that the United States had developed all the hall-

<hr>

[6]Joseph P. Kennedy, "Present Policy is Politically and Morally Bankrupt," *Vital Speeches* (January 1, 1951), pp. 170–73.

marks of empire, Garrett added that the United States, like previous empires, feels itself to be "a prisoner of history." For beyond fear lies "collective security," and the playing of the supposedly destined American role upon the world stage. Garrett concluded:

It is our turn.
Our turn to do what?
Our turn to assume the responsibilities of moral leadership in the world.
Our turn to maintain a balance of power against the forces of evil everywhere—in Europe and Asia and Africa, in the Atlantic and in the Pacific, by air and by sea—evil in this case being the Russian barbarian.
Our turn to keep the peace of the world.
Our turn to save civilization.
Our turn to serve mankind.
But this is the language of Empire. The Roman Empire never doubted that it was the defender of civilization. Its good intentions were peace, law and order. The Spanish Empire added salvation. The British Empire added the noble myth of the white man's burden. We have added freedom and democracy. Yet the more that may be added to it the more it is the same language still. A language of power.[7]

War As the Health of the State

Many libertarians are uncomfortable with foreign policy matters and prefer to spend their energies either on fundamental questions of libertarian theory or on such "domestic" concerns as the free market or privatizing postal service or garbage disposal. Yet an attack on war or a warlike foreign policy is of crucial importance to libertarians. There are two important reasons. One has become a cliché, but is all too true nevertheless: the overriding importance of preventing a nuclear holocaust. To all the long-standing reasons, moral and economic, against an interventionist foreign policy has now been added the imminent, ever-present threat of world destruction. If the world should be destroyed, all the other problems and all the other isms—socialism, capitalism, liberalism, or libertarianism—would be of no importance whatsoever. Hence the prime importance of a peaceful foreign policy and of ending the nuclear threat.

The other reason is that, apart from the nuclear menace, war, in the words of the libertarian Randolph Bourne, "is the health of the

[7]Garet Garrett, *The People's Pottage* (Caldwell, Idaho: Caxton Printers, 1953), pp. 158–59, 129–174. For more expressions of conservative or classical liberal antiimperialist critiques of the Cold War, see Doenecke, *Not to the Swift*, p. 79.

State." War has always been the occasion of a great—and usually permanent—acceleration and intensification of State power over society. War is the great excuse for mobilizing all the energies and resources of the nation, in the name of patriotic rhetoric, under the aegis and dictation of the State apparatus. It is in war that the State really comes into its own: swelling in power, in number, in pride, in absolute dominion over the economy and the society. Society becomes a herd, seeking to kill its alleged enemies, rooting out and suppressing all dissent from the official war effort, happily betraying truth for the supposed public interest. Society becomes an armed camp, with the values and the morals—as the libertarian Albert Jay Nock once phrased it—of an "army on the march."

It is particularly ironic that war always enables the State to rally the energies of its citizens under the slogan of helping it to defend the country against some bestial outside menace. For the root myth that enables the State to wax fat off war is the canard that war is a defense *by* the State *of* its subjects. The facts, however, are precisely the reverse. For if war is the health of the State, it is also its greatest danger. A State can only "die" by defeat in war or by revolution. In war, therefore, the State frantically mobilizes its subjects to fight for *it* against another State, under the pretext that *it* is fighting to defend them.[8]

In the history of the United States, war has generally been the main occasion for the often permanent intensification of the power of the State over society. In the War of 1812 against Great Britain, as we have indicated above, the modern inflationary fractional-reserve banking system first came into being on a large scale, as did protective tariffs, internal federal taxation, and a standing army and navy. And a direct consequence of the wartime inflation was the reestablishment of a central bank, the Second Bank of the United States. Virtually all of these statist policies and institutions continued permanently after the war was over. The Civil War and its virtual one-party system led to the permanent establishment of a neomercantilist policy of Big Government and the subsidizing of various big business interests through protective tariffs, huge land grants and other subsidies to railroads, federal excise taxation, and a federally controlled banking system. It also brought the first imposition of federal conscription and an income tax, setting dangerous precedents

---

[8]For more on a libertarian theory of foreign policy, see Murray N. Rothbard, "War, Peace and the State," in *Egalitarianism As A Revolt Against Nature and other Essays* (Washington, D.C.: Libertarian Review Press, 1974), pp. 70–80.

for the future. World War I brought the decisive and fateful turn from a relatively free and laissez-faire economy to the present system of corporate state monopoly at home and permanent global intervention abroad. The collectivist economic mobilization during the war, headed by War Industries Board Chairman Bernard Baruch, fulfilled the emerging dream of big business leaders and progressive intellectuals for a cartelized and monopolized economy planned by the federal government in cozy collaboration with big business leadership. And it was precisely this wartime collectivism that nurtured and developed a nationwide labor movement that would eagerly take its place as junior partner in the new corporate State economy. This temporary collectivism, furthermore, served as a permanent beacon and model for big business leaders and corporatist politicians as the kind of permanent peacetime economy that they would like to impose on the United States. As food czar, Secretary of Commerce, and later as President, Herbert C. Hoover helped bring this continuing monopolized statist economy into being, and the vision was fulfilled in a recrudescence of wartime agencies and even wartime personnel by Franklin D. Roosevelt's New Deal.[9] World War I also brought a permanent Wilsonian global intervention abroad, the fastening of the newly imposed Federal Reserve System and a permanent income tax on society, high federal budgets, massive conscription, and intimate connections between economic boom, war contracts, and loans to Western nations.

World War II was the culmination and fulfillment of all these trends: Franklin D. Roosevelt finally fastened upon American life the heady promise of the Wilsonian domestic and foreign program: permanent partnership of Big Government, big business, and big unions; a continuing and ever-expanding military-industrial complex; conscription; continuing and accelerating inflation; and an endless and costly role as counterrevolutionary "policeman" for the entire world. The Roosevelt-Truman-Eisenhower-Kennedy-Johnson-Nixon-Ford-Carter world (and there is little substantive difference among any of these administrations) is "corporate liberalism," the corporate State fulfilled.

It is particularly ironic that conservatives, at least in rhetoric support-

---

[9]Numerous revisionist historians have recently developed this interpretation of twentieth-century American history. In particular, see the works of, among others, Gabriel Kolko, James Weinstein, Robert Wiebe, Robert D. Cuff, William E. Leuchtenburg, Ellis D. Hawley, Melvin I. Urofsky, Joan Hoff Wilson, Ronald Radosh, Jerry Israel, David Eakins, and Paul Conkin—again, as in foreign policy revisionism, under the inspiration of William Appleman Williams. A series of essays using this approach may be found in Ronald Radosh and Murray N. Rothbard, eds., *A New History of Leviathan* (New York: Dutton, 1972).

ers of a free-market economy, should be so complacent and even admiring of our vast military-industrial complex. There is no greater single distortion of the free market in present-day America. The bulk of our scientists and engineers has been diverted from basic research for civilian ends, from increasing productivity and the standard of living of consumers, into wasteful, inefficient, and nonproductive military and space boondoggles. These boondoggles are every bit as wasteful but infinitely more destructive than the vast pyramid building of the Pharaoh. It is no accident that Lord Keynes's economics have proved to be the economics par excellence of the corporate liberal State. For Keynesian economists place equal approval upon all forms of government spending, whether on pyramids, missiles, or steel plants; by definition all of these expenditures swell the gross national product, regardless of how wasteful they may be. It is only recently that many liberals have begun to awaken to the evils of the waste, inflation, and militarism that Keynesian corporate liberalism has brought to America.

As the scope of government spending—military and civilian alike—has widened, science and industry have been skewed more and more into unproductive goals and highly inefficient processes. The goal of satisfying consumers as efficiently as possible has been increasingly replaced by the currying of favors by government contractors, often in the form of highly wasteful "cost-plus" contracts. Politics, in field after field, has replaced economics in guiding the activities of industry. Furthermore, as entire industries and regions of the country have come to depend upon government and military contracts, a huge vested interest has been created in continuing the programs, heedless of whether they retain even the most threadbare excuse of military necessity. Our economic prosperity has been made to depend on continuing the narcotic of unproductive and antiproductive government spending.[10]

One of the most perceptive and prophetic critics of America's entry into World War II was the classical liberal writer John T. Flynn. In his *As We Go Marching*, written in the midst of the war he had tried so hard to forestall, Flynn charged that the New Deal, culminating in its wartime embodiment, had finally established the corporate State that important elements of big business had been seeking since the turn of the twentieth century. "The general idea," Flynn wrote, was "to reorder the society by making it a planned and coerced economy instead of a free one, in which business would be brought together into great guilds

---

[10]On the economic distortions imposed by the military-industrial policies, see Seymour Melman, ed., *The War Economy of the United States* (New York: St. Martin's Press, 1971).

or an immense corporative structure, combining the elements of self-rule and government supervision with a national economic policing system to enforce these decrees. . . . This, after all, is not so very far from what business had been talking about. . . ."[11]

The New Deal had first attempted to create such a new society in the National Recovery Administration and the Agricultural Adjustment Administration, mighty engines of "regimentation" hailed by labor and business alike. Now the advent of World War II had reestablished this collectivist program—"an economy supported by great streams of debt under complete control, with nearly all the planning agencies functioning with almost totalitarian power under a vast bureaucracy." After the war, Flynn prophesied, the New Deal would attempt to expand this system permanently into international affairs. He wisely predicted that the great emphasis of vast governmental spending after the war would continue to be military, since this is the one form of government spending to which conservatives would never object, and which workers would also welcome for its creation of jobs. "Thus militarism is the one great glamorous public-works project upon which a variety of elements in the community can be brought into agreement."[12]

Flynn predicted that America's postwar policy would be "internationalist" in the sense of being imperialist. Imperialism "is, of course, international . . . in the sense that war is international," and it will follow from the policy of militarism. "We will do what other countries have done; we will keep alive the fears of our people of the aggressive ambitions of other countries and we will ourselves embark upon imperialistic enterprises of our own." Imperialism will ensure for the United States the existence of perpetual "enemies," of waging what Charles A. Beard was later to call "perpetual war for perpetual peace." For, Flynn pointed out, "we have managed to acquire bases all over the world. . . . There is no part of the world where trouble can break out where . . . we cannot claim that our interests are menaced. Thus menaced there must remain when the war is over a continuing argument in the hands of the imperialists for a vast naval establishment and a huge army ready to attack anywhere or to resist an attack from all the enemies we shall be obliged to have."[13]

One of the most moving portrayals of the change in American life wrought by World War II was written by John Dos Passos, a lifelong

[11]John T. Flynn, *As We Go Marching* (New York: Doubleday, Doran & Co., 1944), pp. 193–94.

[12]*Ibid.*, pp. 198, 201, 207.

[13]*Ibid.*, pp. 212–13, 225–26.

radical and individualist who was pushed from "extreme left" to "extreme right" by the march of the New Deal. Dos Passos expressed his bitterness in his postwar novel, *The Grand Design:*

At home we organized bloodbanks and civilian defense
and imitated the rest of the world by setting up
concentration camps (only we called them relocation
centers) and stuffing into them
    American citizens of Japanese ancestry . . . without
benefit of habeas corpus . . .
    The President of the United States talked the
sincere democrat and so did the members of Congress.
In the Administration there were devout believers in
civil liberty. "Now we're busy fighting a war; we'll
deploy all four freedoms later on," they said. . . .
    War is a time of Caesars. . . .
    And the American people were supposed to say thank
you for the century of the Common Man turned over for
relocation behind barbed wire so help him God.
    We learned. There are things we learned to do
    but we have not learned, in spite of the Constitution
and the Declaration of Independence and the great
debates at Richmond and Philadelphia
    how to put power over the lives of men into the
hands of one man
    and to make him use it wisely.[14]

Soviet Foreign Policy

In a previous chapter, we have already dealt with the problem of national defense, abstracting from the question of whether the Russians are *really* hell-bent upon a military attack upon the United States. Since World War II, American military and foreign policy, at least rhetorically, has been based upon the assumption of a looming threat of Russian attack—an assumption that has managed to gain public approval for global American intervention and for scores of billions in military expenditures. But how realistic, how well grounded, *is* this assumption?

First, there is no doubt that the Soviets, along with all other Marxist-Leninists, would *like* to replace all existing social systems by Communist regimes. But such a sentiment, of course, scarcely implies any sort of realistic threat of attack—just as an ill wish in private life can hardly

[14]John Dos Passos, *The Grand Design* (Boston: Houghton Mifflin Co., 1949), pp. 416–418.

be grounds for realistic expectation of imminent aggression. On the contrary, Marxism-Leninism itself believes that a victory of communism is inevitable—*not* on the wings of outside force, but rather from accumulating tensions and "contradictions" within each society. So Marxism-Leninism considers internal revolution (or, in the current "Eurocommunist" version, democratic change) for installing communism to be inevitable. At the same time, it holds any coercive external imposition of communism to be at best suspect, and at worst disruptive and counterproductive of genuine organic social change. Any idea of "exporting" communism to other countries on the backs of the Soviet military is totally contradictory to Marxist-Leninist theory.

We are not saying, of course, that Soviet leaders will never do anything contrary to Marxist-Leninist theory. But to the extent that they act as ordinary rulers of a strong Russian nation-state, the case for an imminent Soviet threat to the United States is gravely weakened. For the sole alleged basis of such a threat, as conjured up by our cold warriors, is the Soviet Union's alleged devotion to Marxist-Leninist theory and to its ultimate goal of world Communist triumph. If the Soviet rulers were simply to act as Russian dictators consulting only their own nation-state interests, then the entire basis for treating the Soviets as a uniquely diabolic source of imminent military assault crumbles to the ground.

When the Bolsheviks took power in Russia in 1917, they had given little thought to a future Soviet foreign policy, for they were convinced that Communist revolution would soon follow in the advanced industrial countries of Western Europe. When such hopes were dashed after the end of World War I, Lenin and his fellow Bolsheviks adopted the theory of "peaceful coexistence" as the basic foreign policy for a Communist State. The idea was this: as the first successful Communist movement, Soviet Russia would serve as a beacon for and supporter of other Communist parties throughout the world. *But* the Soviet State *qua* State would devote itself to peaceful relations with all other countries, and would not attempt to export communism through inter-State warfare. The idea here was not just to follow Marxist-Leninist theory, but was the highly practical course of holding the survival of the existing Communist State as the foremost goal of foreign policy: that is, never to endanger the Soviet State by courting inter-State warfare. Other countries would be expected to become Communist by their own internal processes.

Thus, fortuitously, from a mixture of theoretical and practical grounds of their own, the Soviets arrived early at what libertarians consider to be the only proper and principled foreign policy. As time went on, furthermore, this policy was reinforced by a "conservatism" that comes upon all movements after they have acquired and retained power for any length of time, in which the interests of keeping power over one's nation-state begins to take more and more precedence over the initial ideal of world revolution. This increasing conservatism under Stalin and his successors strengthened and reinforced the nonaggressive, "peaceful coexistence" policy.

The Bolsheviks, indeed, began their success story by being literally the only political party in Russia to clamor, from the beginning of World War I, for an immediate Russian pullout from the war. Indeed, they went further and courted enormous unpopularity among the public by calling for the defeat of "their own" government ("revolutionary defeatism"). When Russia began to suffer enormous losses, accompanied by massive military desertions from the front, and the war became extremely unpopular, the Bolsheviks, guided by Lenin, continued to be the only party to call for an immediate end to the war—the other parties still vowing to fight the Germans to the end. When the Bolsheviks took power, Lenin, over the hysterical opposition of even the majority of the Bolshevik central committee itself, insisted on concluding the "appeasement" peace of Brest-Litovsk in March 1918. Here, Lenin succeeded in taking Russia out of the war, even at the price of granting to the victorious German army all the parts of the Russian empire which it then occupied (including White Russia and the Ukraine). Thus, Lenin and the Bolsheviks began their reign by being not simply a peace party, but virtually a "peace-at-any-price" party.

After World War I and Germany's defeat, the new Polish State attacked Russia and succeeded in grabbing for itself a large chunk of White Russia and the Ukraine. Taking advantage of the turmoil and of the civil war within Russia at the end of the war, various other national groups—Finland, Estonia, Latvia, and Lithuania—decided to break away from the pre–World War I Russian empire and declare national independence. Now, while Leninism pays lip service to national self-determination, to Soviet rulers, from the very beginning, it was clear that the boundaries of the old Russian State were supposed to remain intact. The Red Army reconquered the Ukraine, not only from the Whites, but also from the Ukrainian nationalists, and from the indigenously Ukrainian anarchist army of Nestor Makhno as well. For the rest, it was clear that Russia, like Germany in the 1920s and 1930s, was a "revisionist" country vis à vis the postwar settlement at Versailles. That is, the lodestar of both Russian and German foreign policy was to recapture their pre–World War I borders—what they both considered the "true" borders of their respective States. It should be noted that *every* political party or tendency in Russia and Germany, whether ruling the State or in opposition, agreed with this aim of full restoration of national territory.

But, it should be emphasized, while Germany under Hitler took strong measures to recapture the lost lands, the cautious and conservative Soviet rulers did absolutely nothing. Only after the Stalin-Hitler pact and the German conquest of Poland did the Soviets, now facing no danger in doing so, recapture their lost territories. Specifically, the Russians repossessed Estonia, Latvia, and Lithuania as well as the old Russian lands of White Russia and the Ukraine that had been eastern Poland. And they were able to do so without a fight. The old pre–World War I Russia had now been restored with the exception of Finland. But Finland was prepared to fight. Here the Russians demanded not the reincorporation of Finland as a whole, but only of parts of the Karelian Isthmus which were ethnically Russian. When the Finns refused this demand, the "Winter War" (1939–1940) between Russia and Finland ensued, which ended with the Finns conceding only Russian Karelia.[15]

On June 22, 1941, Germany, triumphant over everyone but England in the West, launched a sudden, massive, and unprovoked assault on Soviet Russia, an act of aggression aided and abetted by the other pro-German States in Eastern Europe: Hungary, Romania, Bulgaria, Slovakia, and Finland. This German and allied invasion of Russia soon became one of the pivotal facts in the history of Europe since that date. So unprepared was Stalin for the assault, so trusting was he in the rationality of the German-Russian accord for peace in Eastern Europe, that he had allowed the Russian army to fall into disrepair. So unwarlike was Stalin, in fact, that Germany was almost able to conquer Russia in the face of enormous odds. Since Germany otherwise would have been able to retain control of Europe indefinitely, it was Hitler who was led by the siren call of anti-Communist ideology to throw away a rational and prudent course and launch what was to be the beginning of his ultimate defeat.

The mythology of the cold warriors often concedes that the Soviets were not internationally aggressive *until* World War II—indeed, they are compelled to assert this point, since most cold warriors heartily approve the World War II alliance of the United States with Russia against Germany. It was during and immediately after the war, they

[15]For an illuminating view of the Russo-Finnish conflict, see Max Jakobson, *The Diplomacy of the Winter War* (Cambridge: Harvard University Press, 1961).

assert, that Russia became expansionist and drove its way into Eastern Europe.

What this charge overlooks is the central fact of the German and associated assault upon Russia in June 1941. There is no doubt that Germany and her allies launched this war. Hence, in order to defeat the invaders, it was obviously necessary for the Russians to roll back the invading armies and conquer Germany and the other warring countries of Eastern Europe. It is easier to make a case for the United States being expansionist for conquering and occupying Italy and part of Germany than it is for Russia's actions—after all, the United States was never directly attacked by the Germans.

During World War II, the United States, Britain, and Russia, the three major Allies, had agreed on joint three-power military occupation of all the conquered territories. The United States was the first to break the agreement during the war by allowing Russia no role whatever in the military occupation of Italy. Despite this serious breach of agreement, Stalin displayed his consistent preference for the conservative interests of the Russian nation-state over cleaving to revolutionary ideology by repeatedly betraying indigenous Communist movements. In order to preserve peaceful relations between Russia and the West, Stalin consistently tried to hold back the success of various Communist movements. He was successful in France and Italy, where Communist partisan groups might easily have seized power in the wake of the German military retreat; but Stalin ordered them not to do so, and instead persuaded them to join coalition regimes headed by anti-Communist parties. In both countries, the Communists were soon ousted from the coalition. In Greece, where the Communist partisans almost *did* seize power, Stalin irretrievably weakened them by abandoning them and urging them to turn over power to newly invading British troops.

In other countries, particularly ones where Communist partisan groups were strong, the Communists flatly refused Stalin's requests. In Yugoslavia, the victorious Tito refused Stalin's demand that Tito subordinate himself to the anti-Communist Mihailovich in a governing coalition; Mao refused a similar Stalin demand that he subordinate himself to Chiang Kai-shek. There is no doubt that these rejections were the beginning of the later extraordinarily important schisms within the world Communist movement.

Russia, therefore, governed Eastern Europe as military occupier after winning a war launched against her. Russia's initial goal was not to communize Eastern Europe on the backs of the Soviet army. Her goal was to gain assurances that Eastern Europe would not be the broad highway for an assault on Russia, as it had been three times in half a century—the last time in a war in which over twenty million Russians had been slaughtered. In short, Russia wanted countries on her border which would not be anti-Communist in a military sense, and which would not be used as a springboard for another invasion. Political conditions in Eastern Europe were such that only in more modernized Finland did non-Communist politicians exist whom Russia could trust to pursue a peaceful line in foreign affairs. And in Finland, this situation was the work of one far-seeing statesman, the agrarian leader Julio Paasikivi. It was because Finland, then and since, has firmly followed the "Paasikivi line" that Russia was willing to pull its troops out of Finland and not to insist on the communization of that country—even though it had fought two wars with Finland in the previous six years.

Even in the other Eastern European countries, Russia clung to coalition governments for several years after the war and only fully communized them in 1948—after three years of unrelenting American Cold War pressure to try to oust Russia from these countries. In other areas, Russia readily pulled its troops out of Austria and out of Azerbaijan.

The cold warriors find it difficult to explain Russian actions in Finland. If Russia is always hell-bent to impose Communist rule wherever it can, why the "soft line" on Finland? The only plausible explanation is that its motivation is security for the Russian nation-state against attack, with the success of world communism playing a very minor role in its scale of priorities.

In fact, the cold warriors have never been able either to explain or absorb the fact of deep schisms in the world Communist movement. For if all Communists are governed by a common ideology, then every Communist everywhere should be part of one unified monolith, and one which, given the early success of the Bolsheviks, would make them subordinates or "agents" of Moscow. If Communists are mainly motivated by their bond of Marxism-Leninism, how come the deep China-Russia split, in which Russia, for example, keeps one million troops at the ready on the China-Russia frontier? How come the enmity between the Yugoslav and Albanian Communist States? How come the actual military conflict between the Cambodian and Vietnamese Communists? The answer, of course, is that once a revolutionary movement seizes State power, it begins very quickly to take on the attributes of a ruling class with a class interest in retaining State power. The world revolution begins to pale, in their outlook, to insignificance. And since State elites can and do have conflicting interests in power and wealth, it is not surprising that inter-Communist conflicts have become endemic.

Since their victory over German and associated military aggression in World War II, the Soviets have continued to be conservative in their military policy. Their only use of troops has been to *defend* their territory in the Communist bloc, rather than to extend it further. Thus, when Hungary threatened to leave the Soviet bloc in 1956, or Czechoslovakia in 1968, the Soviets intervened with troops—reprehensibly, to be sure, but still acting in a conservative and defensive rather than expansionist manner. (The Soviets apparently gave considerable thought to invading Yugoslavia when Tito took it out of the Soviet bloc, but were deterred by the formidable qualities for guerrilla fighting of the Yugoslav army.) In no case has Russia used troops to extend its bloc or to conquer more territories.

Professor Stephen F. Cohen, director of the program in Russian Studies at Princeton, has recently delineated the nature of Soviet conservatism in foreign affairs:

That a system born in revolution and still professing revolutionary ideas should have become one of the most conservative in the world may seem preposterous. But all those factors variously said to be most important in Soviet politics have contributed to this conservatism: the bureaucratic tradition of Russian government before the revolution; the subsequent bureaucratization of Soviet life, which proliferated conservative norms and created an entrenched class of zealous defenders of bureaucratic privilege; the geriatric nature of the present-day elite; and even the official ideology, whose thrust turned many years ago from the creation of a new social order to extolling the existing one . . .

In other words, the main thrust of Soviet conservatism today is to preserve what it already has at home and abroad, not to jeopardize it. A conservative government is, of course, capable of dangerous militaristic actions, as we saw in Czechoslovakia . . . but these are acts of imperial protectionism, a kind of defensive militarism, not a revolutionary or aggrandizing one. It is certainly true that for most Soviet leaders, as presumably for most American leaders, detente is not an altruistic endeavor but the pursuit of national interests. In one sense, this is sad. But it is probably also true that mutual self-interest provides a more durable basis for detente than lofty, and finally empty, altruism.[16]

Similarly, as impeccable an anti-Soviet source as former CIA Director William Colby finds the overwhelming concern of the Soviets to be the defensive goal of avoiding another catastrophic invasion of their territory. As Colby testified before the Senate Foreign Relations Committee:

[16]Stephen F. Cohen, "Why Detente Can Work," *Inquiry* (December 19, 1977), pp. 14–15.

You will find a concern, even a paranoia, over their [the Soviets'] own security. You will find the determination that they shall never again be invaded and put through the kinds of turmoil that they have been under and many different invasions . . . I think that they . . . want to overprotect themselves to make certain that that does not happen . . .[17]

Even the Chinese, for all their bluster, have pursued a conservative and pacific foreign policy. Not only have they failed to invade Taiwan, recognized internationally as part of China, but they have even allowed the small offshore islands of Quemoy and Matsu to remain in Chiang Kai-shek's hands. No moves have been made against the British and Portuguese-occupied enclaves of Hong Kong and Macao. China's invasion of Communist Vietnam turned out to be a brief incursion followed by unilateral withdrawal. Similarly, China had previously taken the unusual step of declaring a *unilateral* cease-fire and withdrawal of forces to its border after having triumphed easily over Indian arms in their escalated border war.[18]

Avoiding A Priori *History*

There is still one thesis common to Americans and even to some libertarians that may prevent them from absorbing the analysis of this chapter: the myth propounded by Woodrow Wilson that democracies must inevitably be peace-loving while dictatorships are inevitably warlike. This thesis was of course highly convenient for covering Wilson's own culpability for dragging America into a needless and monstrous war. But apart from that, there is simply no evidence for this assumption. Many dictatorships have turned inward, cautiously confining themselves to preying on their own people: examples range from premodern Japan to Communist Albania to innumerable dictatorships in the Third World today. Uganda's Idi Amin, perhaps the most brutal and repressive dictator in today's world, shows no signs whatever of jeopardizing his regime by invading neighboring countries. On the other hand, such an indubitable democracy as Great Britain spread its coercive imperialism across the globe during the nineteenth and earlier centuries.

The theoretical reason why focussing on democracy or dictatorship

---

[17]Quoted in Richard J. Barnet, "The Present Danger: American Security and the U.S.-Soviet Military Balance," *Libertarian Review* (November 1977), p. 12.

[18]See Neville Maxwell, *India's China War* (New York: Pantheon Books, 1970). Neither is China's reconquest and suppression of national rebellion in Tibet a valid point against our thesis. For Chiang Kai-shek as well as all other Chinese have for many generations considered Tibet as part of Greater China, and China was here acting in the same conservative nation-state manner as we have seen guiding the Soviets.

misses the point is that *States—all* States—rule their population and decide whether or not to make war. And *all* States, whether formally a democracy or dictatorship or some other brand of rule, are run by a ruling elite. Whether or not these elites, in any particular case, will make war upon another State is a function of a complex interweaving web of causes, including temperament of the rulers, the strength of their enemies, the inducements for war, public opinion. While public opinion has to be gauged in either case, the only real difference between a democracy and a dictatorship on making war is that in the former, *more* propaganda must be beamed at one's subjects to engineer their approval. Intensive propaganda is necessary in any case—as we can see by the zealous opinion-moulding behavior of all modern warring States. But the democratic State must work harder and faster. And also the democratic State must be more hypocritical in using rhetoric designed to appeal to the values of the masses: justice, freedom, national interest, patriotism, world peace, etc. So in democratic States, the art of propagandizing their subjects must be a bit more sophisticated and refined. But this, as we have seen, is true of *all* governmental decisions, not just war or peace. For all governments—but especially democratic governments—must work hard at persuading their subjects that all of their deeds of oppression are *really* in their subjects' best interests.

What we have said about democracy and dictatorship applies equally to the lack of correlation between degrees of internal freedom in a country and its external aggressiveness. Some States have proved themselves perfectly capable of allowing a considerable degree of freedom internally while making aggressive war abroad; other States have shown themselves capable of totalitarian rule internally while pursuing a pacific foreign policy. The examples of Uganda, Albania, China, Great Britain, etc., apply equally well in this comparison.

In short, libertarians and other Americans must guard against *a priori* history: in this case, against the assumption that, in any conflict, the State which is more democratic or allows more internal freedom is necessarily or even presumptively the victim of aggression by the more dictatorial or totalitarian State. There is simply no historical evidence whatever for such a presumption. In deciding on relative rights and wrongs, on relative degrees of aggression in any dispute in foreign affairs, there is no substitute for a detailed empirical, historical investigation of the dispute itself. It should occasion no great surprise, then, if such an investigation concludes that a democratic and relatively far freer United States has been more aggressive and imperialistic in foreign affairs than a relatively totalitarian Russia or China. Conversely, hailing a State for being less aggressive in foreign affairs in no way implies that the observer is in any way sympathetic to that State's internal record. It is vital—indeed, it is literally a life-and-death matter—that Americans be able to look as coolly and clear-sightedly, as free from myth at their government's record in foreign affairs as they are increasingly able to do in domestic politics. For war and a phony "external threat" have long been the chief means by which the State wins back the loyalty of its subjects. As we have seen, war and militarism were the gravediggers of classical liberalism; we must not allow the State to get away with this ruse ever again.[19]

A Foreign Policy Program

To conclude our discussion, the primary plank of a libertarian foreign policy program for America must be to call upon the United States to abandon its policy of global interventionism: to withdraw immediately and completely, militarily and politically, from Asia, Europe, Latin America, the Middle East, from *everywhere*. The cry among American libertarians should be for the United States to withdraw now, in every way that involves the U.S. government. The United States should dismantle its bases, withdraw its troops, stop its incessant political meddling, and abolish the CIA. It should also end all foreign aid—which is simply a device to coerce the American taxpayer into subsidizing American exports and favored foreign States, all in the name of "helping the starving peoples of the world." In short, the United States government should withdraw totally to within its own boundaries and maintain a policy of strict political "isolation" or neutrality everywhere.

The spirit of this ultra-"isolationist," libertarian foreign policy was expressed during the 1930s by retired Marine Corps Major General Smedley D. Butler. In the fall of 1936, General Butler proposed a now-forgotten constitutional amendment, an amendment which would delight libertarian hearts if it were once again to be taken seriously. Here is Butler's proposed constitutional amendment in its entirety:

1. The removal of members of the land armed forces from within the continental limits of the United States and the Panama Canal Zone for any cause whatsoever is hereby prohibited.
2. The vessels of the United States Navy, or of the other branches of the armed service, are hereby prohibited from steaming, for any reason whatsoever except on an errand of mercy, more than five hundred miles from our coast.

---

[19]For a critique of recent attempts by cold warriors to revive the bogey of a Soviet military threat, see Barnet, *The Present Danger*.

3. Aircraft of the Army, Navy and Marine Corps is hereby prohibited from flying, for any reason whatsoever, more than seven hundred and fifty miles beyond the coast of the United States.[20]

Disarmament

Strict isolationism and neutrality, then, is the first plank of a libertarian foreign policy, in addition to recognizing the chief responsibility of the American State for the Cold War and for its entry into all the other conflicts of this century. Given isolation, however, what sort of arms policy should the United States pursue? Many of the original isolationists also advocated a policy of "arming to the teeth"; but such a program, in a nuclear age, continues the grave risk of global holocaust, a mightily armed State, and the enormous waste and distortions that unproductive government spending imposes on the economy.

Even from a purely military point of view, the United States and the Soviet Union have the power to annihilate each other many times over; and the United States could easily preserve all of its nuclear retaliatory power by scrapping every armament except Polaris submarines, which are invulnerable and armed with nuclear missiles with multi-targeted warheads. Bur for the libertarian, or indeed for anyone worried about massive nuclear destruction of human life, even disarming down to Polaris submarines is hardly a satisfactory settlement. World peace would continue to rest on a shaky "balance of terror," a balance that could always be upset by accident or by the actions of madmen in power. No; for anyone to become secure from the nuclear menace it is vital to achieve worldwide nuclear disarmament, a disarmament toward which the SALT agreement of 1972 and the SALT II negotiations are only a very hesitant beginning.

Since it is in the interest of all people, and even of all State rulers, *not* to be annihilated in a nuclear holocaust, this mutual self-interest provides a firm, rational basis for agreeing upon and carrying out a policy of joint and worldwide "general and complete disarmament" of nuclear and other modern weapons of mass destruction. Such joint disarmament has been feasible ever since the Soviet Union accepted Western proposals to this effect on May 10, 1955—an acceptance which only gained a total and panicky Western abandonment of their own proposals![21]

[20] *The Woman's Home Companion* (September 1936), p. 4. Reprinted in Mauritz A. Hallgren, *The Tragic Fallacy* (New York: Knopf, 1937), p. 194*n*.

[21] On the details of the shameful Western record in these negotiations, and as a corrective to the portrayals in the American press, see Philip Noel-Baker, *The Arms Race* (New York: Oceana Publications, 1958).

The American version has long held that while we have wanted disarmament plus inspection, the Soviets persist in wanting only disarmament without inspection. The actual picture is very different: since May 1955, the Soviet Union has favored any and all disarmament and unlimited inspection of whatever has been disarmed; whereas the Americans have advocated unlimited inspection but accompanied by little or no disarmament! This was the burden of President Eisenhower's spectacular but basically dishonest "open skies" proposal, which replaced the disarmament proposals we quickly withdrew after the Soviet acceptance of May 1955. Even now that open skies have been essentially achieved through American and Russian space satellites, the 1972 controversial SALT agreement involves no actual disarmament, only limitations on further nuclear expansion. Furthermore, since American strategic might throughout the world rests on nuclear and air power, there is good reason to believe in Soviet sincerity in any agreement to liquidate nuclear missiles or offensive bombers.

Not only should there be joint disarmament of nuclear weapons, but also of all weapons capable of being fired massively across national borders; in particular bombers. It is precisely such weapons of mass destruction as the missile and the bomber which can never be pinpoint-targeted to avoid their use against innocent civilians. In addition, the total abandonment of missiles and bombers would *enforce* upon every government, especially including the American, a policy of isolation and neutrality. Only if governments are deprived of weapons of offensive warfare will they be forced to pursue a policy of isolation and peace. Surely, in view of the black record of all governments, including the American, it would be folly to leave these harbingers of mass murder and destruction in their hands, and to trust them never to employ those monstrous weapons. If it is illegitimate for government ever to employ such weapons, why should they be allowed to remain, fully loaded, in their none-too-clean hands?

The contrast between the conservative and the libertarian positions on war and American foreign policy was starkly expressed in an interchange between William F. Buckley, Jr., and the libertarian Ronald Hamowy in the early days of the contemporary libertarian movement. Scorning the libertarian critique of conservative foreign policy postures, Buckley wrote: "There is room in any society for those whose only concern is for tablet-keeping; but let them realize that it is only because of the conservatives' disposition to sacrifice in order to withstand the [Soviet] enemy, that they are able to enjoy their monasticism, and pursue their busy little seminars on whether or not to demunicipalize the garbage collectors." To which Hamowy trenchantly replied:

It might appear ungrateful of me, but I must decline to thank Mr. Buckley for saving my life. It is, further, my belief that if his viewpoint prevails and that if he persists in his unsolicited aid the result will almost certainly be my death (and that of tens of millions of others) in nuclear war or my imminent imprisonment as an "un-American.". . .

I hold strongly to my personal liberty and it is precisely because of this that I insist that no one has the right to force his decisions on another. Mr. Buckley chooses to be dead rather than Red. So do I. But I insist that all men be allowed to make that decision for themselves. A nuclear holocaust will make it for them.[22]

To which we might add that anyone who wishes is entitled to make the personal decision of "better dead than Red" or "give me liberty or give me death." What he is *not* entitled to do is to make these decisions *for* others, as the prowar policy of conservatism would do. What conservatives are really saying is: "Better *them* dead than Red," and "give me liberty or give *them* death"—which are the battle cries not of noble heroes but of mass murderers.

In one sense alone is Mr. Buckley correct: in the nuclear age it *is* more important to worry about war and foreign policy than about de-municipalizing garbage disposal, as important as the latter may be. But if we do so, we come ineluctably to the reverse of the Buckleyite conclusion. We come to the view that since modern air and missile weapons *cannot* be pinpoint-targeted to avoid harming civilians, their very existence must be condemned. And nuclear and air disarmament becomes a great and overriding good to be pursued for its own sake, more avidly even than the demunicipalization of garbage.

[22]Ronald Hamowy and William F. Buckley, Jr., *"National Review:* Criticism and Reply," *New Individualist Review* (November 1961), pp. 9, 11.

PART III

Epilogue

15

A Strategy for Liberty

Education: Theory and Movement

AND SO WE HAVE IT: a body of truth, sound in theory and capable of
application to our political problems—the new libertarianism. But now
that we have the truth, how can we achieve victory? We face the great
strategic problem of all "radical" creeds throughout history: How can
we get from here to there, from our current State-ridden and imperfect
world to the great goal of liberty?

There is no magic formula for strategy; any strategy for social change,
resting as it does on persuasion and conversion, can only be an art
rather than an exact science. But having said this, we are still not bereft
of wisdom in the pursuit of our goals. There *can* be a fruitful theory,
or at the very least, theoretical discussion, of the proper strategy for
change.

On one point there can scarcely be disagreement: a prime and necessary condition for libertarian victory (or, indeed, for victory for *any*
social movement, from Buddhism to vegetarianism) is *education:* the
persuasion and conversion of large numbers of people to the cause.
Education, in turn, has two vital aspects: *calling people's attention* to the
existence of such a system, and converting people to the libertarian
system. If our movement consisted only of slogans, publicity, and other
attention-getting devices, then we might be *heard* by many people, but

it would soon be discovered that we had nothing to say—and so the hearing would be fitful and ephemeral. Libertarians must, therefore, engage in hard thinking and scholarship, put forth theoretical and systematic books, articles, and journals, and engage in conferences and seminars. On the other hand, a mere elaboration of the theory will get nowhere if no one has ever heard of the books and articles; hence the need for publicity, slogans, student activism, lectures, radio and TV spots, etc. True education cannot proceed without theory *and* activism, without an ideology and people to carry that ideology forward.

Thus, just as the theory needs to be carried to the attention of the public, so does the theory need *people* to hold the banner, discuss, agitate, and carry the message forward and outward to the public. Once again, both theory and movement become futile and sterile without each other; the theory will die on the vine without a self-conscious movement which dedicates itself to advancing the theory and the goal. The movement will become mere pointless motion if it loses sight of the ideology and the goal in view. Some libertarian theorists feel that there is something impure or disreputable about a living movement with acting individuals; but how can liberty be achieved without libertarians to advance the cause? On the other hand, some militant activists, in their haste for action—*any* action—scorn what seems to be parlor discussions of theory; yet their action becomes futile and wasted energy if they have only a dim idea of what they are being active *about.*

Furthermore, one often hears libertarians (as well as members of other social movements) bewail that they are "only talking to themselves" with their books and journals and conferences; that few people of the "outside world" are listening. But this frequent charge gravely misconceives the many-sided purpose of "education" in the broadest sense. It is not only necessary to educate *others;* continual self-education is also (and equally) necessary. The corps of libertarians must always try to recruit others to their ranks, to be sure; but they must *also* keep their own ranks vibrant and healthy. Education of "ourselves" accomplishes two vital goals. One is the refining and advancing of the libertarian "theory"—the goal and purpose of our whole enterprise. Libertarianism, while vital and true, cannot be merely graven in stone tablets; it must be a living theory, advancing through writing and discussion, and through refuting and combatting errors as they arise. The libertarian movement has dozens of small newsletters and magazines, ranging from mimeographed sheets to slick publications, constantly emerging and dying. This is a sign of a healthy, growing movement, a movement that consists of countless individuals thinking, arguing, and contributing.

But there is another critical reason for "talking to ourselves," *even if* that were all the talking that was going on. And that is *reinforcement*— the psychologically necessary knowledge that there are other people of like mind to talk to, argue with, and generally communicate and interact with. At present, the libertarian creed is still that of a relatively small minority, and, furthermore, it proposes radical changes in the *status quo.* Hence, it is bound to be a lonely creed, and the reinforcement of having a movement, of "talking to ourselves," can combat and over- come that isolation. The contemporary movement is now old enough to have had a host of defectors; analysis of these defections shows that, in almost every case, the libertarian has been isolated, cut off from fellow- ship and interaction with his colleagues. A flourishing movement with a sense of community and *esprit de corps* is the best antidote for giving up liberty as a hopeless or "impractical" cause.

Are We "Utopians"?

All right, we are to have education through both theory and a move- ment. But what then should be the *content* of that education? Every "radical" creed has been subjected to the charge of being "utopian," and the libertarian movement is no exception. Some libertarians them- selves maintain that we should not frighten people off by being "too radical," and that therefore the full libertarian ideology and program should be kept hidden from view. These people counsel a "Fabian" program of gradualism, concentrating solely on a gradual whittling away of State power. An example would be in the field of taxation: Instead of advocating the "radical" measure of abolition of all taxation, or even of abolishing income taxation, we should confine ourselves to a call for tiny improvements; say, for a two percent cut in income tax.

In the field of strategic thinking, it behooves libertarians to heed the lessons of the Marxists, because they have been thinking about strategy for radical social change longer than any other group. Thus, the Marxists see two critically important strategic fallacies that "deviate" from the proper path: one they call "left-wing sectarianism"; the other, and oppos- ing, deviation is "right-wing opportunism." The critics of libertarian "extremist" principles are the analog of the Marxian "right-wing oppor- tunists." The major problem with the opportunists is that by confining themselves strictly to gradual and "practical" programs, programs that stand a good chance of immediate adoption, they are in grave danger of completely losing sight of the ultimate objective, the libertarian goal. He who confines himself to calling for a two percent reduction in taxes helps to bury the ultimate goal of abolition of taxation altogether. By concentrating on the immediate means, he helps liquidate the ultimate goal, and therefore the point of being a libertarian in the first place. If libertarians refuse to hold aloft the banner of the pure principle, of the ultimate goal, *who will?* The answer is no one, hence another major source of defection from the ranks in recent years has been the erroneous path of opportunism.

A prominent case of defection through opportunism is someone we shall call "Robert," who became a dedicated and militant libertarian back in the early 1950s. Reaching quickly for activism and immediate gains, Robert concluded that the proper strategic path was to play down all talk of the libertarian goal, and in particular to play down libertarian hostility to government. His aim was to stress only the "positive" and the accomplishments that people could achieve through voluntary action. As his career advanced, Robert began to find uncompromising libertarians an encumbrance; so he began systematically to fire anyone in his organization caught being "negative" about government. It did not take very long for Robert to abandon the libertarian ideology openly and explicitly, and to call for a "partnership" between government and private enterprise—between coercion and the voluntary—in short, to take his place openly in the Establishment. Yet, in his cups, Robert will even refer to himself as an "anarchist," but only in some abstract cloud-land totally unrelated to the world as it is.

The free-market economist F. A. Hayek, himself in no sense an "extremist," has written eloquently of the vital importance for the success of liberty of holding the pure and "extreme" ideology aloft as a never-to-be-forgotten creed. Hayek has written that one of the great attractions of socialism has always been the continuing stress on its "ideal" goal, an ideal that permeates, informs, and guides the actions of all those striving to attain it. Hayek then adds:

We must make the building of a free society once more an intellectual adventure, a deed of courage. What we lack is a liberal Utopia, a programme which seems neither a mere defence of things as they are nor a diluted kind of socialism, but a truly liberal radicalism which does not spare the susceptibility of the mighty (including the trade unions), which is not too severely practical and which does not confine itself to what appears today as politically possible. We need intellectual leaders who are prepared to resist the blandishments of power and influence and who are willing to work for an ideal, however small may be the prospects of its early realization. They must be men who are willing to stick to principles and to fight for their full realization, however remote. . . . Free trade and freedom of opportunity are ideals which still may rouse the imaginations of large numbers, but a mere "reasonable freedom of trade" or a mere "relaxation of controls" is neither intellectually respectable nor likely to inspire any enthusiasm. The main lesson which the true liberal must learn from the success of the socialists is that it was their courage to be Utopian which gained them the support of the intellectuals and thereby an influence on public opinion which is daily making possible what only recently seemed utterly remote. Those who have concerned themselves exclusively with what seemed practicable in the existing state of opinion have constantly found that even this has rapidly become politically impossible as the result of changes in a public opinion which they have done nothing to guide. Unless we can make the philosophic foundations of a free society once more a living intellectual issue, and its implementation a task which challenges the ingenuity and imagination of our liveliest minds, the prospects of freedom are indeed dark. But if we can regain that belief in the power of ideas which was the mark of liberalism at its best, the battle is not lost.[1]

Hayek is here highlighting an important truth, and an important reason for stressing the ultimate goal: the excitement and enthusiasm that a logically consistent system can inspire. Who, in contrast, will go to the barricades for a two percent tax reduction?

There is another vital tactical reason for cleaving to pure principle. It is true that day-to-day social and political events are the resultants of many pressures, the often unsatisfactory outcome of the push-and-pull of conflicting ideologies and interests. But if only for that reason, it is all the more important for the libertarian to keep upping the ante. The call for a two percent tax reduction may achieve only the slight moderation of a projected tax *increase;* a call for a drastic tax cut may indeed achieve a substantial reduction. And, over the years, it is precisely the strategic role of the "extremist" to keep pushing the matrix of day-to-day action further and further in his direction. The socialists have been particularly adept at this strategy. If we look at the socialist program advanced sixty, or even thirty years ago, it will be evident that measures considered dangerously socialistic a generation or two ago are now considered an indispensable part of the "mainstream" of the American heritage. In this way, the day-to-day compromises of supposedly "practical" politics get pulled inexorably in the collectivist direction. There is no reason why the libertarian cannot accomplish the same result. In fact, one of the reasons that the conservative opposition to collectivism has been so weak is that conservatism, by its very nature, offers not a consis-

---

[1]F. A. Hayek, "The Intellectuals and Socialism," in *Studies in Philosophy, Politics, and Economics* (Chicago: University of Chicago Press, 1967), p. 194.

tent political philosophy but only a "practical" defense of the existing *status quo,* enshrined as embodiments of the American "tradition." Yet, as statism grows and accretes, it becomes, by definition, increasingly entrenched and therefore "traditional"; conservatism can then find no intellectual weapons to accomplish its overthrow.

Cleaving to principle means something more than holding high and not contradicting the ultimate libertarian ideal. It *also* means striving to achieve that ultimate goal as rapidly as is physically possible. In short, the libertarian must never advocate or *prefer* a gradual, as opposed to an immediate and rapid, approach to his goal. For by doing so, he undercuts the overriding importance of his own goals and principles. And if he himself values his own goals so lightly, how highly will *others* value them?

In short, to really pursue the goal of liberty, the libertarian must desire it attained by the most effective and speediest means available. It was in this spirit that the classical liberal Leonard E. Read, advocating immediate and total abolition of price and wage controls after World War II, declared in a speech, "If there were a button on this rostrum, the pressing of which would release all wage and price controls instantaneously, I would put my finger on it and push!"[2]

The libertarian, then, should be a person who would push the button, if it existed, for the instantaneous abolition of all invasions of liberty. Of course, he knows, too, that such a magic button does not exist, but his fundamental preference colors and shapes his entire strategic perspective.

Such an "abolitionist" perspective does not mean, again, that the libertarian has an unrealistic assessment of how rapidly his goal will, in fact, be achieved. Thus, the libertarian abolitionist of slavery, William Lloyd Garrison, was not being "unrealistic" when in the 1830s he first raised the glorious standard of immediate emancipation of the slaves. His goal was the morally proper one, and his strategic realism came in the fact that he did not expect his goal to be quickly reached. We have seen in chapter 1 that Garrison himself distinguished: "Urge immediate abolition as earnestly as we may, it will, alas! be gradual abolition in the end. We have never said that slavery would be overthrown by a single blow; that it ought to be, we shall always contend."[3] Otherwise, as Garrison trenchantly warned, "Gradualism in theory is perpetuity in practice."

---

[2]Leonard E. Read, *I'd Push the Button* (New York: Joseph D. McGuire, 1946), p. 3.

[3]Quoted in William H. Pease and Jane H. Pease, eds., *The Antislavery Argument* (Indianapolis: Bobbs-Merrill Co., 1965), p. xxxv.

Gradualism in theory indeed undercuts the goal itself by conceding that it must take second or third place to other, non- or antilibertarian considerations. For a preference for gradualism implies that these other considerations are more important than liberty. Thus, suppose that the abolitionist of slavery had said, "I advocate an end to slavery—but only after ten years' time." But this would imply that abolition eight or nine years from now, or *a fortiori* immediately, would be *wrong,* and that therefore it is *better* for slavery to be continued a while longer. But this would mean that considerations of justice have been abandoned, and that the goal itself is no longer held highest by the abolitionist (or libertarian). In fact, for both the abolitionist and libertarian this would mean they are advocating the *prolongation* of crime and injustice.

While it is vital for the libertarian to hold his ultimate and "extreme" ideal aloft, this does not, contrary to Hayek, make him a "utopian." The true utopian is one who advocates a system that is contrary to the natural law of human beings and of the real world. A utopian system is one that could not work even if everyone were persuaded to try to put it into practice. The utopian system could not work, i.e., could not sustain itself in operation. The utopian goal of the left: communism— the abolition of specialization and the adoption of uniformity—could not work even if everyone were willing to adopt it immediately. It could not work because it violates the very nature of man and the world, especially the uniqueness and individuality of every person, of his abilities and interests, and because it would mean a drastic decline in the production of wealth, so much so as to doom the great bulk of the human race to rapid starvation and extinction.

In short, the term "utopian" in popular parlance confuses two kinds of obstacles in the path of a program radically different from the status quo. One is that it violates the nature of man and of the world and therefore could not work once it was put into effect. This is the utopianism of communism. The second is the difficulty in *convincing* enough people that the program should be adopted. The former is a bad theory because it violates the nature of man; the latter is simply a problem of human *will,* of convincing enough people of the rightness of the doctrine. "Utopian" in its common pejorative sense applies only to the former. In the deepest sense, then, the libertarian doctrine is not utopian but eminently realistic, because it is the only theory that is really consistent with the nature of man and the world. The libertarian does not deny the variety and diversity of man, he glories in it and seeks to give that diversity full expression in a world of complete freedom. And in doing so, he also brings about an enormous increase in productivity and in the living standards of everyone, an eminently "practical" result generally scorned by true utopians as evil "materialism."

The libertarian is also eminently realistic because he alone understands fully the nature of the State and its thrust for power. In contrast, it is the seemingly far more realistic conservative believer in "limited government" who is the truly impractical utopian. This conservative keeps repeating the litany that the central government should be severely limited by a constitution. Yet, at the same time that he rails against the corruption of the original Constitution and the widening of federal power since 1789, the conservative fails to draw the proper lesson from that degeneration. The idea of a strictly limited constitutional State was a noble experiment that failed, even under the most favorable and propitious circumstances. If it failed then, why should a similar experiment fare any better now? No, it is the conservative laissez-fairist, the man who puts all the guns and all the decision-making power into the hands of the central government and *then* says, "Limit yourself"; it is *he* who is truly the impractical utopian.

There is another deep sense in which libertarians scorn the broader utopianism of the left. The left utopians invariably postulate a drastic change in the nature of man; to the left, man *has* no nature. The individual is supposed to be infinitely malleable by his institutions, and so the communist ideal (or the transitional socialist system) is supposed to bring about the New Communist Man. The libertarian believes that, in the ultimate analysis, every individual has free will and moulds himself; it is therefore folly to put one's hope in a uniform and drastic change in people brought about by the projected New Order. The libertarian would *like* to see a moral improvement in everyone, although his moral goals scarcely coincide with those of the socialists. He would, for example, be overjoyed to see all desire for aggression by one man against another disappear from the face of the earth. But he is far too much of a realist to put his trust in this sort of change. Instead, the libertarian system is one that will at once be far more moral and work much better than any other, *given* any existing human values and attitudes. The more the desire for aggression disappears, of course, the better *any* social system will work, including the libertarian; the less need will there be, for example, for any resort to police or to the courts. But the libertarian system places no reliance on any such change.

If, then, the libertarian must advocate the immediate attainment of liberty and abolition of statism, and if gradualism in theory is contradictory to this overriding end, what *further* strategic stance may a libertarian take in today's world? Must he necessarily *confine* himself to advocating immediate abolition? Are "transitional demands," steps *toward* liberty in practice, necessarily illegitimate? No, for this would fall into the other self-defeating strategic trap of "left-wing sectarianism." For while libertarians have too often been opportunists who lose sight of or undercut their ultimate goal, some have erred in the opposite direction: fearing and condemning *any advances* toward the idea as necessarily selling out the goal itself. The tragedy is that these sectarians, in condemning all advances that fall short of the goal, serve to render vain and futile the cherished goal itself. For much as all of us would be overjoyed to arrive at total liberty at a single bound, the realistic prospects for such a mighty leap are limited. If social change is not always tiny and gradual, neither does it usually occur in a single leap. In rejecting any transitional approaches to the goal, then, these sectarian libertarians make it impossible for the goal itself ever to be reached. Thus, the sectarians can eventually be as fully "liquidationist" of the pure goal as the opportunists themselves.

Sometimes, curiously enough, the same individual will undergo alterations from one of these opposing errors to the other, in each case scorning the proper strategic path. Thus, despairing after years of futile reiteration of his purity while making no advances in the real world, the left sectarian may leap into the heady thickets of right opportunism, in the quest for *some* short-run advance, even at the cost of his ultimate goal. Or the right opportunist, growing disgusted at his own or his colleagues' compromise of their intellectual integrity and their ultimate goals, may leap into left sectarianism and decry *any* setting of strategic priorities toward those goals. In this way, the two opposing deviations feed on and reinforce each other, and are both destructive of the major task of effectively reaching the libertarian goal.

How, then, can we know whether any halfway measure or transitional demand should be hailed as a step forward or condemned as an opportunistic betrayal? There are two vitally important criteria for answering this crucial question: (1) that, whatever the transitional demands, the ultimate end of liberty be always held aloft as the desired goal; and (2) that no steps or means ever explicitly or implicitly *contradict* the ultimate goal. A short-run demand may not go as far as we would like, but it should always be consistent with the final end; if not, the short-run goal will work against the long-run purpose, and opportunistic liquidation of libertarian principle will have arrived.

An example of such counterproductive and opportunistic strategy may be taken from the tax system. The libertarian looks forward to eventual abolition of taxes. It is perfectly legitimate for him, as a strategic measure in that desired direction, to push for a drastic reduction or repeal of the income tax. But the libertarian must never support any new tax or tax increase. For example, he must not, while advocating a large cut in income taxes, also call for its replacement by a sales or other form of tax. The reduction or, better, the abolition of a tax is always a noncontradictory reduction of State power and a significant step toward liberty; but its replacement by a new or increased tax elsewhere does just the opposite, for it signifies a new and additional imposition of the State on some other front. The imposition of a new or higher tax flatly contradicts and undercuts the libertarian goal itself.

Similarly, in this age of permanent federal deficits, we are often faced with the practical problem: Should we agree to a tax cut, even though it may well result in an increased government deficit? Conservatives, who from their particular perspective prefer budget balancing to tax reduction, invariably oppose any tax cut which is not immediately and strictly accompanied by an equivalent or greater cut in government expenditures. But since taxation is an illegitimate act of aggression, any failure to welcome a tax cut—any tax cut—with alacrity undercuts and contradicts the libertarian goal. The time to oppose government expenditures is when the budget is being considered or voted upon; then the libertarian should call for drastic slashes in expenditures as well. In short, government activity must be reduced whenever it can: any opposition to a particular cut in taxes or expenditures is impermissible, for it contradicts libertarian principles and the libertarian goal.

A particularly dangerous temptation for practicing opportunism is the tendency of some libertarians, especially in the Libertarian party, to appear "responsible" and "realistic" by coming up with some sort of "four-year plan" for destatization. The important point here is not the number of years in the plan, but the idea of setting forth any sort of comprehensive and planned program of transition to the goal of total liberty. For example: that in year 1, law A should be repealed, law B modified, tax C cut by 10%, etc.; in year 2, law D should be repealed, tax C cut by a further 10%, etc. The grave problem with such a plan, the severe contradiction with libertarian principle, is that it strongly implies, e.g., that law D should *not* be repealed *until* the second year of the planned program. Hence the trap of gradualism-in-theory would be fallen into on a massive scale. The would-be libertarian planners would have fallen into a position of seeming to oppose any faster pace toward liberty than is encompassed by their plan. And, indeed, there is no legitimate reason for a slower than a faster pace; quite the contrary.

There is another grave flaw in the very idea of a comprehensive planned program toward liberty. For the very care and studied pace, the very all-embracing nature of the program, implies that the State is not really the common enemy of mankind, that it is possible and desirable to *use* the State for engineering a planned and measured pace toward liberty. The insight that the State is the major enemy of mankind, on the other hand, leads to a very different strategic outlook: namely, that libertarians should push for and accept with alacrity *any* reduction of State power or activity on any front. Any such reduction at any time should be a welcome decrease of crime and aggression. Therefore, the libertarian's concern should not be to use the State to embark on a measured course of destatization, but rather to hack away at any and all manifestations of statism whenever and wherever he or she can.

In keeping with this analysis, the National Committee of the Libertarian party in October 1977 adopted a declaration of strategy which included the following:

We must hold high the banner of pure principle, and never compromise our goal. . . . The moral imperative of libertarian principle demands that tyranny, injustice, the absence of full liberty, and violation of rights continue no longer.

Any intermediate demand must be treated, as it is in the Libertarian Party platform, as pending achievement of the pure goal and inferior to it. Therefore, any such demand should be presented as leading toward our ultimate goal, not as an end in itself.

Holding high our principles means avoiding completely the quagmire of self-imposed, obligatory gradualism: We must avoid the view that, in the name of fairness, abating suffering, or fulfilling expectations, we must temporize and stall on the road to liberty. Achieving liberty must be our overriding goal.

We must not commit ourselves to any particular order of destatization, for that would be construed as our endorsing the continuation of statism and the violation of rights. Since we must never be in the position of advocating the continuation of tyranny, we should accept any and all destatization measures wherever and whenever we can.

Thus, the libertarian must never allow himself to be trapped into any sort of proposal for "positive" governmental action; in his perspective, the role of government should only be to remove itself from all spheres of society just as rapidly as it can be pressured to do so.

Neither should there be any contradictions in rhetoric. The libertarian should not indulge in any rhetoric, let alone any policy recommendations, which would work against the eventual goal. Thus, suppose that a libertarian is asked to give his views on a specific tax cut. Even if he does not feel that he can at the moment call loudly for tax abolition, the one thing that he *must not* do is add to his support of a tax cut such unprincipled rhetoric as, "Well, of course, *some* taxation is essential . . . ," etc. Only harm to the ultimate objective can be achieved by rhetorical flourishes which confuse the public and contradict and violate principle.

Is Education Enough?

All libertarians, of whatever faction or persuasion, lay great stress on education, on convincing an ever-larger number of people to become libertarians, and hopefully, highly dedicated ones. The problem, however, is that the great bulk of libertarians hold a very simplistic view of the role and scope of such education. They do not, in short, even attempt to answer the question: After education, what? What then? What happens after X number of people are convinced? And how many need to be convinced to press on to the next stage? *Everyone?* A majority? Many people?

The implicit view of many libertarians is that only education is needed because everyone is an equally likely prospect for conversion. *Everyone* can be converted. While logically, of course, this is true, *socio*logically this is a feeble strategy indeed. Libertarians, of all people, should recognize that the State is a parasitic enemy of society, and that the State creates an elite of rulers who dominate the rest of us and extract their income by coercion. *Convincing* the ruling groups of their own iniquity, while logically possible (and perhaps even feasible in one or two instances), is almost impossible in practice. How much chance is there, for example, of convincing the executives of General Dynamics or of Lockheed that they should not take government largesse? How much likelihood is there that the President of the United States will read this book, or any other piece of libertarian literature, and then exclaim: "They're right. I've been wrong. I resign."? Clearly the chances of converting those who are waxing fat by means of State exploitation are negligible, to say the least. Our hope is to convert the mass of the people who are being victimized by State power, not those who are gaining by it.

But when we say this, we are also saying that beyond the problem of education lies the problem of power. After a substantial number of people have been converted, there will be the additional task of finding ways and means to remove State power from our society. Since the State will not gracefully convert itself out of power, other means than education, means of pressure, will have to be used. What particular means or what combination of means—whether by voting, alternative institutions untouched by the State or massive failure to cooperate with the State—depends on the conditions of the time and what will be found to work or not to work. In contrast to matters of theory and principle, the particular tactics to be used—so long as they are consistent with the principles and ultimate goal of a purely free society—are a matter of pragmatism, judgment, and the inexact "art" of the tactician.

Which Groups?

But education is the current strategic problem for the foreseeable and indefinite future. An important strategic question is *who:* If we cannot hope to convert our rulers in substantial numbers, *who* are the most likely prospects for conversion? which social, occupational, economic, or ethnic classes?

Conservatives have often placed their central hopes in big businessmen. This view of big business was most starkly expressed in Ayn Rand's *dictum* that "Big Business is America's most persecuted minority." Persecuted? With a few honorable exceptions, big business jostles one another eagerly to line up at the public trough. Does Lockheed, or General Dynamics, or AT&T, or Nelson Rockefeller feel persecuted?

Big business support for the Corporate Welfare-Warfare State is so blatant and so far-ranging, on all levels from the local to the federal, that even many conservatives have had to acknowledge it, at least to some extent. How then explain such fervent support from "America's most persecuted minority?" The only way out for conservatives is to assume (a) that these businessmen are dumb, and don't understand their own economic interests, and/or (b) that they have been brainwashed by left-liberal intellectuals, who have poisoned their souls with guilt and misguided altruism. Neither of these explanations will wash, however, as only a glance at AT&T or Lockheed will amply show. Big businessmen tend to be admirers of statism, to be "corporate liberals," not because their souls have been poisoned by intellectuals, but because a good thing has thereby been coming their way. Ever since the acceleration of statism at the turn of the twentieth century, big businessmen have been using the great powers of State contracts, subsidies and cartelization to carve out privileges for themselves at the expense of the rest of the society. It is not too farfetched to assume that Nelson Rockefeller is guided far more by self-interest than he is by woolly-headed altruism. It is generally admitted even by liberals, for example, that the vast network of government regulatory agencies is being used to cartelize each industry on behalf of the large firms and at the expense of the public. But to salvage their New Deal world-view, liberals have to console themselves with the thought that these agencies and similar "reforms," enacted during the Progressive, Wilson, or Rooseveltian periods, were launched in good faith, with the "public weal" grandly in view. The idea and genesis of the agencies and other liberal reforms were therefore "good"; it was only in practice that the agencies somehow slipped into sin and into subservience to private, corporate interests. But what Kolko, Weinstein, Domhoff and other revisionist historians have shown, clearly and thoroughly, is that this is a piece of liberal mythology. In reality, all of these reforms, on the national and local levels alike, were conceived, written, and lobbied for by these very privileged groups themselves. The work of these historians reveals conclusively that there *was* no Golden Age of Reform before sin crept in; sin was there from the beginning, from the moment of conception. The liberal reforms of the Progressive–New Deal–Welfare State were designed to create what they did in fact create: a world of centralized statism, of "partnership" between government and industry, a world which subsists in granting subsidies and monopoly privileges to business and other favored groups.

Expecting the Rockefellers or the legion of other favored big businessmen to convert to a libertarian or even a laissez-faire view is a vain and empty hope. But this is not to say that *all* big businessmen, or businessmen in general, must be written off. Contrary to the Marxists, not all businessmen, or even big businessmen, constitute a homogeneous economic class with identical class interests. On the contrary, when the CAB confers monopoly privileges on a few large airlines, or when the FCC confers a monopoly on AT&T, there are numerous other firms and businessmen, small and large, who are injured and *excluded* from the privileges. The conferring of a monopoly of communications on AT&T by the FCC, for example, for a long while kept the now rapidly growing data communications industry stagnating in infancy; it was only an FCC decision to allow competition that enabled the industry to grow by leaps and bounds. Privilege implies exclusion, so there will always be a host of businesses and businessmen, large and small, who will have a solid economic interest in ending State control over their industry. There are therefore a host of businessmen, especially those remote from the privileged "Eastern Establishment," who are potentially receptive to free-market and libertarian ideas.

Which groups, then, could we expect to be particularly receptive to libertarian ideas? Where, as the Marxists would put it, is our proposed "agency for social change"? This, of course, is an important strategic question for libertarians, since it gives us leads on where to direct our educational energies.

Campus youth is one group that has been prominent in the rising libertarian movement. This is not surprising: college is the time when people are most open to reflection and to considering basic questions of our society. As youth enamored of consistency and unvarnished truth, as collegians accustomed to a world of scholarship and abstract ideas, and not yet burdened with the care and the often narrower vision of adult employment, these youngsters provide a fertile field for libertarian conversion. We can expect far greater growth of libertarianism on the nation's campuses in the future, a growth that is already being matched by the adherence of an expanding number of young scholars, professors, and graduate students.

Youth in general should also be attracted by the libertarian position on subjects that are often closest to their concerns: specifically, our call for complete abolition of the draft, withdrawal from the Cold War, civil liberties for everyone, and legalization of drugs and other victimless crimes.

The media, too, have proved to be a rich source of favorable interest in the new libertarian creed. Not simply for its publicity value, but because the consistency of libertarianism attracts a group of people who are most alert to new social and political trends, and who, while originally liberals, are most alert to the growing failures and breakdowns of Establishment liberalism. Media people generally find that they cannot be attracted to a hostile conservative movement which automatically writes them off as leftists and which takes uncongenial positions on foreign policy and civil liberties. But these same media persons can be and are favorably disposed to a libertarian movement which wholeheartedly agrees with their instincts on peace and personal liberty, and then links up their opposition to Big Government in these areas to government intervention in the economy and in property rights. More and more media people are making these new and illuminating connections, and they of course are extremely important in their influence and leverage on the rest of the public.

What of "Middle America"—that vast middle class and working class that constitute the bulk of the American population—and which is often at polar opposites from campus youth? Do we have any appeal for them? Logically, our appeal to Middle America should be even greater. We direct ourselves squarely to the aggravated and chronic discontent that afflicts the mass of the American people: rising taxes, inflation, urban congestion, crime, welfare scandals. Only libertarians have concrete and consistent solutions to these pressing ills: solutions that center on getting them out from under government in all these areas and turning them over to private and voluntary action. We can show that government and statism have been responsible for these evils, and that getting coercive government off our backs will provide the remedies.

To small businessmen we can promise a truly free-enterprise world, shorn of monopoly privilege, cartels, and subsidies engineered by the State and the Establishment. And to them and to the big businessmen outside the monopoly Establishment we can promise a world where their individual talents and energies can at last have full room to expand and to provide improved technology and increased productivity for them and for us all. To various ethnic and minority groups we can show that only under liberty is there full freedom for each group to cultivate its concerns and to run its own institutions, unimpeded and uncoerced by majority rule.

In short, the potential appeal of libertarianism is a multi-class appeal; it is an appeal that cuts across race, occupation, economic class, and the generations; any and all people not directly in the ruling elite are potentially receptive to our message. Every person or group that values its liberty or prosperity is a potential adherent to the libertarian creed.

Liberty, then, has the potential for appealing to all groups across the public spectrum. Yet, it is a fact of life that when things are going smoothly, most people fail to develop any interest in public affairs. For radical social change—a change to a different social system—to take place, there must be what is called a "crisis situation." There must, in short, be a breakdown of the existing system which calls forth a general search for alternative solutions. When such a widespread search for social alternatives takes place, then activists of a dissenting movement must be available to supply that radical alternative, to relate the crisis to the inherent defects of the system itself, and to point out how the alternative system would solve the existing crisis and prevent any similar breakdowns in the future. Hopefully, the dissenters would also have provided a track record of predicting and warning against the crisis that now exists.[4]

Furthermore, one of the characteristics of crisis situations is that even

---

[4]Thus, Fritz Redlich writes, ". . . often the soil [for the triumph of an idea] must have been prepared by events. One can remember how difficult it was to disseminate the idea of an American central bank prior to the crisis of 1907 and how relatively easy it was thereafter." Fritz Redlich, "Ideas: Their Migration in Space and Transmittal Over Time," *Kyklos* (1953), p. 306.

the ruling elites begin to weaken their support for the system. Because of the crisis, even part of the State begins to lose its zest and enthusiasm for rule. In short, a failure of nerve by segments of the State occurs. Thus, in these situations of breakdown, even members of the ruling elite may convert to an alternative system or, at the least, may lose their enthusiasm for the existing one.

Thus the historian Lawrence Stone stresses, as a requirement for radical change, a decay in the will of the ruling elite. "The elite may lose its manipulative skill, or its military superiority, or its self-confidence, or its cohesion; it may become estranged from the non-elite, or overwhelmed by a financial crisis; it may be incompetent, or weak or brutal."[5]

Why Liberty Will Win

Having set forth the libertarian creed and how it applies to vital current problems, and having sketched which groups in society that creed can be expected to attract and at what times, we must now assess the future prospects for liberty. In particular, we must examine the firm and growing conviction of the present author *not only* that libertarianism will triumph eventually and in the long run, but also that it will emerge victorious in a remarkably short period of time. For I am convinced that the dark night of tyranny is ending, and that a new dawn of liberty is now at hand.

Many libertarians are highly pessimistic about the prospects for liberty. And if we focus on the growth of statism in the twentieth century, and on the decline of classical liberalism that we adumbrated in the introductory chapter, it is easy to fall prey to a pessimistic prognosis. This pessimism may deepen further if we survey the history of man and see the black record of despotism, tyranny, and exploitation in civilization after civilization. We could be pardoned for thinking that the classical liberal upsurge of the seventeenth through the nineteenth centuries in the West would prove to be an atypical burst of glory in the grim annals of past and future history. But this would be succumbing

---

[5]Lawrence Stone, *The Causes of the English Revolution, 1529–1642* (New York: Harper & Row, 1972), p. 9. Similar is Lenin's analysis of the features of a "revolutionary situation":

". . . when there is a crisis, in one form or another, among the 'upper classes,' a crisis in the policy of the ruling class, leading to a fissure through which the discontent and indignation of the oppressed classes burst forth. For a revolution to take place, it is usually insufficient for 'the lower classes not to want' to live in the old way; it is also necessary that 'the upper classes should be unable' to live in the old way . . ." V. I. Lenin, "The Collapse of the Second International" (June 1915), in *Collected Works*, vol. 21 (Moscow: Progress Publishers, 1964), pp. 213–214.

to the fallacy of what the Marxists call "impressionism": a superficial focus on the historical events themselves without a deeper analysis of the causal laws and trends at work.

The case for libertarian optimism can be made in a series of what might be called concentric circles, beginning with the broadest and longest-run considerations and moving to the sharpest focus on short-run trends. In the broadest and longest-run sense, libertarianism will win eventually because it and only it is compatible with the nature of man and of the world. Only liberty can achieve man's prosperity, fulfillment, and happiness. In short, libertarianism will win because it is true, because it is the correct policy for mankind, and truth will eventually out.

But such long-run considerations may be very long indeed, and waiting many centuries for truth to prevail may be small consolation for those of us living at any particular moment in history. Fortunately, there is a shorter-run reason for hope, particularly one that allows us to dismiss the grim record of pre-eighteenth-century history as no longer relevant to the future prospects of liberty.

Our contention here is that history made a great leap, a sea-change, when the classical liberal revolutions propelled us into the Industrial Revolution of the eighteenth and nineteenth centuries.[6] For in the pre-industrial world, the world of the Old Order and the peasant economy, there was no reason why the reign of despotism could not continue indefinitely, for many centuries. The peasants grew the food, and the kings, nobles, and feudal landlords extracted all of the peasants' surplus above what was necessary to keep them all alive and working. As brutish, exploitative, and dismal as agrarian despotism was, it could survive, for two main reasons: (1) the economy could readily be maintained, even though at subsistence level; and (2) because the masses knew no better, had never experienced a better system, and hence could be induced to keep serving as beasts of burden for their lords.

But the Industrial Revolution was a great leap in history, because it created conditions and expectations which were irreversible. For the first time in the history of the world, the Industrial Revolution created a society where the standard of living of the masses leapt up from subsistence and rose to previously unheard of heights. The population of the West, previously stagnant, now proliferated to take advantage of the greatly increased opportunities for jobs and the good life.

The clock cannot be turned back to a preindustrial age. Not only

---

[6]For a more extended historical analysis, see Murray N. Rothbard, "Left and Right: The Prospects for Liberty," in *Egalitarianism as a Revolt Against Nature, and Other Essays* (Washington, D.C.: Libertarian Review Press, 1974), pp. 14–33.

would the masses not permit such a drastic reversal of their expectations for a rising standard of living, but return to an agrarian world would mean the starvation and death of the great bulk of the current population. We are stuck with the industrial age, whether we like it or not.

But if that is true, then the cause of liberty is secured. For economic science has shown, as we have partially demonstrated in this book, that *only* freedom and a free market can run an industrial economy. In short, while a free economy and a free society would be desirable and just in a preindustrial world, in an industrial world it is also a vital *necessity*. For, as Ludwig von Mises and other economists have shown, in an industrial economy statism simply does not work. Hence, given a universal commitment to an industrial world, it will eventually—and a much sooner "eventually" than the simple emergence of truth—become clear that the world will have to adopt freedom and the free market as the requisite for industry to survive and flourish. It was this insight that Herbert Spencer and other nineteenth-century libertarians were perceiving in their distinction between the "military" and the "industrial" society, between a society of "status" and a society of "contract." In the twentieth century, Mises demonstrated (a) that all statist intervention distorts and cripples the market and leads, if not reversed, to socialism; and (b) that socialism is a disaster because it cannot plan an industrial economy for lack of profit-and-loss incentives, and for lack of a genuine price system or property rights in capital, land, and other means of production. In short, as Mises predicted, neither socialism nor the various intermediary forms of statism and interventionism can work. Hence, given a general commitment to an industrial economy, these forms of statism would have to be discarded, and be replaced by freedom and free markets.

Now this was a much shorter run than simply waiting for the truth, but to the classical liberals at the turn of the twentieth century—the Sumners, Spencers, and Paretos—it seemed like an unbearably long run indeed. And they cannot be blamed, for they were witnessing the decline of classical liberalism and the birth of the new despotic forms which they opposed so strongly and steadfastly.They were, alas! present at the creation. The world would have to wait, if not centuries then at least decades, for socialism and corporate statism to be shown up as utter failures.

But the long run is now here. We do not have to prophesy the ruinous effects of statism; they are here at every hand. Lord Keynes once scoffed at criticisms by free-market economists that his inflationist policies would be ruinous in the long run; in his famous reply, he chortled that "in the long run we are all dead." But now *Keynes* is dead and we are alive, living in *his* long run. The statist chickens have come home to roost.

At the turn of the twentieth century, and for decades thereafter, things were not nearly that clear. Statist intervention, in its various forms, tried to preserve and even extend an industrial economy while scuttling the very requirements of freedom and the free market which in the long run are necessary for its survival. For half a century, statist intervention could wreak its depredations through planning, controls, high and crippling taxation, and paper money inflation without causing clear and *evident* crises and dislocations. For the free-market industrialization of the nineteenth century had created a vast cushion of "fat" in the economy against such depredations. The government could impose taxes, restrictions, and inflation upon the system and not reap rapid and evidently bad effects.

But now statism has advanced so far and been in power so long that the cushion is worn thin; as Mises pointed out as long ago as the 1940s, the "reserve fund" created by laissez-faire has been "exhausted." So that now, whatever the government does brings about an instant negative feedback—ill effects that are evident to all, even to many of the most ardent apologists for statism.

In the Communist countries of Eastern Europe, and now China, the Communists themselves have increasingly perceived that socialist central planning simply does not work for an industrial economy. Hence the rapid retreat, in recent years, away from central planning and toward free markets, especially in Yugoslavia. In the Western world, too, State capitalism is everywhere in crisis as it becomes clear that, in the most profound way, the government has run out of money: increasing taxes will cripple industry and incentives beyond repair, while increased creation of new money will lead to a disastrous runaway inflation. And so we hear more and more about the "necessity of lowered expectations from government" from among the State's once most ardent champions. In West Germany, the Social Democratic party has long since abandoned the call for socialism. In Great Britain, suffering from a tax-crippled economy and aggravated inflation—what even the British are calling the "English disease"—the Tory party, for years in the hands of dedicated statists, has now been taken over by a free-market-oriented faction, while even the Labor party has been drawing back from the planned chaos of galloping statism.

But it is in the United States that we can be particularly optimistic, for here we can narrow the circle of optimism to a short-run dimension.

Indeed, we can confidently say that the United States has now entered a permanent crisis situation, and we can even pinpoint the years of origin of that crisis: 1973–1975. Happily for the cause of liberty, not only has a crisis of statism arrived in the United States, but it has fortuitously struck across the board of society, in many different spheres of life at about the same time. Hence, these breakdowns of statism have had a synergistic effect, reinforcing each other in their cumulative impact. And not only have they been crises of statism, but they are perceived by everyone to be caused by statism, and not by the free market, public greed, or whatever. And finally, these crises can only be alleviated by getting the government out of the picture. All we need are libertarians to point the way.

Let us quickly run down these areas of systemic crisis and see how many of them dovetailed in 1973–1975 and in the years since. From the fall of 1973 through 1975 the United States experienced an inflationary depression, after forty years of alleged Keynesian fine-tuning which was supposed to eliminate both problems for all time. It was also in this period that inflation reached frightening, double-digit proportions.

It was, furthermore, in 1975 that New York City experienced its first great debt crisis, a crisis that resulted in partial default. The dread *name* "default" was avoided, to be sure; the virtual act of bankruptcy was instead called a "stretchout" (forcing short-term creditors to accept long-term New York City bonds). This crisis is only the first of many state and local bond defaults across the country. For state and local governments will be increasingly forced into unpleasant "crisis" choices: between radical cuts in expenditure, higher taxes that will drive businesses and middle-class citizens out of the area, and defaulting on debt.

Since the early 1970s, too, it has become increasingly clear that high taxes on income, savings, and investment have been crippling business activity and productivity. Accountants are only now beginning to realize that these taxes, combined especially with inflationary distortions of business calculation, have led to an increasing scarcity of capital, and to an imminent danger of consuming America's vital stock of capital without even realizing it.

Tax rebellions are sweeping the country, reacting against high property, income, and sales taxes. And it is safe to say that any further increases in taxes would be politically suicidal for politicians at every level of government.

The Social Security system, once so sacred in American opinion that it was literally above criticism, is now seen to be as fully in disrepair as libertarian and free-market writers have long warned. Even the Establishment *now* recognizes that the Social Security system is bankrupt, that it is in no sense a genuine "insurance" scheme.

Regulation of industry is increasingly seen to be such a failure that even such statists as Senator Edward Kennedy have been calling for deregulation of the airlines; there has even been considerable talk about abolition of the ICC and CAB.

On the social front, the once sacrosanct public school system has come under increasing fire. Public schools, necessarily making educational decisions for the entire community, have been generating intense social conflicts: over race, sex, religion, and the content of learning. Government practices on crime and incarceration are under increasing fire: the libertarian Dr. Thomas Szasz has almost single-handedly managed to free many citizens from involuntary commitment, while the government now concedes that its cherished policy of trying to "rehabilitate" criminals is an abject failure. There has been a total breakdown of enforcement of such drug laws as prohibition of marijuana and laws against various forms of sexual relations. Sentiment is rising across the nation for repeal of all victimless crime laws, that is, laws that designate crimes where there are no victims. It is increasingly seen that attempts at enforcement of these laws can only bring about hardship and a virtual police state. The time is fast approaching when prohibitionism in areas of personal morality will be seen to be as ineffective and unjust as it was in the case of alcohol.

Along with the disastrous consequences of statism on the economic and social fronts, there came the traumatic defeat in Vietnam, culminating in 1975. The utter failure of American intervention in Vietnam has led to a growing reexamination of the entire interventionist foreign policy that the United States has been pursuing since Woodrow Wilson and Franklin D. Roosevelt. The growing view that American power must be cut back, that the American government cannot successfully run the world, is the "neoisolationist" analogue of cutting back the interventions of Big Government at home. While America's foreign policy is still aggressively globalist, this neoisolationist sentiment did succeed in limiting American intervention in Angola during 1976.

Perhaps the best sign of all, the most favorable indication of the breakdown of the mystique of the American State, of its moral groundwork, was the Watergate exposures of 1973-1974. It is Watergate that gives us the greatest single hope for the short-run victory of liberty in America. For Watergate, as politicians have been warning us ever since, destroyed the public's "faith in government"—and it was high time, too. Watergate engendered a radical shift in the deep-seated attitudes of *everyone*—regardless of their explicit ideology—toward government itself. For, in the first place, Watergate awakened everyone to the invasions of personal liberty and private property by government—to its bugging, drugging, wiretapping, mail covering, agents provocateurs—even assassinations. Watergate at last desanctified our previously sacrosanct FBI and CIA and caused them to be looked at clearly and coolly. But more important, by bringing about the impeachment of the President, Watergate permanently desanctified an office that had come to be virtually considered as sovereign by the American public. No longer will the President be considered above the law; no longer will the President be able to do no wrong.

But most important of all, government *itself* has been largely desanctified in America. No one trusts politicians or government anymore; all government is viewed with abiding hostility, thus returning us to that state of healthy distrust of government that marked the American public and the American revolutionaries of the eighteenth century.

For a while, it looked as if Jimmy Carter might be able to accomplish his declared task of bringing back people's faith and trust in government. But, thanks to the Bert Lance fiasco and to other peccadilloes, Carter has fortunately failed. The permanent crisis of government continues.

The conditions are therefore ripe, now and in the future in the United States, for the triumph of liberty. All that is needed is a growing and vibrant libertarian movement to explain this systemic crisis and to point out the libertarian path out of our government-created morass. But, as we have seen at the beginning of this work, that is precisely what we have been getting. And now we come, at last, to our promised answer to the question we posed in our introductory chapter: Why *now?* If America has a deep-seated heritage of libertarian values, why have they surfaced *now*, in the last four or five years?

Our answer is that the emergence and rapid growth of the libertarian movement is no accident, that it is a function of the crisis situation that struck America in 1973–1975 and has continued ever since. Crisis situations always stimulate interest and a search for solutions. And this crisis has inspired numbers of thinking Americans to realize that government has gotten us into this mess, and that only liberty—the rolling back of government—can get us out. We are growing because the conditions are ripe. In a sense, as on the free market, demand has created its own supply.

And so that is why the Libertarian party received 174,000 votes in its first try for national office in 1976. And that is why the authoritative newsletter on Washington politics, *The Baron Report*—a report that is in no sense libertarian-oriented—denied, in a recent issue, media claims of a current trend toward conservatism in the electorate. The report points out, to the contrary, that "if any trend in opinion is evident, it's toward libertarianism—the philosophy that argues against government intervention and for personal rights." The report adds that libertarianism has an appeal to both ends of the political spectrum: "Conservatives welcome that trend when it indicates public skepticism over federal programs; liberals welcome it when it shows growing acceptance of individual rights in such areas as drugs, sexual behavior, etc., and increasingly reticence of the public to support foreign intervention."[7]

The strength of the current libertarian movement is demonstrated by the intensity of recent attacks upon it by defenders of statism left, right, and center. From mid-March through mid-June 1979, the liberal Catholic *Commonweal*, the leftist *Nation*, and the right-wing *National Review*, each attacked libertarianism after its own fashion, and each proclaimed the supremacy of the State over the individual. *Commonweal*'s editorial in its March 16 issue, entitled "In Defense of Government," summed up all of their concerns by bewailing the fact that not for generations "have there been so many intelligent people bent upon proclaiming that the state is the enemy."

Toward a Free America

The libertarian creed, finally, offers the fulfillment of the best of the American past along with the promise of a far better future. Even more than conservatives, who are often attached to the monarchical traditions of a happily obsolete European past, libertarians are squarely in the great classical liberal tradition that built the United States and bestowed on us the American heritage of individual liberty, a peaceful foreign policy, minimal government, and a free-market economy. Libertarians are the only genuine current heirs of Jefferson, Paine, Jackson, and the abolitionists.

And yet, while we are more truly traditional and more rootedly American than the conservatives, we are in some ways more radical than the radicals. *Not* in the sense that we have either the desire or the hope of remoulding human nature by the path of politics; but in the sense that only we provide the really sharp and genuine break with the encroaching statism of the twentieth century. The Old Left wants only more of what we are suffering from now; the New Left, in the last analysis, proposes only still more aggravated statism or compulsory egalitarianism and uni-

[7] *The Baron Report* (February 3, 1978), p. 2.

formity. Libertarianism is the logical culmination of the now forgotten "Old Right" (of the 1930s and '40s) opposition to the New Deal, war, centralization, and State intervention. Only we wish to break with *all* aspects of the liberal State: with its welfare *and* its warfare, its monopoly privileges *and* its egalitarianism, its repression of victimless crimes whether personal *or* economic. Only we offer technology without technocracy, growth without pollution, liberty without chaos, law without tyranny, the defense of property rights in one's person and in one's material possessions.

Strands and remnants of libertarian doctrines are, indeed, all around us, in large parts of our glorious past and in values and ideas in the confused present. But only libertarianism takes these strands and remnants and integrates them into a mighty, logical, and consistent system. The enormous success of Karl Marx and Marxism has been due not to the validity of his ideas—all of which, indeed, are fallacious—but to the fact that he dared to weave socialist theory into a mighty system. Liberty cannot succeed without an equivalent and contrasting systematic theory; and until the last few years, despite our great heritage of economic and political thought and practice, we have not had a fully integrated and consistent theory of liberty. We now have that systematic theory; we come, fully armed with our knowledge, prepared to bring our message and to capture the imagination of all groups and strands in the population. All other theories and systems have clearly failed: socialism is in retreat everywhere, and notably in Eastern Europe; liberalism has bogged us down in a host of insoluble problems; conservatism has nothing to offer but sterile defense of the status quo. Liberty has never been fully tried in the modern world; libertarians now propose to fulfill the American dream and the world dream of liberty and prosperity for all mankind.

Appendix:

The Libertarian Movement

IN THE LAST HALF-DOZEN YEARS, the growing and expanding libertarian movement has evolved into an infrastructure of groups, organizations, periodicals, and institutions, each performing different and vital functions that contribute to the overall goal. This appendix provides an annotated outline of these groups and institutions.

1. *The Libertarian Party*
   1516 P Street, NW
   Washington, D.C. 20005

The Libertarian party is the political-action arm of the movement. Its candidates in 1978 gained a 1.25 million votes throughout the country, and it elected a member of the Alaska House of Representatives. Its 1976 presidential ticket of Roger MacBride and David Bergland was on the ballot in 32 states and garnered 174,000 votes—more than any party besides the Democratic and Republican. It is the major mass organization and focus for libertarian activity. Its bimonthly newspaper, *LP News*, the LP platform, and numerous LP position papers on critical issues are available at the above address.

2. *Young Libertarian Alliance*
   1516 P Street, NW
   Washington, D.C. 20005

The youth affiliate of the Libertarian party. It organized scores of college campuses in 1976 on behalf of the MacBride-Bergland ticket. The YLA issues a tabloid newspaper, *Outlook*, which has had hundreds of thousands of copies distributed throughout the country.

3. *Students for a Libertarian Society*
   1620 Montgomery Street
   San Francisco, California 94111

A new student organization which organizes libertarian clubs on college campuses. Devoted to ideology and activity, but not affiliated or associated with any political party.

4. *Libertarian Review*
   1620 Montgomery Street
   San Francisco, California 94111

This is the most important monthly magazine for libertarians and those interested in libertarianism. Hard-hitting, professional, devoted to libertarian analyses of current national and world problems as well as news of the movement, interviews, and books reviews.

5. *The Libertarian Forum*
   Box 341
   Madison Square Station
   New York, New York 10010

A hard-hitting bi-monthly newsletter featuring editorials and articles by the editor, Murray N. Rothbard, and others, presenting a libertarian analysis of current events as well as news and critiques of the movement.

6. *The Center for Libertarian Studies*
   200 Park Avenue South
   Suite 911
   New York, New York 10003

The focal point for libertarian scholarship. The CLS holds annual Libertarian Scholars Conferences, and other conferences on special topics. It publishes the *Journal of Libertarian Studies*, a quarterly scholarly journal devoted to all the scholarly disciplines which impinge upon libertarianism; *Occasional Papers*, a series of original and reprint pamphlets; *In Pursuit of Liberty*, a periodical newsletter of CLS activities; and an *Austrian Economics Newsletter*, devoted to news of the free-market "Austrian School" of economics.

7. *Reason Magazine*
   Box 40105
   Santa Barbara, California 93103

A professionally done libertarian monthly, with a moderate approach to political problems.

8. *Frontlines*
   Box 40105
   Santa Barbara, California 93103

New monthly newsletter with news, gossip, and opinion about the libertarian movement.

9. *Literature of Liberty*
   1700 Montgomery Street
   San Francisco, California 94111

A scholarly quarterly journal which provides bibliographical essays by leading scholars, as well as informative abstracts of all articles in scholarly journals which serve to advance the discipline of libertarianism. Indispensable for keeping up with what is happening in the scholarly literature.

10. *Laissez-Faire Books*
    206 Mercer Street
    New York, New York 10012

The leading libertarian bookstore and a means for mail-order purchases of books. Issues a periodic catalogue of its offerings, with annotations and brief reviews of new books.

Then there are numerous other organizations, foundations, and publications which are not designedly libertarian, but which often take stands in a strongly libertarian direction. Among the best of these are:

11. *The National Taxpayers Union*
    325 Pennsylvania Avenue, SE
    Washington, D.C. 20003

The National Taxpayers Union is a nationwide membership organization that lobbies in Washington for lower taxes and lower government spending in every area.

12. *The Campaign for Political Rights*
    201 Massachusetts Avenue, NE
    Room 112
    Washington, D.C. 20002

A coalition of organizations, including the Libertarian party, dedicated to ending spying on political dissidents by the FBI, CIA, and other intelligence agencies.

13. *Amnesty International*
    2112 Broadway, Room 309
    New York, NY 10023

An international organization dedicated to exposing and struggling against the incarceration and torture of political prisoners by any government in the world.

14. *Association of Libertarian Feminists*
    41 Union Square West
    Suite 1428
    New York, New York 10003

This group was founded by 1972 Libertarian party vice presidential candidate Tonie Nathan, the only woman in United States history to have received a vote in the electoral college. ALF is a national organization concerned with feminist issues as well as libertarianism.

15. *Inquiry Magazine*
    1700 Montgomery Street
    San Francisco, California 94111

A highly respected biweekly that concentrates on analyzing civil liberties and foreign policy questions from perspectives that will be of interest to libertarians. Edited by long-time libertarian activist Williamson Evers.

16. *Center for Independent Education*
    c/o Institute for Humane Studies
    1177 University Drive
    Menlo Park, California 94025

CIE is the only organization devoted solely to the libertarian objective of privatizing our educational system. It sponsors scholarly papers and conducts conferences which analyze the private alternatives to public education.

17. *Cato Institute*
    1700 Montgomery Street
    San Francisco, California 94111

A rapidly growing public policy research foundation dedicated to "preserving and extending social and economic freedom." In addition to producing public policy studies, the Cato Institute holds seminars and produces "Byline," a daily radio program that is heard on over one hundred stations across the country. Several prominent libertarians are among its staff.

Index

Index